Fat, Gluttony and Sloth

Fat, Gluttony and Sloth

Obesity in Medicine, Art and Literature

David Haslam & Fiona Haslam

LIVERPOOL UNIVERSITY PRESS

First published 2009 by
Liverpool University Press
4 Cambridge Street
Liverpool L69 7ZU

British Library Cataloguing-in-Publication data
A British Library CIP record is available

ISBN 978-1-84631-094-2 limp
ISBN 978-1-84631-093-5 cased

Typeset in Kuenstler and Frutiger
Page design by R. J. Footring Ltd, Derby
Printed and bound in the European Union by Bell & Bain Limited, Glasgow

Contents

Colour illustrations

Refer to index entries for illustrations in text.

Foreword

Stamped on the barrel of a US rocket launcher are the words 'Point towards the enemy'. Clearly good advice: failing to do so can make you very unpopular with what is left of your platoon. The problem with obesity is identifying the 'enemy'. Depending on which newspaper you read this can be the government, food industry, advertising moguls, schools, Jamie Oliver or fat people themselves. Speaking as a founder member of the fat fraternity, it is very tempting to blame others for personal girth. In truth, if the 'enemy' is to be identified it is probably as much 'within' as 'without'. None of this makes it any easier to read statistics on obesity, which are so dreadful you instinctively reach for a nice, comforting Gross Mac.

With a total lack of pomposity, preaching or valueless invective the Haslams manage to show not only that obesity has been around for a very long time, for which there is good evolutionary reason, but also how societal changes make it less of a value and more a gooey millstone around the neck of future generations. None of this is done with malice. Humour is always in the forefront but with empathy. Funny Fat Folks are often sad and exploited by society's need to point fingers. Seriously overweight humans are no longer confined to circuses as they were in past times, when most people were thin by force of circumstance. Overweight people are all around us. In fact, if the latest statistics are anything to go by, many of 'us' might at another time have found ourselves sharing space with the circus's 'The Fat Female from Farringdon'.

This is a hugely important book. It is at once honest, funny, alarming but also optimistic. It says there is a way out of this conundrum and makes refreshing reading, quite different from the self-congratulatory criticism politicians often serve up with low-calorie, indigestible readability and regurgitatively impossible calls for action.

I recommend every person genuinely concerned over the obesity epidemic read this book, and laugh a little. By my reckoning, given the population of the UK alone, there should be around 60 million readers. Afterwards, at least if nothing else, they will know which way to point their rocket salad launcher.

Ian Banks

Professor on European Men's Health, Leeds Metropolitan University
President, Men's Health Forum
Council member, British Medical Association
International author and presenter on obesity and men's health

Picture credits

Images are from the collection of the authors except the following:

Bridgeman Art Library, London: 9-8 details from Netherlandish Proverbs/ Private Collection/Christies, 12-24 courtesy of the Warden and Scholars of New College, Oxford

Cameron Collection: 2-5, 2-7, 2-8, 2-11, 4-2, 4-3, 4-4, 4-5, 5-1, 5-2, 5-3, 5-6, 7-3, 8-2, 9-7, 9-9, 11-1, 11-2, 11-3, 11-4, 11-7, 11-8, 11-10, 11-11, 11-12, 12-4, 12-5, 12-6, 12-16, 12-23

Emma Donnelly: 10-12 collection of the artist

Joanna Mallin-Davies/photo Sissle Honore: 10-11

Library of Congress: 12-22

Newarke House Museum, Leicester: 12-15

Private collections: 2-4, 2-6, 2-10, 6-2, 6-3, 7-2, 7-11, 8-1, 8-3, 8-4, 8-5, 8-6, 8-7, 8-8, 9-1, 9-2, 9-4, 9-6, 10-1, 10-2, 10-3, 10-4, 10-5, 10-6, 10-8, 10-9 20th Century Fox, 11-5, 11-6, 12-1, 12-3, 12-4, 12-5, 12-6, 12-13, 12-14 Brian Osman, 12-19, 12-21, 13-1, 13-2, 13-3, 13-4, 13-5, 13-6, 13-7, 13-8, 13-9, 13-10 Universal, 13-11, 13-12 Warner Bros/First National, 13-13, 13-15 Cineman, 13-16 Warner Bros, 13-7 Universal, 13-18 Universal/Studio Canal/ Miramax, 13-18 United Artists, 13-9, 14-4, 14-5

Rosslyn Chapel Trust/photo Antonia Reeve: 9-5, 14-1

Victoria Art Gallery, Bath and North East Somerset Council: 12-8, 12-9, 12-10

Colour plates

Bridgeman Art Library, London: C-12/Private Collection/Christies, C-21 courtesy of the Warden and Scholars of New College, Oxford

Gayle Chong Kwan: C-10

Jenny Saville/Courtesy of the Gagosian Gallery, New York: C-15

Kevin Kallaugher: C-20

Martin Kippenburger: C-16

Private collections: C5, C-6, C-7, C8, C-9, C-11, C-13, C-14, C-18, C-19, C-23, C-26

The Times Syndication: C-22

CHAPTER 1

Introduction

> Death always chuses to assume,
> To usher mortals to the tomb:
> He'll lay aside the poison'd cup,
> Which, at one certain, hasty sup,
> He often drinks Life's current up;
> And will our nature undermine
> E'en on the food on which we dine;
> Nay, with slow, pois'nous power, control
> The operations of the bowl;
> Season the Glutton's daily feast,
> And fat him as we fat a beast;
> Smile grimly, o'er each rich repast,
> Till the gorg'd Corm'rant bursts at last.[1]

In a few decades' time, obesity may no longer exist. In the meantime, it kills more people in the developed world than terrorism, climate change or war. The current adult population of the UK will lose a cumulative 100,000,000 years of life, enough to take the world back to the Cretaceous era. The obesity 'time-bomb' which detonated last century is set to result in an explosion of premature death; as soon as the United States, in the vanguard, starts to realise the full extent of the epidemic, there will be no expense spared in conquering the foe. When medical science sets out to deal with a disease, as it did with smallpox, then it can effectively be eliminated.

Astonishing changes in the patterns of a disease can be induced by lifestyle alone. For instance, the rates of cot death were slashed by the 'Back to Sleep' campaign; the number of victims of road traffic accidents was vastly reduced in the 1970s by the 'Clunk click, every trip' safety campaign promoting the wearing of seat-belts. Widespread changes in behaviour can be induced across a whole population, as demonstrated by smoking bans. Governments will finally stop procrastinating, and get obesity in their sights, when they realise that there is a moral and economic imperative to make sweeping changes to the way their populations eat and the way they behave. Food producers, advertisers and retailers will realise that their shareholders' dividends depend upon their ability to fulfil the 'healthy food' niche. Genuinely nutritious foods will become 'more palatable' by scientific intervention and this will encourage people to switch to them. Nutrition science will produce food that tastes sweeter and fattier than ever, but which can be eaten in typical American vast quantities without ill effect, as it will contain minimal calories. The necessary changes are obvious, and have been stated *ad nauseam* in reports, policy documents and White Papers. One day soon someone in power will be brave enough to take decisive action and actually implement them.

The pharmaceutical industry is crucial in eradicating obesity. Twenty years ago one of the most common causes of hospital admission was for perforated peptic ulcer; nowadays these are hardly ever seen, due to advances in drug treatment. The description of the nature of the 'crisis' suffered by pneumonia victims after nine days of illness is found in books by Jane Austen, for example, not medical books, thanks to the discovery of antibiotics. The pharmaceutical industry may be motivated by the chance to save mankind or it may be interested in shareholders' profits; either way, overcoming obesity is high on its agenda. Safe and effective anti-obesity drugs already exist, but are not widely prescribed, and anti-diabetes drugs are already being used which induce dramatic weight loss, as opposed to the traditional weight gain caused by insulin and other agents. The drug development pipeline is crammed with anti-obesity agents which will work in novel and exciting ways. New drugs may emerge from the study of familiar brain systems, but also of so-called 'orphan' receptors, whose functions are unknown; greater understanding of brain physiology and function will lead to the discovery of new compounds regulating arousal, appetite and weight change. There is even an anti-obesity vaccine being studied, which stimulates a person to produce antibodies to ghrelin, the 'hunger hormone'.

Surgery for obesity is developing rapidly, so that gastric bypass is now routinely performed by keyhole surgery. The bypass has the effect of shrinking the stomach to 20 ml and reducing the length of the bowel, to limit absorption of food. If our genetic evolution were quick enough to keep pace with the evolution of the environment, it would do the same, that is, produce smaller stomachs and shorter bowels. Bariatric surgery could therefore be considered merely assisted evolution. In March 2009, a gut enzyme, MGAT2, was identified in mice which is secreted as soon as fatty food touches the small bowel, alerting the body to be ready to lay down fat. Mice with the genes responsible for producing the enzyme 'knocked out' were leaner than their counterparts and less prone to diabetes.[2] By making the duodenum obsolete, bariatric surgery may be inadvertently curing diabetes by modifying the metabolism, and the eradication of MGAT2 may be the method. Gastric bypass on lean patients with diabetes seems to cause the diabetes to resolve even in the absence of weight loss, raising the possibility of patients presenting to their GP with diabetes being offered an operation to cure it, in the same way as a hernia or piles.

The science of gene manipulation is advancing rapidly. The authors of a literature review for the Foresight Programme's project on obesity suggest, with regard to obesity, that:

> Optimists forecast that in ten years' time scientists will reliably and cheaply test for a thousand different genes, and foresee patients' records available on networked metabolic and genetic databases that allow 'cyber physicians' to diagnose, treat and monitor patient illness in a tailored way.[3]

Children are already being born with the breast cancer gene having been deliberately eliminated, in order to avoid serious illness, and as many obesity genes have been discovered (as reported weekly in the press), it will one day be possible to genetically engineer babies to remove any genetic predisposition to obesity. The Foresight authors go further in predicting a world in which obesity has been banished. Their review quotes Inayatullah (2003): '*Homo technicus* will be a fusion of biology and technology at the atomic level. Its living and non-living materials will be indistinguishable.' They go on to state:

> Nanomedicine may increase our ability to regulate signals in the bloodstream, and to adjust how individual cells respond to them in the body. Nanoscale sensors could improve our understanding of how different foods travel through and are used by the body, which may enable adjustment of food molecules or digestion processes, for example to reduce absorption of sugars or storing of fat around the body.

Fat people themselves will have a role in their own extinction. Not only do obese people die prematurely, but obesity increases the chances of infertility, reduced libido and erectile dysfunction; and when two fat individuals form a relationship, the risks multiply. Even if pregnancy does occur, the risk of miscarriage, stillbirth and maternal death are increased.

When obesity has been successfully eradicated, it, like smallpox, will be consigned to the history books, art, literature and other media. Hence the importance of this book in documenting its rise, prior to its fall.

Chambers' *Twentieth Century Dictionary* defines 'fat' as 'plump, fleshy; well-filled out; thick, full-bodied; corpulent; obese; having much, or of the nature of, adipose tissue or the substance it contains; oily, fruitful or profitable; rich in some important constituent; gross, fulsome'. The dictionary almost makes 'fat' seem like a desirable accessory, especially when the quality or state of being fat, i.e. 'fatness', is then considered, with its 'fullness of flesh, richness and fertility'. Only when the word becomes attached to a noun does it give out a different, negative, message: a fat-head is a dullard; fat-brained means stupid, whilst, as an adverb, 'fatly' becomes 'grossly' or 'in a lumbering fashion'.

From a medical point of view, fatness and to be fat have no positive connotations. Fatness, corpulence or obesity is a threat to the individual and to society as a whole, and there is more of it about than there used to be. Fat is a big issue.

In 1727 Thomas Short, the physician and social observer, wrote: 'I believe no Age did ever afford more Instances of Corpulency than our own'.[4] The words have become more relevant with each passing year since then, and today an obesity epidemic is under way. So, the epidemic is a modern phenomenon; obesity is not. The origins of obesity itself can be traced back at least 25,000 years, to the times of the hunter-gatherers. Survival of the fittest dictated that those who stored energy in the most efficient way – as part of their inherited genetic make-up – would survive the times of fast and famine that would inevitably follow times of plenty. Such individuals ensured the continued dominance of those credited with this so-called 'thrifty gene'. Only recently has natural selection played false by favouring inefficient phenotypes or individuals who fail to store energy in adipose tissue or 'fat depots', whilst those who do lay down visceral fat deposits in the abdomen are condemned to premature death. In order to fight obesity, individuals must fly in the face of evolution and instinct by consciously countermanding the strong urge to eat to survive and to be inactive in order to conserve energy to hunt and flee from danger.

There has been a linear increase in average body mass index (BMI)[5] over the last century; this increase has led into the obesity epidemic of the late twentieth and early twenty-first centuries. There can have been no major evolutionary changes in such a short period of time and consequently there is a great deal of debate about the actual underlying cause or causes of the problem. The epidemic has caught the nation by surprise, and the science behind obesity is still in its infancy. Scientists have very little idea of the origin or cause of insulin resistance, which is the fundamental physiological defect in the metabolic syndrome that denotes one group of individuals who are at high risk of becoming obese.

The importance and significance of an epidemic of obesity is illustrated in tragic proportions by the group of Pima Indians living in South Dakota. The Pima Indians of the Sierra Madre mountains in Mexico still demonstrate the healthy physique common to 'undeveloped' races, but a genetically identical cohort who moved to South Dakota at least 2000 years ago and were influenced by modern Western culture and more sedentary lifestyles have developed appalling levels of obesity and diabetes. The group who moved to South Dakota 'made the desert bloom' through the use of irrigation. They were fine runners, and their descendants were used as scouts by the US army. They hit upon times of great poverty when the American settlers cut off their water supplies in order to irrigate their own farms. But with the advent of the Second World War, their economy boomed as they were conscripted into the army or worked in munitions factories, earning more money than ever before. These factory workers had sedentary jobs, more money for food and access, for the first time, to modern 'Western' diets; they gained weight, becoming, reportedly, the fattest people on earth. They are now suffering an 80 per cent obesity rate and a major epidemic of type 2 diabetes affecting half the population. Meanwhile, in the Sierra Madre mountains in Mexico, the original community of Pima Indians still have the healthy lifestyle of their ancestors and remain fit and lean, with lower than average rates of diabetes.

The Nauru Islanders of the South Pacific (who live on what was known as 'Bird-Shit Island') went from poverty to great wealth when it was discovered that phosphates in the bird droppings were effective as a fertiliser. All the top soil from their land was removed, mines were excavated and the phosphate sold, bringing untold wealth to the country. This was spent on cars (although there were no roads), alcohol and food. The inhabitants have now run out of bird shit and the island is a wasteland of bed-rock. Alcoholism, traffic deaths and obesity are rife and, according to the World Health Organization, the island – along with Tonga – now has the largest obesity problem in the world and the prevalence of type 2 diabetes is 45 per cent. The same phenomenon is occurring in the cases of some former Eastern bloc countries that now have access to Western-style fast-food restaurants.

In the late eighteenth century, phrenologists considered the brain to be a 'jig-saw' of separate organs, amongst which was the organ of *gustativeness*. This, according to one authority, 'rules our love of eating'; another maintained that it 'guides our palates as to flavours'.[6] In the twenty-first century, various kinds of research into the physiological causes of obesity and the means of rectifying it are being undertaken and assessed. It has been found that leptin, for example, a hormone secreted by adipose tissue, communicates with the hypothalamus in the brain, telling individuals to stop eating when they are satisfied. The name itself comes from the Greek word *leptos*, meaning 'thin'. Ghrelin does the opposite: it stimulates hunger. Resistin, discovered in 2001, so named because of its role in insulin resistance, is another hormone under investigation, as is adinopectin, which is a beneficial protein derived from adipose tissue, the level of which decreases in obesity. It, too, is thought to be linked with insulin resistance.

The genetic influence on obesity is hotly argued. It is effected by two separate mechanisms: a person's natural genetic make-up, inherited from their parents, but also by way of abnormal gene mutations (still at present being identified) that predispose to extreme obesity. Some are particularly rare, such as a mutation in the human leptin receptor gene which causes obesity and pituitary dysfunction, and a mutation in the melanocortin-4 receptor gene which leads to early-onset obesity and diabetes. Others are being discovered which are common enough to affect the general population. DNA samples obtained from participants in the Framingham Heart Study show that up to 10 per cent of individuals may have a genotype predisposing to obesity.[7] One such gene, known as FTO, contributes to obesity in the general population and explains why some people put on weight easily whilst others with a similar lifestyle stay slim. It is not a gene 'for obesity' but one that contributes to the risk of becoming obese. This is, thus, a gene–environment association. Certainly obesity does seem to exhibit a familial association but the environmental element in the association cannot be ignored. Further studies into the biological function and exact role of genes in obesity may lead to the development of designer drugs that will help people to control their weight.

Many social changes have occurred during the past few decades which are likely to have contributed to the rise in obesity levels, with or without any genetic input. Almost all fat children suffer from 'simple' obesity and have no identifiable organic disease. Unusual syndromes, such as Prader–Willi and Laurence–Moon-Biedl, in which obesity features, have other stigmata, and endocrine disorders such as Cushing's disease and hypothyroidism are likewise associated with other anomalies.

A newly found system in the brain and adipose tissue called the endocannabinoid system is of interest. It was discovered by the observation that users of cannabis have a surge in appetite, and if the cannabinoid receptor in the brain is blocked, people tend to ingest less food. A new drug, rimonabant, is based on this system and was licensed in 2006 in the UK for use in inducing weight loss, in the context of improving overall risk. It has been suggested that the endocannabinoid system has prehistoric relevance. If our ancestors were given access to large amounts of food, they would eat as much as possible with a view to surviving the next famine or drought. It is thought possible that the endocannabinoid system is involved with facilitating this functional 'overeating'. The system, normally dormant, may be switched on in certain individuals, leading to overindulgence and consequent obesity. Unfortunately, due to an over-reaction by a small panel of European administrators, rimonabant itself has entered the growing category of historical remedies, and the thousands of patients benefiting from improvements in their weight, and diabetes in particular, have been left at increased risk because of its withdrawal from use.

Some commentators believe that enough is already known about the simple causes of obesity to be able to manage it effectively without vast sums of money being spent on research that may explain only a tiny fraction of cases of morbid obesity. It is known that poor diet and sedentary behaviour lead to obesity, and that changes in the 'obesogenic environment' and alterations in lifestyle by the individual can control the epidemic, whatever new molecules or genes are discovered.

There is, however, another option or way of looking at the problem. The Western world is faced with an epidemic that, if unchecked, will result in a catastrophically reduced life expectancy. Uniquely amongst chronic diseases, lack of scientific knowledge is not a barrier to the successful treatment of an individual suffering from obesity. Enough is known about what causes it, about appetite and fat regulation, its outcome, and what to do about it in terms of diet, activity, drugs and surgery. We know this by studying history. Much more can be learned from the past relating to the condition and to discover how the UK has reached such a parlous state. There is not an aspect of obesity today that does not have a relevant backdrop in history, but if we are to learn from the past, the past should not be hidden or ignored.

Britain is at present in the throes of an obesity epidemic, and is at risk of following in the footsteps of the United States, where there is now an epidemic of diabetes as a result of obesity; the prevalence of diabetes in some states exceeds 10 per cent of the population. Many writers and physicians over the centuries have made it their life's work to teach mankind how to preserve health and warn of the dire consequences of ignoring the need for both a good diet and to be active. We in the Western world have chosen to disregard their wisdom, with catastrophic results. Life expectancy had been improving for centuries; advances in hygiene, science, public health and medicine have enabled us to live longer and to lead more productive lives. Obesity, on its own, is threatening to herald a reduction in life expectancy in coming generations. The number of overweight people in the world has overtaken the number of malnourished for the first time.

There is growing evidence that today's generation of children is heavier than any previous generation. According to the Department of Health, 9.5 per cent of children were regarded as obese in 1995 and this had risen to 13.7 per cent by 2007. Many overweight schoolchildren remain so into adult life[8] and this has other implications. In 2005, a newsletter from a primary care trust informed family physicians that the veterinary department at the Zoological Society of London did not have computerised tomography or magnetic resonance scanners suitable for oversize patients: instead, doctors were advised to contact the equine/large-animal units at either Cambridge University Veterinary School or the Animal Health Trust in Newmarket.[9] Elsewhere, it has been stated that larger needles may be necessary for gluteal intramuscular injections; standard-size needles have been found inappropriate because of the amount of fat at the injection site.[10] In 2008, as part of a 'one person, one fare' initiative, Canadian Airlines was forbidden to charge extra to passengers who needed more space because of a disability – including obesity – and was forced to provide extra seats to obese individuals at no extra cost.

An understanding of the public perception of obesity is assisted by the study of art and literature. Obese people are currently the subject of discrimination, and it is widely recognised that obesity is linked with deprivation. Historically, however, the opposite was the case: corpulence was traditionally an index of social status and indicated that one was successful and could afford to eat well. Thinness was derided as a mark of penury. 'Portraits of the Restoration and Augustan eras show Englishmen proud to display a good embonpoint or an ample corporation while fleshiness in females was suggestive of allure and fertility.'[11] This book surveys the history and perceptions of obesity; it is not intended to engage with critical theory and analysis, although opinions expressed on some aspects would, by definition, be open to debate and question. The intention is to present historical facts and to document historical conceptions and the views and reasoning of important medical figures in order to shed light on modern representations and management of obesity. The focus is generally on Britain, although Europe and America are included.

Outline of the book

Chapter 2 sets out the medical understanding of obesity, and in particular the physical and psychological disorders associated with the condition. In looking at the health of some people who may be called 'super-obese' it also gives examples of those who have achieved some celebrity, past and present, by dint of their weight, and in particular ends with a case history of Daniel Lambert. In the eighteenth century, Lambert, a well known figure who was distinguished for his corpulence, reluctantly travelled to London to be on show there, and stayed in the city for some months. After his untimely death at the age of 39 years, whilst visiting Stamford, Lincolnshire, his waistcoat, which could fit round seven men, and other artefacts, were put on display in a museum in the town. These have recently been removed from display, such advertising of obesity being considered politically incorrect. Sadly, the discrimination is against those who are fat regardless of any other good attributes they might possess. It would seem that an opportunity to celebrate the unique lifestyle of a well respected and popular personality has been lost because of misguided censorship. In addition, the opportunity to present some of the clinical consequences of extreme obesity has also been missed.

Chapter 3 continues with the theme and discusses individuals who gained sufficient weight for them to be able to make a living from putting themselves on show. The study of freak shows and their modern equivalents gives some insight into the characters of those involved. Television programmes show super-obese individuals undergoing humiliation and interrogation in their search for a normal body size. Gastric banding or bypass is an entirely appropriate treatment for their condition, but the global broadcasting of their plight is nothing more than a modern-day freak show.

In order to give some context to the ensuing discussions, Chapter 4 describes from a historical perspective the attitudes to food and drink people have had. Periods of fast and famine have been replaced by an era when food is cheaper, more plentiful and available in super-sized portions almost everywhere, at any time of day or night, though it is often less healthy than it was in former times.

The next three chapters look at how obesity has been viewed by the medical profession, from the point of view of diet, physical activity and pharmacology. The Salerno Medical School brought the writings of Hippocrates to the West. The *Regimen Sanitatis Salernitanum*, a book of instructive verse probably compiled in the thirteenth century, recognised that 'Health consists of the moderate use of the air we breathe, of food and drink, activity and repose, sleep and waking, and of the passions of the soul, that use being called the diet'.[12] The general concept of health has not changed. There is no new diet under the sun. George Cheyne, during the Enlightenment, lost a remarkable amount of weight on the 'lettuce diet', a form of modified fast. William Banting came to prominence in the 1860s with his diet 'low in farinaceous food', proclaimed as the forerunner of the Atkins diet. Any new diet is based upon a particular idiosyncrasy or 'fad' but, in the absence of any new evolutionary food or digestive system, each one has historical precedents. Any diet, drug or device may seem startlingly new and promising, but many have been around before. 'The rejuvenation of diets is as much a part of the culture of slimming as the rejuvenation of the dieter.'[13]

It is particularly important to consult the history books when considering the drug treatment of obesity. Fortunately, at the present time, safe and effective anti-obesity drugs are available but only because of the lessons learnt from the past. Anti-obesity pills have a bad reputation because of dangerous amphetamine-based compounds used until the end of the last century. Prior to that, an enormous range of ineffective 'quack' remedies was in use; earlier still, potentially fatal drugs such as arsenic and mercury were prescribed. Modern drugs are still tainted by the memory of these substances and they are under-used today partly because of the reputation of their dubious antecedents.

Moving on from medicine and fat, Chapters 8 and 9 look at the deadly sins of gluttony and sloth. In 1995, Andrew Prentice and Susan Jebb wrote a landmark paper entitled 'Gluttony or Sloth?'[14] The only way of answering the question posed as to which of the two is the root cause of obesity is by referring to the history books to assess the changes in physical activity and food intake that have occurred, not just over a few decades but over hundreds of years. Sanctorius (1561–1636) spent 30 years monitoring his body functions and correlating these with his state of health to create the concept of 'insensible weight loss'. The changes in activity following the Industrial Revolution, with the consequent reduction in manual labour, compared with the increasing availability of food, are important considerations in coming to a conclusion on the 'gluttony versus sloth' argument. The history of gluttony itself is loaded with historical baggage of religious and moral significance.

Chapter 10 examines how what are considered to be desirable body shapes and sizes have varied across both time and culture. Fatness has not always, nor everywhere, been shunned. What are the ideal body size and shape? Fashion magazines, for example, show 'designer' bodies, but fashion is a hard and ever-changing taskmaster. The Greeks thought that the ideal male body was that of the god Apollo, and that the goddess Venus had the body of the ideal woman. Times and fashions have changed and these ideals no longer hold sway, but following the tide of fashion has a bearing on a person's self-image and may lead, in some instances, to eating disorders. Today, obesity in women is associated with reduced job and marriage prospects; thinness is admired – thin is in, stout is out – although a tendency to enhance certain body parts such as breasts and bottoms is growing. In a very superficial sense, there is an obsession with thinness in models and actresses, in contrast to Renaissance values whereby beauty was ascribed to Rubenesque curves. In the 1950s Marilyn Monroe and Jane Russell were the pin-ups of the era, whereas today they would be considered plump, compared to Kate Moss or Luisel Ramos, whose tragic death during Uruguay's fashion week, after days of starvation, sparked the 'size zero' controversy. A review of *Vogue* and *Ladies' Home Journal* from 1901 to 1980 revealed that the breast to waist ratio amongst their models, used as a measure of body shape preference, ranged from 2.0 in 1910, to 1.1 in 1925, 1.5 in 1950 and 1.25 in 1981.[15]

Generally, fatness implies loss of control. It courts pity, contempt and distaste. Prejudice and discrimination against those who are overweight are widespread in the West, although there are areas of the world where obesity is admired. In Mauritania, for example, many girls are still force-fed at puberty to make them more alluring to men and thus enhance their marriage prospects, and in India 'Bollywood' film stars are admired for their plumpness. Others, such as Japanese sumo wrestlers, are particularly noted and frequently admired for their size.

Chapters 11 to 13 look at the ways in which corpulence has been presented in literature, art and film. Works of art and literature mirror the age in which they were produced, and social attitudes to obesity and its effect on the individual concerned are reflected in numerous graphic and literary works. Chapter 11 includes children's literature in its purview. The story of 'Piggy' in William Golding's *Lord of the Flies*, first published in 1954, exemplifies the psychological trauma suffered by the obese child. Being obese invites dislike, criticism, ridicule and rejection. The disparaging name 'Piggy' is symbolic of attitudes to overweight children. Many such children resort to comfort eating as a source of consolation – and further weight gain. Paradoxically, many older adults fondly remember Billy Bunter of the *Magnet* comic, in spite of his objectionable characteristics; his contemporary school-mates merely tolerated him.

Stereotypical images of obese figures abound in graphic satire and cartoons, and these are looked at in Chapter 12. Although there may well be an element of hyperbole in many of these images, they are based on some public perception of the truth. If it were not so, the message to be conveyed would not be understood. Picture postcards, which first appeared towards the end of the nineteenth century, became more popular and less sophisticated after the First World War. Crude pictures with dubious captions became well known and were sent from many seaside resorts. Fat ladies and *double entendres* abounded. The allure of the ladies thus portrayed was questionable, but the public perception of fat females as figures of fun continues.

More recent works of fiction draw attention to eating disorders such as bulimia, anorexia and night-eating syndrome. The characters so afflicted mirror people in real life who struggle to cope with stress, problems with self-image and psychological disturbances. Representations of obese individuals in films likewise mirror real people. The real lives and fictional roles played by large actors are looked at in Chapter 13. Sadly, many died young.

The epilogue presents the 'Dance of Death', a scene portrayed in various works of art from the Middle Ages onwards. Artists portrayed how death was in the midst of life, was no respecter of persons and could occur at any time, without warning.

We have been warned about the effects of obesity, of how it leads to almost a decade of loss of life for an individual, and directly to cardio-vascular disease, diabetes and stroke. It is also a major factor in around 20 different forms of cancer, respiratory disease, mental health problems, infertility and complications of pregnancy, and even joint diseases. Apart from the cost of obesity to the individual in terms of physical and psychological health, there is a great financial cost to the nation for the treatment of the diseases arising from the condition.

Looking back over thousands of years is highly revealing. Present-day food, fashion, fads and fat cannot be dissociated from history. The works of our forefathers should be revisited, and lessons learnt from mistakes made in the past. Once again, the preservation of health should be the priority. Is looking back, therefore, the way forward?

CHAPTER 2

Obesity and the obese

Some celebrated gentlemen of extreme corpulence

> Till within a short time of his death, this wonderful man enjoyed an excellent state of health.[1]

Why was it, then, that, despite such excellent health, Daniel Lambert [2-1] (whose case is detailed at the end of this chapter) died suddenly, in 1809, weighing 52 stone 11 pounds (739 pounds) at the tender age of 39? This was remarkably young, even by the standards of the time.

> While this extraordinary person lived, his immense bulk and other peculiarities made him not only an object of surprise and wonder to the multitude, but of curious and interesting speculation to the man of science and the medical practitioner.[2]

Almost two centuries later, Walter Hudson, of Brooklyn, weighed 1197 pounds, although the act of weighing him broke the industrial scale being used. He had a 110-inch waist and a 106-inch chest, but he was found by his doctors to be extraordinarily healthy. He was never sick for a day of his adult life; his heart, lungs and kidneys functioned normally, and his cholesterol and blood sugar levels would have been healthy for a 21-year-old. 'Walter Hudson's health was nothing short of remarkable – not merely remarkable for someone his size, but remarkable period.' Newspaper reports said 'He possesses a morbidly obese body that is mind bogglingly sound.'[3] Hudson, however, died in 1991, at the age of only 47.

The truth is that although Daniel Lambert and Walter Hudson may not have suffered specific illnesses, obesity itself is a chronic medical condition and an independent risk factor for diseases such as heart disease and stroke; even if an obese person is ostensibly healthy, vascular and metabolic

DANIEL LAMBERT, Of Surprising Corpulency

Mr DANIEL LAMBERT of Leicester.
Weighs 39 Stone 12 lbs.
Pub.d Aug.t 31. 1806 by R.S.Kirby London House Yard & J.Scott Strand.

2-1
Two contemporary pictures of
Daniel Lambert.

changes are almost certainly progressing covertly. In other words, it is impossible to be as obese as individuals such as Lambert and Hudson and be otherwise genuinely healthy.

Other celebrated gentlemen of extreme corpulence followed similar clinical paths, enjoying apparently good health, but dying quickly and prematurely. Daniel Lambert took over the mantle of the fattest ever Englishman from Edward Bright [2-2], a grocer from Malden in Essex, who weighed 44 stone at the time of his death, and who was 'one of the finest specimens on record, as his extreme corpulency was combined with the utmost activity of both body and mind'.[4] Bright's family had a history of corpulence and he was said to have taken a great deal of exercise until within the last two years of his life.

> He could walk very well, and nimbly too, having great strength of muscle; and could not only ride on horseback, but would sometimes gallop, after he was grown to between thirty and forty stones' weight.[5]

He ate moderately and was 'fond of ale' as a young man, but in later life 'his chief liquor was small beer, of which he commonly drank about a gallon a day'. Even so, although Edward Bright, like Daniel Lambert and Walter Hudson, 'enjoyed for the most part of his life, as good health as any man', he died at only 29 years of age. In 1749, he started to display symptoms of possible heart failure – extreme shortness of breath, with fevers and

Engraved for the London Magazine. P.82.

Mr. Edward Bright.

2-2
Edward Bright. *Right:* The wager between Mr Codd and Mr Hants of Maldon, for which seven 'hundred' men (inhabitants of the Dengie Hundred) were buttoned in Edward Bright's waistcoat.

inflammation of the legs – and was treated by blood letting; he finally died, of an unconnected illness, typhus, on 10 November 1750.[6]

Also in the eighteenth century, John Lowe, a bookseller from Weymouth, was transformed from his 'marked leanness of body' by the advice of his worried physicians, who provided him with every kind of nutritious food. This led him into such indulgent habits that he soon grew 'as remarkably heavy and corpulent as he was before light and slender', and 'His bulk, probably from the extraordinary contrast in appearance, excited the astonishment of every spectator'. But having been transformed from a healthy individual of normal weight into an unhealthy obese one, he succumbed, 'suffocated by fat, paid the debt of nature in the 41st year of his age in October, 1793'.

In the nineteenth century, the Glaswegian William Campbell, known as the 'Scotch Giant', was landlord of the Duke of Wellington public house in Highbridge, Newcastle, following a period when he had been on exhibition at the Egyptian Hall in London. He came close to achieving similar dimensions to Daniel Lambert, but his lifespan was far shorter – he died at age 26, on 26 May 1878, after what was considered to be 'a short illness'.[7] Mr Baker of Worcester, supposed to be larger than Mr Bright, was interred in a coffin that was larger than the hearse intended to carry it.[8] The cause of death at age 54, weighing 52 stone, of Roger Byrne of Rosenalis, Queen's

County, Ireland, probably the fattest Irishman of the nineteenth century, was recorded simply as 'excessive fatness'.[9]

Even many of the celebrated super-obese individuals renowned for their relative longevity still succumbed earlier than would have been expected of their normal-weight counterparts.[10]

Longevity and weight

Greek and Latin writers looked back to a time when their predecessors routinely lived 1000 years:

> Manetho who wrote the Egyptian history, Berosus who wrote the Chaldean, Mochus, Hestiaeus, and Jerom the Egyptian, who wrote the Phoenician antiquities, give their concurrent testimony to this truth. Hesiod also, Hecataeus Hellanicus, Accusilaus, Ephorus and Nicolaus, relate, that among the first race of men, some lived to a thousand years.[11]

Lucretius wrote:

> The nerves that join'd their limbs were firm and strong,
> Their life was healthy, and their age was long,
> Returning years still saw them in their prime,
> They wearied e'en the wings of measuring time.[12]

Hippocrates recognised that obese men died early. James Mackenzie, writing in the eighteenth century, believed that Hippocrates and others aimed to improve diet and lifestyle in an effort to restore the lost years:

> Nothing can be more obvious than that the avowed longevity of the primeval race necessarily infers [sic] the salubrity of their food. And in fact, we find that bread, milk, and the fruits of the earth, dressed in a plain and simple manner, together with water to drink, were the aliments of Adam's family.[13]

It is said that the current obesity epidemic may result in modern children having a shorter life expectancy than their parents. Although the claim that the ancients had a lifespan of 1000 years is probably due to differences in measuring spans of time, rather than actual longevity, there is no doubt that some aspects of twenty-first-century life, including obesity, conspire to reduce a person's allotted time. It is well established that obesity leads to premature death; obese individuals will lose, on average, a decade of life. Some 30,000 deaths are estimated to occur in the UK each year as a direct consequence of obesity, and in the US this figure is 10-fold greater.

The famous Bogalusa Heart Study in 1992 looked at autopsies of children and young adults who died of any causes, whether or not they were related to obesity or heart disease, and discovered that the greater the level of obesity, the more inflammatory changes developed in the arterial wall as a precursor to overt cardiovascular disease. Contemporary science reveals increased resistance to insulin in overweight and obese individuals, which leads to poor control of blood sugar, abnormal cholesterol profiles and raised blood pressure, none of which causes symptoms initially, but all lay foundations for serious disease in the future.

In Lambert's day, the obvious external manifestation of obesity-related disease was limited to functional disability, more often than not mechanical phenomena caused by the workload of hauling an increased bulk around, such as the development of breathlessness on exertion. It is now well recognised that obesity increases the risk of diabetes by up to 100-fold, and the chances of high blood pressure, heart attack and stroke many times, not to mention the likelihood of cancer, liver disease, arthritis, depression, infertility, sleep apnoea, accidental injury, blindness and even Alzheimer's disease. Most overweight and obese people progress slowly through the stages of obesity, and experience illness in later years, but those in the extreme stages of obesity, sometimes called 'super-obese', usually succumb tragically early, and display entirely different co-morbidities.[14]

The greater the degree of obesity, the correspondingly greater is the risk of premature death from a variety of chronic diseases. It is therefore hardly surprising that celebrated super-obese individuals such as Daniel Lambert and Walter Hudson demonstrated a dramatic reduction in duration of life. They represent the distant end of a spectrum of excess weight, sedentary behaviour, disordered eating, poor health and, ultimately, early death. Their experience is valuable from an analytical point of view, as they represent a small, unique cohort, which can be used to observe the effects of almost unimaginable levels of adiposity on the human metabolism, which always includes a hastening of death by many decades. Often the death of such individuals is in dramatic clinical circumstances, due to the rapid deterioration in health which occurs when the multiple systems of the body fail simultaneously and catastrophically owing to the enormous metabolic and mechanical burden. In other instances, death is accompanied by major accident or injury, or hastened by practical problems involved in seeking medical aid for individuals too large to ride in an ambulance or, indeed, even to leave their house. Stories of heroic firemen knocking down walls to extricate individuals from their beds or rescuing them from beneath floorboards have become legendary. Dolly Dimples (discussed in Chapter 3) demonstrated the obese person's preponderance to accidental injury, falls and fractures:

> Dressed in delicate pink and decorated with a fragrant tea rose corsage, I emerged from the museum prepared to brave the pelting rain that was falling. With feminine grace I tossed my pink cape over my shoulders and stepped out into the rain, and as I did my feet took off in separate

directions while I, oxenlike, plopped to the ground. With my face pushing into the sidewalk, my whole world collapsed. Seven strong sons of Mexico restored me to my feet, but not to my dignity.

On another occasion:

I rose to move the fan and, of course, I could not see the slippers I had cast off. As I stepped forward I tripped over my own shoes and collapsed on the floor.

A fractured tibia resulted.[15]

Body fat

It took two surgeons, Giovanni Battista Morgagni and William Wadd, to discover that, rather than adiposity itself representing a risk factor for disease, it was the anatomical presence of fat within the omentum of the bowel that was a precursor of illness. Morgagni had discovered, by post-mortem dissection, that sudden premature death was often accompanied by abdominal obesity. Moreover, in his *Epistola anatoma clinica XXI: De Sedibuset Causis Morborum per Anatomen indagata* (*The Seats and Causes of Diseases Investigated by Anatomy*) of 1765 he suggested that the position of the fat was crucial.[16] Wadd confirmed this in the early nineteenth century. In 1829 Wadd described his findings of visceral fat at post-mortem in one patient:

The omentum was a thick fat apron. The whole of the intestinal canal was embedded in fat, as if melted tallow had been poured into the cavity of the abdomen; and the diaphragm and the parietes of the abdomen must have been strained to their very utmost extent, to have sustained the extreme and constant pressure of such a weighty mass. So great was the mechanical obstruction … that the wonder is, not that he should die, but that he should live.[17]

Wadd was ahead of his time in recognising that fat, not only by its existence but by its location, was a serious threat to health, but he was mistaken in describing it as just a 'weighty mass' causing 'mechanical obstruction'.

The different location of the fat naturally leads to a different shape of the obese individual. In the 1940s, the French physician Dr Jean Vague introduced the concept of android versus gynoid obesity [2-3]:[18] men traditionally carry fat abdominally, assuming the dangerous 'apple' shape, whereas women often resemble the 'pear', and carry fat on the buttocks, hips and thighs, where it is metabolically inactive, and carries few risks, apart from the mechanical effects of extra weight on the joints of the lower limb.[19]

The fatty adipose tissue which is most dangerous is that which is described as intra-abdominal or visceral, wrapped around the gut, in the omentum of the bowel. This collection of fatty tissue is far from being a functionless mass but is now considered to be the most active endocrine

2-3
The apple and pear shapes (pear from Taylor postcard, published by Bamforth).

gland in the body. Rather like an ant hill, at first glance it appears to be a large inert entity, but on closer inspection it is a frenzy of activity; substances are entering, leaving and being structurally altered. Hormones are being absorbed and changed, disrupting the natural hormonal axis of the body; for example, in women it can cause polycystic ovarian syndrome, which includes hirsutism, irregular periods and infertility. Cancer of the lining of the womb and postmenopausal breast cancer can result from this hormonal disruption in women, and cancer of the prostate and testicles in men. Adipose tissue secretes dangerous toxic chemicals called adipocytokines, which, when combined with the high insulin levels, produce a toxic brew that leads to further health problems.

The gender-specific aspects of obesity

Although it was not until the middle of the twentieth century that Dr Vague differentiated between 'apples' and 'pears', the gender-specific aspects of obesity had been known for thousands of years. Over 3000 years ago Hippocrates wrote 'men who are constitutionally very fat are more likely to die quickly than those who are thin'.[20] The differences between the risks of obesity to men as opposed to women were well recognised by the Greeks, who realised that obese women were frequently infertile, whereas obese men had a shortened life expectancy.[21]

In the nineteenth century, the link between maleness and obesity was more clearly defined. According to the famed writer and wit Jean Anthelme Brillat-Savarin:

> There is one kind of obesity that centres round the belly; I have never noticed it in women: since they are generally made up of softer tissues, no part of their body is spared when obesity attacks them. I call this type of fatness Gastrophoria, and its victims Gastrophores. I myself am in their company; but although I carry around with me a fairly prominent stomach, I still have well-formed lower legs, and calves as sinewy as the muscles of an Arabian steed.[22]

He is describing the typical, and dangerous, male 'apple' shape. (One notable 'apple' was Mr William Banting, discussed in Chapter 5.)

Some of the gynaecological conditions associated with obesity are described below (page 24).

The metabolic syndrome

The condition known by clinicians as metabolic syndrome, syndrome X or insulin resistance syndrome describes the clustering of risk factors for chronic disease which coexist in obese individuals, predominantly raised blood pressure, abnormal cholesterol and lipids, and impaired control of blood glucose, which often leads to frank type 2 diabetes.

Metabolic syndrome was first formally described by Gerald Reaven, Emeritus Professor of Medicine at Stanford, in his American Diabetes Association Banting lecture in 1988.[23] He described how adipose tissue, skeletal muscle and liver become resistant to the effects of insulin. Insulin is the hormone that enables tissues to take up glucose from the blood stream, to be used for energy. Resistance to it leads to the potential for raised blood sugar and, whilst the beta islet cells of the pancreas can respond, a compensatory increase in secretion of insulin (hyperinsulin-aemia). When the pancreas can no longer respond because of beta-cell failure and increasing demands for insulin, blood glucose rises unchallenged and type 2 diabetes develops. The tendency towards heart disease and stroke is simultaneously increased as a result of the raised blood pressure, an abnormal lipid profile and greater 'stickiness' of the blood. Other organs of the body, such as the ovaries, kidneys and brain, react badly to raised insulin levels. Reaven described these organs as 'innocent bystanders' of the hyperinsulinaemic state. This is why obesity leads to such widespread co-morbidities.

Physical diseases linked with obesity

Over the past few centuries, it has become clear to physicians and writers that poor diet, sedentary behaviour and obesity lead to illness, even if the victims remain unaware of their condition, as was the case with many super-obese individuals. It slowly became recognised that the obese state was an unhealthy one. The connection between disparate conditions associated with corpulency was also documented, but of course the underlying science was, until recently, far from understood.

In 1806 Dr Shadrach Ricketson, a physician from New York, compiled the thoughts of some of the leading physicians of the day regarding health issues, and pointed out the initially hidden diseases, and even death, that we now see as the commonplace results of overeating:[24]

> Let not the drunkard, the epicure, or the voluptuary say, that because he feels no immediate bad effects from his excesses, none are ever to follow: he may be assured, that if he persevere, weakness, disease, and, perhaps death, will, sooner or later, be the inevitable consequence....
>
> ... as a neglect of this attention to the quantity of food proportioned to the necessity of each individual, is sooner or later, followed with the most serious consequences. To the strong and robust, inflammatory diseases happen, and all such as proceed from plenitude and acrimony combined, as the gout, and many other chronic indispositions....

> Fulness of blood, and corpulency, are the disagreeable effects of glut-
> tony, which progressively relaxes the stomach, and punishes the offender
> with head-ach, fever, pain in the bowels, diarrhoea, and other disorders.

Ricketson not only recognised overeating as the cause of disease but promoted good nutrition over and above drugs for its management:

> Moderation and temperance have, from their importance, been not
> improperly called 'the golden means of preserving health'. A proper
> attention to diet, as well as to pure air, is no less important and
> necessary in the cure, than in the prevention of diseases, and in the
> preservation of health in general. Hence, many disorders prove incurable
> by medicine, without a well regulated diet and regimen: to which, those
> of a chronic nature often yield, more than to the whole materia medica.[25]

Diabetes

Diabetes[26] is the chronic disease most closely associated with obesity and is
such a common illness that it is not surprising that many celebrated individuals have suffered from it. It has probably been known to doctors since
1552 BC, as the Ebers papyrus [2-4] – the largest and most comprehensive
of many ancient Egyptian medical papyri from around that date – refers
to 'excessive urination', followed by prescriptions of 'A medicine to drive
away the passing of too much urine' and 'To eliminate urine which is too
plentiful'. Expert opinion varies, but most consider this to be a reference to
diabetes rather than infection.

It is said in Hindu writings that black ants were detecting diabetes
thousands of years ago. Records from c. 1500 BC describe people with a

2-4
The Ebers papyrus, of
1552 BC, now held in the
University of Leipzig.

mysterious and deadly disease that caused intense thirst, enormous urine output and wasting away of the body. A diagnostic sign was the attraction of ants and flies to the urine of the victims.

For thousands of years, although the mysterious condition was recognised, there was no name or cure. The conditions we now know to be type 1 and type 2 diabetes were, though, recognised to be different; children with the disease were noted to die quickly, often within days of onset, whereas adults struggled with devastating complications. Attempted cures ranged from herbs to 'cataplasms to the hypochondrium over the kidneys' to venesection.[27] About 1000 AD, Greek physicians prescribed exercise, preferably on horseback, to 'employ moderate friction' and alleviate excess urination.[28] Apollonius of Memphis may have introduced the name 'diabetes' around 250 BC, meaning literally 'to go through' or siphon, describing the drainage patients experienced of more fluid than they can consume.

In the second century AD, the Greek physician Aretaeus the Cappadocian gave a more detailed description of diabetes, and for the first time linked it with weight:

> Diabetes is a wonderful affection, not very frequent among men, being a melting down of the flesh and limbs into urine. Its cause is of a cold and humid nature as in dropsy. The course is a common one, namely the kidneys and bladder; for the patients never stop making water, but the flow is incessant, as if from the opening of aqueducts. The nature of the disease then is chronic, and it takes a long period to form, but the patient is short-lived if the constitution of the disease be completely established; for the melting is rapid, the death speedy. Moreover, life is disgusting and painful; thirst unquenchable; excessive drinking, which however is disproportionate to the large quantity of urine for more urine is passed; and one cannot stop them either from drinking or making water.
>
> Or if for a time they abstain from drinking, their mouth becomes parched and their body dry; the viscera seem as if scorched up; they are affected with nausea, restlessness, and a burning thirst as if scorched by fire, and at no distant term they expire.
>
> Hence the disease appears to me to have got the name diabetes, as if from the Greek word which signifies a siphon, because the fluid does not remain in the body, but uses the man's body as a ladder whereby to leave it.[29]

It is now widely accepted that around 80 per cent of cases of type 2 diabetes are due to excess weight, but it was only relatively recently that the connection was highlighted. Many authors, such as Nathan Buchan in 1795, blamed 'hard drinking' for the condition, but corpulence was much less emphasised. Robert Thomas was ahead of his time, in 1811, in noting not only the presence but also the site of body fat in cases of diabetes, and in highlighting the function of dangerous metabolically active visceral fat:

The fat within the thorax, abdomen, and pelvis, in some instances has seemed entirely converted into a gelatinous-like matter somewhat of an amber colour.... The subcutaneous fat is found in general much diminished.[30]

2-5
Elvis Presley.

Because diabetes is so closely linked with obesity, certain lifestyles predispose to the illness, which may be why the likes of Elvis Presley [2-5] were victims. Elvis was known for his gluttony; his favourite dishes allegedly included squirrel fried in butter, and the famous Denver Fool's Gold Loaf. One portion of the latter consisted of an entire loaf of bread with two tablespoons of butter, a pound of bacon, a large jar of peanut butter and a jar of jam. On one much-recounted occasion Elvis and his entourage flew 1000 miles in his private jet just to sample these treats, which were washed down with Pepsi. David Adler's *Life and Cuisine of Elvis Presley* tells of his culinary exploits, including his favourite foods: buttery biscuits, six-egg omelettes served with a pound of burnt bacon, pecan-crusted catfish, smoked back ribs, beefburgers, smoked pork sandwiches, fried dill pickles, grits and cheese, bologna cups, sweet potato pie, barbecue pizza, turnip greens, fried peanut butter and banana sandwiches, 16-pound T-bone steaks, 8-ounce filets of salmon, banana pudding, triple-layer fudge cake, not to mention his $4000 caviar-and-scotch breakfasts in Vegas.[31] Given both the quality and quantity of this intake, combined with a sedentary lifestyle, the onset of obesity was almost inevitable, with diabetes hard on its heels. Elvis died of a presumed heart attack in Memphis on 16 August 1977 aged only 42, partly due to his diabetes, not helped by his habitual drug abuse. His last meal was four scoops of ice-cream and several chocolate-chip cookies.

Cass Elliot, otherwise known as Mama Cass of the chart-topping 1960s pop group The Mamas and the Papas, reportedly another person with diabetes, succumbed to heart failure due to fatty myocardial infiltration from obesity, during a solo tour to London on 29 July 1974, age only 32. She had spent years yo-yo dieting and her doctor, when interviewed later, created an urban myth by referring to her eating habits, claiming that she probably choked on a sandwich.

Cardiovascular disease

Galen was the first person to recognise the function of blood, but it was William Harvey in 1616 who realised that blood circulates the body, rather than being produced by the heart. The pressure under which human blood flowed was first measured in 1847, by Carl Ludwig, using catheters inserted into the arteries, but the modern sphygmomanometer was invented in 1881.[32] Blood pressure is increased in obesity for a number of reasons, including salt retention by the kidneys in response to high circulating insulin levels and increased sympathetic tone. Celesta Geyer, otherwise known as Dolly Dimples (see Chapter 3), the circus fat lady, demonstrated the risks: she was given a prognosis of 'a matter of hours' after collapsing with breathlessness and swollen ankles with a massively raised blood pressure of 240/132 mmHg.[33] A combination of excellent medical care and a 'diet or die' philosophy saved her life. She embarked upon a weight loss diet, eventually losing 433 pounds and resuming a normal cardiovascular status.

It has been said that the condition now known as angina (chest pains caused by an insufficient flow of blood to the heart) was first described by Edward Hyde in 1607; however, it is possible that Hippocrates had the condition in mind when he wrote:

> some persons, from repletion, especially such as are gross, sweat profusely in their sleep, which gives them no great uneasiness in the beginning; tho', in process of time, it becomes the cause of pain and distempers. And it is observable, that they are most apt to fall into this disorder, who, from a long habit of idleness, come, of a sudden, to use exercise.[34]

The actual term 'angina' was first used by William Heberden, on 21 July 1768, when he read his paper entitled 'Some Account of a Disorder of the Breast' at the Royal College of Physicians:

> There is a disorder of the breast, marked with strong and peculiar symptoms, considerable for the kind of danger belonging to it.... The seat of it and sense of strangling and anxiety with which it is attended may make it not improperly be called angina pectoris.

The connection between angina and obesity was emphasised much later. Dr Robert Thomas of Salisbury wrote in 1811:[35]

> It is found to attack men much more frequently than women, particularly those who have short necks, who are inclinable to corpulency, and who at the same time lead an inactive or sedentary life … he should endeavour to counteract any disposition to obesity, which has been considered as a predisposing cause.[36]

Thomas also wrote of 'paralysis', or stroke, in 1811,[37] linking it with 'full plethoric habit'.

By 1897 physicians such as William Osler [2-6] were describing the causative factors of angina: 'it is an attendant rather of ease and luxury than of temperance and labor: on which account, though occurring among the poor … more wise men than fools are its victims'. The connection between diabetes and angina was not observed by Osler, but it was noted by others, including Wilhelm Ebstein in 1895, in a paper that appeared in the *Berliner Klinische Wochenschrift*. Osler did, though, present a case study of 'Mr L, aged 55 years, merchant, who for a week had had attacks of severe pain in the region of the heart'. Although Mr L was said to be 'a stout, large-framed man' his stoutness was not worthy of comment with regard to his 'severe attack of angina pectoris, accompanied with vomiting and sweating'.

2-6
William Osler.

Gynaecological conditions linked with obesity

Hippocrates had observed that obese women tended to infertility, and various authors since have linked weight with ovarian and uterine pathology.

Giovanni Battista Morgagni describes a female patient with severe obesity and *virili aspectu*, or virile (manly) aspect. The abdomen is noted to be prominent and to contain a large amount of fat accumulated in the intra-abdominal spaces and at the level of the ribcage, with a raised diaphragm. The 'virile aspect' of the unfortunate woman may well have indicated polycystic ovarian syndrome (PCOS), in which abdominal obesity is linked with hyperandrogenism – hirsutism, acne and alopecia in response to raised levels of testosterone. The syndrome is also linked with insulin resistance and diabetes.

Dr William Buchan, writing in 1795, warned against overeating and sedentariness in females as a precursor to gynaecological complaints:

> we find, that such girls as lead an indolent life, and eat great quantities of trash, are not only subject to obstructions of the menses, but likewise glandular obstructions; as the scrophula or king's evil, &c.[38]

According to Buchan, 'for women of a gross or full habit ... a spare thin diet' was called for, with only a small beer for enjoyment and a teaspoonful of the tincture of black hellebore.

In 1811, Robert Thomas gave dire warning about amenorrhoea, or lack of periods, in women of child-bearing age, and recognised the link with endometrial cancer:

> When they happen to disappear suddenly in women of a full plethoric habit, such persons should be careful to confine themselves to a more spare diet than usual; they should likewise take regular exercise, and keep their body open by a use of some mild laxative.... Should any scirrhous or cancerous affection of the uterus take place on a stoppage of menstrual flux, as sometimes happens, all that can be done in such a case is to have recourse to palliatives, such as opium, hyoscyamus, and hemlock, which may be combined.[39]

Respiratory disorders

Sleep apnoea is increasing in prevalence with the rise in levels of obesity. It was documented as being linked with the condition as early as the fourth century BC.

Hippocrates wrote of abnormal sleep patterns before the recognition of sleep apnoea:

> Others, when their diet bears not too great a proportion to their exercise, not only sleep well at night, but are likewise drowsy in the day; the repletion still increases, and their nights begin to grow restless; their sleep afterwards becomes disturbed with frightful dreams of battles.[40]

The connection between obesity and respiratory disorders was recognised by Celsus, in the first century AD, who said 'The obese are throttled by acute diseases and breathing difficulties; they often die suddenly, which rarely happens in the thinner person'.[41] Robert Thomas also described respiratory disorders related to abdominal obesity:

> Corpulency, when it arrives at a certain height, becomes an absolute disease. The increase of the omentum particularly, and the accumulation of fat about the kidneys and mesentery, swell the abdomen, and obstruct the motions of the diaphragm; whence one reason of the difficulty of breathing, which is peculiar to corpulent people.[42]

Joe was the obese, sleepy, red-faced boy described by Charles Dickens in *The Pickwick Papers* (1837) (see Chapter 11), whose attributes gave rise to a condition now known as the Pickwickian syndrome. C. Sidney Burwell and his colleagues coined the term 'Pickwickian syndrome' in 1956 because of the resemblance of a patient of theirs to Joe [2-7]. This obese person had apparently sought advice for his condition after falling asleep during a game of poker, when he had been dealt a full house; he had thus failed to take advantage of his situation! The term is more or less synonymous with the now more generally used 'obstructive sleep apnoea', although 'Pickwickian syndrome' is reserved for the more severe late stage condition, with signs of

2-7
Joe from Dickens' *Pickwick Papers*, drawn by Phiz: detail from picture captioned 'The fat boy awake on this occasion only'.

impending heart failure. The term 'apnoea' comes from the Greek word for 'want of breath'. In sleep apnoea syndrome, the sufferer stops breathing for 10 seconds or more at a frequency of over 30 times a night, during normal sleep periods. Consequently, the level of oxygen in the blood falls and the sufferer wakes frequently, without being aware of waking. This causes daytime sleepiness and, in some instances, mental confusion, dry mouth and morning headache.

Massive obesity often restricts movement of the chest wall, and so causes hypoventilation (shallow breathing), hypoxia (low blood oxygen level) and hypercapnia (carbon monoxide retention). The body tries to compensate for the lack of oxygen by increasing the proportion of red blood cells in the blood (polycythaemia, associated with a red face and ruddy cheeks). The high levels of red blood cells increase the risk of venous thrombosis and pulmonary embolism. The chronic shortage of oxygen leads to pulmonary hypertension, right-sided heart failure and peripheral oedema (swelling of the feet and lower legs – or 'dropsy'). Sleep during the night is disturbed and the patient nods off uncontrollably during the day. Burwell's patient's condition had many of these features; he improved after he lost 39 pounds.[43]

It has been suggested that Shakespeare's Falstaff [2-8] suffered from sleep apnoea.[44] One of Prince Hal's courtiers describes Falstaff as 'snorting like

2-8
Falstaff.

a horse', to which Hal remarks, 'Hark, how hard he fetches breath'.[45] Such breathing results from a sharp intake of breath following a period of apnoea.

In 1829, William Wadd described contemporary cases of sleepiness associated with obesity. One man who weighed 23 stone (320 pounds) 'was withal so lethargic that he frequently fell asleep in company. He felt so much inconvenience and alarm...'. His condition improved with dieting, by which he reduced his weight to 15 stone (210 pounds).[46]

Sleep apnoea is not a new condition, though treatment has certainly changed since that used by Dionysius, tyrant of Heracleia in Pontus in the fourth century BC, at the time of Alexander the Great. It was said of him: 'He was an unusually fat man, which increased at length to such a degree that he could take no food which was not introduced into his stomach by artificial means.'[47] Aelianus, a contemporary historian, wrote that Dionysius, 'through daily gluttony and intemperance, increased to an extraordinary degree of Corpulence and Fatness, by reason whereof he had much adoe to take breath'. Dionysius lived in fear of suffocating whilst asleep. On his physicians' recommendation he therefore employed attendants to thrust long, thin needles through his sides into his belly (through the fat and into the flesh) to awaken him every time he fell asleep, enabling him to breathe. In California, the airways in the neck are being stented with incompressible cylinders to prevent sleep apnoea, rendering sharp painful needles in the flanks obsolete.

Skin complaints

Obesity leads to many skin complaints, including skin tags, candidiasis, ulcers, cancers, a discolouration called acanthosis nigricans, and psoriasis.

The physician George Cheyne confessed to dreadful skin complaints as a result of his own gross obesity and reported that his own blood was 'one impenetrable mass of glew ... every vein and artery like so many black puddings', so that his 'legs broke out all over in scorbutick ulcers'.[48]

In 1795 Dr William Buchan documented the effect on the skin in 'sedentary and studious' individuals:

> Sedentary artificers are not only hurt by pressure on the bowels, but also on the inferior extremities, which obstructs the circulation in these parts, and renders them weak and feeble ... from whence proceed the scab, ulcerous sores, foul blotches, and other cutaneous disorders, so common among sedentary artificers.[49]

Liver disorder

Buchan also described the effect of obesity on the liver, now known as non-alcoholic steatohepatitis (NASH), which closely resembles alcoholic liver disease, but with obesity as the primary aetiological factor: 'Hence sedentary people are frequently afflicted with schirrous livers'.[50]

Obesity and mental health

The term 'jolly' is often applied to fat people. In some cases this is an accurate label, in others an assumption. 'A malign or dour human being who weighs more than three hundred pounds seems a contradiction in terms.'[51] The emotional complexities within the persona of the fat person have been extensively studied. In her book *The Secret Lives of Fat People*, psychologist Mildred Klingman controversially tackled the paradox of the 'jolly' fat person:

> Being jolly is the fat person's ticket to acceptance. It is important that the rest of us think you're happy. If you're happy then there's nothing seriously wrong with you. You're not a freak. The jollity masks your rage and pain, neither of which is acceptable. It's an emotional disguise, even as loose clothes camouflage the physical reality.[52]

In 2002, researchers at the University of Texas set themselves the task of finding out, once and for all, whether fat people are more jolly. They came up with an emphatic 'No!'[53] They analysed body mass index and studied eight indicators of mental health, including overall happiness, relationship satisfaction and optimism, and discovered that 'In no case did we observe better mental health among the obese. In sum, the obese were not more jolly.' The connections between depression and obesity are explored below.

Anti-fat discrimination is well known amongst the public but, historically, even physicians attending obese patients have been less than complimentary about their subjects. In 1839, Dr J. G. Milligan described obesity as the external manifestation of 'indolence and apathy ... and laxity of fibre'.[54]

Jean Frumusan, writing in 1922, described two different obese phenotypes, the florid obese and the torpid obese:

> the *florids* are those who apparently enjoy blooming health. Their appetite is good, complexion vivid, corpulence does not affect their vivacity and they are the first to boast of their perfect health.

Whereas the torpids are described as:

> pale and puffy, whose flesh is swollen as if by liquids. The mucous membranes are pallid and discoloured, the eyes dull, the walk slow and indolent.... It is from the torpids that the vast army of neurasthenics of all kinds is incessantly recruited, and it is quite exceptional if they do not suffer from the neurosis of fear. Their emotivity is always exaggerated, and although cloaked by an apparent indifference, their exaggerated sensitivities makes their lives a perpetual tragedy.[55]

The physician George Dupain, writing in Sydney in 1935, was scathing about his obese patients: 'Psychologically the obese patient is non-emotional and possesses very little initiative, courage and self-confidence'.[56]

Grafe points out, in referring to Kimpton's *Metabolic Diseases*, published in 1934:

They [obese people] are usually kind hearted, and mean well. Live and let live is their motto. Mental dullness and narrow intellectual interests are part of the picture.

Fatness and foolishness are often synonymous. In the presence of excessive fatness it is difficult to preserve intelligence. In the majority of cases fat people are stupid, easy-going, mulish types. But they can be freed from their bulky embonpoint and their brains relieved from the burden of stupidity.[57]

Another specialist, Francis Xavier Dercum, of Philadelphia, added to the medical field surrounding obesity, personality and mental health. In 1888 he described what was later called Dercum's syndrome, almost exclusively found in women, in which a distinct pattern of obesity coincided with depression and fatigue. The four cardinal signs were later described in the *Journal of the American Medical Association* in 1938:[58] adiposity, asthenia, pain and psychic disturbances. His original work was based on the case of a 51-year-old woman,[59] an Irish widow 'who died both alcoholic and syphilitic'. At the age of 48 her arms began to enlarge, and in June 1887 the enlargement affected the shoulders, arms, back and sides of the chest. 'In some places the fat was lobulated, in others it appeared as though filled with bundles of worms'.[60] He presented three more cases in 1892 [2-9]:

Evidently the disease is not simple obesity. If so, how are we to dispose of the nervous elements present?... Inasmuch as fatty swelling and pain are the most prominent features of the disease, I propose for it the name Adiposis Dolorosa.[61]

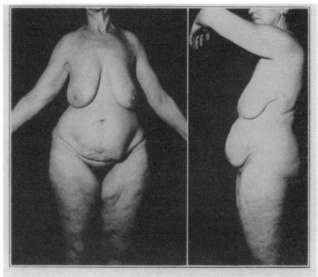

Fig. 1 (case 1).—Adiposis dolorosa. Note lumpy, encapsulated masses of fat on thighs and abdomen, forming an overhanging apron of fat. The upper half of the body is relatively thin (after weight loss of 10 Kg.).

2-9
Figure 1 from Dercum's 1892 paper in the *American Journal of the Medical Sciences*, showing adiposis dolorosa.

The name itself implies sadness and melancholy. It is clear from historical and contemporary literature that obesity and depression are linked.

Depression and obesity

It is worth looking at the possible causes of depression in obesity, a subject which is still unclear, despite modern medical research. It is often thought that depression in people who are overweight is simply due to extreme unhappiness at being fat, loathing of the figure staring back from the other side of the mirror, and inability to follow the same activities and pursuits as leaner people, but there is more to it than that. The repetitive 'yo-yo' cycle of dieting and subsequent weight gain probably has a more profound depressant effect than merely being overweight or obese, because of the additional stigma of failure, whereas successful dieting can improve psychological function.[62] Some authorities suggest that low-calorie diets themselves may have a direct link with depression.[63]

There is little doubt that depression and obesity coexist. Many notable studies have demonstrated poor ratings for mental well-being in obese individuals; one of these compared levels of depression found in different chronic diseases and revealed increased depression and anxiety in obese individuals similar to or to a greater degree than among patients with metastatic malignant melanoma or tetraplegia.[64] A landmark study[65] tested the relationship more closely in 40,000 men and women; it looked at body weight, clinical depression, suicide ideation and suicide attempts. In women, obesity increased the risks of a diagnosis of major depression by 37 per cent, but in men obesity *decreased* this risk by 37 per cent. Similarly, a higher BMI in women dramatically increased the risk of suicide ideation and suicide attempts, but significantly decreased the risks in men, in whom being underweight was associated with significantly higher risks of depression and suicide. The exact reason for this is unknown, but it is thought that depressed men smoke more heavily, which may keep their weight down.

Depression in obese individuals may result from the attitudes, perceptions and reactions of other people to the obese state. There are profound social stigmata linked with obesity in today's society, which discriminates against fat people, starting early in childhood, when obese children are believed by their peers to be lazy, dirty, stupid, ugly, cheats and liars. Often, however, depression may be a precursor to obesity in an individual.

The connection between obesity and depression is convincingly presented in medical literature, far more closely in women than in men, but the phenomenon has not been closely analysed in super-obese individuals. There are certainly specific gender differences between those individuals noted for their extreme obesity; the historical figures who exhibited themselves and were famed for their size were invariably male, such as Daniel Lambert and Edward Bright. Writers and scholars who were noted for their obesity, such as William Banting and George Cheyne, likewise were male – not surprising, given the social constraints of the day – whereas the majority of circus and carnival performers were female (Chapter 3). There are numerous possible reasons for this: for instance, women may have been more popular as performers for reasons of sexuality or social factors, or it may simply have been that extremely fat men naturally shy away from self-exhibition more than their female counterparts.

In terms of gender-related propensity to depression, Dr George Cheyne [2-10], one of the most famous men in eighteenth-century Britain, was the exception to the rule. He weighed 448 pounds at his peak, and suffered from severe bouts of depression. He described his condition as 'a *Disgust* or *Disrelish* of worldly *Amusements* and *Creature-Comforts* … tumultuous, overbearing *Hurricanes* in the Mind'.[66] But there is little other evidence to suggest that the rule is invalid. Carrie Akers apparently made no effort whatsoever to appear outwardly cheerful. A performing fat lady and dwarf, her downright bad temper earned her the nickname 'Quarrelsome Carrie',[67] in contrast to a notable fat male dwarf who displayed the opposite tendency – Jimmy Camber, jester to the grandfather of James I, who was said to be three feet high with a waist circumference of six feet.[68]

2-10
George Cheyne.

Eating disorders and disordered eating

'Emotional eating' is a term used to describe comfort eating at times of stress, pressure or negative emotional state; it is eating that does not rely on the usual stimulus of hunger. This behaviour may date back to childhood, in particular to the time of breast-feeding, when nourishment and comfort were closely associated.[69] Many individuals binge on crisps or chocolates when common sense tells them to stop, but they feel unable to resist until the packet is empty.

There are two well defined eating disorders that commonly lead to obesity: binge-eating disorder and night-eating syndrome. Binge-eating disorder comprises the following features:[70]

- There are recurrent episodes of eating objectively large amounts of food within a discrete period of time, accompanied by a subjective sense of lack of control during each episode.
- The episodes are associated with three or more of the following: eating much more rapidly than normal; eating until feeling uncomfortably full; eating large amounts of food when not feeling physically hungry; eating alone because of being embarrassed by how much one is eating; feeling disgusted with oneself, depressed, or very guilty after overeating.
- There is marked distress over the binge-eating.
- The binge-eating occurs, on average, at least two days a week for six months.

- The binge-eating is not associated with the regular use of inappropriate compensatory behaviours (e.g., purging, fasting, excessive exercise).

Approximately 2.5 per cent of adult women and 1.1 per cent of men are thought to suffer from binge-eating disorder, most but not all of whom are obese.[71] The prevalence amongst patients attending obesity clinics (i.e. those at the upper end of the obesity spectrum) is 20–30 per cent. Depression and personality disorders are linked with binge-eating, but it is unclear whether the abnormal eating pattern pre-dates the psychological condition or vice versa.[72]

Dr Albert Stunkard is the specialist who first described binge-eating disorder, in the middle of the twentieth century, and he has written about the patient who made him consider its existence, a man named Hyman Cohen:[73]

> 'everything seemed to go blank. I just said "what the Hell" and started eating.' He started with cake, pieces of pie and cookies, then set out on a furtive round of the local restaurants, then went to a delicatessen, bought another $20 of food 'until my gut ached. I'll drink beer, maybe six or eight bottles to keep me going, then I'll want more food. I don't feel in control any more. I feel like Hell. I should be punished for the shameful act I've performed.'

2-11
Lord Byron.

George Gordon Byron (Lord Byron) [2-11] was a sufferer of binge-eating disorder. He was born with a club foot and was lame, and he suffered from various complaints during his lifetime, before dying of malaria at the age of 36. He tended to obesity and tried many ways to reduce his weight, as he described in a letter:

> I have taken every means to accomplish the end, by violent exercise and fasting…. I wear seven waistcoats, and a great Coat, run and play cricket in this Dress, till quite exhausted by excessive perspiration.[74]

His diet was frugal and at times he became a 'leguminous-eating ascetic'. The cycle of weight loss and regain cited in his letters and journals has led to a posthumous diagnosis of binge-eating disorder. He describes his various dietary regimens but admitted in 1823:

> for several months I have been following a most abstemious regime, living almost entirely on vegetables; and now that I see a good dinner, I cannot resist temptation though tomorrow I shall suffer for my gourmandise, as I always do.[75]

The health of the super-obese

Many of the illnesses and diseases traditionally linked with obesity, as described above, hardly feature in the medical histories of super-obese or celebrated obese individuals, usually because they did not survive long enough to develop them. The most common chronic condition or terminal event amongst this group is heart failure (also called congestive cardiac failure) – when the heart does not pump efficiently enough to maintain adequate blood circulation, leading to swelling of the legs and breathlessness, as the body becomes waterlogged. Eventually, the heart is under such strain to circulate blood round a massive frame that it stops, and death ensues. The diagnosis probably explains the sudden death of previously 'healthy' obese individuals such as Lambert and Bright. Hudson had certainly suffered from symptoms of the condition before his premature death.

Another example was Jon Brower Minnoch (1941–83), reputed at the time to be the heaviest man who ever lived, who claimed to be 'in no way handicapped' by his weight of over 1400 pounds with a BMI of 105.3 kg/m^2, even though it took 13 people to roll him over in bed. Minnoch was born and raised in Bainbridge Island, Washington, where, in adult life, he drove the island's only taxi cab – a notoriously sedentary occupation. He had a reputation as a 'warm and funny family man' and, according to a friend:

> The Island loved Jon and as far as I know, his fame for his weight was only a big story across the water; back home on Bainbridge, Jon was just Jon – married to skinny little 110 pound Jeanette, and father to two normal sized children.[76]

His endocrinologist, Robert Schwartz, estimated that he carried around 900 pounds of excess fluid due to congestive cardiac failure, which led to generalised oedema and swelling. He was hospitalised and put on a 1200-calorie-a-day diet, inducing a world record weight loss of 924 pounds but, reputedly owing to further accumulation of fluid due to heart failure and oedema, he regained weight, reaching 952 pounds. He had suffered from weight problems even as a child, weighing 292 pounds as a 12-year-old, and 392 pounds at age 22. Minnoch died at age 42, despite having once again lost weight on a 500-calorie-a-day diet.

The *Guinness Book of Records* has listed the world's most super-obese people for many years. But in 2003, *Dimensions Magazine* took over the job of documenting such individuals, by issuing a list which it called the 900 Club: a hall of fame of all those individuals in history with an authenticated weight of over 900 pounds, with a brief biography. It is striking, if not surprising, that these individuals usually died at an early age. Of those with a biography available, the average age at death was 43 years, a loss of life of over 30 years. Carol Yager topped the list, as the heaviest human being who ever lived; she died age in 1994, in her thirty-fourth year, having weighed around 1600 pounds at her peak. She became famous because of her appearances on the *Jerry Springer Show* and her recurrent attempts to diet: at one stage in her life she lost 500 pounds – said to be mostly fluid, owing to the development of oedema due to heart failure[77] – only to regain it.

The youngest incumbent of the hall of fame was Michael Edelman, of New York, whose mother estimated his weight to be 1200 pounds, although his highest officially recorded weight was only 994 pounds. Michael was obese throughout his life, being forced to leave school at age 10 because he was too large to sit behind a desk. His 700-pound mother would feed him a breakfast of four bowls of cereal, toast, waffles, cake and a quart of soda, and his bedtime snack was a whole pizza 'with all the works'. Mother and son were evicted from their home by forklift truck, leading to media attention and approaches from diet companies. Michael did indeed lose weight; he had developed a friendship with Walter Hudson and was badly traumatised by his death. This is said to have induced a 'pathological fear of eating' and led to his death from 'starvation', weighing 600 pounds, at age 28.

The diagnosis of heart failure looms large amongst members of the 900 Club. Although only around 12 per cent of cases of heart failure in the general population are caused by obesity, it appears to be almost ubiquitous in those individuals famed for their super-obesity. Patrick Deuel became celebrated in 2005 as the Half Ton Man; he appeared in television documentaries and the media weighing 1072 pounds and undergoing gastric bypass surgery. His lead doctor, Fred Harris, said 'If we hadn't gotten him here, he'd be dead now'; his wife, Edith, described how 'His body was just so sick, he was just hanging on by his fingernails'. The conditions from which he suffered were listed as 'heart failure, diabetes, pulmonary hypertension and arthritis'.[78]

Descriptions of heart failure as a cause of death vary. Minnoch was said to have had massive generalised oedema, respiratory and cardiac failure, and to have died of multi-organ failure. Baby Ruth Pontico, the circus fat lady (Chapter 3), died of operative complications, inhaling and choking upon her own vomit on recovering from anaesthetic following the removal of a tumour from her leg, but the cause of death was listed as heart failure.[79] Johnny Alee lost the chance to be registered as the largest human being who ever lived because he refused to be weighed. He died of obesity-related heart failure at the age of 34. Alee was born in 1853 and at around the age of 10 began to eat at 'an exceptional rate'. At 15 he was unable to fit through his front door. Eventually, at an estimated 1132 pounds, which would have been a world record if formally accredited, he fell through his floorboards and his heart failed.

Robert Earl Hughes' gross obesity [2-12] was responsible for his death at only 32, in 1958. He was, at the time, officially the fattest human being ever, having been medically examined, and weighed in at 1069 pounds, with a waist circumference of 124 inches. After giving up his job as a farm hand because of his weight, he joined the Gooding Amusement Company and spent his life in a reinforced mobile home. His parents blamed whooping cough at the age of three months for his 'glandular' problems and

2-12
Robert Earl Hughes.

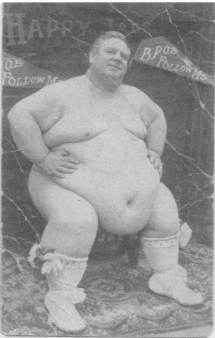

2-13
Happy Jack Eckhart.

ill-health dogged the rest of his life. He caught measles in July 1958, which led to acute renal failure, and premature death in a hospital car park in Bremen, Indiana, as the doors into the building would not admit him, and no suitable beds were available if they had. He was buried in a piano case in Mount Sterling, Illinois.

Happy Jack Eckhart [2-13] was an exception to the rule of early death by heart failure, as he lived to the age of 62. He died in 1939, when the vehicle carrying him was hit by a freight truck and he sustained the sort of internal injuries and rib fractures that, ironically, obese individuals are relatively protected against. Unfortunately, his obese state delayed the onset of medical care, as he could not be lifted into an ambulance. Happy Jack had been one of the most popular and best-known fat men, and was genuinely said to be happy, despite his limited lifestyle. He had started life as an impressive 19-pound baby in Lafayette, Indiana, and began his show-business career as a 10-year-old, touring with Barnum and Bailey, amongst others.

Detailed information about Baby Flo is hard to find, apart from her name, Flora Mae Jackson, her reputed weight, of 850 pounds, and her age of 35 at her premature death in 1965.

The cause of super-obesity is almost always overeating and lack of physical activity, although various excuses are often made. Minnoch blamed 'massive generalised edema' as the cause of his weight, rather than a

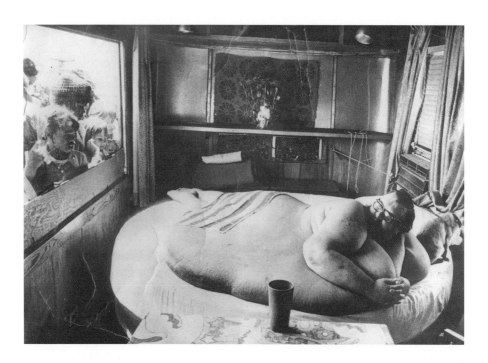

consequence; Francis Lang's excuse [2-14] was the 'munchies', brought on as a side-effect of the narcotics to which he became addicted following his traumatic spell in the Korean War. Agoraphobia, obsessive-compulsive disorder and depression are said to have sealed Walter Hudson's fate, as they caused him to spend the best part of 27 years in bed for fear of facing the outside world. At age 13 and already weighing 300 pounds, Hudson suffered a fall which caused such severe injuries that he remained confined to bed for months. In later life he admitted that the episode 'may have got me thinking that it was easier just to stay in bed'.[80] Manuel Uribe claimed to be Mexico's fattest man, at 1235 pounds, and achieved fame as the subject of a television series. At age 41, he had been bed-ridden for five years, and was told by his doctor 'Your heart is in trouble, your lungs are in trouble, and you are just months away from breaking into ulcers everywhere';[81] he then started to lose weight on a high-protein diet. He blamed his morbid obesity on an unspecified 'hormonal problem'. Half Ton Man Patrick Deuel blamed 'genetics'. Rosalie Bradford, the *Guinness Book of Records* record holder for greatest weight loss (for losing 950 pounds), suffered appalling hardships as a child[82] and cited food addiction as an exacerbating feature in her obesity. Carol Yager claimed to have gained weight deliberately as a child to discourage the sexual attacks of a close family member.

However, one man with an excuse for his size was Mills Darden, who suffered from the pituitary disorder acromegaly and was, medically speaking, a giant. His height was variously reported as 8 feet or 7 feet 6 inches, but he clearly attained an abnormally great stature. He was born in 1799, and his life is the subject of legend. According to a biography in 1930, he was discovered as a baby by 'an old negro woman', abandoned at an old mill – hence his forename; his surname originated from the first words she spoke to him, to comfort him: 'Dar den'. The truth, however, is much more mundane; he was born to John and Mary Darden, in North Carolina. He was reticent about his great size and shunned publicity. He never allowed himself to be weighed and his proportions are known only because of his devious fellow villagers. Darden was transported in a specially constructed cart, as he was too big for normal forms of transport. The suspension of the carriage was by way of springs, whose compression, with Darden *in situ*, was measured by the curious onlookers. Once Darden had dismounted, they filled the cart with rocks to replicate the compression of the springs, and concluded that he was just over 1000 pounds.

For obvious reasons, the 900 Club does not include children. Christine Corrigan, one of the most well publicised cases of obesity in childhood, died of congestive heart failure due to morbid obesity in 1996, at age 13, reportedly weighing about 680 pounds. She was discovered after her death, allegedly surrounded by empty fast-food cartons, and at autopsy a television remote control was said to have been discovered hidden between the folds of her flesh.

It is no coincidence that 25 out of the 28 members of the 900 Club are American, including the entire top eight, as the United States has by far the worst obesity problem in the world. Amongst the remainder, Mohammed Naaman was a Kenyan, who attained 1055 pounds at his peak, and fathered 21 children; G. Hopkins was a Welshman; and Joselina de Silva, who sneaked into the list at number 28, despite weighing only 895 pounds, was a Brazilian who died from double pneumonia at age 37.

In America, there is already an epidemic of diabetes following on from the epidemic of obesity, and there will soon be an epidemic of heart disease and premature death. But as the prevalence of super-obesity increases, the likelihood is that heart failure rates in this group will also sky-rocket as a result.

A life history of Daniel Lambert

Daniel Lambert [2-15; C-1, C-2] was born in Blue Boar Lane, Leicester, on 13 March 1770. His father was keeper of Bridewell prison, and Daniel was a fit, athletic child, known for his ability as a swimmer; he even taught local children to swim in the River Soar. He was passionate about all sports as a child, especially racing, cock-fighting and fishing. At age 14 he became apprentice to a firm of engravers.

> At the age of nineteen, he began to imagine he should be a heavy man, but had not previously perceived any indications that could lead him to suppose he should ever attain the excessive corpulence for which he was afterwards distinguished. He always possessed extraordinary muscular power, and at the time we are speaking of, could lift great weights, and carry five hundred weight with ease.[83]

He was also known for acts of great heroism and strength. He rescued a friend's dog from the grasp of a giant dancing bear, by beating it into submission with his fist, and saved a colleague from being crushed to death under the wall of a burning building.

During riots in 1791 the engraving business which employed him was destroyed, and he followed in his father's footsteps as gaol keeper, but:

> within a year … his bulk received the greatest and most rapid increase. This he attributed to the confinement and sedentary life to which he was now obliged to submit, which produced an effect so much the more striking, as from his attachment to sport, he had previously been in the habit of taking a great deal of exercise.[84]

Daniel Lambert's excess weight has been said to have been 'due to disease', but without any record of symptoms or signs relating to an underlying condition this is pure conjecture. What is certainly a matter of record is that his weight increased dramatically as he graduated from being a highly active adolescent to assume an increasingly sedentary life. He clearly also had a genetic predisposition to weight gain; his uncle, the gamekeeper to the Earl of Stamford, and his paternal aunt were said to have been 'very heavy'.

By 1793 his weight had increased to 32 stone, yet he remained active, walking long distances with ease, was a keen huntsman and continued teaching swimming to youngsters in his native town: 'His power of floating was so great, owing to his uncommon bulk, that he could swim with two men of ordinary size on his back'.

As his weight increased, he became more and more sedentary:

> He was fond of riding before his weight prevented him from enjoying that exercise … before his increasing size prevented him partaking in the sports of the field, he never could be prevailed upon, when he returned home at night from these excursions, to change any part of his clothes.[85]

As gaoler he was renowned for his compassion and sincerity, even by the prisoners:

> he never forbore to make the greatest exertions to assist them at the time of their trials. Few left the prison without testifying their gratitude, and tears often spoke the sincerity of the feelings they expressed.

Lambert worked at the gaol until its closure in 1805, and he was granted an annuity of £50 for life as 'a declaration of the universal satisfaction which he had given in the discharge of the duties of his office'.

In April 1806, he reluctantly decided to exhibit himself in London, at 53 Piccadilly, for an entrance fee of 1s:

> Finding, at length, that he must either submit to be a close prisoner in his own house, or endure all the inconveniences without receiving any of the profits of an exhibition, Mr Lambert strove to overcome his repugnance, and determined to visit the metropolis for that purpose. As it was impossible to procure a carriage large enough to admit him, he had a vehicle constructed expressly to convey him to London, where he arrived in the spring of 1806, and fixed his residence in Piccadilly.

One description of him at this time states that:

> When sitting, he appears to be a stupendous mass of flesh, for his thighs are so covered by his belly that nothing but his knees are to be seen, while the flesh of his legs, which resemble pillows, projects in such a manner as to nearly bury his feet.[86]

He was renowned not only for his corpulence, but also for his politeness, humour and courteous bearing; the stories of his wit are well documented, as is his scathing treatment of rude visitors and hecklers, one of whom he threatened to throw out of the window into Piccadilly.

After five months he returned to Leicester, to tour various local towns.

Daniel Lambert had displayed no symptoms of his illness before his sudden, unexpected death at 9 a.m. on Wednesday 21 June 1809 at the Waggon and Horses in Stamford, where he had travelled to watch, and be exhibited at, the races.

His medical history was remarkable only because of his apparently excellent state of health, which was remarked upon by his visitors and admirers:

> While this extraordinary person lived, his immense bulk and other peculiarities made him not only an object of surprise and wonder to the multitude, but of curious and interesting speculation to the man of science and the medical practitioner. It was impossible to behold his excessive corpulence without being astonished that he was not suffocated by such an accumulation of fat; but when the spectator ascertained that his breathing was perfectly free, and his respiration not in the least obstructed, even in sleep, that astonishment was proportionally augmented.
>
> Till within a short time of his death, this wonderful man enjoyed an excellent state of health, and felt perfectly at ease either while sitting up or lying in bed.... His respiration was as free as that of any moderate-sized person. He was a teetotaller, never ate more than one dish at meals, never suffered pain, never snored, could awake within five minutes of any time he pleased, never retired before 1 am, never slept for more than 8 hours, never caught a cold. He could sing in a strong tenor voice, and enjoyed the company of the opposite sex.

Another report describes his respiration, giving no hint of sleep apnoea or heart failure:

> He slept without having his bed raised more than is usual with other men, and always with the window open. His respiration was so perfectly free and unobstructed that he never snored.... All the secretions were carried on in him with the same facility as in any other person.

His physician, Dr Heaviside, was of the opinion that his patient was in good health; indeed, he expressed the opinion that 'his life was as good as that of any other healthy man'. Lambert was said to have retained his 'health and spirits till within a day of his death'.

His mental health seemed not to have been adversely affected. He was described as a shrewd and intelligent man who was lively and agreeable in company, vivacious and interesting.

However, on closer inspection of his medical history, Dr Heaviside was clearly aware of underlying health problems, respiratory ones in particular. In 1806, having taken up residence near Leicester Square, 'for the first time, he felt inconvenienced by the air of the metropolis' and the physician ordered him to return home to Leicester. Other symptoms reported were 'an occasional momentary trifling depression of spirits in a morning' and 'inflammatory attacks', the nature of which are not fully documented. So Lambert may have displayed mild signs of heart failure, although his breathing difficulties may have been due to hauling his immense bulk around the polluted streets of the capital. His symptoms, though, gave no indication of his imminent death and his demise at age 39 was surprising and unexpected. Its suddenness would suggest a heart attack as the most likely cause.

After his death at an inn in Stamford, his body was removed by demolishing a wall of the room, and placed in a coffin built on wheels, made with 112 feet of elm. More than 20 men lowered him down a ramp into his grave in St Martin's Churchyard. His gravestone reads:

Altus in Animo in Corpore Maximus.

———

In Remembrance of
that Prodigy in Nature
DANIEL LAMBERT,
A NATIVE OF LEICESTER,
who was possessed of
AN EXALTED AND CONVIVIAL MIND,
and in Personal Greatness
HAD NO COMPETITOR.

HE MEASURED THREE FEET ONE INCH ROUND THE LEG
NINE FEET FOUR INCHES ROUND THE BODY,
AND WEIGHED
FIFTY-TWO STONE ELEVEN POUNDS!

He departed this life
ON THE 21ST OF JUNE,
1809
AGED 39 YEARS

———

*As a Testimony of Respect
this Stone is Erected
by his Friends
in Leicester*

CHAPTER 3

Fat folk on show

Freak shows, carnivals and circuses

> Oh they are fat, so terribly terribly terrifically fat.[1]

Dolly Dimples (Celesta Geyer), the most famous and glamorous of all the carnival fat folk – the 'it lady' of fat circus performers – based her career on advice from Jolly Pearl, another carnival fat lady: 'You know honey, everyone laughs at you now. Don't you think it would be a good idea to make them pay for their fun?'[2] Although she was highly successful, and ultimately happy in her job, the foundation of her career was the assumption that obese individuals are discriminated against, abused and mocked. The fact that she turned this to her advantage is testament to both her talent and her strength of character, which enabled her to make a decent show-business living displaying her body, and fighting off proposals of marriage, whilst tackling hecklers and denigrators head on.

> 'How does your husband make love to you?' I was shocked and infuriated; I never thought that a woman could be so uncouth. Returning the shock to her I said, 'Why, honey, he waits until I go to the bathroom and then follows the stream to the exact spot'.[3]

3-1
Bruce Snowdon.

By contrast, Bruce Snowdon [3-1], better known as carnival performer Howard Huge, had much more positive ambitions to become a 'fat man'. One of the last remaining fat 'freak show' performers, he had been destined to become a lawyer, until, studying some old circus books in his local library, he realised that at 450 pounds he had at least a 100-pound advantage over the performer he was admiring. He consequently signed up to the Ward Hall/Chris Christ 'World of Wonders', heralding a successful show-business and Hollywood career, which included an appearance as himself in Tim Burton's film *Big Fish* (2003).

Obese individuals have always been targets for insensitive comments. In 1860, the Mayor of London is thought to have been the first person ever to be referred to as a 'fat slob', and the descriptive vocabulary of abuse has ballooned since, with increasing obesity levels. In Dolly's case, in her new career, the derogatory comments continued unabated, not only from her audience but also in the sanitised form of the banter and 'ballyhoo' of her 'talker', the person outside the performance booth employed to bring in the punters: 'It takes six men to hug her, and a boxcar to lug her'. Talkers would often use drums to attract attention – literally 'drumming up business'. A show in Rutland, Vermont, in 1941 presented a fat family: Mother, Father, Sister Violet, Baby Ruth, Brother Bill and Brother Burvia, whose average weight was said to be 600 pounds. Their talker promised 10 different vaudeville acts from the one family:

> Ten! The family sings, Willie does a whistling solo, Ruth favors you with a tap dance. Burvia gives a stirring sax solo. Ruth follows with an acrobatic number. Not to be left out Ma and Pa will dance. Sibling rivalry? The family's got it, Will and Burr will have a boxing match. Violet calms things down with a Hawaiian hula so realistic you'll think you're on Waikiki Beach. Ruth provides a soulful song of blues. And last, certainly not least! Will and Violet show you how the jellyrolls shake with a fast, modern jitterbug!

Once again, the talker was overtly offensive about the fat family:

> We've had to bring in a structural engineer to figure out how to hold up the stage floor with all that blubber shaking and shifting putting such a strain on that poor floor.... Oh they are fat, so terribly terribly terrifically fat.[4]

Carnival 'midways' (sideshows) thrived during the late nineteenth and early twentieth centuries. One of the most famous was the Coney Island Dreamland Show, which featured stars of the circuit, such as Zip, the 'pinhead', and Lilliputia, an entire village scaled down to size for 300 performing dwarfs.[5] The history of this type of show dates back to the Bartholomew Fair, which started in London in the early twelfth century[6] and which in the mid-seventeenth century featured freaks such as the three-breasted woman and the two-headed man. The 'Irish Giant' Edward Malone[7] was displayed at the Fair in 1692, described as 'Miracula Naturae'. His bill informed onlookers: 'being so much admired Young man, he was born in Ireland of such a Prodigious Height and Bigness and every way proportionable, the like hath not been seen since the memory of man'.[8] Malone was an early example of display for profit; it is possible that he was not obese (simply large), but in 1830 it is reported that a fat girl and a fat boy were shown at the Fair alongside the 'living skeleton' and a pig-faced woman. The Prussian Fat Boy was another celebrated exhibit.

At some stage in the late eighteenth century (the exact date is unknown), a Welshman by the name of G. Hopkins was said to have been exhibited in 'a London Fair', possibly the Bartholomew Fair, in a sturdy cart pulled by four teams of oxen. Reputed to have weighed 980 pounds, he was displayed in a stall alongside some fattened prize hogs. According to legend, after a particularly large meal, he toppled over, whilst reaching for a remaining morsel, and landed on a nursing sow and her piglets, killing them all.

In the United States, freak shows displaying humans rather than animals became more common from the beginning of the nineteenth century. These human exhibitions were still often known as 'dog and pony shows', in order to avoid tighter legislation relating to showing people, as opposed to dumb animals.

Categories of freak

Different categories of freak[9] were recognised: *born freaks, made freaks* and *novelty acts.* Novelty acts did not rely on any abnormality or physical characteristic, but depended rather on a skill, such as sword swallowing or snake charming. Born freaks relied on their congenital features, such as the original Siamese twins Chang and Eng, the famous pianist, band-leader and 'half-man' Johnny Eck, 'born without a body', and Prince Ranadian, who was born without arms or legs but could roll, light and smoke a cigarette with just his mouth, and had seven children. Made freaks included tattooed women, people with immensely long hair or those who had done something spectacularly odd to themselves to make them noteworthy. Fat folk fitted into neither category: some said they were 'made freaks', self-inflicted by overindulgence and inactivity; others, for example the famous Farmar's Fat Family [3-2],

FARMAR'S FAT FAMILY.   TOTAL WEIGHT - 3773 LBS.

3-2
Farmar's Fat Family.

claimed that they were victims of family history, or underactive endocrine systems, or both, and should be thought of as born freaks. According to Leslie Fiedler: 'Like the Strongs, the Fats also seem different to other freaks, since they, too, begin not with an irreversible fate, but a tendency, a possibility of attaining monstrous size, which they can fight, feed, or merely endure'.[10]

In Britain in the twenty-first century, the debate still rages: there are those, even within the medical profession, who consider that obesity is self-induced through gluttony and sloth, and that sufferers, therefore, have no right to sympathy or National Health Service treatment; others recognise the multifactorial nature of the condition, as well as the medical conse-quences of obesity, which rank it alongside smoking as the major cause of chronic disease.

A further distinct category of freak is the 'gaff': a normal person fraudu-lently made up as a freak, such as the 'armless' person with normal limbs taped up in a tight shirt or, for instance, the 'Siamese twins' Adolph–Rudolph,[11] with different facial features (which would not have been possible for genuine Siamese twins), who disguised their four normal legs in one pair of trousers [3-3]. Many fat men and ladies, and even children, would pad their costumes to increase their apparent bulk, and use lighting on stage to exaggerate their size.

3-3
Adolph–Rudolph.

'Modern' fat folk

There is a great deal of debate concerning who would qualify as the very first of the 'modern' fat men or women. As far back as the 1860s the *New York Clipper* weekly entertainments newspaper posted advertisements for John Powers, the Kentucky Fat Boy; he had an older, and heavier, sister, Mary Jane, who was exhibited at B. T. Barnum's New York Museum in 1867. The identity and impressive weight of the Powers siblings is recorded for posterity. John weighed 485½ pounds at age 17 years, whereas Mary tipped the scales at 782 pounds, despite, at 5 feet 2 inches, being over 14 inches shorter than her brother. Mary Powers [3-4] was the fat lady in residence at Barnum's Museum at the time of the great fire of 1868, which destroyed the premises and persuaded Barnum to tour as a circus instead. The Powers siblings set up their own travelling show in Cincinnati, playing fairs with a midget and two bears, before eventually settling in Philadelphia as museum exhibits.

3-4
Mary Powers.

The American author Sarah Orne Jewett published the novel *Deep-haven* in 1877, only nine years after the Barnum fire, and during the time when the Powers siblings were touring. In it she describes a circus's visit to a small town in New England in which one character, Mrs Kew, sees a poster of 'The Kentucky Giantess' advertised as weighing 650 pounds. She is persuaded to visit by the ballyhoo:

'Walk in and see the wonder of the world, ladies and gentlemen, – the largest woman ever seen in America, – the great Kentucky giantess!'

The Kentucky giantess sat in two chairs on a platform, and there was a large cage of monkeys just beyond…. 'Why, she isn't more than two thirds as big as the picture,' said Mrs. Kew, in a regretful whisper; 'but I guess she's big enough; doesn't she look discouraged, poor creatur'?

In spite of the advertisement to the contrary, the Kentucky Giantess admits to weighing less than 400 pounds: 'I believe I'd rather die than grow any bigger. I do lose heart sometimes, and wish I was a smart woman and could keep house.' Mrs Kew's companion feels guilty at being seen gawping at a fat woman, and fixes her gaze firmly on the monkeys.

It is almost certain that Jewett is not describing an actual meeting with Mary Powers; in her introduction to the novel, the author admits that the characters she describes will 'more often than not be searched for in vain'. Furthermore, the fictitious fat lady introduced in this section of text had no link with Kentucky, having merely inherited the moniker from her predecessor in the circus, who had left the show without taking her 'Kentucky Giantess' poster with her. Nevertheless, the scene was clearly based on a meeting with one of the very first circus fat ladies and, unless the name was pure coincidence, it was probably Mary Powers who was her inspiration.

3-5 (above)
Hannah Battersby.

3-6 (right)
John Battersby with 'wife' Hannah.

J. Battersby, 62 North Clark St., Chicago.

MR. & MRS. JOHN BATTERSBY.
Weight, 69 lbs. and 700 lbs.

Lizzie Whitlock is another possible claimant to the title of first fat lady. Although little is known about her career, her gravestone in Batavia, Michigan, states 'Fat Lady of Circus', and she is reputed to have joined the circus in 1867, aged 14, and toured with the Barnum and Bailey Circus at some stage.

However, the woman probably most qualified to be called the first of the modern fat ladies is Hannah Battersby [3-5], born Hannah Crouse in 1842 in Vermont. It is likely that she started being exhibited in 1859, at which time she weighed 500 pounds, and at her peak was thought to weigh around 800 pounds. She married John Battersby, the famous Human Skeleton, and died in Frankfort, Philadelphia, in 1889. Rare individual photographs of Hannah and John reveal the extreme degrees of their personal body morphology, but pictures of them together contrast Hannah's buxom curves and embonpoint with John's bizarre skeletal form [3-6]. It is hard to imagine that this was a marriage made in Heaven, but the commercial possibilities must have been considerable.

The rise and fall of the show

The *Circus Scrapbook* in 1929 bemoaned the fate of the fat woman since the days of Hannah Battersby, and controversially suggested that they may not have had the relaxed personalities indicated by their 'Jolly' monikers (see below, page 50:

> Although the side-show will last as long as the circus itself, I regret to say, that some of the traditional features are losing interest. The fat lady, for instance, is ceasing to interest the public. In the old days no show was complete without her. Thirty years ago, there was a famous rivalry between two famous fat women. They were Kate Keathley and Hannah Battersby. Each weighed 400 pounds, and each got a dollar a week for every pound they carried. Once they got into such heated conversation, that it led to a fight, but there was so much body space between the combatants, that they could not reach each other with their arms. Besides, the exertions threatened them with heart seizure, and their managers were loath to lose such a profitable asset.
>
> Most freaks make equally freakish marriages, and it followed that Hannah married a Living Skeleton, who weighed sixty-five pounds. The alliance was happy and for years they occupied adjoining platforms in the Barnum sideshow. The average fat woman got only $75 or $100 a week. [12]

If this account is to be believed, Hannah was still on display 10 years after her death. A more likely scenario is that, like the Kentucky Giantess, her posters were post-mortem.

According to one contemporary critic, Alfred Trumble, one type of circus freak was particularly scorned:

Bearded women are, as a rule, peevish and a never ending source of annoyance to managers. They demand as many little attentions as a prima donna, and are continually grumbling. Bearded women get from $20 to $35 a week as salary, according to their charms and the lengths of their beards. In spite of the prevailing impression that bearded women are men in disguise there is little doubt but most of them are what they claim to be. The same remark applies to the fat women, with the exception that when you are told their weight you can always afford to deduct at least fifty pounds for every hundred. The pay of fat women is about the same as that of the female Esaus.[13]

As the display of human oddities became more profitable in America during the 1880s and 1890s, 'dime museums' became popular in most cities, sometimes occupying several storeys of a building, and showing permanent artefacts as well as performers and a theatrical show.[14]

Vivid and provocative epithets often followed the names of performers. Lizzie Harris, who weighed 676 pounds, was heralded as the 'Largest Mountain of Flesh Ever Seen'. Captain and Mrs Bates were billed as 'Extraordinary Specimens of Magnified Humanity'.[15]

(The last couple were known more for their height and weight rather than fatness.)

Another craze was for fat lady 'conventions': 'Managers booked in half-a-dozen fat ladies and featured them in various contests – the 50 yard dash in the street outside the museum always drew large crowds'.[16]

In 1893 the World Famous Chicago Show was the catalyst for showmen and small-time carnival operators to group together both to create bigger and better shows and to enjoy security in numbers, and so the golden age of the carnival midway arrived. The good times lasted until the 1960s, when fairground rides became bigger and more popular, at the expense of freak shows. Seeking entertainment from the unfortunate, deformed and disabled became increasingly frowned upon. But during the intervening decades, the shows flourished, and the ability to exhibit at least one fat person was essential to their success.

As part of their business, performers were allowed to sell postcards and *cartes de visite* to their audiences. These would often find their way into family albums in well-to-do houses, alongside photographs of nephews, nieces and even royalty. Such cards have provided unique historical information about many of the performers, both from the pictures themselves and from the unique information scribbled on the back by the punter.

Unique selling points

Because of the relative abundance of fat folk, the individual performers had to have their own unique selling point. This invariably included

3-7
Colosse Tatouée.

exaggerating their advertised weight (the opposite of what we expect today) – as there was no ready way of checking the precise figure – and often wearing loose clothes, or even using padding to enhance their figure. One European fat lady with two strings to her bow advertised herself as the 'Colosse Tatouée' [3-7], leaving no doubt as to whether at least one aspect of her 'freak' appeal was made or born. A show in the 1970s, by which time most gimmicks had already been exhausted, featured 'Lee Klozsey's Man Eating Chicken Show'; punters were attracted by a sign promoting 'Real Alive 7 ft Tall 250 lb Man Eating CHICKEN' only to find a tall, fat man eating from a bucket of chicken take-away! Other means of attracting publicity and stealing the limelight from rival shows included displaying obese individuals together, or accentuating the level of obesity by contrasting the fat person with a midget or 'living skeleton', as with Hannah and John Battersby, mentioned above.

Chauncey Morlan [3-8, 3-9] was a popular performer of the 1860s, whose image appears on several *cartes de visite* from an early age, revealing him as a clothes-conscious and fashionable young man, rather than the sort of boy who would put up with the oversized cotton bloomers sported by

3-8
Chauncey Morlan.

3-9
Mr and Mrs Morlan.

3-10
Annie Bell.

many of his counterparts.[17] Whether his relationship with fat lady Annie Bell [3-10] was just a show-business gimmick or whether these two similar young people genuinely attracted each other is open to conjecture, but the pair were married amongst much razzmatazz at a ceremony celebrating the union of 'The World's Heaviest Married Couple', who had a combined weight of 1132 pounds.

At the other end of the scale, John Craig's bride, Princess Tiny, could not have been more different from her 792-pound husband colossus: she measured only 21 inches tall at age 18 and weighed 15 pounds [3-11]. Other fat folk were put in incongruous situations to provide added curiosity value. For example, in 1894 the Ringling Brothers showed 'ME and HIM' in a boxing match: Fred Howe weighed 435 pounds at only 5 feet 4 inches, whereas George Moore was around quarter his weight, but 7 feet 2 inches tall [3-12]. Both pugilists in this mismatch were 22 years old. In 1918, the Polack Brothers' show featured Buster and Nellie, the 'Boxing Fat Twins' – 'One-Half Ton of Fat' – and another incongruous situation pitted an unnamed fat lady against a (stuffed) horse.

The mental health of fat folk: the paradox of the 'jolly' fat person

The association between obesity and depression (as well as other mental health disorders) was looked at in Chapter 2. Obesity is of interest to the medical profession for one reason only: the fact that it leads to co-morbidities

3-11
John Craig with wife
Princess Tiny.

3-12
Fred Howe and George
Moore, the pugilists.

such as type 2 diabetes, heart disease and many other life-threatening conditions. Freaks, by definition, occupy the very far end of the spectrum of obesity, and individuals of such immense bulk are therefore of scientific interest as *in vivo* examples of what would otherwise be academic extrapolation of disease processes. Scholars such as George Cheyne (Chapter 2) and William Banting (Chapter 5) were able to document their own obese condition in a scientifically clinical manner, whereas performers generally were not: their underlying medical histories come to light only by studying the newspaper column inches or the occasional autobiography or interview. Their intimate details generally remain private and their medical details unknown, just like their true personalities, which are deemed irrelevant once the moniker 'Jolly' is added to their name. A series of medical confessions would probably take the gloss off the show. Punters might have been put off by the realisation, for instance, that Jolly Pearl sat on a specially customised commode throughout her performance to mask her incontinence, and by the fact that she was unable to move to, or fit on, an ordinary toilet.

'Celebrated' fat ladies seem often to have evidence of an underlying depressive illness whereas men generally do not. In fat women, the prefix of 'Jolly', 'Happy' or some similar adjective seems very often to mask melancholy or depressive tendencies. Daniel Lambert was renowned for being cheerful and for his easy-going temperament, and Happy Jack Eckhart appears to have been true to his name. Baby Ruth Pontico, Katy Dierlam, Dolly Dimples and others reveal a variety of mental health problems in their past. Albert Stunkard described the depression found in one of his female patients, Phyllis Baker, who confessed a childhood of almost un-relieved gloom and to feeling like 'a great mass of gray–green, amorphous material. Then at times I feel like a sloth. And just now, when I got up on the examining table, I felt like an elephant.'[18]

At least the public persona of performing fat ladies lived up to their monikers of 'Jolly' and 'Happy', even if only for the benefit of the fee-paying audience. According to Fiedler:

> we do not remember them as melancholy … having been as brain-washed by the rest of us into believing that laughter and obesity go hand in hand. Faced by the camera, at any rate, they guffaw, giggle, and slap their quivering thighs like the very embodiment of zest and joy.[19]

It is clear from historical and contemporary literature that obesity and depression are linked. What is less clear is whether circus fat folk and pro-fessional entertainers fulfil the mental and psychological characteristics expected of them by dint of their obesity. Famous cheery monikers of circus fat men and ladies were intended either to reflect the personality or the characteristics of their owner, or impose upon them an artificial veneer for the benefit of the punters. Such names included Dainty Dora and Dainty Dotty, Winsome Winnie, Bonnie Bess, Happy Jack and Happy Val (a man), Diamond Kitty, Baby Ruth, Baby Viola, Baby Dumpling and Baby Bliss, and Jolly Ray, Jolly Ollie and Jolly Joe [3-13], and many more.

In relation to another aspect of mental health, it is interesting to compare the criteria for binge-eating disorder (see pages 31–32) to the autobio-graphical details of Celesta Geyer, better known as Fat Lady Dolly Dimples.

- 'I was barely able to squeeze through the bus door. I guess I should have paid a double fare but I didn't. For the trip I was well stocked with prob-ably the biggest bag of food that ever accompanied anyone on a bus. The regular stops added to my eating pleasure too, for I was able to pick up "travelling snacks" at each one.'
- Her lack of self-control was so severe that her mother insisted that, on shopping trips, as well as Celesta carrying her own bag, she brought a shopping bag as well so that she carried one in each hand. 'In this way my left, as well as my right hand was engaged. She did this to keep me from eating everything I had bought before I got home. It was a clever device of hers but I soon learned that she would willingly stop when I asked for a rest. It was during these rest periods that I sneaked a caramel into my mouth. This would satisfy the craving for something to eat until we got home. And then I could appeal to Mother for refreshments since I had worked so hard marketing.'

3-13
Clockwise from top left:
Winsome Winnie,
Bonnie Bess, Diamond Kitty,
Baby Viola, Baby Bliss and
Jolly Joe.

- 'I never forgot to eat. I did not want to lose precious time for lunch so I learned to operate my machine with one hand, peddle the treadle with my feet and eat sandwich after sandwich from my other hand, never missing a stitch or a bite.'

- 'Usually I'd had my fill with three or four [pint bottles of sarsaparilla], then I'd watch the horses draw the canal barges into and out of the city. When this attraction wore off I'd return to the bottling plant and continue the consumption. The usual number of pints ran to six or seven per day. As I set this down I cannot help but think of the 1,050 calories I flushed down with this little assault.'

- 'For almost fifty years I was addicted to food. Like the poor souls who are caught in the horrible clutches of alcohol and narcotics, I was caught in the clutches of my own jaws.'

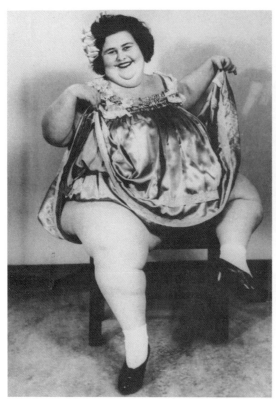

3-14
Dolly Dimples before and
after weight loss.

- 'Quietly I stole downstairs into the kitchen and with the precision of a
  marauder I attacked the icebox. Stuffed like a Christmas bird I returned
  to bed and to sleep.'[20]

Combined with the lack of any compensatory behaviour, this evidence
points to a clear diagnosis of binge-eating disorder. Treatment depends
upon the successful management of the emotional cause. The fact that
Dolly Dimples was ultimately successful in losing weight [3-14], and
maintaining that weight loss, indicates that she overcame her underlying
depression, which she describes openly in her book, having found a successful loving long-term relationship with husband Frank.

Dolly Dimples seems to have suffered from depression and eating disorder despite her stage persona. The aetiological factors of both obesity and
depression are too multifactorial and complex for any reliable conclusion to
be drawn, and different circumstances will have affected each individual.

The stereotype image of the 'gormless' exhibit is propagated in the book
Freak Show by Robert Bogdan (1988), who holds Baby Ruth Pontico (see
below), Dolly Dimples and others up to ridicule, among the category of

'Huge women [who] wore dainty, little girl's outfits, danced soft shoe, and chuckled'. Baby Ruth could not have danced a soft shoe shuffle if her life depended on it, and Dolly Dimples, far from being held up for mockery, was revered and considered to be the 'it girl' of fat ladies.

Other health hazards lay in wait for the super-obese of this era, as they do today: Baby Ruth Pontico was born Ruth Smith, in Kempton, Indiana, in 1904, and at her peak claimed a weight of 815 pounds, despite being 'a light eater'. She performed for Royal American Shows and the Ringling Brothers Circus.[21] She was married to Joe Pontico, a 130-pound balloon-seller in Madison Square Gardens, who, according to legend, first set eyes on Ruth from 100 feet away and exclaimed 'That's my woman!' There was certainly a family history of obesity from both parents: her mother was a Ringling Brothers' fat lady weighing 600 pounds and her father weighed 255 pounds. She had a reputation for being cheerful and friendly, and always willing to lend a hand, but her external veneer was said to hide deep unhappiness at the effect her weight had on her ability to lead a normal life. She demonstrated the obese person's susceptibility to accidents by falling through her sister's floor, having to be hauled out with a crane, and, on another occasion, through the steps of the railroad coach in which she was forced to travel because of her size. Her gross obesity eventually led to large fatty deposits developing on the insides of both knees, which affected her mobility so drastically that a surgeon recommended their removal. Obesity is known to add greatly to surgical and anaesthetic risks, and Ruth was no exception: on coming round from the anaesthetic gas, she vomited and choked to death before her attendants could roll her over. She was 37 years old.

Obesity and eroticism

Circus fat ladies have been described as 'the most erotically appealing of all freaks, with the possible exception of male dwarfs'.[22] Female obesity has often been regarded as sexually desirable; the abbreviation BBW, standing for big beautiful woman, is widely recognised in personal advertisements. Mildred Klingman explains the sexual dynamics often displayed by fat people:

> that an ordinary man would prefer a fat woman comes as something of a surprise to most people. There are many such men.... 'Sure I like 'em big. I don't want to have to shake the sheets to find my woman.'[23]

Helen Melon, also known as actress Katy Dierlam, took to the stage as a performing fat lady and was interviewed in depth during the 1992 season at Coney Island for the book *Bodies Out of Bounds*.[24] She is clearly a charismatic person and an accomplished performer. However, it is obvious from her comments that she feels that her wit and banter, as well as her overt

3-15
Alice Wade.

sexual energy, set her apart from what she considers to be the 'traditional sideshow fat lady' role. Helen Melon's stage surname has sexual connotations, and her opening routine involves touching her breasts and shimmying her hips at the audience: 'Take a good long look'. However, she displays most of the traditional elements of the sideshow fat lady to perfection: the exaggerated weight, the amusing stage name, the girlish attire. So why should one assume that the famous fat ladies from the past were any less erotic?

In the early 1900s, sexuality was not mentioned in polite company, yet under the surface sexually adventurous and immoral behaviour was rife. In the sideshows, exhibits such as the tattooed lady would use their uniqueness as an excuse to show more flesh than would normally be appropriate in public. Fat ladies were no different.

> Sometimes patrons were allowed to touch the limbs of Fat Ladies or pull the whiskers of Bearded Ladies. It was deeply arousing to Victorians to touch a strange woman in a legitimate, respectable setting, and it was a tantalizing and disturbing sight for the other spectators, especially adolescents. A wondrously titillating dialectic emerged, in which performers were alluring as well as repulsive.[25]

A glance at Alice Wade – 'Alice from Dallas' – in the many postcard images available does not suggest a shrinking violet, more an open invitation, as she reclines on a sofa in a silk negligee revealing bare arms and thighs [3-15]. In later, more permissive eras, performers such as Dainty Dotty [3-16] and Miss Baby Dumpling were far more overtly provocative, appearing naked behind fans, '400 lbs of fun'.

Helen Melon explains the basis of the eroticism as 'the memory of having been cuddled against the buxom breast of a warm, soft Giantess, whose bulk, to our 8 lb, 21 inch infant selves – must have seemed as mountainous as any 600 lb Fat Lady to our adult selves'. Similarly, other fat ladies of renown, such as Jolly Pearl, were renowned for their sexual banter and ability to deal with hecklers just as well as Helen Melon, so it seems that she is from exactly the same mould as her predecessors. She

briefly, but importantly, gives some history and autobiography in the interview, revealing weight gain through childhood and adolescence, a degree of yo-yo dieting, and eventual mental health problems: 'a series of crises, including a period of alcohol dependency complicated by severe agoraphobia, led to her current weight'.[26]

Children on show

In 1862, B. T. Barnum held a grand national baby show for the 'Finest Babies, Twins, Triplets, Quaterns or Fat Babies', for the considerable prize of $2000 in cash. The show, advertised as the 'Greatest Galaxy of Human Wonders Ever Beheld', included 'Thirty Two Pairs of Twins, Four Triplets and numerous Fat Babies'.[27]

3-17
Elizabeth Daltrey (with,
below, details printed on
reverse of card).

Fat babies and children attracted enormous interest as junior freaks or medical curiosities, their condition often referred to as 'congenital corpulency'. However, many babies suffering from the condition, judged by modern criteria, seem merely a little plump. 'The Tomkins Child' was displayed as a curiosity of medicine despite his cute but ordinary appearance. Elizabeth Daltrey, the Fat Girl of Bethnal Green [3-17], would fit in unnoticed into most modern school playgrounds. Britain produced a healthy crop of such youngsters. However, maybe the most notable feature of fat children, on viewing collections of postcards and *cartes de visite*, is that they would not earn much money today, as many do not appear fat to modern eyes, and seem typical of youngsters seen every day.

There have, though, been genuine cases of enormous obesity in children on record, including an unnamed girl of four who weighed 256 pounds.[28] In October 1788, at an inn in York, the 'Worcestershire Girl' died at the age of only five years. She had a beautiful face and was quite active despite tipping the scales at around 200 pounds; she measured more round the breast and waist than her height of four feet.[29] In 1862 it was reported that William Abernethy weighed 308 pounds at age 13 and had a 57-inch waist.[30] One of the most famous adolescents to have been publicly displayed for his

3.18
Johnny Trunley,
'The Peckham Fat Boy',
January 1917.

3.19
Adelina Guttilla.

JOHNNY TRUNLEY,
THE PECKHAM FAT BOY
Age 18 years.   Height 5ft. 8in   Weight 36 stone.

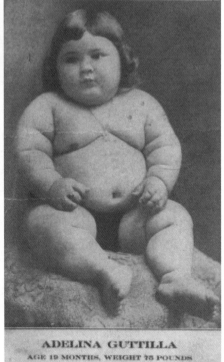

ADELINA GUTTILLA
AGE 19 MONTHS, WEIGHT 75 POUNDS

phenomenal weight was Johnny Trunley, 'The Peckham Fat Boy' [3-18], who claimed to be 36 stone (504 pounds) at age 18.

The arguments surrounding the display to the public of obese children are complex. Children such as Adelina Guttilla (75 pounds at 19 months) had no choice about participating in shows from an early age [3-19], regardless of the mental health consequences. Thomas Sabin was considered to be a great blessing to his parents on account of his weight, as he was a means for them to earn the substantial sum of £10 a week. At two years old he weighed eight stone (112 pounds) and, remarkably, as his weight increased, his stated age remained constant. A specialist from London could offer no assistance to Thomas, so the life of a showman was the next best option. If such obese children had grown up in a normal family and school environment, they may well have been bullied and picked upon, causing irreparable damage; removing them from such negative sentiments may, paradoxically, have protected them psychologically. Traditional upbringing, however, was replaced with life in a goldfish bowl, which may have had its own damaging effects. In any event, treating or controlling the childhood obesity does not seem to have been an option for these children.

For one of the greatest displays of childhood obesity, the British showmen looked to America, to Lovely Lucy Moore [3-20], who, whilst on display on tour in England, was billed as weighing 47 stone 10 pounds – 'the World's Record and still Growing'. The domestic opposition looked frankly unimpressive in comparison: Collosso, the Scottish Giant Fat Boy, was a dour-looking adolescent, and Miss Ivy [3-21], the Lancashire Fat Girl, was a plump young lady with a fringe and bob-cut to accentuate her round face and large neck. Lenny Mason [3-22], the Leicester Fat Boy, would not have looked particularly out of place today in Blackpool, where he was 'On view at 83 Central Beach'. Judging by the comments scribbled on the back of his photographs by his admirers, he seems to have escaped without too much psychological trauma from growing up obese – apparently he was a very pleasant and healthy young man:

> This is just like him, we have seen him, he is ten years old. We could see that he was real, he is a lovely boy; nearly caught on with him. He weighs 21 stone. The Champion Fat Boy of the World. We felt him, he was solid as a rock, such a lovely face and skin. I weigh 10 st 11 lb.

Another says:

> Something soft and cuddly.... He has not once been ill all his life, his father is there giving his tale all about him. I felt like sticking a pin in him just to see if he would go pop.

3-20
Lucy Moore.

3-21
Miss Ivy.

3-22
Lenny Mason, the Leicester
Fat Boy.

CHAPTER 4

A brief history of food and drink

Nothing helps scenery like ham and eggs.[1] (Mark Twain)

Any consideration of fatness or obesity must be accompanied by a consideration of food: its use and misuse. 'What men eat and drink is shaped not only by cooking techniques and equipment, but by agriculture and animal husbandry, by the availability of water and fuel, by knowledge of botany, biology, and the ecology of plants, insects and animals.'[2] Success or failure in the quest for food has shaped the development of mankind both socially and politically. To this might be added his physical and, according to the writer Anthelme Brillat-Savarin, his intellectual development. 'Tell me what a man eats and I'll tell you the kind of a man he is', wrote Brillat-Savarin in the early nineteenth century in his meditations upon cooking as an art and eating as a pleasure.[3] He felt that a nation that thought critically about its food would do likewise about its art, music and literature. On this basis, he condemned Americans as having no taste in art and no taste in food.

The food of early man and early civilisations

Early man was a hunter and gatherer of food; his diet was low in fat and derived mainly from slowly absorbed carbohydrates. Later he added the flesh of wild animals to his diet, and his nutritional status was determined partly by his skill in hunting and partly by his environment. The sporadic nature of his success in hunting animals meant that he often had to withstand times of famine by living on his own fat reserves, and those individuals most favourably genetically programmed to cope efficiently with the variability of energy sources would survive preferentially. Such individuals are said to have possessed the 'thrifty gene', which enabled them to lay down food efficiently as fat – although no such specific gene exists. Efficient storage and slow release of energy were life-preserving mechanisms. The origins of overeating were genetically predetermined during the same period. A successful day's hunting might provide twice as much animal flesh as was immediately necessary, but to waste food would have been inefficient. Eating more than a person's hunger dictated allowed excess intake to be laid down as fat, improving the chances of survival through less successful hunting trips. Two zebras are better than one!

Gradually, early man learnt how to cultivate seeds and to herd, rather than hunt, animals. In colder climates, animals were usually slaughtered before the winter set in, when it would have been difficult to house and feed them. Meat therefore had to be preserved and this was done either by salting or by drying. Although the meat (or fish) itself might have been successfully preserved by these methods, its flavour was not, but this, it was discovered, could be enhanced by the addition of certain grasses or herbs and, later, by the addition of spices. Man also discovered the process of fermentation, by which he produced a form of wine and beer (alcohol is discussed below).

Over the centuries, man's skills and knowledge of husbandry and agriculture developed. Tablets found in Babylon give a record of some of the foods available circa 2400 BC. Garlic, onions, chickpeas, plants of the bean family, lentils, turnips, lettuce, cress, leeks, mustard, thyme, pears and figs are amongst those mentioned. Sheep, goats, cows and pigs (descended from wild boars) were recorded and wild deer, gazelle and wild boar were hunted, birds snared and fish netted.[4] The Egyptians cultivated wheat in the fertile land in the Nile Valley and discovered how to make leavened bread. They had originally made bread from wheat flour mixed with water, flattened and shaped into cakes and baked on a hot stone until it was crisp on the outside. Accidental addition of yeast spores, possibly blown by the wind, made the bread rise. As they did not know the origin of the 'leaven', they kept back a small portion of dough each day to make a further supply that would also rise. 'Number of breads' became a measure of wealth and for hundreds of years payment for work was in bread and beer.[5]

Originally 'diet', to our prehistoric ancestors, merely implied eating what was there to be eaten. Moses is considered by many to be the original writer on diet, documenting those things suitable for consumption. According to Leviticus:

> Of all the animals that live on land, these are the ones you may eat: You may eat any animal that has a split hoof completely divided and that chews the cud.... Of all the creatures living in the water of the seas and the streams, you may eat any that have fins and scales. But all creatures in the seas or streams that do not have fins and scales ... you are to detest. These are the birds you are to detest and not eat because they are detestable: the eagle, the vulture....[6]

Prescriptions about diet became medical as well as religious. Writing about the origins of cooking and food preparation (and the link to health), Hippocrates stated:

> in the beginning man made use of the same food with the beasts, and it was the many distempers brought upon him by such indigestible aliment, which taught him, in length of time, to find out a different diet, better adapted to his constitution…. the distempers arising from the coarse aliment which men at first made use of, obliged them to study the most proper method of preparing bread from grain, and of dressing other vegetables as should render them more wholesome.[7]

The Western world

In the Western world, it is said that our ancestors ate practically everything that had wings, from a bustard to a sparrow, including herons, egrets and bitterns, and everything that swam, from a porpoise to a minnow. Early monarchs gave elaborate and expensive dinners that included such dishes as peacocks, porpoises and large venison pasties. 'Four and twenty blackbirds baked in a pie' may not have been just for nursery rhymes.

In early modern times, sumptuary laws were enacted. The evils which were supposed to have arisen 'through the excessive and over-many sorts of costly meats' were to be curbed:

> no man, of what estate or condition so ever he be, shall cause himself to be served in his own house or elsewhere, at dinner, meal, or supper, or at any other time, with more than two courses, and each mess of two sorts of victuals at the utmost, be it of flesh or of fish, with the common sort of pottage, without sauce or any other sorts of victuals. And if any man choose to have sauce for his mess he may, provided it be not made at great cost; and if fish or flesh be to be mixed therein, it shall be of two sorts only at the utmost, either fish or flesh, and shall stand instead of a mess, except only on the principal feasts of the year, on which days every man may be served with three courses.[8]

In 1363, it was enacted that the servants of gentlemen, merchants and artificers should have only one meal of flesh or fish in the day, and that their other food should consist of milk, butter and cheese. In Scotland, an Act of Parliament of 1433 forbade the consumption of pies and baked meats (which had only recently been introduced) to all under the rank of baron. At the same time, the manner of living of all orders in Scotland was prescribed.

Such rules of the early 'nanny state' soon fell into disuse. Certainly by the time George Neville was installed as Archbishop of York in 1466 no thought of curbing appetites seems to have been in evidence. At the time of his enthronement, 3500 people sat down for a feast that lasted over several days; 80 oxen, 6 wild bulls, 1004 sheep, 300 calves, 2000 pigs, 400 harts, bucks and does, 2300 capons and 3000 geese were just some of the items on the bill of fare, along with 8 seals and 4 porpoises.[9]

Vegetables were not commonly added to the diet until Elizabethan times and fruit was not widely available; a sixteenth-century act forbade street fruiterers from selling plums and apples because the sight of them offered such a temptation to apprentices and servants that they were led to steal their employers' money in order to gratify their longing.[10]

In the eighteenth century, both men and women were great meat eaters and an English dinner was a protracted affair. Food preparation was labour intensive in households of even modest size. At one time, servants and families ate at the same table, the servants at the bottom end – 'below the salt' – and the family at the top. Later, separate tables were used or separate rooms, a practice that resulted in the servants eating in the kitchen and the family in the dining room. In some houses the kitchens were on the lower ground floor, which led to the terms 'above' and 'below' stairs or to the separation of the social classes as 'upstairs and downstairs'. This inferior status often extended to the food served. For example, the 'humble pie' of former times was a pie made out of the 'umbles' or entrails of the deer. This dish was placed on the second or lower part of the table, whilst the venison pie was served on the dais or upper table. In some households the umbles of the deer were the 'perks' of the gamekeeper.

In larger households stocks of essential food and drinks had to be stored. The housekeeper retained a large bunch of keys for access to the innumerable cupboards, cellars, pantries and storerooms. Pickles, preserves, honey, beer, butter and cheese were produced 'in-house'. Even simple remedies for various illnesses were prepared; and the lady of the manor often kept ready-stocked medicine chests for males, females and horses.

The cleansing and cooking of some pigs killed by her farmer husband led Ann Hughes to describe the process as 'a messie job that I doe mislyke, butte they bee verrie goode when cooked'.[11] On such occasions all the servants were assembled to prepare the animals for cooking. The insides had to be cleaned and boiled for three days and the flitches rubbed with a mixture of salt, black sugar, saltpetre and soda. Lard had to be made and the tongues, hearts, lungs and livers were baked in the oven with sweet herbs and onion.[12] Nothing, it seems, was wasted. Parson James Woodforde of Norfolk, for one, might have wished it to be otherwise when on 17 February 1763 he noted in his diary:

> I dined at the Chaplain's table with Pickering and Waring, upon a roasted Tongue and Udder.... N.B. I shall not dine on a roasted Tongue and Udder again very soon.[13]

Woodforde, who had a living in Norfolk, wrote in his diary about the people in nearby country villages during the second half of the eighteenth century.

He recorded details of the lives of ordinary men and women far removed from the affairs of state, which impinged little upon the countryside. He wrote about sport, gossip, travelling by coach, the price of a new wig, his servants, the local gentry and food. Food played a major role in the parson's life – certainly in his diary. It appears that it took 10 days for news of the fall of the Bastille to reach him, but his recording of this momentous occasion took up no more space in his diary than a record of what he had for breakfast and how he had bought an extra large crab from a travelling fisherman. The diary contains almost daily references to the food consumed. For example:

> July 31, 1787.... We had for Dinner some Veal, Beans and Ham, and a piece of Boiled Beef, a Green Goose and some tarts.

> May 11, Monday 1789.... We had Macceral to day for Dinner being the first we have seen any where this Season, 5d. apiece, but the Spring is so very backward that there are no green-gooseberries to eat with them.

> May 21, Thursday 1789.... We had for Dinner some Skaite, and a nice Neck of Pork rosted and Apple Sauce, and Tarts and Tartlets....

On Wednesday 27 May 1789 three guests stayed for dinner, at which they dined upon:

> 3 nice spring Chicken boiled and a Tongue, a Knuckle of Veal, a fine Piece of rost Beef and a plumb Pudding. A green Goose rosted and Asparagus and green Apricot Tarts.

The meal following the public presentation of a child in church is described as follows:

> January 28, 1780 – We had for dinner a Calf's Head, boiled Fowl and Tongue, a Saddle of Mutton rosted on the Side Table, and a fine Swan rosted with Currant Jelly Sauce for the first course. The second Course a couple of Wild Fowl called Dun Fowls, Larks, Blamange, Tarts etc. etc. and a good Desert of Fruit after amongst which was a Damson Cheese.

Alcohol in various forms invariably accompanied these meals. On 23 October it is noted that a tub of brandy and a tub of rum were brought to the parsonage and this was 'bottled off' between eight and ten o'clock the next morning. The parson drank a medicinal glass of port as a strengthening cordial twice a day. (Tea was bought from smugglers and cost between 9s and 10s.6d a pound, whereas a tub of gin – 19 bottles and 1 pint – obtained from the same source, cost £1.16s and half an anchor of rum £1.15s.)

Whereas such meals as those described above would probably be considered excessive in modern times, by the lights of the seventeenth and eighteenth century they might even be perceived as modest. However,

4-1
'The Fat Kitchin; The Lean Kitchin'. Anonymous nineteenth-century print.

during the first half of the nineteenth century the diet of the poor people in the towns was bad. The greater part of their nourishment came from bread, potatoes and strong tea. Later in the century, the consumption of bread and potatoes declined, and there was a steady rise in the sale of meat, milk, flour and vegetables, in line with a general rise in the standard of living.

The kitchens pictured [4-1] tell their own tale: in the first, everyone is well fed. The pot is boiling over a blazing fire and meat and game hang by the side of the fireplace. The diners have eaten well; the corpulent man seated at the table rubs his paunch with satisfaction and a tankard of ale is raised in good cheer. The second scene depicts a sad state of affairs. The diners here are thin, underfed and gloomy; even the dog is emaciated and is jumping up in search of a spare morsel of food. Only bowls of soup seem to be available, apart from a few small game birds which hang by the fire. It follows, in this print, that good health equates with healthy eating and thinness is due to inadequate nutrition.

Alcohol consumption

All countries in every age have prepared an intoxicating drink of some kind. The art of brewing, or preparing an exhilarating or intoxicating beverage by means of a process of fermentation, was known and practised by the Egyptians many hundreds of years before the Christian era, and afterwards by the Greeks and Romans and the ancient Gauls. The Greeks and the Romans had worshipped at the feet of Bacchus – the god of the grapevine – and the grape and wine are frequently mentioned in the Bible. Pliny the Elder said that the Egyptians made wine from corn and gave it the name *zythum*, which in Greek would mean a drink made from barley.[14] The Greeks learnt from the Egyptians and drank barley wine or beer in their daily lives as well as on festive occasions. Pliny also said:

> The natives who inhabit the west of Europe have a liquor with which they intoxicate themselves, made from corn and water. The manner of making this liquid is somewhat different in Gaul, Spain, and other countries; and it is called by different names, but its nature and properties are everywhere the same. The people of Spain in part, brew this liquor so well that it will keep good a long time. So exquisite is the cunning of mankind in gratifying their vicious appetites, that they have thus invented a method to make water itself produce intoxication.[15]

The art of malting and making beer was introduced into Britain by the Romans. Beer and vinegar were the ordinary beverages of the soldiers under Julius Caesar. The vinegar was made strong and diluted with water when the soldiers were on the march; before the introduction of beer, water, milk and mead were drunk in most households. The Romans were also fond of their wine and planted vineyards wherever they conquered. After the fall of the Roman Empire and the Dark Ages, the Church became the vintner of note. Its wine was used not only for religious purposes but also for medicinal and 'monastic' use. Some monasteries even had their own 'labels' and made spirits from fruit such as quince or plum. Those in charge of the infirmaries infused their wine with herbs for medicinal purposes, and at some monasteries brothers were advised to get drunk once a month to maintain a good level of health.[16] Teaching from the Bible had no doubt strengthened ideas about the medicinal properties of their products: 'Stop drinking only water, and use a little wine because of your stomach and your frequent illnesses'.[17] Other quotations from the Bible, however, give warning of the dangers of intoxicating drinks. Proverbs states 'Wine is a mocker and beer a brawler; whoever is led astray by them is not wise'.[18] And more:

> Who has woe? Who has sorrow?
> Who has strife? Who has complaints?
> Who has needless bruises? Who has bloodshot eyes?
> Those who linger over wine,
>   who go to sample bowls of mixed wine.
> Do not gaze at wine when it is red,
>   when it sparkles in the cup,
>   when it goes down smoothly!
> In the end it bites like a snake
>   and poisons like a viper.
> Your eyes will see strange sights
>   and your mind imagine confusing things.
> You will be like one sleeping on the high seas,
>   lying on top of the rigging.
> 'They hit me,' you will say, 'but I'm not hurt!
> They beat me, but I don't feel it!
> When will I wake up
>   so I can find another drink?'[19]

And Luke says 'for he will be great in the sight of the Lord. He is never to take wine or other fermented drink, and he will be filled with the Holy Spirit even from birth'.[20]

In spite of such warnings, a Benedictine monk, Dom Pierre Pérignon, who was the cellar master at the Abbey of Hautvillers in the seventeenth century, developed his champagne by experimenting with different blends of grapes. The idea of frugality in monasteries was dealt a heavy blow and images of rotund monks became commonplace.

Monasteries were remarkable for the strength and purity of their ales brewed from malt, prepared by the monks with great care and skill. The waters of Burton on Trent were famous in the thirteenth century (and are to the present day) and found to be especially good for brewing by some monks who held land in the neighbourhood. Mary Queen of Scots was one beneficiary of this beverage; when she was confined in Tutbury Castle, her secretary asked 'At what place near Tutbury beer may be provided for her majestie's use?' Sir Ralph Sadler, governor of the Castle, replied 'Beer may be had at Burton, three miles off'. In 1630 Burton beer had reached London, being sold in Ye Peacocke in Gray's Inn Lane and, according to the *Spectator*, was in great demand amongst the visitors at Vauxhall.[21]

Drinking alcohol had traditionally been viewed as a good thing: drinking was convivial, wine nutritious, invigorating and medicinal, but lack of self-control led to excessive drinking and its attendant problems. This seemed to be especially so during the eighteenth century, when drinking was also noted to be competitive. 'I was always ambitious', confessed man-about-town William Hickey, 'of sitting out every man at the table when I presided'. Many peers, such as Addison and Bolingbroke (as well as members of the Commons, notably at that time Charles James Fox), lived up to the term 'drunk as a lord'. One ordinary man, Thomas Turner, a shopkeeper and diarist, wrote as follows after a night of revelry:

> we continued drinking like horses, as the vulgar phrase is, and singing till many of us were very drunk, and then we went to dancing, and pulling wigs, caps and hats; and thus we continued in this frantic manner, behaving more like mad people than they that profess the name of Christians.[22]

George Cheyne, the eighteenth-century physician, described how cravings for alcohol grow:

> They begin with the weaker wines; These, by Use and Habit, will not do; They leave the Stomach sick and mawkish; they fly to stronger Wines, and stronger still, and run the Climax from Brandy to Barbados Waters, and double-distill'd Spirits, till at last they find nothing hot enough for them.[23]

The Quaker physician John Coakley Lettsom later described how what had initially been consumed for its benefits

> gains attachment, and a little drop of brandy, or gin, and water, becomes as necessary as food; the female sex, from natural delicacy, acquire this custom by small degrees, and the poison being admitted in small doses, is slow in its operations, but not less painful in its effects.[24]

Soldiers returning from the Low Countries early in the eighteenth century had introduced gin (which they had christened 'Dutch courage') into England and it soon proved to be a panacea for many of the hardships that life had to offer in the form of dirt, disease and poverty. It was not taxed initially because the use of fermented barley in its production provided a market for farmers. In addition, the distillers had a powerful political lobby. Its price therefore was low and sales of gin soon overtook those of the traditional drink of beer or ale for members of the working class; the more wealthy members of society drank wine, punch or brandy. The effects on society of cheap gin were disastrous – socially, morally and economically – especially in London, although other trading cities were not immune. Its popularity increased rapidly between 1720 and 1750. Drunkenness in itself was not regarded as a vice, but its consequences were. As Seneca had said, 'drunkenness does not produce but discovers faults'. The first attempt at regulation to remedy the state of affairs caused by the availability of cheap gin was a parliamentary bill of 1729 that required each retailer to take out a licence costing £20, and put a duty of 5s a gallon on gin. The result of this was to encourage the making of inferior products, sold under the name of 'parliamentary brandy' in an attempt to avoid paying the duty on it. However, the sale and consumption of gin still flourished.

A bill of 1735 imposed greater taxes and licence charges upon retailers in a further attempt to curtail the distribution of gin. The preamble to this bill laid out the reason for its introduction:

> Whereas the Drinking of Spirituous Liquors or Strong Waters is becoming very common, especially amongst the People of lower and Inferior Ranks, the constant and excessive Use whereof tends greatly to the Destruction of their Healths rendying [sic] them unfit for useful Labour and Business, Debauching their Morals, and inciting them to perpetrate all manner of Vices....[25]

The enacted bill led to angry reprisals. Again, gin was sold under other names, such as 'Ladies Delight', 'Cuckold's Comfort', 'King Theodore of Corsica' and 'Strip-me-Naked', and it was difficult to enforce the law. In 1743 the act was repealed. Other duties were imposed but the crime rate, poverty and ill-health increased, much of this blamed on the consumption of gin. A paragraph printed in the *Old Whig* of 26 February 1736 read as follows:

> We hear that a strong-water shop was lately opened in Southwark, with the inscription on the sign:
>
> > 'Drunk for 1d.
> > Dead drunk for 2d.
> > Clean straw, for nothing'

A letter writer to the *Gentleman's Magazine* of 20 January 1743 observed that:

> Since Spirituous Liquors became common, the Baking Trade has very much decreas'd and what the Landed Interest has gained by them, it has lost in Bread and Beer, beside Meat, Butter, Cheese and other Eatables ... [Spirituous liquors] obstruct the carrying on of Trade in every Branch....

William Hogarth had literally drawn attention to the consequences of excessive consumption of alcohol in the form of gin in his engraving *Gin Lane* (1751) [4-2], which highlights the evils perpetrated in a society under the influence of gin. In *Gin Lane*, Hogarth points graphically to the total disintegration of a well ordered and well fed society such as the one depicted in *Beer Street*, its companion print [4-3]. The difference between the two is due to the consumption of gin rather than the traditional English beer. In *Beer Street* the rotund English butcher holds aloft a large leg of beef in one hand and a foaming tankard of beer in his other. He calmly smokes his pipe. In this scene, only the French sign-writer appears malnourished and the pawnbroker's establishment is the only one in a state of disrepair.

4-2 (left)
William Hogarth's *Gin Lane*
(1751).

4-3 (right)
William Hogarth's *Beer Street*
(1751).

Gin Lane is set in the slum district of St Giles' Parish, Westminster, where, in 1750 at least, every fourth house was a gin-shop, and numerous brothels and places for receiving stolen goods existed. The only thriving establishment seems to be that of the pawnbroker, where the prosperous-looking owner, 'Mr Gripe' (the name being slang for a usurer), is profiting from the more profligate habits of his clients. Underneath the pawnbroker's establishment, the Gin Royal tavern sports the words that Hogarth borrowed from the *Old Whig* of 1736, 'Drunk for 1d...'. Two charity girls or orphans wearing badges inscribed with the letters 'G.S.' representing St Giles' Parish can also be seen drinking. Criticism had been made of some charity schools that failed to guide and protect vulnerable young people under their care. Hogarth draws attention to this in his print.

The images portrayed in *Gin Lane* supported the argument of Hogarth's friend and magistrate Henry Fielding, that drunkenness, especially through the drinking of gin by the poor, was one of the chief causes of crime, immorality and poor health. Although Hogarth's scene was one of hyperbole and open to many interpretations, its intention was to show the effects of drunkenness in one print, an exercise in propaganda based on reality. The efforts of Fielding and Hogarth, amongst others, to draw attention to the deplorable state of affairs led to the introduction of yet another government bill, the so-called Tippling Act, against the sale of cheap gin. Legislation was enacted in 1751 restricting licensing of premises and imposing further duties on the sale of spirituous liquors. Infringements were more rigorously checked and penalties imposed. This time, legislation was more effective and the problems gradually diminished.

Unfortunately, the twenty-first century has ushered in a new era of drinking which seems to be more allied to Hogarthian times.

> Those who routinely see the consequences of drink-fuelled violence in offences of rage, grievous bodily harm and worse on a daily basis are in no doubt that an escalation of offences of this nature will inevitably be caused by the relaxation of liquor licensing which the government has now authorised.

This quotation is from a paper from the Council of Her Majesty's Circuit Judges, published in *The Times* on 10 August 2005. 'Our city centres are abandoned to drunk, noisy louts', stated a headline in the same newspaper. The new licensing laws referred to have allowed prolonged and more flexible opening hours in public houses and other licensed premises but binge-drinking and under-age drinking are now becoming a cause for concern. According to *The Times* (4 August 2005), 'Overall alcohol consumption has risen by 10% in a year, according to new Government figures, and sales of "alcopops", targeted at young drinkers have grown even faster.'

Second World War and rations

The diet of the ordinary British people was already changing during the early part of the twentieth century, with an increase in the consumption of fruit and vegetables (other than potatoes), butter and eggs. The nation's demand for bread fell to nearly half what it had been a century earlier. Children were encouraged to drink milk and in 1934 a scheme based on the Milk Act of that year dictated that children at elementary schools each had a third of a pint of milk a day for ½d, the difference between this and the market price being shared by the government and the Milk Marketing Board. There was a steady improvement in the rate of growth of children and in their general physical condition.

By 1939, more information about the relationship between food and health was available. Much of this was through popular women's magazines, often with an American influence. Such items as canned fruits and vegetables, tomato juice, fruit juices and milk bars became popular. Then came the Second World War. 'Adults kept fit and children grew strong and healthy.'[26] It has already been stated that diet is shaped by availability. This was especially so during the Second World War, when Britain, as a nation, had to think critically about its food, though perhaps not quite in the way that Brillat-Savarin would have considered necessary.

Food was rationed in Britain from January 1940 to 1954 and items that had been taken for granted pre-war were either no longer available or in short measure. Rationing began gradually. The Ministry of Food controlled

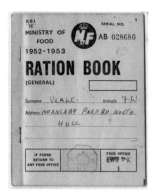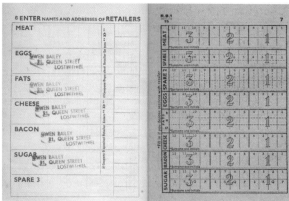

4-4
Cover and inside pages of a
British post-war ration book.

the food supplies and nutritionists were employed to advise the public on the best use to make of their rations. 'Food Facts' were written in the newspapers and shown on cinema screens, and recipe leaflets were available and read out and discussed on the wireless (as the radio was then generally known). Cookery demonstrations were given in marketplaces and shops and from mobile vans.

Housewives were encouraged to fight on the 'Kitchen Front', armed with their ration books – small booklets containing coupons to be cut out as items of food were purchased [4-4]. Marguerite Patten in *Victory Cookbook* (2003) records the rations for one adult per week:

> Bacon and ham 4 oz. (100 gm)
> Meat to the value of 1*s*.2*d*.
> Butter 2 oz. (50 gm)
> Cheese 2 oz. (50 gm) sometimes 4 oz. and up to 8 oz. (225 gm)
> Margarine 4 oz. (100 gm)
> Cooking fat 4 oz. – sometimes less
> Milk 3 pints (1800 ml) sometimes 2 pints. Some skimmed, dried milk
> was available.
> Sugar 8 oz. (225 gm)
> Preserves 1 lb. every 2 months
> Tea 2 oz.
> Eggs 1 shell egg per week. Dried eggs – 1 tin each 4 weeks.
> Sweets/chocolates 12 oz. (350 gm) each 4 weeks.[27]

Sausages were not rationed but were scarce, and offal was originally un-rationed but sometimes formed part of the meat ration. Some items varied as the years passed. Oranges (if available) could be bought for children to eat instead of tea. Many children never saw a banana until the war had ended. The few that were imported were reserved for children with coeliac disease, whose diet was very limited before gluten-free wheat was available (they could digest bananas when they were brown and soft). Sweets and chocolate were rationed, and items like potato crisps, fizzy drinks and real ice cream were not in the shops.

During the war years housewives learnt how to make the best of their rations and nothing was wasted. Vegetable peelings, apple cores, stale bread and any 'left-overs' were put in 'pig bins', which were strategically placed throughout towns and villages; the contents were then taken to local pig farms, boiled up and used to feed the animals (which would then become part of the meat ration). Many homes kept a few chickens in the back garden; their eggs supplemented the rations and the occasional roast chicken was a treat. Vegetable plots or allotments flourished as people were urged to 'Dig for Victory' and many people supplemented their rations with home-grown fruit and vegetables wherever possible. The Land Army recruited women who helped on the farms in many ways whilst the men were at war. The national diet during years of food rationing was a healthier one than that consumed by many people today. Obesity was not a problem during the war years; this came later.

Directly or indirectly, the war had a far-reaching influence on our knowledge of the function of food and of food problems. It was directly responsible for a great deal of investigation on the technical side, into methods of preparation, preservation, storage and transport. This led to an interest in scientific aspects of food and nutrition and to the establishment of research departments.[28] Through research came, for example, the realisation that vitamins might be an important part of ordinary diets.

The post-war years

Arguably, an obesity problem seems to have started in the 1970s, initially in the United States, where farming at that time was in decline, with rising costs and falling profits for the farmers. Food prices were soaring; bad weather had led to smaller crops, protein feed for animals was in poor supply due to failure of the anchovy fish catches off the coast of Peru and the US dollar was devalued. American food was cheaper abroad and subsequent food shortages in America called for crisis management. An aggressive campaign to free farmers from many of the existing rules and regulations in the growing and marketing of their crops led to soaring production of corn and soybean.

Worldwide sugar prices were high, but food scientists in Japan had discovered a cheaper substitute that was six times sweeter than cane sugar: high-fructose corn syrup. This was a boon to the manufacturers of convenience foods, who, by this time, had developed a sizeable market in the United States. Not only was the cost of sweetener reduced, but the new substance also helped to preserve frozen food and even enhanced the looks and taste of the final product.

Palm oil, or 'tree lard', was another product the use of which had been transformed by new technologies. By the mid-1970s it had become a viable commercial fat, 'fit for everything from frying french fries to making margarine to baking cookies and bread and pies'.[29] With the comparatively cheap price of palm oil, its year-round availability, tastiness and the added bonus of a long supermarket shelf-life, its use seemed assured. The only disadvantage seemed to be that to achieve a better texture or good 'mouth feel', more of it would be needed. This meant extra calories in the final product. For mainly political reasons, the fact that palm oil is a highly saturated fat, known by medical experts to be bad for the cardiovascular system, was largely ignored.

American hamburgers, now known worldwide, had arrived on the scene in the early twentieth century. The first fast-food chain, White Castle, which sold hamburgers, french fries and colas, was founded in 1916 in Kansas and this and other chains thrived. It was not until after the Second World War, however, that 'fast foods' became a significant part of the American landscape; McDonald's was born. In 1948, Brothers Richard and Maurice McDonald conceived the idea for a fast-food outlet where customers were served at a window and took their food away to eat elsewhere, thereby eliminating many overhead charges. Initially only hamburgers, cheeseburgers, french fries and beverages were served. Their operations were later franchised and 'drive-in' McDonald's developed in many states of America. Other fast-food enterprises followed suit and different menus were devised, including chicken, pizzas and tacos – all usually accompanied by french fries and colas.

Calorie-dense convenience foods were becoming more affordable and popular, and they offered choice and freedom from the kitchen. Fast-food outlets such as McDonald's and Burger King continued to flourish. Astute marketing persuaded consumers to eat more, and larger portions were provided. 'Large-sizing was a new kind of marketing magic.'[30] Sales soared with 'super-sizing', 'super-value' and 'more for less' items. The chains benefited from the 'new and better' cheaper fats and sweeteners and could reduce prices and still offer larger portions. 'Bigness' in food items became 'bigness' in consumers. It was acceptable; it was about power. There were no limits. Take-away meals and 'snacking' meant that dense, high-calorie food of seemingly infinite variety was available anywhere, at any time, and at a price that most people could afford. Schools were encouraged to give franchises to fast-food producers in exchange for help with the provision of sports equipment – a cynical offer to help children to exercise more to overcome weight problems caused by the very products on sale.

An obesity epidemic in America was born.

In 1974, McDonald's opened its first restaurant in Britain. Customers travelled many miles to visit the new palace of consumerism. Thirty years later, 1235 such restaurants were operating in the UK and 30,000 worldwide. Other fast-food establishments followed suit, such as Pizza Hut, Burger King and Kentucky Fried Chicken. To compound the calorie-rich consumption of convenience food, Coke and Pepsi changed their sweetening agent from a 50–50 blend of sugar and corn syrup to 100 per cent high-fructose corn syrup in the early 1980s.

The obesity epidemic seems to have arrived in Britain along with the fast-food outlets.

Research in the late 1990s showed that an increase in fructose consumption in convenience foods, pastries, snacks and soda pop was directly associated with an increase in obesity. A study carried out by a group of nutritionists from the Department of Medicine at the Children's Hospital in Boston, Massachusetts, in 2001 found that one extra drink of high-fructose corn syrup a day added 0.18 points to a child's body mass index, 'regardless of what else they ate or how much they exercised'.[31] High-calorie consumption, though, is only one aspect of the obesity problem. Calorie expenditure through lifestyle and lack of exercise is another, and this will be considered in Chapters 6 and 9.

CHAPTER 5

Addressing obesity – diet

Proper exercise, food and drugs maintain or restore the body's economy, which is health. (Hippocrates[1])

The restriction of the quantity of food is absolutely the first postulate for anyone wishing to get rid of superfluous fat superinduced by too plentiful nourishment. (Wilhelm Ebstein[2])

A healthy lifestyle and keeping fit are not new concepts. This chapter traces the history of the medical views of obesity, in particular in relation to diet.

The ancient world

The ancient Egyptians were concerned with diet as a means of preserving health and recognised that quantity as well as quality of food was important. Their method of maintaining health by redressing the balance of food ingested was fairly primitive; they were said by the ancient Greek historian Diodorus Siculus to 'prevent distempers by glisters, purging, vomiting or fasting every second, third or fourth day', because 'the greatest part of the aliment we take is superfluous, which superfluity is cause of our distempers'.[3] Herodotus agreed that 'the Egyptians vomit and purge themselves thrice every month, with a view to preserve their health, which in their opinion is chiefly injured by their aliment'.[4]

Pythagoras [5-1] promoted a different approach; rather than eating too much, followed by vomiting or fasting, he recommended moderation as conducive to health, and maintained that 'no man, who values his health, ought to trespass on the bounds of moderation, either in labour, diet or concubinage'.[5] Until the term 'vegetarian' was coined in 1847, 'Pythagorean' was used instead, as homage to the originator of the diet. Iccus, a physician

5-1
Pythagoras.

who came after Pythagoras, was a proponent of his beliefs. The phrase 'the repast of Iccus' came to be used to describe a plain, temperate meal.

The word 'diet' derives from the Greek *diaita*, meaning 'way of life', and the science of dietetics has existed since the time of Hippocrates (c. 460–377). Hippocrates [5-2] considered that length of life depended not so much on a good physical constitution as on the best use of the following practical applications:

1 to divide the day properly between sleeping and waking
2 to adjust air to the needs of the body
3 to take more or less food and drink according to age, temperament and whether one is lean or fat
4 to know oneself
5 to exercise and rest
6 to be able to rule and moderate one's emotions.

5-2
Hippocrates.

Those who followed these directions would have a long life and would seldom need a physician. These rules are just as relevant today.

In addition to the above 'practical applications', Hippocrates' theory of the 'nature of man' was based upon bodily 'type', according to the combination of four humours:

1 choler, or yellow bile, caused a choleric temperament, corresponding to the basic element of fire (hot and dry)
2 phlegm, or mucus, caused a phlegmatic temperament, corresponding to the basic element of water (cold and wet)
3 black bile caused a melancholic temperament, corresponding to earth (cold and dry)
4 blood caused a sanguine temperament, corresponding to air (hot and wet).

These humours should be kept in balance, as maladjustment caused sickness.

The Greeks valued the practice of taking exercise, bathing and having adequate sleep. Sexual advice was given too; for example, intercourse should be more frequent in winter than summer.

Hippocrates' theories on the preservation of health were centuries ahead of his time. He correctly identified the energy balance equation, that is, the difference between calories ingested and energy burnt off by physical activity. Any surplus of energy ingested compared with energy spent will induce weight gain, and vice versa:

> It is very injurious to health to take in more food than the constitution will bear, when, at the same time, one uses no exercise to carry off this excess.... if an exact proportion could be adjusted between the quantity of aliment taken in to nourish every individual, and the measure of exercise sufficient to carry off such quantity, so that the one should not exceed or fall short of the other, such adjustment would fix the true

standard of health, and distempers might with certainty be avoided. For as aliment fills, and exercise empties the body, the result of an exact equipoise between them must be, to leave the body in the same state they found it, that is, in perfect health.

He would have recognised the fundamental root of today's obesity epidemic, as he believed that it was possible to observe the smallest excesses on either side of the energy balance and prevent any imbalance from going further 'and increasing into a distemper, for most distempers do not seize people suddenly, but grow by degrees':

I have discovered those symptoms by which every excess, either of food above exercise, or exercise above food, may be known in its beginning, and prevented from breaking out into a distemper, which will prove nearly of the same benefit to mankind, as if a just equilibrium between diet and exercise could have been found out.[6]

Hippocrates' disciple and son-in-law Polybus continued the theme, but for the first time hinted that rules of diet and exercise might benefit fat individuals wishing to reduce their weight, although the medical necessity to lose weight was not considered:

persons of a gross relaxed habit of body, the flabby, and red-haired, ought always to use a drying diet.... Such as are fat, and desire to be lean, should use exercise and fasting; should drink small liquors a little warm; should eat only once a day, and no more than will just satisfy their hunger.[7]

Contrary to this, the great physician Celsus, who lived under Tiberius, suggested that a healthy individual, rather than follow temperance and moderation at all times, should 'sometimes indulge himself at feasts; … sometimes eat and drink more than is proper', leading to suggestions that he was a 'patron of gluttons and drunkards'.[8]

The fundamental concept of ancient medicine therefore was that a good diet ensured health, since food could cause disease or restore health through its effect on the balance of humours. Purging, bleeding and the use of drugs were drastic remedies, to be used only when diet could no longer help achieve this balance. This reasoning was presented by a body of like-minded physicians who regarded themselves as superior to 'the existing mishmash of soothsayers, magicians, quacks and folk practitioners, those practising what might loosely be called religious, mystical or traditional modes of healing'.[9]

Galen later codified the Hippocratic corpus of work. Galen was born in AD 129, in Pergamum, where a large religious centre had been established with a sanctuary dedicated to Aesculapius. Aesculapius was the son of Apollo and acted as a bridge between the divine and human. He thought that dreams predicted the future and advised on courses of action accordingly. Galen's father received such a sign when his son was aged 17 and was advised to send Galen to study medicine. After obligingly under-going medical training, Galen returned to Pergamum and took up the rather lowly task of becoming doctor to the gladiators. During this time, he experimented with diets for healing and building up the strength of the gladiators. He also conducted some research into the properties of various plants and minerals used medicinally. He then went to Rome, where he gave lectures and anatomy demonstrations and eventually became personal physician to Marcus Aurelius, the Emperor.

Galen followed the basic principles of the Hippocratic tradition but added the belief that, beyond a reliance on diet, everyone had it in their power to control their own way of life. This gave to food a moral dimen-sion that went along with the contemporary Stoic views of life. Moderation and balance were essential in the pursuit of truth and the ultimate good. Galen's most important dietary treatise is *On the Power of Foods*, written about AD 180. In this, foods are classified carefully according to their powers: salty or sweet, good or bad for the stomach, promoting one or other of the humours, sharp or bitter, sour or watery, easy or difficult to digest, slow or quick to pass through the body, costive or laxative, com-posed of fine or thick particles, cooling or heating. It also contains recipes; Galen thought that a good doctor should also be a good cook. For example, a hot and drying recipe – probably containing pepper and wine – could counteract indigestion due to excess phlegm brought on by overeating. A good doctor would learn what foods best suited different patients and pathologies. An individual's body make-up had thus to be assessed. It was recognised that persons who were naturally very fat were apt to die earlier than those who were slender. Galen believed that fat people could be made thinner by warm baths, exercise, little sleep (on hard beds), proper evacua-tions and eating only one meal a day. Galen recounted one of the earliest case studies of the treatment of obesity:

> I reduced a huge fat fellow to a moderate size in a short time, by making him run every morning until he fell into a profuse sweat; I then had him rubbed hard, and put into a warm bath; after which I ordered him a small breakfast, and sent him to the warm bath a second time. Some hours after, I permitted him to eat freely of food, which afforded but little nourishment; and lastly, set him to some work which he was accustomed to for the remaining part of the day.[10]

Galen's rules on nutrition for the elderly were strict:

> Old people should avoid every sort of food that produces thick or glewy juices, as unfermented bread, cheese, pork, beef, eels and oysters, and likewise everything that is hard to digest … otherwise it will occasion obstructions in the liver, spleen and kidneys.[11]

In the first century AD Plutarch, although not a physician himself, made the connection between weight and health, observing that 'thin people are generally the most healthy; we should not therefore indulge our appetites with delicacies or high living, for fear of growing corpulent'. He also said 'The body is a ship which must not be overloaded'. Some centuries earlier, Aristotle agreed: 'Drink or food above or below a certain amount destroys the health'.[12]

The Middle Ages

The classical framework for understanding the workings of the body held sway throughout the Middle Ages. Guides to healthy living were considered important in order to keep disease at bay. In the twelfth century such guides were the *regimen sanitatis*. Ideally, a physician was supposed to provide each patient with his own regimen, which would be determined by his body 'type' and lifestyle. In addition, age, heredity and environment had to be taken into account; sensible eating, relaxation and avoidance of stress were important aspects of a healthy lifestyle. Only the rich could afford such individual assessment, however. For example, in 1424, Gilbert Kymer, an Oxford doctor, composed a *Dietarium de Sanitatis Custodia* for his patron, Humphrey, Duke of Gloucester. This contained 26 chapters of advice about diet, digestion, exercise and the dangers of sexual excess.

However, shorter and more general works became accessible, such as John Lydgate's *Dietary, or Rules for Health*. Lydgate was a fifteenth-century monk and poet. Some advice for a healthy life is set out in his poem 'Doctrine for Pestilence':

> For helthe of body keep fro cold thyn hed,
> Ete no raw mete, take good heed herto,
> Drynk holsom wyn, feede thee on lyht bred,
> With an appetite ryse from thi mete also,
> With women aged fleshly have na a do,
> Upon thy sleep drynk nevyr of thi cuppe,
> Glad toward bedde and at morwe, bothe too,
> And use nevir late for to suppe.
>
> Temperat diet kindly digestioun,
> The golden sleep braiding upon pryme,
> Naturall appetite abydyng his sesoun,
> Foode according to the complexioun,
> Stondying on iiij, flewme or malencolie,
> Sanguey, colre, so conveid bi resoun,
> Voidyng al trouble of forward maladie.[13]

Overindulgence at mealtimes was generally discouraged, as this would disrupt the digestive processes and upset the body humours. The physician

5-3
Chaucer's *Canterbury Tales*.

in Chaucer's *Canterbury Tales* (begun about 1387) [5-3] was perhaps typical of the times:

> He knew the cause of every malady,
> If it were 'hot' or 'cold' or 'moist' or 'dry',
> And where it came from, and from which humour.[14]

Foods could be categorised in similar fashion to the body – hot, cold, moist or dry – and were therefore recommended according to the patient's perceived needs. For example, the melancholy man should abstain from fried and salt meats, drink light wines and eat boiled eggs. Phlegmatic men should not eat uncooked vegetables, whilst the choleric might take nettles and wild hops but may find spices and strong wines 'provocative'.

The ideal state of body and mind seem to have been achieved by the widow in Chaucer's 'Nun's Priest's Tale':

> Her diet matched the cottage where she lived,
> So too much eating never made her sick;
> Her only medicine was a temperate diet,
> And exercise, and a contented heart.
> …
> She never touched wine, neither white nor red;
> Most of the food she ate was white and black –
> Milk and brown bread, in which she found no lack,
> Grilled bacon and an egg or two sometimes.

Other characters in Chaucer's *Canterbury Tales* provide examples of the bodily types categorised at the time, which, altogether, sum up the whole of mankind. The Franklin was a country gentleman and freeman landowner:

> Sanguine his temperament; his face ruddy.
> He loved his morning draught of sops-in-wine,
> Since living well was ever his custom,

> For he was Epicurus' own true son
> And held with him that sensuality
> Is where the only happiness is found.
> And he kept open house so lavishly
> His bread and wine were always of the best,
> Like his wine-cellar, which was unsurpassed,
> Cooked food was never lacking in his house,
> Both meat and fish, and that so plenteous
> That in his home it snowed with food and drink,
> And all the delicacies you could think.

In contrast, the Reeve was a 'thin and bilious man' – a choleric individual:

> His legs were very long, and very lean,
> And like a stick; no calf was to be seen.

The physician:

> In his own diet he was temperate,
> For it was nothing if not moderate,
> Though most nutritious and digestible.

The monk:

> He was a lord full fat and in good point;
> His eyen bright, and rolling in his heed,
> … He was not pale as a for-pyned ghost
> A fat swan loved he best of any roast.

An anonymous writer in 1400 penned the following lines:

> Gentyll bakers make good breade for good breade doth comfort a mannes herte.
>   Sodon breade and breade baken upon a stone or yron is not laudable.
> Burnt breade and harde crustes doth engender melancholy humours.

In most regimens, moderation in drinking alcohol was stressed. Many dangers lay in store for the heavy drinker, especially, according to one Elizabethan traveller, to the drunkard, who snored if the attendant fumes on his breath had no means of escape. Fynes Moryson described precautionary measures taken by persons whom he encountered in Germany:

> They seldome or never drinke with their hats on, for sitting in a warme stove bare-headed, they find their heads more speedily eased of the vapours that arise from drinking. Many of [them] going to sleepe, doe by the advice of the Physitian, put little stones into their mouthes, to keepe them open … that the heate of the inward parts may have vent.[15]

By the same token, the shirt should be kept open to enable body heat to escape.

It is reasonably well accepted that, these days, obese individuals, on reporting their calorific intake, will document their food intake, albeit inaccurately, but often ignore liquids, as being inconsequential. In 1086, the obese William the Conqueror took this to extremes by avoiding food altogether. He was said to have been unable to ride his horse due to his excess weight, and therefore pioneered a weight-loss diet consisting entirely of alcohol. His attempts to get back in the saddle must have proved effective as he died in a riding accident within a year, but the role of an alcohol diet in his decline is undocumented.

Renaissance and Enlightenment

> Man's mind is so avidious, although he have eaten enough, when he seeth better meat come before him against his appetite he will eat.

> Abstinence is the best remedy for overeating.

Dr Andrew Borde, who wrote the above aphorisms, appreciated the virtues of a good diet and of hygiene in achieving and maintaining health and he laid down many rules associated with this aim. Borde was born about 1490 and was educated at Oxford. He became a Carthusian monk at an early age – a strict order in which he remained for 20 years. The brothers were strict vegetarians who fasted at least one day a week on bread and water, and even when not fasting ate sparsely. When Borde was released from his orders he went abroad to study medicine. He returned to England and at one stage was appointed as physician to Henry VIII, who considered himself to be an amateur physician. Borde was noted for his ready wit and humour and his love of good living and was the subject of many broadside ballads. The term 'Merry Andrew' was originally applied to Andrew Borde, a name which became used for a zany or harlequin – one who accompanied a quack doctor or charlatan on his travels – no doubt with the connection to King Henry in mind. Such an individual attracted and entertained a crowd in the marketplaces on behalf of his master, who then sold his 'specifics' or 'universal remedies' to the unwary.

Although Borde enjoyed good living, he advocated a healthy lifestyle and wrote a *Breviary of Health*, published in 1547. The right environment, hygiene and a moderate amount of sleep formed part of his health plans, 'for it doth make parfyte digestion; it doth nourish the blood and doth qualify the heat of the liver, it doth restore nature and doth animate and doth comfort natural and animal and spiritual powers of man'. On rising each morning, Borde gave instructions that one should stretch the arms, legs and body and should wash in cold water.

In his *Breviary of Diet* he offered further advice. Many different meats and drinks should not be taken at dinner or supper, he said, and only two or three dishes were recommended, three at the most: 'Two meals a day is sufficient for a rest man, and a labourer may eat three times a day, and he that doth eat after, liveth a beastly life'. At supper, light meats should be eaten and one should go to bed with neither a full nor an empty stomach. One meal should be digested before the next one was taken. As for drinking, 'Good wine moderately drunken doth actuate and doth quicken a man's wits; it doth comfort his heart; it doth scour the liver; it doth engender good blood; it doth comfort and nourish the brain'. But, he added, 'All sweet wines and grass wines doth make a man fat'. Water was generally unwholesome at that time and ale brewed from malt and water was the drink taken by most people, but Borde disapproved of the addition of hops, which had just been introduced from the Low Countries.

A good diet as a contribution to good health continued to form a large part of medical thinking. In the seventeenth century, Thomas Sydenham, a well respected physician who had built up a practice in London that was famous throughout Europe, had an interest in the natural history of disease. His opinion with regard to corpulence was that it was a lifestyle issue:

> chronic diseases proceed from ourselves, or errors in diet; and although corpulency may be ranked amongst the diseases arising from original imperfections in the functions of some of the organs, yet it must be admitted also, to be most intimately connected with our habits of life. For which reason, the inconveniencies arising from it, are to be removed by dietetic remedies.

Yet another physician, Tobias Venner, had definite ideas about diets. In his treatise of 1660, *Via Recta ad Vitam Longam*, Venner set out to demonstrate the 'right way and best manner of living for attaining a long and healthful life'. He described three types of diet that were usually taken: the 'Accurate or Precise' diet, the 'Vulgar' diet and the 'Subvulgar' diet. The Accurate diet was that 'which is taken in a certain measure, order, and number, and at fixed times, and they also such as are agreeable to his nature and constitution of body'.

A Vulgar diet was the opposite of the Accurate and was one in which no respect or consideration was given for the type of person taking the food:

> no choice of meats, no set or fixed time of eating: for sometimes they eat liquid meats, sometimes hard, sometimes grosse, sometimes fine, sometimes salt, sometimes fresh, sometimes temperate, sometimes intemperate, sometimes of evill juyce, and sometimes of good: so they fill and glut themselves, sometimes they rise with an appetite, sometimes they eat twice, sometimes thrice, sometimes four times, or oftener in a day.[16]

A Subvulgar diet was a mean between the other two: meals were eaten at set times 'with some respect and choice had of the meals'. This was the diet recommended by Venner 'for healthy men to observe'. He counselled that one should not eat unless 'the appetite was certaine' and that 'all such as are truly respective of the preservation of their health, that they oppresse not their stomacks with untimely or immoderate eating'. According to Venner, some people need only one meal a day. This should be taken at suppertime if not too late; it is 'very hurtful to go to bed within 3 hours after a full Supper'. If two meals were taken, the usual time for dinner was 11 o'clock, with supper about six hours later, allowing an hour for a meal. The elderly, 'those that are past their declining age, and entered within the limit of old age, as those be, that are past 60 or 63 years, may eat 3 or 4 times a day, or oftener, a little at a time'.[17]

Venner has words of warning for those who are in their youthful age, 'having grosse bodies, and a phlegmatic temperature'. They should never exceed three meals a day, but content themselves with two at the most.

Venner's treatise posed many questions and answers. One such reads: 'Why ought such as are of a phlegmatick constitution of body, to be more sparing in their Diet than others, for keeping their bodies in health?' The reason is, according to the author:

> because they naturally abound with much moisture, which by liberall feeding would so increase, that their bodies quickly become excessively grosse and moist aliments, as Porke, Fish etc. which fill the body with cold, grosse and phlegmatick humors, are very hurtful for them. Wherefore it is good for the phlegmatick to accustome themselves for the most part to meats of hot and dry substance, to be sparing in their feeding and drinking, and to fast sometimes a whole day and night together, that the natural and internal heat may in some measure consume their moist superfluous and excremental humours.[18]

Dieting was a serious matter and required great consideration of the body's humours. Fasting and a sparse diet were all very well for 'fat and full' bodies, but could be 'hurtful to dry and cholerick individuals'. Dieting, according to Venner, was best undertaken in the spring and summer, and should be altered according to the temperature of the season and the age and constitution of the body.

Another question posed by Venner was whether a fat and corpulent state of body is worse for health than a lean. His answer was that the former condition is worse, for it is more subject to sickness, and it is 'for all corporall actions far more unapt'. Diseases to which a fat and gross body was liable to succumb included 'Apoplexie, Epilepsie, Shortnesse and heavinesse of breath, sownings, and sudden death'. A warning is given to those who grow gross and fat while young, that is, before 25 years of age: they seldom live to be old. This was an early recognition that obesity is a threat to health and longevity.

The first medical discourses addressing the topic of corpulency date from the seventeenth century, a time when fat was fashionable. Medical men, such as Venner, began to draw attention to the dangers of excess weight, which, although rare, became increasingly defined as a pathological state. It has been said that by calling attention to the dangers of excess weight, medical professionals were to a great extent responsible for generating a nascent fear of fat. Their recommendations for weight loss are ultimately to blame for the gradual shift in meaning of the word 'diet' from a general programme of health maintenance to a regimen designed specifically to reduce excess weight.

Recommendations for 'curing' excess weight revisited much of the advice given in earlier times, with the use of purgatives, emetics and sudorifics (substances that cause sweating). In 1670, Johann Friedrich Held offered advice based on the prevailing chemical understanding of fat. He advised the consumption of less meat, hence less fat. Anything that would speed the passage of food through the body was of benefit, and therefore substances that increased salivation such as mercury or chewing tobacco helped to initiate speedy digestion; vomits, clysters and laxatives all helped to clear the body quickly and so prevent the accumulation of fat. Thus drugs seemed to be the first line of action with regard to reduction in weight; a reduction in food intake was not necessarily a consideration initially. This is contrary to the position today, when diet and physical activity are the first considerations, followed by the use of drugs.

Held was probably the first person to define obesity by belt size, insisting that a waistline of over 3 feet (36 inches) with a full stomach is technically obese. Today, the recommended waist measurements are less than 40 inches for a man and less than 35 inches for a woman, but contemporary men and women are generally larger than their predecessors.

The nineteenth century

> A good cook is half a physician, for the chief physic (the counsel of a physician except) doth come from the kitchen; wherefore the physician and the cook for sick men must consult together.[19]

Dr William Kitchiner, who had studied medicine at the University of Glasgow but practised in other spheres, including music and cookery, wrote a book entitled *Cook's Oracle*, first published in 1817, which went into six editions. It includes 600 recipes devised by the doctor, with health, the science of nutrition and economy in mind. He became an accomplished cook and took great pains with the quantity and quality of the food prepared and with the exact timing of its preparation. Guests invited to his house for dinner were not allowed to be late; if the meal was ready to be served, he took his place at table and the doors were closed to late arrivals. He wrote at the end of his book:

> We now have made in one design
> The Utile and Dulce join,
> And taught the poor and men of wealth
> To reconcile their tastes to health.
> Restrain each forward appetite
> To dine with prudence and delight,
> And, careful all our rules to follow,
> To masticate before they swallow.
> 'Tis Hygeia guides our pen
> To warn the greedy sons of men
> To moderate their wine and meat
> And eat to live, not live to eat.

Kitchiner went on to write (amongst other works) *The Art of Invigorating and Prolonging Life, by Food, Clothes, Air, Exercise, Wine, Sleep etc.* The author continues in the same vein, arguing that all sorts of disorders may be produced so long as persons live too fully and use too little exercise. They are warned that, if they do so, they will very soon make themselves ready for the undertaker.

> Most chronic diseases arise from too much food and too little exercise, – both of which lessen the weight of the heart and the quantity of blood; – the first by causing fatness; the second by a diminution of the blood's motion.[20]

Problems with indigestion and flatulence, Kitchiner continues, are caused by overindulgence and certain idiosyncrasies of the person's constitution:

> Salt, Pepper, and Mustard, ay, Vinegar too,
> Are quite as unwholesome as Curry I vow,
> All lovers of Goose, Duck, or Pig, he'll engage,
> That eat it with Onion, Salt, Pepper or Sage,
> Will find ill effects from't, and therefore no doubt
> Their prudence should tell them, – best eat it without!
> But, alas! These are subjects on which there's no reas'ning,
> For you'll still eat your Goose, Duck, or Pig, with its seas'ning;
> And what is far worse – not withstanding his huffing,
> You'll make for your Hare and your Veal a good stuffing:
> And I fear, if a Leg of good Mutton you boil
> With Sauce of vile Capers, that Mutton you'll spoil;
> And tho', as you think, to procure good Digestion,
> A mouthful of Cheese is the best thing in question:
> In *Gath* do not tell, nor in *Askelon* blab it,
> You're strictly forbidden to eat a *Welsh Rabbit*.
> And Bread, 'the main staff of our life,' some will call
> No more nor no less, – than 'the worst thing of all.'[21]

The same book includes some cautionary hints to man to keep him healthy and the author advises him to avoid all manner of distressing symptoms caused by overeating. The remedy lies within his own powers:

> The Stomach, that great Organ, soon,
> If overcharg'd, is out of tune,
> Blown up with Wind that sore annoys
> The Ear with most unhallow'd noise!!
> Now all these Sorrows and Diseases
> A man may fly from if he pleases;
> For rising early will restore
> His powers to what they were before,
> Teach him to Dine at Nature's call,
> And to Sup lightly, if at all;
> Teach him each morning to preserve
> The active brain, and steady nerve;
> Provide him with a share of Health
> For the pursuit of fame, or wealth;
> And leave the folly of Night Dinners
> To Fools and Dandies, and Old Sinners!!!

Surgeon William Wadd wrote his *Cursory Remarks on Corpulence; or Obesity as a Disease* in 1816, at about the same time as Kitchiner was writing. In the Preface to this book, he describes a colleague who had a 'tendency to corpulence' who sought his advice. According to Wadd, this man approached his thirtieth year before experiencing any great inconvenience from his bulk. Then:

> inactivity, somnolency, depression of spirits and an inaptitude for study began to produce anxiety in him. By an abstemious mode of living, and a light vegetable diet he became lighter, more capable of mental exertion, and improved in general health – but when he resumed his former habits, his complaints returned in full force.

'The corpulent grow dull, sleepy and indolent because of the accumulation of fat in the omentum', Wadd writes. 'Respiration is impeded, the ability to exercise is reduced and pressure on the blood vessels obstructs the circulation.'[22] Ultimately, death may result. Wadd goes on to tell his readers that George III's jubilee year of 1809 produced the fattest ox and the most corpulent man (referring to Daniel Lambert, who died in that year – see Chapter 2) ever heard of in the history of the world. It was conjectured by some that for one fat person in France or Spain, there were 100 in England.

It was conceded that there was sometimes a hereditary predisposition to obesity. This was often accompanied by a cheerful nature but was also associated with 'free indulgence at table'. Superior nourishment was a form of privilege – part of a class system. 'The poor', Dr John Arbuthnot had said, 'are seldom encumbered. Spare diet and labour will keep constitutions, where this disposition is the strongest, from being fat.' Nonetheless, 'The restriction of the quantity of food is absolutely the first postulate for anyone wishing to get rid of superfluous fat superinduced by too plentiful nourishment.'[23]

Changing attitudes: the rise of slimming

Thomas Wood became the first weight-loss diet celebrity guru in 1770, when visitors from the length and breadth of Britain visited him, and admirers worldwide wrote asking for slimming advice, on what he called 'abstemious warfare'. He took an immense amount of trouble visiting the homes of his followers for a friendly chat, and to regale them with stories of fat people undergoing ghastly deaths. His advice was always 'Eat sparingly of plain food. Avoid fermented liquors, relishings, salt meats and sauces. Take regular exercise.'[24]

Wood was a Billericay miller, born in 1719, who had avoided fruit and vegetables with a passion, in favour of fat meat, cheese, puddings and quarts of ale. By age 40, he was 25 stone, and known as 'Monster Miller', but remained ostensibly healthy. By 43, however, he started suffering from obesity-related co-morbidities: arthritis, gout, indigestion and a 'raging thirst' – possibly diabetes. He also suffered almost suicidal depression. In 1767, on the recommendation of 'a worthy clergyman in the neighbour-hood', he followed the regimen advised by Luigi Cornaro set out in his book *The Life of Cornaro*, which was written in the sixteenth century but was still in print in the eighteenth century and often quoted. Wood went on a diet, cut out meat and cheese, and ate predominantly a pudding of his own invention: crushed sea-biscuit, skimmed milk, and eggs, boiled in a cloth, starting with breakfast at 4 o'clock each morning. His exercise regimen in-volved digging the garden, riding and working the mill. He was transformed 'from a monster to a person of moderate size; from the condition of an un-healthy, decrepit, old man, to perfect health, and to the vigour and activity of youth'.[25] He died in 1783.

In British and American culture today, the goal of any dietary regimen is generally the elimination of body fat. The science that underpins this had its roots in the mid-nineteenth century, when medical officers appointed by the British government sought to eliminate problems with malnutrition among the poor. Reformation of the relief system of food distribution for the poor was constrained by cost; the largest amount of nourishment was to be provided at the least cost. A fat pauper would be seen as a symbol of government waste; thus fatness became stigmatised. The results of the early scientific studies of nutrition and alimentation were used for the management of pauper diets. The publication of the findings of such studies and nutritional recommendations for an efficient workhouse diet spread, and manuals of domestic medicine and pamphlets on health matters

5-4
Banting's *Letter on
Corpulence.*

disseminated information into middle-class homes. In addition, insurance companies, which were looking for quantifiable standards of health, fixed upon body size as an easy means of assessing physical welfare. Diet, weight and life span assumed new importance and efficient bodies, devoid of excess fat, became the desirable norm. Losing weight gained in popularity.

Other means of treating corpulence were those directed towards regulating the quality as well as the quantity of food and drink consumed. This approach gained much attention after a pamphlet entitled *Letter on Corpulence, Addressed to the Public by Wm. Banting* was published in 1863 [5-4]. This might be described as the first commercially available diet book. William Banting was a fashionable London 'cabinet maker' or undertaker, who, from his early years, had a dread of growing fat. He became so in his thirties and was unable to shed his excess weight, which he called a 'lamentable disease'. By the age of 65, he weighed 202 pounds (his height was 5 feet 5 inches). His initial, unsuccessful attempts to lose weight are described in his *Letter*:

> much exercise, gallons of physic, the waters of Leamington, lived on sixpence-a-day, spared no expense on consultations with the best authorities in the Land, the evil still gradually increased.... [Eventually I could] not stoop to tie my shoe; I have been compelled to go downstairs slowly backwards to save the jar of increased weight upon the ankle and knee joints.

When deafness was added to his list of ailments, an ear, nose and throat surgeon, 'the celebrated aurist' Mr William Harvey, successfully cured his hearing by suggesting a diet (something of a forerunner of the Atkins diet); he cut out bread, sugar, beer and potatoes, and lost over 12 inches from his waist. Banting's diet, unlike modern low-carbohydrate diets, permitted seven units of alcohol per day. Thus this particular diet entailed the removal (as far as possible) from his diet all saccharine, starchy and fat food, a reduction in liquids and the substitution of meat or fish and fruit in moderate quantities at each meal plus a daily draught of an antacid mixture. Banting described the diet in his *Letter*:

> *For Breakfast, at 9.0 A.M.* I take five to six ounces of either beef, mutton, kidneys, broiled fish, bacon, or cold meat of any kind except pork or veal; a large cup of tea or coffee (without milk or sugar), a little biscuit, or one ounce of dry toast; making together six ounces solid, nine liquid.

> *For Dinner, at 2.0 P.M.* Five or six ounces of any fish, except salmon, herrings, or eels, any meat except pork or veal, any vegetable, except potato, parsnip, beetroot, turnip, or carrot, one ounce of dry toast, fruit out of a pudding not sweetened, any kind of poultry or game and two or three glasses of good claret, sherry, or Madeira – Champagne, port, and beer forbidden; making together ten to twelve ounces solid, and ten liquid.

For Tea, at 6.0 P.M. Two or three ounces of cooked fruit, a rusk or two, and a cup of tea without milk or sugar; making two to four ounces solid, nine liquid.

For Supper, at 9.0 P.M. Three or four ounces of meat or fish, similar to dinner, with a glass or two of claret or sherry and water; making four ounces solid and seven liquid.

For nightcap, if required, A tumbler of grog – (gin, whisky or brandy, without sugar) – or a glass or two of claret or sherry.

Although doubtful about its benefits initially and fearing that he had little left to live for, after a short while Banting said that anyone 'who would desire a better table' must be an extraordinary person. Under this regimen he lost 46 pounds in weight in a few weeks, with consequent improvement in his health and restoration of his hearing, the loss of which had been caused by adipose tissue in his throat compressing the Eustachian tubes. At his death, more than 58,000 copies of his *Letter* had been sold, and 'banting' or 'to bant' became the words associated with his method of reducing weight. Many tried to follow this advice, but it was found not to suit everyone. It followed that the regimen should be undertaken only under medical supervision and that a physician should also supervise the amount of bodily exercise advised in addition to the diet.

Banting, and the verb to Bant, were alternately revered and lampooned in the pages of *Punch* and other journals of the day [5-5].

BANTING IN THE YEOMANRY.

5-5
Banting in the Yeomanry.

Harvey stated that every patient under treatment for the disease of corpulence should be weighed regularly, while the condition of his health was carefully watched. He added:

> Particular heed is to be taken that the appetite does not fail, the power of digestion fall off, constipation take place, the action of the heart become enfeebled, or the blood get impoverished. On the part of both physician and patient, firmness of purpose and steady perseverance will be needed.

He also stipulated that weight loss should not be allowed to progress more rapidly than at the rate of a pound a week, much slower than most modern dietary regimens.

Banting's diet did not meet with uniform acclaim. The German doctor, Dr Wilhelm Ebstein, published his treatise *Corpulence and Its Treatment on Physiological Principles* in 1884. In the Preface to the first edition, he wrote: 'The treatise aims more particularly at substituting for the so-called Banting remedy or cure by avoidance of fat something better and more in harmony with the natural conditions'. He regarded the 'Banting cure' as 'objectionable'. At best, he stated, it can be applied only temporarily, because while many patients find their bulk reduced, they feel weak and wretched. Others develop 'a temporary insuperable loathing for the regimen of flesh, or are attacked by dyspeptic affections, rendering a further persistence in the diet impossible for the time being and exceedingly difficult for the future'.[26]

Ebstein quotes Cantani of Naples, who describes the influence of corpulency on mental energy as highly injurious. 'Fat', Cantani wrote, 'quenches the divine flame of the mind even before old age has deprived it of the oil of cerebral nourishment'.[27] Ultimately, premature death may occur. Cantani went further than Banting in his recommended dietary restrictions, by excluding all fats from the diet and, in addition, barring all farinaceous preparations, all saccharine foods, as well as sweet and aromatic fruits. These diets, although leading to a reduction in weight, could not be tolerated for any length of time and the risk of gaining weight again once the diet was relaxed was great.

Ebstein conceded that Banting's dietary system was less condemnatory of fats than were some subsequent diets because, although he condemned pig's meat, he allowed ham, all fish except salmon, and poultry. Hippocrates, Ebstein reminded his readers, had taught that to lose their embonpoint people must eat fat; Hippocrates had remarked that 'dishes must be succulent, for in this way we are easiest sated'. Ebstein suggested that some parts of the body are predisposed to accumulate fat and, he said, layers of fat may acquire monstrous proportions; for example, it may be inches thick under the skin, especially on the paunch, upper part of the thigh and breasts. The caul, liver and heart also accumulate fat.

Ebstein describes three stages in the acquisition of obesity, a term he uses to denote the high and highest degrees of corpulency. The first stage is when the person may be envied and admired for his stoutness and his embonpoint. His body is fuller and the outlines 'rounded off'. He appears healthy and in exuberant spirits. At this stage, his muscular system keeps pace with the increase of his fat. The second stage is when the corpulent person becomes ridiculed and a laughing stock; he may even laugh at himself. For example, the ancient Greeks had jeered at the obese Silenus in the procession held in honour of his foster-child Bacchus, and Falstaff is the embodiment of low comedy (see Chapter 11). Slight inconveniences such as shortness of breath and an increase in perspiration are ignored, but become serious when the third stage is reached. Then, 'the plump face shines like the full-moon, and three men cannot span the paunch'. Falstaff bemoans his own fate at this stage: 'A man of my kidney.... That am as subject to heat as butter; a man of continual dissolution and thaw.'[28] The gait becomes unwieldy and bloated features provoke the derision of the lean. The gravity of the situation becomes more evident to the corpulent themselves and associated problems such as anaemia, gout and diabetes may occur.

Ebstein makes the issue quite plain when he states that as people have eaten or drunk themselves into the state of corpulency, they must forego these pleasant habits of life once and for all. A permanent change in habits is essential. He declares, 'In the overwhelming majority of cases, obesity in human beings is nothing more than the analogue of the fattening process in animals'. However, a cure cannot be expected 'in a few weeks or a couple of months'. A regimen is for life. Fat is an essential part of Ebstein's diet because fats in the stomach alleviate feelings of hunger and thirst. Fats must, though, be taken in moderation, but the would-be gourmet could occasionally indulge in foods such as salmon or pâté de foie gras and this might reconcile him to other deprivations. These deprivations or sacrifices included most carbohydrates, sugar, sweets of all kinds and potatoes, but a small quantity of bread (3–3½ ounces) was allowed each day, as were vegetables such as asparagus, spinach, cabbage and legumes. No meats were excluded from the diet and even bacon fat was allowed, as were fat roast pork and mutton; if no other fat was available, bone marrow should be added to soups. Sauces could be made juicy with butter. The daily allowance of fat was, on average, 2–3½ ounces. The quantity and quality of the food varied with bodily stature, weight and the person's pursuits.

Three meals a day were allowed under Ebstein's regimen: breakfast, dinner and supper. Dinner (at midday) was the most important meal and 'its value must not be impaired by luncheons or so-called second breakfasts.... Under all circumstances he [the patient] must abstain from a so-called evening meal or afternoon tea.' Beer was barred, but two or three glasses of either red or white light wine could be taken with dinner. Ebstein goes on to say that the diet should be arranged so that the sufferer not only tolerates it but even relishes it.

Exercise did not form the major part of Ebstein's regimen. In this respect, he quoted Banting, who found to his great chagrin that when he rowed a heavy boat daily for two hours he acquired muscular power – but also a fabulous appetite. As he yielded to this, he gained more weight. Other forms of exercise such as riding and labouring had the same effect, so that although Ebstein recommended habitual exercise in moderation for the sake of general health, 'of themselves alone these exercises cannot make good the baneful effects of an improper dietary system'.

Dr Thomas King Chambers, Honorary Physician to HRH The Prince of Wales, bemoaned the fact that there is no natural food for humans to eat. As he states in his *Lessons in Cookery* (1878, described as the *Hand-Book of the National Training School for Cookery. To Which Is Added the Principles of Diet in Health and Disease*) man has 'prehensile organs … teeth, jaws, feet and nails' which do not fit him for 'grappling with the difficulties which the adoption of special kinds of food prepared by nature entails':

> He can neither tear his prey conveniently, nor crack many nuts, nor grub roots, nor graze. His digestive viscera in middle life are too bulky and heavy to qualify him for the rapid movements of the carnivora; and they are not long enough to extract nourishment from raw vegetables. To judge by form and structure alone, the natural food of an adult man must be pronounced to be *nothing*.

Chambers recognised the changes in physiology associated with ageing, now known as sarcopenia, which refers to the decrease in muscle mass caused by a reduction in activity levels, which should be countered by a reduction in intake:

> Everybody who has passed the age of fifty (or thereabouts) with a fairly unimpaired constitution will act wisely in diminishing his daily allowance of solid food. At the 'grand climacteric' (as this turn of life is pompously called) the movements of nutrition are retarded, and the constructive and evacuating actions of the system being diminished, there is less call for materials of repair.… The saving up an appetite for the enjoyment of an abundant repast may be conceded as a harmless folly in our juniors, but it is a shame to a gray head.

Chambers recommended alcohol for the elderly:

> in the decline of life the advantages derived from fermented liquors are more advantageous, and the injuries it inflicts less injurious than in youth.… Alcohol calmly arrests the energies of the nervous system which would fret the tissues to decay.… We shrink, rightly enough from being shelved just when the rewards of our exertions are becoming due; and we do not care to rival the centuries of the olive or the yew, unless we can, like them, 'renew our age' and bear fruit unto the end. Here, then, alcohol steps in as a help in need.[29]

Developments in the United States

In 1909, Horace Fletcher, a Fellow of the American Association for the Advancement of Science, suggested in his book *The New Glutton or Epicure* that women held some of the blame for the development of weight problems through their 'aggressive hospitality' in begging friends to eat and drink more than they wanted, just to satisfy their own generous impulses. He felt that overeating wasted the body's economy because of the necessity for the passage of waste 'through some twenty to twenty-five feet of convoluted intestinal canal'. 'This', he claimed, 'is a great tax upon available mental and physical power'. To really appreciate food and for the best digestion, Fletcher recommended mastication. (William Gladstone had famously urged his children to 'Chew your food thirty-two times to each mouthful'.) Fletcher added that the food should be masticated thoroughly, until taste was eliminated. This form of 'buccal digestion' became popular; it was said by Fletcher to 'save an undue waste of food, the burden of overweight, and above all things, the *waste of disease*'.[30]

Henry James apparently practised this manner of eating:

> James was lying on his sick bed in London in December 1915. 'What's the matter with him now?' asked the butler.
> 'Gastric,' said Minnie.
> 'Aye,' said Burgess, fastening his belt buckle with a click. 'All that Fletcherising done it.'[31]

Henry James had met Fletcher 10 years previously and had been converted by the doctor to his recommendations that food should be masticated until it was reduced to a liquid before being swallowed. One memorable day Fletcher had visited the author at Lamb House, and their lunch was a solemn ritual in which priest and acolyte vied with each other for merit. The servants could hardly keep straight faces as they watched the two men virtuously chewing each forkful of their roast beef 60 times. The tempo of conversation was necessarily slow and the meal inordinately long.

Fletcher himself stated that the quantities and kinds of food were no reliable guide to the number of mastications required: 'Some morsels of food will not resist thirty-two mastications, while others will defy seven hundred'. However, the doctor claimed that cheerfulness was as important as chewing; one must be industrious with one's munching and cheerful about it.

A friend of Horace Fletcher's was John Harvey Kellogg [5-6]. From simple beginnings working at the Seventh-Day Adventist Press at the age of 12, he went on to study medicine and in 1876 held a directorship of the Adventist Battle Creek sanatorium. Kellogg was keen to find a healthy pre-digested food for his patients at the sanatorium and at this time a contemporary named James Caleb Jackson was baking flour and water in thin sheets until

5-6
John Harvey Kellogg and his
famous flakes.

it was brittle, grinding it up and baking it again – and again. Kellogg added
several different grains to a version of his own and his brother, Will, added
sugar, malt and grain. By 1906, the resultant cornflakes were selling so
well that the brothers set up a company for that product alone. Here was a
product that was a medicine, pure, digestible and wholesome.

Kellogg went on to treat obesity with a low-fat diet of lean meat, green
vegetables and pure water. Water cures and electrotherapy became part of
his remit, along with many other 'gadgets' for reducing body weight. He also
embraced 'Fletcherism' and bran, and he counted calories; every portion of
food at the sanatorium was weighed. A low-calorie, high-bulk, moderate-
protein diet with daily baths and exercise became the rage, spreading from
Battle Creek across America.

Over the years, many methods of dieting have come and gone. 'Reducing
has become a national pastime … a craze, a national fanaticism, a frenzy',
wrote one journalist in 1925, but perhaps the best advice is still that given
by Cornaro: 'That of all parts of a feast, that which one leaves, does one
most good'.

CHAPTER 6

Addressing obesity – physical exercise

> Cardan condemns exercise as prejudicial to health; and that by comparing the longevity of trees to the ordinary duration of animal life, he attributes the long life of the first to their immobility.[1]

Cardan, otherwise known as Hieronymus Cardanus, was born in Pavia, Italy, in 1500, and is one of the most important writers on the preservation of health and longevity. He also cured the Archbishop of St Andrews of 'a dangerous illness'. He was an admirer of Luigi Cornaro, the Italian nobleman who changed his debauched lifestyle when in his forties, and lived to be over 100 years of age, but Cardan was no admirer of Hippocrates or Galen and blamed them for mistakes in their work, the proof of which was that Galen only lived until age 77, 'which cannot properly be called old age'. Cardan, however, reached only 75. He was unique amongst health writers, in being vehemently opposed to physical activity. Mackenzie stated:

> He exclaims, for example, against using any exercise that can fatigue a man in the smallest degree, or throw him into the most gentle sweat, or in the least accelerates his respiration; and gravely observes, that trees live longer than animals, because they never stir from their places.[2]

Modern science disagrees wholeheartedly with Cardan: sedentariness is associated with obesity, but is also an independent risk factor for cardiovascular disease, as well as cancer and other illnesses. As one expert states:

> The human body has evolved to accommodate vigorous physical activity, and inactivity can be regarded as the abnormal, rather than normal. It should not, therefore, be surprising that inactivity is associated with ill health.[3]

In the distant past of our hunter-gatherer ancestors, vigorous activity was necessary for survival; energy was used for hunting and self-defence, so it was a precious commodity, not to be wasted. Although obesity is known to have existed in prehistoric times, as depicted by the Venus of Willendorf and other such statuettes (see Chapter 10), man's ancestors were generally fit and lean. Intensive physical activity was a normal part of life before machines, and preserving energy was a more pressing concern. The inventor of the wheel would not have known what a vicious circle he was creating.

Those people who eat whenever food is available and who rest until called into urgent action are becoming overweight and obese. Having survived preferentially, by courtesy of their 'thrifty' genotype, they are now being deselected by nature, suffering increased rates of heart disease, diabetes, cancer and ultimately premature death. This chapter examines the changing role of physical activity within a person's life throughout history, from being a necessary aspect of life, to being vital for the preservation of health, then being a means of regaining lost health, and ultimately playing an important role in the treatment of obesity.

The history of physical activity and its relation to health reflects the environmental and secular changes which have occurred over thousands of years. Once a vital element of life, activity has become less of a necessity with the invention of machines and the progression of technology, but it remains an important aspect of health. It has now been relegated to the status of a trivial aspect of our daily routine, but simultaneously elevated to become a vital part of the solution to the obesity epidemic. Until recently, those people in any society most able to call upon the latest advances have always been those at the top of the social scale, the rich and affluent, who, naturally, also became the first group to succumb to the problems associated with obesity and lack of physical fitness. Recent trends, however – a reduction in manual labour, an increase in cheaper and widely available labour-saving devices, alongside a revolution in eating habits – have led to the more deprived members of society developing the most serious and debilitating obesity-related problems. As the drivers for exercise have altered over the course of history, so the scholarly advice offered to the population has been revised and the ability to indulge in active pursuits has changed.

Writers in different eras have had different attitudes to physical activity, just as they have concerning diet (Chapter 5). Whereas the modern method is to promote diet and physical activity in novel and unconventional ways, early texts dwell more on the inclusion of food, air and exercise as part of a fulfilling, balanced existence.

The ancient world

Misogug was High Priest of Synopolis.[4] He used his influence to demand clinical action against disease rather than mere discussion of its nature – personal medical care as opposed to epidemiology – and became dissatisfied with the physicians of the country for their 'long and unintelligible harangues on the nature of distemper instead of giving directions for a cure'. He also complained darkly of their 'not altogether unblemished characters'. Misogug had a drastic solution: he struck off half of his physicians from practising and conferred the degree of doctor on the rest, after examining them on their different modes of treating patients. One such examination is described:

> A venerable old man appeared one morning before his tribunal; and Misogug inquired what were his theory and practice of medicine? He expected from the man a profound display of erudition, mixed up with the jargon of his art, and already, in imagination, felt himself fatigued and disgusted at his long and learned references. The old man, trembling, told him that he could neither read nor write, and yet had been so happy as never to occasion the death of a single person during the whole course of his life. 'Good heavens!' exclaimed Misogug, with amazement ... '– what a wonder! – pray what are the secrets or prescriptions which you make use of?' 'They are very simple,' replied the old man; 'I never prescribe either purges or blood letting, and the only medicines which I prescribe are oxymel, juleps and exercise.'[5]

The old man's grasp of the basics of preservation of health without recourse to drugs also included light diet – 'never rise from table with a cloyed and overloaded stomach' – and earned him the appointment of chief physician.

The ancient Greeks had their own theories on exercise and health. The philosopher Pythagoras was said to have been the first to recommend universal moderation and temperance as conducive to health: 'no man who values his health, ought to trespass on the bounds of moderation, either in labour, diet or concubinage'.[6] Iccus, a follower of Pythagoras, also wrote of temperance and exercise for the preservation of health, and recommended the union of gymnastics with the most sober regimen to preserve health.[7] Herodicus taught the infirm to regulate their exercise to prolong life. Although the practice of 'seasoning youths for the fatigues of war and hardening champions for combat' using exercise and training dates back to Hercules, Herodicus is hailed as the inventor of the 'medicinal gymnastic'. Plutarch wrote of him: 'he was the first that blended the gymnastic art with physic in such a manner as protracted to old age his own life, and the lives of others afflicted with the same distemper'.[8]

Hippocrates wrote volumes on the subject of exercise for the maintenance of good health. His six 'articles', the indispensable elements necessary to the life of man, were 'air, aliment, exercise and rest, sleep and wakefulness, repletion and evacuation, together with the passions and affectations of the mind'.[9] Too much sleep 'relaxes the body, oppresses the head, and makes a man look as if he was parboiled'.[10] On evacuation, he wrote:

> When it becomes necessary to cleanse the body, those who are thin,
> and bear vomiting well, ought to take a puke; but those who are fleshy
> and hard to vomit should be purged downwards. And it is in general to
> be observed that a puke, where it agrees, is best in summer, and a purge
> in winter.

On exercise, his teaching was extremely balanced. Moderate exercise is
beneficial for the preservation of health, but too much or too little can be
harmful:

> The complaints which arise from immoderate labour are cured by
> rest; and those which proceed from sloth are removed by exercise. If
> the whole body should rest a great deal longer than usual, it will not
> become stronger for that rest.... The feet, by a long state of rest are dis-
> qualified for much walking, and the other limbs, by long inaction, lose
> in a great measure their use.... Those who seldom use any motion, are
> wearied by the smallest exercise.[11]

Because physical activity was being recommended during this era in order
to preserve health, rather than combat obesity, the nature of the tasks prescribed do not appear unduly arduous in a modern context:

> Reading aloud and singing ... and of all exercises walking seems the
> most natural to men in good health. Universally speaking, moderate
> exercise gives strength to the body, and vigour to the senses. Exercise is
> wholesomest and best before meals.[12]

Hippocrates agreed with Pythagoras that moderation in all things was
crucial to good health: 'Every excess is an enemy to nature: In labour, meat,
drink, sleep, and commerce with the sex, a just mediocrity and moderation
should be observed'.[13]

As mentioned in the previous chapter, Hippocrates correctly identified
the energy balance equation: any surplus of ingested energy compared with
energy spent will induce weight gain. A follower of Hippocrates, Polybus,
went one step further and introduced the subject of fat into the equation.
He suggested exercise as a possible remedy, that is, as a means to regain
health, rather than just a method of preserving it.

Celsus taught along similar lines and differentiated between the suitable
modes of activity for different individuals:

> The meagre should be plumped up by very gentle exercise, and long
> intervals of rest ... fat persons should be made thinner by warm
> bathing, strong exercise, hard beds, little sleep, proper evacuations,
> acids, and one meal a day.[14]

He pays particular attention to one source of physical exertion: 'commerce
with the fair sex', which is 'neither too wantonly to be indulged, nor too

timorously to be shunned. When moderate it renders the body lively, but too frequently it wastes and enervates.'[15]

Plutarch had good advice for those with a sedentary occupation, and his teachings have increased relevance today, as activity has been systematically removed from work and leisure lives. Whereas modern man is advised to reverse the consequences of obesity by walking 10,000 steps per day, or performing 60–90 minutes of brisk exercise every 24 hours, Plutarch's advice seems ludicrously lenient and simple (a reflection on the mildness of the condition in that time). Plutarch noted of 'men of letters' that they benefit 'from reading aloud every day' and 'we ought therefore to make that exercise familiar to us.... The voice moves gently upon the thoughts of another, and glides smoothly along without that vehemence which generally attends disputations'. But he adds a warning not to overdo it (as with any exercise):

> But tho' reading aloud is a very healthful exercise, violent vociferation may prove pernicious, as it has frequently been the cause of bursting some blood vessel.... It is carefully to be observed that this exercise of reading aloud ... must not be used immediately after repast or fatigue, for such an error has proved hurtful to many.

The thought that reading aloud too vigorously could be harmful would baffle modern middle-aged squash players, or veteran rugby players, who are unlikely to be convinced about changing to reading aloud for their adrenaline rush.

Socrates, by contrast, recommended more brisk activity, and directly contradicted Cardan's later call for immobility:

> Idleness and sloth have always been looked upon as a plentiful source of distempers, and the man who thinks to procure himself health by indolence, is like him who, by continuing to be silent, hopes to mend his voice. Besides, the very end and aim of health, which is action, is destroyed by sloth; what is his health good for, who never does anything to help himself or his friends?[16]

Socrates' recommendation was dancing, although only for health purposes. Dancing for enjoyment was 'inconvenient as it took up too much room, whereas to a man who used the exercise of singing, or reading aloud, a chamber large enough to fit in, was sufficient.'

Another advocate of dancing was Ptolemy VII, son of Alexander the Great, who was so fat that when he walked he had to be supported on both sides, but when drunk he would 'forget his gross bulk and execute wild dances on top of his couch'.[17]

In the fifth century AD, Caelius Aurelianus advised the taking of food with little nutrition in it and enjoined the patient to take exercise – to ride on horseback, or take a sea voyage, to read aloud and to give the limbs motion by walking quickly.

Galen was a believer in the use of diet and exercise to prolong life. He offered such advice to those at both extremes of life, starting in childhood: 'The child be then taught to use moderate exercise but not too violent lest it should stint his growth'. Having helped his followers to grow up healthy and achieve great longevity, he did not let them then relax into indolence or sloth. Galen recounts the case of Antiochus the Physician:

> when he was above fourscore years old, walked from his house, three stadia to the forum, where the principal citizens of Rome met every day; and in his road visited such patients as lay near him. He had a small room in his house, warmed with a stove in winter, and temperate in summer, in which his body was well chafed and rubbed, after going to stool every morning. He used some gentle exercise before dinner which was very moderate, beginning always with something that was opening. His supper was either some light spoon meat, or a fowl with the broth in which it was boiled. And thus he lived with all his senses perfect, and all his limbs sound, to extreme old age.

Antiochus was practising what doctors still encourage today: the building of physical activity into daily life, wherever possible. Then, as now, no one particular form of physical activity is appropriate for everybody, as people have different skills and body habitus, as well as occupation, income and time pressures. Although Galen taught that exercise was essential to live a long life, he accepted that different individuals required different amounts and types of exercise: 'I know some men, who, if they abstained three days from labour were sure to be ill; others I was acquainted with, who enjoyed a good state of health tho' they used little or no exercise'. He describes an acquaintance who kept fit because of 'his trade of walking much about the city to buy and sell several things, and by being of a quarrelsome disposition, and fighting frequently', and another whom he was 'obliged to restrain from exercise, because he used it to excess'. He concluded: 'I have restored health to several persons of a cold temperament, by rousing them from a lazy life, and by persuading them to labour'.

Galen, like Plutarch, was concerned about the health of sedentary individuals – 'statesmen, and students, whose employments engross too much of their time' – and he provided three rules for such individuals to ensure a balanced lifestyle:

1 After any extraordinary attendance or meditation, they should live more abstemiously than usual. He gave himself as an example: 'when at any time he was fatigued and spent with business, he chose the most simple food he could think of, which was commonly bread alone'.
2 Common diet should be plain and simple, and such that can be easily digested.
3 Some portion of their time should be set apart for exercise every day (whatever their engagements may be).

Galen sums up his own advice succinctly:

> I beseech all persons not to degrade themselves to a level with the brutes, or the rabble, by gratifying their sloth, or by eating and drinking promiscuously whatever pleases their palates; or by indulging their appetites of every kind. But whether they understand physick or not, let them consult their reason, and observe what agrees, and what disagrees with them, that, like wise men, they may adhere to the use of such things as conducive to their health, and forbear everything which, by their own experience they find to do them hurt.

Thus the ancient physicians and scholars laid down the ground rules on the necessity of physical activity to ensure a long, healthy and productive life: to balance energy input and output, to balance exercise with rest and to exercise every day. It was asserted that each individual should perform exercises appropriate to himself, that moderate or light exercise is often better than vigorous exertion for maintenance of health and that physical activity in childhood and old age is essential. The difference today is that rather than to preserve health, physical activity is widely used to regain lost health and to fight obesity. 'Fat' was rarely encountered by the ancients and its role as a precursor of disease was poorly understood. 'Modern' writers became increasingly aware of obesity in the context of ill-health, and gradually adapted the theories of the ancient writers to reflect this.

Thomas Cogan, who was educated at Oxford in the early sixteenth century, drew upon the theories of Galen and Hippocrates and others. He interpreted their writings, especially on exercise, for his own audience: 'Flowing water does not corrupt, but that which standeth still; even so animal bodies exercised are for the greatest part healthful; and such as be idle are subject to sickness'.

The eighteenth century

In 1710, the sycophant Bernardino Ramazzini was certain that the health of a good prince was crucial to the nation's health and 'is the greatest blessing imaginable to the public':

> The constitution of the prince should be carefully studied, and well understood by his physician; and his diet, exercise, and evacuations ought to be regulated accordingly.... Manly exercises, suitable to their high rank, according to the custom of the country, and especially riding on horseback should be recommended to princes. They should also indulge themselves in other innocent and genteel recreations, and never fail to admit young people to partake of their diversions.

Another person to reinvent the theories of the ancient physicians was Francis Fuller, in the early eighteenth century, who, harking back to

Herodicus, published his own *Medicina gymnastica*, which recommended exercise as the principal remedy in 'consumption, dropsy, and hypochondriacal disorders', but also in the preservation of health. Horse riding in particular was high on Fuller's list of beneficial pursuits, being 'as useful to preserve, as to recover health'. Although horse riding is still undertaken as a healthy form of physical activity, Fuller's other favourite, friction by the flesh brush – also widely prescribed by the ancient physicians – has fallen out of favour. He says:

> It is very strange that this exercise of chafing the skin, which was in such universal request among the antients, and which they put into practice almost every day, should be so totally neglected and slightened by us, especially when we consider that their experience agrees so exactly with our modern discoveries in the oeconomy of nature.

Dr Thomas King Chambers would later recommend 'Rise at 7. Rub the body well with horse-hair gloves, have a cold bath, take a short turn in the open air.'

George Cheyne stated his views on exercise in 1724: 'The studious, the contemplative, the Valetudinary, and those of weak nerves – if they aim at Health and Long Life, must make Exercise in a good air, a part of their Religion'. Exercise, Cheyne maintained, should be taken whatever the state of the weather:

> I do not allow the state of the weather to be urged as an objection to the prosecution of measures so essential to Health, since it is in the power of every one to protect themselves from cold by clothing, and the exercise may be taken in a chamber with the windows thrown open, by actively walking backwards and forwards, as sailors do on ship-board.[18]

Richard Mead wrote about exercise and health in his volume entitled *Monita et praecepta medica* in 1751, a work which revealed remarkable insight into the causes and management of ill-health. His teachings seem to indicate that exercise is vital to health, but must under no circumstances be enjoyable. He also recommended 'friction' as a remedy: 'Old men … should also be well rubbed with a flesh brush every morning to supply that exercise which, for want of strength, they cannot use, tho' their health requires it'. Whereas Pythagoras had recommended moderation in all things, including concubinage, Mead issued a stern warning against such forms of recreational exertion:

> The frigidity of men advanced in years, is a faithful monitor, that points out to them the folly of forcing themselves to exert a vigour which they have lost, vainly expecting raptures, but finding only an irksome labour that will shorten their days.

But apart from this somewhat monastic view of life, Mead gave some good advice:

> Moderate labour supplies a poor man with wholesome food, and at the same time gives him an appetite to relish, and strength to digest it; without goading his lust or inflaming his passions. His sleep is sound and refreshing, undisturbed with corroding cares: And his healthy and hardy offspring nursed up in temperance, soon grows fit to partake of that labour which made the parents happy.

It has recently been documented that obese mothers with poor dietary and lifestyle habits prior to conception confer metabolic dysfunction on their babies from birth, imprinting a predisposition to obesity and subsequent health problems from an early age: epigenetics. This was recognised by Mead, in a remarkable passage, which also documents the reduced life expectancy associated with obesity, a fact which has only recently been re-established:

> How different are the effects produced by the sloth and luxury of the rich! To enable them to eat, their stomachs require high fauces which heat and corrupt their blood, pamper their vicious inclinations, and render them obnoxious to various diseases. The excess of the day destroys the sleep of the night. Their children are tainted in their mother's womb, with distempers which afflict their whole lives, and hardly permit them, diseased and decrepit, to arrive at the threshold of old age.

From this passage Mead also provides a clear description of the class divide at the time between the hard-working and temperate poor and the slothful rich, who would suffer from their greed with diseases such as gout and obesity.

James Mackenzie, an Edinburgh physician, retired from practice in the middle of the eighteenth century and provided a useful overview of the theories surrounding physical activity developed by his predecessors. As well as studying the ancient physicians' views on the preservation of health, he also drew up his own succinct commentary on diet and exercise with respect to health:

> As the human body is a system of pipes, through which fluids are perpetually circulating; and as life subsists by this circulation, contrived by infinite wisdom to perform all the animal functions, it is obvious that exercise must be necessary to health, because it preserves the circulation by assisting digestion, and throwing off superfluities. Besides, we see every day that the active are stronger than the sedentary; and that those limbs of labouring men which happen to be most exercised in their respective occupations, grow proportionally larger, and firmer than those limbs which are less employed.[19]

In 1791, the Methodist minister John Wesley gave good advice to those individuals with sedentary occupations:

> the lungs may be strengthened by loudspeaking.... The studious ought to have stated times for exercise, at least two or three hours a-day.... They should frequently shave and frequently wash their feet.... Those who read or write much, should learn to do it standing; otherwise it will impair their health.[20]

The nineteenth century

In 1829 Dick Humelbergius Secundus' counsel reflected his era and his class: he advised the dinner party circuit on how to avoid the complications arising from dining too heartily. He recommended moderate physical exercise as a means of earning a healthy meal, stating that the appetite must be 'purchased at some trouble': 'It is not in a hackney coach, a cabriolet, nor even in an elegant landau that you ought to repair to the place of invitation for a rural dinner, but on foot. Ladies alone, have the privilege of being carried to the appointed place'.[21] He likened the body to 'the best constructed machine [which] will occasionally become deranged … and must be put in immediate repair': 'It has been discovered that the body perspires but little, while the stomach is too full, or too empty; that full diet is prejudicial to those who use little exercise, but indispensably necessary to those who labour much'.

William Wadd also witnessed the obesity more commonly encountered in the more affluent and privileged classes in the early nineteenth century. In his *Comments on Corpulency* he recounts the story of two affluent cousins in the court of Louis XV:

> there were two fat noblemen, the Duke de L—, and the Duke de N—. They were both at the levee one day, when the king began to rally the former on his corpulency: 'You take no exercise, I suppose,' said the king. 'Pardon me, Sire,' said de L—, 'I walk twice a day round my cousin de N—'.[22]

William Kitchiner, the author of *The Cook's Oracle* discussed in Chapter 5, eloquently described the changing role of physical activity as a reaction to the changing environment. He wrote: 'The Art of Invigorating the Health, and improving The Strength of Man, has hitherto only been considered for the purpose of training him for Athletic Exercises'. But he thought that there might be some advantage to be gained by adopting a similar plan:

> to animate and strengthen enfeebled Constitutions – prevent Gout – reduce Corpulency – cure Nervous and Chronic Weakness – Hypochondriac and Bilious Disorders etc. – to Increase Enjoyment, and prolong the duration of Feeble Life – for which Medicine, unassisted by DIET AND REGIMEN, – affords but very trifling and temporary help.[23]

He argued that experience had taught the value of training and that pugilists would not willingly take part in fights without such preparation. The principal rules, he considered, were 'to go to bed early, rise early, take as much Exercise as you can in the open air, without fatigue – to eat and drink moderately of plain nourishing Food – and especially – to keep the mind diverted, and in as easy and cheerful a state as possible'.[24]

Another authority on obesity, Wilhelm Ebstein, described the vicious circle associated with increased weight, lack of physical fitness and the reduced ability to exercise as corpulence progresses:

> There are even some stout people, who despite more copious perspiration and a slight shortness of breath still remain lusty pedestrians and knock about whole days in the hunting-field. But the matter becomes serious when they reach the stage in which the 'plump face shines like the full moon, and three men cannot span the paunch'. Such people of the Falstaff type with bellies of a hundred pounds are subject to many discomforts.[25]

Ebstein compares the lifestyle exhibited by humans with that displayed by dogs:

> The collie with sufficient bodily exercise does not grow fat on a perfectly adequate diet, consisting of flesh and fat with a sparing supply of carbohydrates. The lap-dog on the contrary, which besides flesh is also fed on delicacies and sweets, that is on carbohydrates, is observed to become rapidly plump and fat, although not to be an underrated part is here certainly played by the quiet and comfortable life led by this variety.[26]

Despite Ebstein's view of the importance of exercise, he correctly asserts that, as a means of losing weight, exercise alone has relatively limited effect:

> Exercise is known to improve fitness, and reduce the risk of disease, but because of the preferential build up of muscle at the expense of fat, weight is often maintained or increased, although waist circumference may well be reduced. Physical activity is regarded as an excellent way of improving health, and maintaining weight loss, but must be combined with dietary interventions in order to successfully induce weight loss.

Ebstein uses William Banting (see Chapter 3) as an example:[27]

> That bodily and excessive exercise also miss the mark, *Banting* himself has given us a most decided proof. He rowed a heavy boat a couple of hours daily and acquired muscular power, but also – a fabulous appetite. And as he yielded to this, he gained more and more in weight; nor did riding and toiling like a day-labourer bring him anywhere nearer to the wished-for goal.... We may and in fact should recommend to the corpulent physical action as well as everything else which, when applied in a rational and discreet way, otherwise promotes the assimilation of material. In such exercises they will also find beneficial and harmless sources of relief ... but of themselves alone these exercises cannot make good the baneful effects of an improper dietary system.

One of the foremost writers on diet in the mid-nineteenth century was Dr Thomas King Chambers (see Chapter 5), but even as a diet expert he gave some profound advice on the benefits of physical activity. As an illustration of the energy balance equation, he lists the food which would be required for a man to climb a ladder 'two miles and one-third high': three pounds and a half of lean beef at a cost of 3s.6d, or little more than half a pound of suet worth about 5½d. Chambers correctly cites schools as important places to gain exercise and he recommended 'an hours run on the playground'. His opinion is reflected by most modern experts, who denounce the selling of school playing fields, the demise of the walk to school, the replacement of PE by numeracy and literacy, and the banning of competitive sports on grounds of political correctness.

Chambers also advised that:

> Violent exertion also of mind or body before and after meals should be avoided.... Aesthetic pursuits, drawing, dancing, singing may be made so as to combine relaxation and amusement.... To the full development of the digestive organs, muscular exertion in the open air is essential, and is doubly valuable when it is of pleasurable character.... It is even more necessary for girls than boys that a sufficient playground should be attached to places of education, for they cannot be allowed to wander about the country like their brothers. In town, gymnastics or riding on horseback may be made substitutes for games ... there is no exercise for girls so good as rowing a light oar or sculling. It opens the chest, throws back the shoulders, straightens the back, and insures the shoulder straps of the dress not impeding movement, so that the liver and stomach gain space to act. Many a sculpturesque figure will acknowledge her debt to her boat for her beauty.[28]

Boys may balance their exertions with 'a glass of well brewed beer at dinnertime'[29] but are warned against 'gorging themselves with pastry and sweetstuff at the confectioner's, as practiced [sic] habitually by schoolboys, and often by girls when they get the chance'. Such gorging 'lays the foundation not only for indigestion in after years, which is its least evil, but also for a habit of indulgence, which is a curse through life'.

As well as warning about overindulgence, Chambers also warns about excessive exercise, and paints a harsh picture of the typical sportsman: 'a well-born and well-bred athlete, stupid, immoral, selfish, case-hardened by his brute strength against the finer emotions of pity and honour, and blind to intellectual pleasures'. Modern athletes would be entitled to take exception to his views! He also warns that athletes 'lay a foundation for disease in after years, and thus shorten life', and he highlights the likelihood of 'the dropping down dead on the stage of an athlete, apparently in the height of healthy vigour'.[30] Much more appealing than vigorous athleticism is an inclination to billiards, skittles, quoits, rowing and running.[31] Additionally, mountaineering is recommended as a worthwhile pursuit and for women the use of 'dumb-bells, in private before putting on the stays'.

The twentieth century

Notwithstanding Ebstein's and Chambers' advice that weight can success-fully be lost and maintained only by a combination of diet and exercise, many weight-loss regimens have been entirely exercise based. In 1933, F. A. Hornibrook published *The Culture of the Abdomen. The Cure of Constipation and Obesity*. The contemporary author Arnold Bennett was a devotee, writing in the Foreword:

> I know a middle-aged man who suffered for thirty years from ill health…. One day he bought a book by Mr F A Hornibrook … [which] set forth a series of short exercises. The fellow began to do the exer-cises…. In three months he had lost thirty pounds avoirdupois…. I can vouch for the case. For the man was myself.

Hornibrook pointed out that obesity was a product of modern life, and remarked upon 'the general tendency to obesity and enlargement of the abdomen in middle life amongst civilized people, their absence amongst the uncivilized'. Rather than putting this down to differences in diet, or the necessity of performing physical activity in more primitive societies as a function of daily life, he ascribed it, harking back to Socrates' advice, to 'the practice of native dancing as a form of body cultivation by the uncivil-ized races and the neglect of any similar form of exercise by the civilized peoples'. Sadly, according to Hornibrook, 'modern' dancing is unable to capture the same elements:

> Ballroom dancing is regarded by its devotees as the best of all exercises. The healthy individual can certainly derive exercise and amusement therefrom, but for the underfed, effete, and jaded victims of fashion it yields little…. In contrast to this, we observe the dance systems of natives. Inherent in these dances is the subconscious effort to make every part of the body participate in outward manifestations of energy and movement, and the native mind early recognized that when the abdomen and buttocks took up voluntary and regularized muscular training the whole body reacted beneficially.[32]

Hornibrook does give some good advice more appropriate to 'civilized' people than taking up native dancing. He promotes the habit of building sustainable forms of activity into daily life, just as modern activity special-ists recommend:

> Probably the greatest obstacle to reform in personal hygiene is encoun-tered in the disinclination to be shaken out of the groove of habit. It is easier to exist in laziness than to live in activity…. The settled pro-gramme of heavy meals far in excess of the body's needs, the constant whip of alcohol, the sedentary existence, perhaps interrupted by ill-judged and spasmodic outbursts of energy … sum up the life of a large section of middle-aged men of business.

Hornibrook's work represents a departure from the balanced lessons taught by writers and physicians of earlier eras, and was intended for those who 'cannot hide the protuberant belly or the ponderous buttocks which handicap fat people in their cumbrous waddle through life' and is based on correct posture, simple exercises, native dancing and an absolute obsession with bowel function:

> Some exercises are appropriated to different parts of the human body; as running and walking for the legs and thighs; shooting with bows and arrows for the arms; stooping and rising at bowls.

The development of sport

To replace physical exercise carried out in ordinary life and to recreate the sentiments of bloodthirsty battle, formal sport developed. The first Olympic Games were held in 776 BC and comprised a race from one end of the stadium to the other; the first winner was Corobus, a chef. Later, more races and sports such as wrestling, boxing and chariot races were added. The ancient Olympics continued until 339 BC, to be revived in 1896 in Athens.

Playing football is said to be so instinctive that kicking a ball around has been done for thousands of years, notably in China and Japan. Ancient Greeks and Romans played variations on football, which sometimes involved carrying the ball. It is said that football was played in London in 1175 by youths 'playing with a ball in wide open spaces'. The game fell foul of royalty, however, in 1314, when Edward II passed a statute banning the game, 'in consequence of the great noise in the City caused by hustling over large balls, from which many evils arise'. Edward III did likewise, ordering his sheriffs to suppress the game; James I banned 'fute bali' in 1424, as did James II in 1457.

Despite the healthy nature of sports such as football, one later professional footballer who was particularly memorable for his 'cat-like' agility and his huge bulk was William 'Fatty' Foulkes [6-1], who played for England, and was Chelsea Football Club's first superstar, despite measuring 6 foot 3 inches and weighing 22 stone. Born in 1874 in Dawley, Shropshire, Foulkes won two Cup medals with Sheffield United before moving to the London club as its first goalkeeper and first captain in 1905. During an away game against Burton, Foulkes decided to go early for the hotel dinner, and before the rest of the team came down he had cleared the portions of pie from all of his team-mates' plates, giving rise to the famous taunt still beloved of modern terraces, 'Who ate all the pies?' If Foulkes was ever mocked by his fellow players, he would simply sit on them as a punishment.[33]

6-1
William 'Fatty' Foulkes.

Although it is said that modern rugby was invented when William Webb Ellis picked up and ran with the ball during a game of football in 1823, sports involving carrying the ball have been round a lot longer. The Irish have Caid, played with a bull's scrotum, the Welsh Criapen, the Cornish 'hurling to goales', the West Country 'hurling over country', East Anglians 'Campball' and the French 'La Soule'. Similar games existed among Maoris, Faroe Islanders, Polynesians and Eskimos. Many modern rugby players, such as the All Black superstar Jonah Lomu at his peak, were designated as obese as measured by body mass index (BMI), despite hardly carrying an ounce of fat. This demonstrates the flawed nature of BMI as a measure of the clinical risk of obesity, compared with the simpler and more accurate measure of waist circumference.

A game involving the hitting of a ball from one pre-designated place to another has taken place in every civilisation, but the game of golf, origin-ally called 'goff', dates back to the fifteenth century. Known in Scotland as 'gowf', the early game took place on the rolling sandy links of Aberdeen, St Andrews and Leith, on the east coast, although an Act of Parliament was passed to prevent the game being played there on a Sunday.[34] Golf was also a passion of F. A. Hornibrook, who remarked:

> To approach golf in any but a spirit of enthusiasm is to confess oneself heretic or madman.... It calls the man from the city, the maid from the mill, it lures the matron from the cares of her nursery and the book-worm from his armchair.

However, he warned anyone who might be considering taking up the game in order to lose weight that 'Carrying a somewhat weighty abdomen around the countryside one or two days a week will not help in any way to improve his condition or lessen his burden'.[35] Hornibrook also had a warning for various sports enthusiasts except those undertaking his beloved native dancing:

> No amount of exercise undertaken by normal individuals will give them the physical peculiarities of the opposite sex; thus a lazy flabby man ... will never present the 'full-bottomed' appearance of the lady of quality or the sweating peasant in the harvest field; nor will the most active gymnast ever induce her protuberant posterior to fly away during her flights on the trapeze.

Tennis is often said to have been an invention of the ancient Egyp-tians, Greeks or Romans, but probably dates back to French monks in the eleventh or twelfth century who played handball against the monastery wall. Both Louis IV and the Pope tried to ban it. Henry VII and VIII were avid players, and promoted the game of 'real' or 'royal' tennis and the building of more courts.[36]

Cricket is thought to have developed before the Norman invasion of England in its most primitive form of a missile and a stick. There is evi-dence of cricket being played in Guildford, Surrey, in 1550, but it was not until 1611 that two youths were fined for playing the game in Sidlesham,

6-2
W. G. Grace.

Sussex.[37] The first great cricketer was William Gilbert (W. G.) Grace [6-2], who was born in 1848 in Bristol. His tremendous gifts, especially his phenomenal batting, were largely responsible for the elevation of cricket to its present status from just another nineteenth-century game. According to record, 'athletic' was not a word that came to mind when contemplating Grace in his prime, though a slim young man was said to have preceded the pot-bellied genius who in middle age was far too heavy for any horse to bear.[38] The famous English test batsman Colin Milburn took on the mantle of W. G. Grace, in terms of both talent and build, weighing 18 stone. His career was ended when he lost an eye in a traffic accident. Sadly, he died of a heart attack at the age of 49 years. Journalist Michael Simkins, in his autobiographical book *Fatty Batter*, describes Milburn's approach to the wicket down the pavilion steps:

> He barrels down, two at a time, his huge stomach wobbling up and down each tread like a giant blancmange, the flesh straining against the flimsy buttons of his cricket shirt. He seems an amalgam of every fat kid who has ever sat in the corner of a school changing room having gym shoes thrown at him by his classmates.[39]

The emergence of the physical fix

Sport has undoubtedly played its part in maintaining the physical health of millions of participants over the years, although it was not designed to do so. The word 'gymnasium' is derived from the Greek *gymnos*, meaning 'naked', as that was the state in which sporting participation was carried out [6-3]. In the modern gym it is unusual to find naked people apart from in the sauna and showers, and rather than being the site of gladiatorial contests they are now merely places where affluent people go, particularly in the weeks after Christmas, to perform vigorous (and often unnatural) exercises in order to lose the weight gained over the festive season.

Many weight loss regimens have included such vigorous exertion. For example, the 'Newmarket plan' was to 'wrap the "victim" in heavy "sweaters", and send him on a smart gallop. On his return he is regaled with a tumblerful of strong Epsom salts.'[40] The 'compression' system consisted of wearing a *bon conteur* belt and running at top speed until exhausted. The distance run was then measured out. The following day, the same programme was carried out, but the distance to be run increased, and the belt tightened, and so on.[41]

In 1892, Edwin Checkley introduced his 'Natural Method of Physical Training', designed to promote muscular strength to combat obesity. Born a weakling, he declared 'Nobody thought I was really worth rearing'.[42] He vigorously encouraged muscular activity, whilst simultaneously warning

6-3
In ancient Greece athletic events were performed naked.

against 'muscle-molding schemes that make men die in middle life ... not for that wise average morsel [sic] who wishes simply to feel light and strong'.[43] The wrong sort of exercise 'prescribed to many an ambitious victim of physical weakness is altogether too heroic', comprising 'chest expanders, boxing machines, and rowing appliances ... you pull this and push that so many times a day and you get to be a little amateur Samson'. This was futile: 'the illusion disappears and is gone'.[44] Checkley, however, made the mistake of assuming that exercise of a particular part of the body would reduce fat in that same region:

> This dissipation of fat is local; that is to say it disappears in localities in which muscles are active.... A large number of people, while of seemly proportions in other respects, grow an abdomen that is exceedingly ugly and becomes in time a great inconvenience. This is because, while the general activity of the person is considerable, their abdomen is kept free from muscular action....
>
> Perhaps eating excessively renders them continually cautious about bending, and at first signs of a protruding abdomen in a person otherwise slender the protrusion is patted and petted as a kind of symbol of health, when, in fact, it is sometimes, if not very often, a threatening sign. It is at least a prophecy of too much fat, and as such should be looked at askance.[45]

Yet Checkley was advanced enough to realise that 'all the fat of the abdomen is not superficial like most of the fat of the body, but is largely internal', reflecting modern concepts of visceral fat as an active endocrine organ.

In Checkley's world, women and children were cases apart from the more important patient – the man – and dismissed in a few paragraphs:

> women, especially if their health is not fair, should [exercise] with caution.... Avoid the chances of shock to the pelvic region.... Among women who have borne children ... or passed middle age, the distended abdomen often brings much distress. Nothing certainly could be uglier, more utterly destructive of grace or distinction in manner....
>
> [Women's] endurance in shopping is often a surprise to men. But the endurance is an illusion. The fact is that women wreck their nervous system at 'bargain counters'. They should be able to bear the physical strain of standing, but their general strength is so poorly developed that they are actually unfit to do the feats they call on their nervous vitality to perform.

And as for children, 'Girls who run are liable to be accused of rudeness'. More sensibly:

> If children are made to do moderate exercise at spading or shovelling or sweeping, the effect upon their back will be a reward for the efforts made by both trainer and trained. *Useful* exercise thus ranks above all others, because it means something and has a double influence....

It might, therefore, be commended that people cultivate the habit of themselves performing little physical tasks such as might ordinarily be relegated to servants.[46]

F. Cecil Russell likened sedentariness in humans to that in cattle:

When the muscular movements of a healthy animal are restrained, a genial temperature kept up, and an ample supply of food containing much amylaceous or oily matter, an accumulation of fat in the system rapidly takes place; this is well seen in the case of stall-fed cattle. On the other hand when food is deficient, and much exercise is taken, emaciation results.[47]

Thomas King Chambers[48] attempted to explain the notable leanness of the French at the time by referring to their levels of constant activity:

he is of an excitable temperament – speaking as much by gesture as by mouth – almost every word spoken being accompanied by some movement of the hands or body. There is consequently a greater demand for much carbon and hydrogen, the chemical constituents of the fat which is consumed by the action of the lungs and liver as well as the muscles.

Physical exertion, however, was deemed an unnecessary and unpleasant distraction amongst the makers of quack remedies of the same age. Most seemed – if the advertisements were to be believed – to work miraculously, without relying on dietary or exercise regimens which might put off potential customers with the thought of having to work to lose weight [6-4].

Lillian Russell provided the exception that proved the rule in 1909, describing the necessary '250 rollovers each morning'.[49] If exercise was recommended as part of commercial remedies, it was as a means of selling gadgets and devices which made the unpleasant task more acceptable, often by contriving to introduce exercise in the most sedentary form possible. An example was the 'Health Jolting Chair' [6-5], 'the most ingenious, scientifically conceived, complete and useful exercising apparatus in existence'.

Hundreds of devices and gadgets were patented in order for health-conscious individuals to avoid any unpleasantness in losing weight and improving health. The simplest were the various girdles, corsets, rubber garments and belts with the mechanical function of compressing the obese abdomen 'imperceptibly' to ensure 'slimness and beauty'. Ten dollars would buy Dr Thomas' 'Human Mould' [6-6], direct from New York. According to Dr Thomas:

Last year I conceived the idea that if I could develop my physical strength sufficiently, I could by the aid of certain apparatus of my invention fly through the air like a bird. To accomplish this purpose it was necessary that I cultivate my muscular and nervous system to the highest degree possible.... The apparatus I now term the Human Mould is a part of the apparatus I finally developed.... I did not fly but

Our Improved Obesity Belt.

AND ABDOMINAL SUPPORTER.

PERSONS suffering from an accumulation of fat about the abdomen (commonly called *Pot Belly or Large Stomach*) should wear one of our Improved Obesity belts while taking treatment. This belt will cause the fat about these parts to be absorbed and it is surprising to see in what a short time the size of the abdomen is reduced after wearing the belt for a little while.

It is also a good supporter in Female Weakness, as it supports the Abdominal Viscera, and relieves congestion.

There are a number of cheaper and worthless belts advertised as Obesity Bands, etc. They do as much good as a towel wrapped around the abdomen. Our belt is made of the *best* material; contains flexible steel "stays" to hold it in position, and is held down by hose supporters (as shown on the annexed cut) to prevent it from slipping up around the waist.

It is light and comfortable and is worn without any inconvenience whatever. Each one is "hand made" and guaranteed to give perfect satisfaction.

DIRECTIONS.—Adjust the belt and buckle just tight enough to support the abdomen. Some prefer to wear it over a light undergarment. It should be taken off before retiring and replaced again the first thing in the morning. A considerable reduction is noticed after wearing it a couple of weeks and great relief is experienced immediately after it is adjusted. It forms a natural support and is invaluable in Prolapsus Uteri (falling of the womb) often curing this trouble when other methods fail. The Belt is made so that it can be shortened as reduction takes place.

HOW TO SEND PROPER MEASUREMENTS.

Take snug measurements around the body under all clothing and next to the skin.

State measurement around the waist corresponding to the dotted line (on the annexed cut.)

A to A...inches
Measurement around the abdomen corresponding to the dotted line

B to B...inches
Measurement around the abdomen corresponding to the dotted line

C to C...inches
Measurement of depth in front from A to

C... inches
The Belt should not be deeper than 8 or 10 inches in front to be comfortable, especially when in a sitting position.

(Note.—We do not keep these belts in stock, but make each one to order according to measurements sent, and begin work at once on same as soon as the order is received.)

Please return this blank containing your measurements when you send in your order for the Belt.

PRICE, Obesity Belt for Ladies, **$3.50,** by mail postpaid.

PRICE, Obesity Belt for Gentlemen, **$3.75,** by mail postpaid.

OPEN MESH BELT.—We make a special Summer Belt of open mesh netting. It is very durable but light and cool and just the thing for summer use.
Price of Summer Belt for ladies,   **$4.00,** | Price of Summer Belt for gentlemen,   **$4.50**
If you wish to see a sample of the open mesh netting used in Summer Belt, send 2 cents for postage and we will send you a sample of same.
If you want the Belt sent by registered mail please add 8c. extra for registering. This will insure safe and speedy delivery.

6-4
Advertisement for the 'Obesity Belt'. The belt was claimed to do more than simply support and mould. The advertisement states 'This belt will cause the fat about these parts to be absorbed and it is surprising to see in what short a time the size of abdomen is reduced'.

THE HEALTH JOLTING CHAIR
is the most **ingenious, scientifically conceived, complete,** and **useful EXERCISING APPARATUS** in existence.

In operation, the levers at the side of the Chair being moved backward and forward, a motion is given to the seat that exercises the abdominal organs of its occupant in a manner similar to that given by the motion of a trotting horse. It confers physical benefits even superior to saddle exercise. The Chair can be so regulated as to exercise the arms, chest, or abdominal organs, singly or together, to any desired degree, being suited to all grades of strength, ranging from that of the most vigorous athlete to that of the helpless invalid. It is suited to both sexes and to all ages.

It is undoubtedly the best-known means for taking **all necessary HEALTH GIVING** exercise when **convenience, expedition, economy, safety,** or direct exercise of the essentially important nutritive organs of the body is desired. For the reason

DR. JULIAN P. THOMAS' HUMAN MOULD
MARVELOUS FAT-REDUCER AND STRENGTH-BUILDER

FOR WOMEN: Reduces Fleshy Hips and Waists 1 to 2 Inches a Week, Gives Grace of Carriage, and Robust, Beauteous Health. Makes Women as Strong as Athletes.
FOR MEN: Turns Fat Into Muscle, Straightens and Squares Shoulders, Builds the Body Strong Against Disease. Makes Men as Powerful as Giants.

This is an improved model of the apparatus with which Dr. Thomas made the world's record lift of 1,257,000 lbs. in 30 minutes, and is creating a sensation in New York not only among stout men and women, but among thin and sickly people. It brings health and normal weight and figure to all. By simply bending, then straightening the knees, an enormous force is exerted, which *melts fat, strengthens the body and perfects the figure* to normal proportions.

SOLD ON TRIAL
Dr. Thomas knows by experience that his wonderful invention never fails to satisfy when used according to instructions, hence makes this liberal offer: On receipt of $10 he will send one complete Human Mould durably made of best materials with nickel trimmings, tested resistance spring and full instructions for use. If you are not entirely satisfied return by express collect in ten days and your money will be refunded.

JULIAN P. THOMAS, M.D.
Dept. B
522 W. 37th St.
NEW YORK

6-5
Advertisement for the Health Jolting Chair.

6-6
Advertisement for Dr Julian Thomas' 'Human Mould'.

I produced a lightness of movement due to increased strength that was astonishing, and when my leg gets entirely well I will resume my aerial experiments.

How Dr Thomas injured his leg, and whether it was due to a mishap with his Mould, is left to the reader's imagination.

In 1916, the journal *The World's Work* recognised the role of the reduction in manual labour as a causative factor in obesity, in an article entitled 'What Can a Fat Man Do?', by Charles Phelps Cushing.[50] Starting with the premise that 'A man is fat because he does the things a fat man does – sits around too much, eats too much, sleeps too much, and loathes activity', the article quotes Professor Graham Lusk, of Cornell Medical College:

> That great class of human beings whose business it is to sit at their desks or to watch machinery, and who may walk to and from their work, require 2,500 calories. In their class are included writers, draughtsmen, tailors, physicians, and other professional men, clerks, accountants, etc. Mental effort is accomplished without any increase in the quantity of energy required. Individuals who stand at their work, such as bakers, dentists, car conductors, decorators, and glass workers, require about 3,000 calories. If muscular labor be constant, more is required. Thus, carpenters making tables, and painters painting furniture require 3,300 calories. Farmers require 3,500 calories, stone masons 4,500, lumbermen 5,000, and a man riding in a bicycle race during twenty-three hours requires 10,000 calories.

A typical businessman of the day, however, might eat the following:

> Breakfast: Grape fruit, two soft boiled eggs, buttered toast, and coffee with cream and sugar. Luncheon: Ham sandwich and a glass of milk. Dinner: Soup, small steak and fried potatoes, bread and butter, apple pie and a cup of coffee.

This degree of intake might seem monastic in modern Western society, but in 1916 this was grossly excessive:

> With this information at hand, it is no difficult feat to prove against the fat man a charge of overeating.... Set down, in round numbers, the nutritional calories that this totals, and you will find that our typical business man is consuming more than enough to nourish him.

Cushing's solution is illustrated by examples of exemplary practice in physical activity:

> Reducing by exercise; Grand opera singers have a tendency towards obesity. Mme Fremstad, the well known operatic star, endeavors to overcome this by hard manual labor on her farm.

Cushing rails against weight reduction by violent exercise, 'which does more harm than good', whilst promoting moderate exercise in conjunction with a proper diet. To demonstrate best practice, he shows a picture of an obese man, dressed in a skimpy leotard, throwing a medicine ball to colleagues, in the snow, supervised by a man in a warm full-length coat and porkpie hat [6-7]. An opposing regimen is now advised; the introduction of physical activity into daily life, rather than scheduled exercise, is more likely to result in long-term health gains.

6-7
Cushing's medicine ball exercise.

Exercise, the perfect physique and discrimination

At the end of the nineteenth century, Bernarr Macfadden founded *Physical Culture* magazine, which combined the narcissistic adoration of the perfect body with health preservation, dietary and lifestyle advice. Born Bernard Adolphus McFadden, on 16 August 1868, to an abusive, alcoholic father and an ailing, 'melancholy' mother, he was an orphan by age 11, and not expected to live long. Soon after, he was placed with a farmer, and grew fit and strong by performing heavy manual labour, only to revert back to a 'physical wreck' on gaining employment as an office clerk. His reaction was to begin regular exercise, including walking and lifting weights, and 'natural methods' of diet and lifestyle, based on observations of the animal kingdom. He was 5 foot 6 inches and 145 pounds, and possessed a powerful upper body, incredible stamina and energy and a forceful personality. In 1894 he changed his name to Bernarr, which sounded more like a lion's roar than just plain Bernard, and set himself up as a physical trainer. He wrestled, sold a patented exercise machine and posed, showing off his impressive musculature. He attended the Chicago World Fair in 1893, before moving to England for two years of lecturing, and in March 1899 published the first edition of *Physical Culture* magazine.[51]

> It appealed particularly to middle-class men and preached an ardent message centered around new physical standards. Artificial gimmicks like corsetry were attacked in favor of an impassioned focus on control of gluttony and vigorous exercise. Advertisements stressed well-muscled men, nearly nude, with large but fat-free bodies.[52]

Ideal weight for the benefits of health was high on the agenda, with many articles and advertisements for gaining and reducing weight, in addition to some first-rate advice:

> Calisthenics all over the House: If housework leaves you little time for special exercises to improve your figure, then do your daily work with movements that will keep your body slim and supple. And what if your figure is already perfect? You can still have the fun of turning drudgery into a game![53]

An article entitled 'Don't be a Desk-Chair Spreader'[54] by Mrs Helen Macfadden warned against 'widening of the hip and thigh' with sedentary work [6-8].

Another by Macfadden himself proclaimed:

> Exercise and the use of all the muscles is always commendable. You cannot build or maintain strength without recognising this requirement. The inclination to romp and play is one of the natural instincts that first of all strengthens and develops the body in childhood. But

"*DESK-CHAIR SPREADER*"
By HELEN MACFADDEN

6-8
From *Physical Culture*,
September 1937.

this overflow of the surging forces of life coming into being in the form of [an] overwhelming desire to dance, sing, and leap about is simply nature's means of forcing us to exercise and use the body throughout its every part.[55]

From today's standpoint, Macfadden's work has sinister overtones, because of the obsession with the perfect body ('Let Sylvia of Hollywood Mold Your Body into a Dream of Loveliness'[56]), with lines of uniformed young people exercising with military precision and frequent quotes from Mussolini. In 1932, articles such as 'Saved from the Black Plague by Shipwreck and Starvation' were printed side to side with 'How I Reduced Seven Pounds in Seven Days' by Gertrude Pugh, and even 'Better Bodies for Mussolini's Young Men; American Games plus Macfadden Training Offer a New Athletic Ideal to Italy'. Rather than being a healthy influence on youth, *Physical Culture* crossed the boundary into anti-fat discrimination, which was reflected in accusations that obese individuals were unpatriotic during the war by eating more than their share. It also coincided with the emergence of the discrimination commonly seen today. A piece penned by Macfadden entitled 'Fatness in Body and Mind' equated obesity with fat-headedness:

> When one is overfed, he is logy and lazy ... there is no such thing as being fat-headed except in the sense that it refers to someone who is dull, slow and stupid ... excessive fat not only makes one slow and sluggish in a physical way, but it frequently has a similar influence mentally. To have an over-fat body is nothing to boast about, but 'fat-headed' is an opprobrious epithet.[57]

An accompanying photograph to a 1936 article showed four young girls and a dog running on the beach [6-9], with the caption 'What is wrong with this

6-9
From *Physical Culture,*
July 1936.

What is wrong with this picture? Just twenty pounds, the
removal of which would make a beauty of the girl at the left

picture? Just twenty pounds, the removal of which would make a beauty of
the girl at the left.'[58] The magazine also wrote of 'The regeneration of a Big
Slob' and 'young hippos'.[59]

Conclusion

It can be seen that sedentariness and physical activity have important roles
in the aetiology and the management of obesity and in the protection of
health and prevention of illness. However, opinions still vary. The truth
about exercise, according to one American psychiatrist, lies in the pleasure
it gives:

> To Hell with Hygeia. It is more often a marker of health than its
> cause – healthy people like to exercise more than unhealthy people. The
> real value of exercise is not in terms of abstract health benefits such as
> longevity, but because it feels good when you do it or when it is over.[60]

CHAPTER 7

Addressing obesity – drug treatments

> A man has but these four things to choose out of – to *exercise* much, to be very *temperate*, to take *physic*, or be *sick*. (Sir William Temple, 1628–99[1])

Historically, the management of weight has been mainly based around the preservation of health by optimum nutrition and physical activity (Chapters 5 and 6). Only as the prevalence of overweight and obesity increased has there been a need for more effective methods of inducing weight loss, hence the introduction of chemical substances designed to reduce the obese body. Modern anti-obesity drugs are well tolerated and effective. They have been scrutinised against strict clinical and scientific criteria, and tried and tested in clinical practice for years.

Obesity is now regarded as one of the major risk factors for serious chronic diseases such as diabetes, cardiovascular disease – including heart attacks and stroke – as well as cancer, infertility, respiratory problems and many others (see Chapter 2). It is in this context that anti-obesity drugs should be judged – by how they affect the markers of disease, especially cholesterol, blood glucose and blood pressure – rather than simply how many pounds they help a person to lose, or how many inches are shed. In this respect, the modern generation of drugs work remarkably well and induce significant improvements in these biochemical markers, to considerable clinical benefit. However, a study of the history of pharmacotherapy reveals that rather than being safe and effective, historical remedies were usually *either* safe *or* effective – sometimes neither, but never both!

An advertisement headed 'Diet Versus Drugs' appeared in the June 1912 edition of *Cosmopolitan* magazine, which illustrated the differing opinions amongst experts in the debate as to what worked best [7-1]. The dietary suggestions were based, quite reasonably, around low-carbohydrate, high-protein options, whereas the choice of other remedies listed displayed

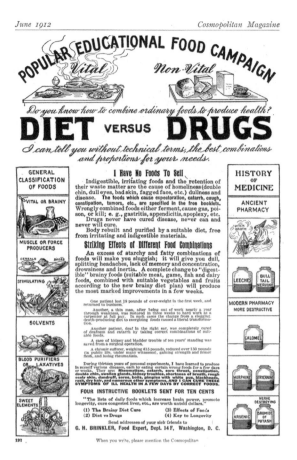

7-1

'Diet Versus Drugs' advertisement from *Cosmopolitan*, June 1912.

a slightly unbalanced argument: witch broth, morphine, strychnine and leeches. The last three listed, however, have all genuinely been used at some stage in history to combat obesity.[2]

Traditionally, in the field of weight-loss pharmacotherapy, manufacturers have concocted a new compound, flogged it mercilessly to both the public and the medical profession, and members of the public have bought it in large quantities, or gone to their healthcare provider for supplies. The reaction of the doctors, however, has varied over the centuries.

William Wadd, the Surgeon Extraordinary to the King in the early nineteenth century, wrote the first books entirely dedicated to the subject of obesity, namely *Wadd on Obesity*, published in 1816, and *Comments on Corpulency*, published in 1829. He summed up the relevant science known at the time, using the device of patients' accounts and case histories, probably sent to him by their personal physicians.

Wadd recounts the case of 'a fat sportsman', who was no longer able to find a horse to carry him, so made a consultation to 'be reduced'. The sportsman explained:

Having had some conversation with you upon the subject before, and hearing that you have made it a matter of study, I am desirous of inquiring your opinion further – as to the safety and treatment by which weight can be diminished by medicine. I am growing heavier and fatter than I wish to be.... The exercise I take does not prevent it at all. I should not quite like to be put on a regimen of abstinence, but upon some system which, with moderate living might gradually bring me back to about my old standard. Now what do you recommend me to do?

Wadd advised the first line remedy: 'Keep your eyes open and your mouth shut'. But the sportsman replied, 'Poh! Nonsense! That won't do for me – give me something to take – have you no pills?' Wadd comments:

The pills this gentleman was in search of, were to counteract the effects of a dose of strong ale, two gallons a day being his moderate allowance. He replied with great good humour 'I see how it is – if I'm ale-ing all day, it follows of course, I must be ail-ing all night. Egad! I can't help it, I should die without it, and I had rather die with it.[3]

Thus Wadd describes the common misapprehensions associated with anti-obesity drugs still held by the public today: the expectation that a 'miracle drug' will undo the damage caused by a poor lifestyle, and work automatically without any alterations in behaviour by the individual. Wadd rejected the fat sportsman's request, in favour of traditional nutrition, physical activity and behavioural advice, as would most modern doctors in the same situation, but there have been recent eras, notably when amphetamines were requested and dispensed like jelly beans, when doctors have not always prescribed with a sufficient degree of responsibility.

For centuries, researchers have searched for the Holy Grail of a drug regimen that will miraculously and without effort banish obesity. Many drugs have failed to live up to this standard, but often claims for them would belie this fact. In the early twentieth century, Lucile Kimball made a bold claim for her remedy: 'I can make your fat vanish by the gallon'. Others promised permanent elegance and beauty. However powerful and effective drugs may be, including the most modern therapies, they must still be accompanied by diet and lifestyle measures, and used only as an adjunct to traditional interventions. Drugs do not make weight loss easier, just more effective.

The ancient world through to the Enlightenment

Some early interventions combined lifestyle and drugs and had the effect of modifying food intake and absorption, but for entirely different reasons than for modern compounds. The Egyptians, Greeks and Romans invented and utilised drastic remedies.[4] Herodotus observed of the Egyptians:

having remarked that the greatest number of diseases proceeded from the abuse of food, they took care every month to consecrate three successive days to make themselves vomit, and cleanse themselves with clysters, to pursue and seize health.

7-2
The *Hoodia gordonii* cactus, an appetite suppressant and potential basis for an anti-obesity drug.

The Greeks 'occasionally resorted to mild means, in order to excite vomiting'. The Romans also induced vomiting, but only in order to enhance their gluttony, rather than their health. These measures demonstrated the misuse and abuse of perfectly acceptable medicinal remedies – in this instance emetics and cathartics – a highly dangerous practice which continues today.

Another ancient medicine is extract of the *Hoodia gordonii* cactus [7-2], which has been used for centuries by the Xhomani Sans bushmen of southern Africa's Kalahari desert to suppress the appetite during long hunting trips. It is currently being assessed by pharmaceutical companies for development, under the experimental name of P57. *Hoodia* may turn out to be the exception that proves the rule, and be a genuine early remedy that is both safe and effective against obesity.

The earliest examples of appetite-moderating drugs were also developed for entirely different purposes than those for the obesity remedies we encounter in the twenty-first century. Appetite suppressants attenuated hunger for the simple reason that hunger was a pointless sensation in the absence of food. Avicenna, the great Persian physician and philosopher, was born in 980, and was the author of 450 books, including *The Book of Healing* and *The Canon of Medicine*, described by William Osler in the nineteenth century as 'the most famous medical textbook ever written'. Avicenna began seeing patients at age 16, having surreptitiously obtained and studied prescriptions from his master, and rose to fame by curing the Sultan of Bukhara from an illness which had baffled the experienced court physicians. Amongst the prescriptions available to Avicenna was an early appetite suppressant, used as a preservative against hunger in times of famine. The recipe was as follows:

> Take of sweet almonds one pound; the like quantity of melted beef suet; of oil of violets two ounces; a sufficient quantity of mucilage; and the roots of marsh-mallows, one ounce: let altogether be brayed in a mortar, and made into bolusses, about the bigness of a common nut.

Those unable to tolerate tablets were offered the liquid form: 'one pound of oil of violets, mixed with melted beef-suet. A person taking this, may fast for ten days without the least hunger'.

One of the first reported case studies relating the deliberate use of harmful compounds for flesh reduction concerned Sancho the Fat. Sancho became King of Leon in 958 AD, but was deposed, allegedly on the grounds that he was deemed too fat to rule. His grandmother, Queen Toda, sought the help of the physician Hisdai ibn Shaprut, who reputedly made his name as a great healer by prescribing opiates to Sancho, which led to his weight loss and his ability to reclaim the throne.[5] If there is any truth in this legend, opiates thus became one of the first in a long line of addictive and dangerous substances used by the medical profession to induce weight loss.

In *The English Physician*, written in 1652 by Nicholas Culpeper [7-3], the renowned herbalist described various herbs that could be used as remedies in obesity. His entry for ash tree reads:

> It is governed by the Sun; and the young tender Tops, with the Leaves taken inwardly and some of them outwardly applied are singular good against the biting of Viper, Adder or any other venomous Beast; and the Water distilled therefrom being taken a small Quantity every Morning fasting is a singular Medicine for those that are subject to Dropsy, or to abate the Gretness of those that are too Gross or fat.

7-3
Nicholas Culpeper.

And for fennel:

> Both Leaves, Seeds and Roots thereof are much used in Drink or Broth, to make People more spare and lean that are too fat.[6]

In 1757 Dr Flemyng recommended diuretics and laxatives in *A Discourse on the Nature, Causes and Cure of Corpulency*,[7] on the grounds that all the excretions produced, along with sweat, contain 'oil', and loss of 'oil' was beneficial. Since then, both categories of drug have been used frequently, and often illegally, for short-term weight loss, in particular the use of diuretics before sporting events for which achieving a precise weight is important, as in wrestling or boxing. The Australian leg-spin bowler Shane Warne was banned from cricket for a year in February 2003 for using the diuretic Moduretic (co-amilozide), in order to lose weight, because of his unhappiness about his appearance.

Mercury, arsenic and other poisons

Other early anti-obesity medications were undoubtedly effective in inducing weight loss, but did so at a cost. Mercury was one of these. It was used for many different medical conditions and, for instance, was a specific for the treatment of syphilis. The great violinist and composer Paganini was obsessed with his health, especially with regard to his basic functions: his bladder and bowels. He used a series of graded tin catheters to evacuate his urine and took mercury for syphilis. This caused ulceration of the gums, resulting in loosening of his teeth, which he then held in place with wires (in some reports said to be violin strings). Although Paganini suffered from Marfan's syndrome and was not obese, some of his problems were caused by mercury, the use of which for the treatment of obesity was extremely successful, although at a grave cost. A patient of William Wadd had been treated with the metal, with severe physical and psychological side-effects:

> mercury, under very judicious advice was administered, till my mouth became affected, and, I may add, my mind also. It brought me to a state such as fits a person for suicide, nervous in the highest degree; with a full conviction that my friendly Doctors wanted to smother me.... Amongst other phantasies, I confidently believed that all below the *lumbar vertebrae* did not belong to me, that the bed I lay in was a ware-house, in short
>> I fancied in my fluttering mood
>> All the diseases which the 'spitals know,
>> For sometimes I would laugh, and sometimes cry,
>> Then sudden waxed wrath, and all I knew not why.'[8]

Large sections of early pharmacopoeias, medical textbooks and encyclo-paedias are devoted to mercury; as one of very few remedies of the age that could boast tangible results, it is not surprising that its use was wide-spread. However, because of its sinister side-effects, and the advances in medicine and pharmacology that were taking place, the metal fell out of favour with clinicians.

One of the sternest critics of the early methods of anti-obesity pharmaco-therapy, including mercury, was F. Cecil Russell, who in 1892, whilst promoting his own vegetable-based corpulency cure, made sure his readers were in no doubt of the dangers wrought by his competitors:

> The use of mercury, for instance, as a cure for obesity and other dis-orders, has entailed upon the human family a train of disorders no physician who is not wholly wedded to the errors of early education, or a slave to the errors of musty books and the edicts of self-constituted medical tribunals, will venture to deny.... The Motherby Mercurial Remedy ... advocates the use of a poison, no other than mercury.[9]

Russell was equally, and not unreasonably, scathing about another physician's attempt to corner the market in obesity treatment using arsenic – Dr Harcourt's Arsenite of Potassa Remedy, otherwise known as arsenic:

> Dr Harcourt, in severe cases, prescribes five drops of a solution of ... Arsenite of Potassa. The policy of administering such a dangerous compound as arsenite of potassa, which contains no less than 80 grains of carbonate of potassa to one pint of water, is questionable, to say the least. Arsenious acid is alike destructive to animal and vegetable life.... Of arsenious acid, Hahnemann writes:
>> 'In long continued small doses, nausea, vomiting, purging, griping, debility, emaciation, and all the effects of slow poisoning occur in succession; a gradual sinking of the powers of life without any violent symptoms; a nameless feeling of illness, failure of the strength, an aversion to food and drink and to all enjoyments of

life…. Under these conditions, I think it well worth to pause and think whether it is worth becoming thin at such a price. Numerous inquiries reach me relative to this, but I unhesitatingly advise all not to entertain the idea of using this diabolical poison for a moment, I don't care by whom it is prescribed.'[10]

Arsenic was still being used in obesity remedies in 1910, in combination with another deadly poison, strychnine, along with caffeine and poke-berry.[11] The Parisian physician Dr Robert Chung, the renowned diet doctor to the 'jet set', boasted Princess Grace of Monaco amongst his clients, and was fond of prescribing pills of 'goats' ovaries, animal brains, and some strychnine … harmless in small doses'.[12]

Russell needs only two lines to write off a treatment reminiscent of the Greek and Roman methods: 'The German drastic (purgative) remedies must be avoided as absolutely dangerous'. Admirable though Russell's condemnation of such effective but highly toxic remedies may have been, his own remedy displayed the opposite characteristics – of being entirely and indisputably safe, but totally ineffectual. It was purported to contain 'the decoction of RAD RUMEX CRISPUS, TINCTURE OF GEOFFROYAE INERMIS, GAVELLES EXTRACT, ACIDUM CITRICUM, MALVA SILVESTRIS'. An analysis of the compound by the British Medical Association revealed only citric acid, iron, ammonium citrate, 'spirit' and water.

Russell's book contains 35 pages condemning the history of obesity cures, five pages advertising the unique and exclusive properties of his own remedy, and 200 pages of testimonials from an admiring public on the brilliance of his cure.

A remedy used by the poet Byron, amongst others, was notable not only for its dangerous nature but also, as with the use of diuretics and laxatives, for its inappropriate use. Byron was famous for his appetites, for both food and sex, each of which at some points in history have been claimed to be addictive. For his gluttony, Byron chose a particularly harmful and addictive cure: tobacco.[13] The curative properties of chewing tobacco were put down to its effect as a sialogogue, or saliva inducer.[14]

The effects of tobacco on weight are well known, not least by the phenomenon of weight gain experienced by individuals attempting to stop smoking. Advertisements for Lucky Strike cigarettes in the 1920s cynically hijacked this fact in an attempt to corner the weight-loss market [7-4, C-3], by inviting the public to try the 'modern way to diet!': 'Light a Lucky when fattening sweets tempt you…. The delicately toasted flame of Luckies is more than a substitute for fattening sweets – it satisfies the appetite without harming the digestion.'[15] And 'Reach for a Lucky instead; you will thus avoid over-indulgence in things that cause excess weight and, by avoiding over-indulgence, maintain a trim figure.' In other advertisements 'a trim figure' was replaced by 'a modern graceful form'. Each full-page

7-4
Lucky Strike advertisement
from the 1920s.

advertisement displayed a fit, healthy young individual, and a sinister shadow of an ageing fat person in the same pose. Remarkably, Lucky Strike cigarettes also claimed to represent 'Your throat protection – against irritation – against cough'.

The poet John Milton, a 'vigorous brain laborer', was also fond of smoking as part of a balanced diet; his supper comprised bread, water, olives and a pipe of tobacco.[16]

Quackery in the nineteenth and twentieth centuries

Many physicians concocted their own versions of anti-obesity remedies. In the nineteenth century, the pharmaceutical panacea for obesity devised by a Monsieur Andry comprised 'ashes of cray-fish, sea sponge, and the pith of sweet briar'.[17] So powerful were the doctor's concoctions that he issued a health warning: 'that they were of so extenuating a nature, that unless administered with great judgement they would cause too great a meagreness'.

William Wadd noted that, with an increasing incidence of obesity, more and more remedies were being invented, not as serious scientific advances but as cynical profit-making ventures. He fired the first warning shots to serious practitioners prior to the golden age of Victorian quackery, and was particularly scathing about herbal, and especially homeopathic, remedies:

> The thousandth part of a grain of arsenic is the largest dose that should be given, and the hundred-thousandth part of a grain is enough in ordinary cases…. A drop of the spirituous tincture of sarsaparilla is said to be a strong dose – and the seven-millionth part of a grain of cucumis colocynthis acts sometimes too powerfully!!… That 'preparations which have the power to act beneficially, in the same ratio necessarily do harm if unskilfully exhibited' is an observation of the learned Mead. A stronger proof of it cannot be given, than in the case of General Vitellis, whose skin hung about him, from the injudicious administration of that common and efficacious remedy – vinegar.[18]

In the middle of the nineteenth century, Wadd had witnessed only the beginnings of drug manufacturers' ability to advertise directly to the public. During the Victorian era, their greater access to the public via newspapers increased the ability of quacks to disseminate their false claims and flog their wares to a naïve population.

French physician Jean Frumusan had similar views to William Wadd and in 1924 in his book *The Cure of Obesity* summed up the problem of chemical interference in obesity and the dishonest advertising of drugs at a time when many anti-obesity drugs falsely claimed major breakthroughs:

> Remedies are certainly not lacking … there is a superabundance of them. But how poor are the results! It is difficult to decide which most to admire: the calm audacity of the lying statements made by those who recommend their wares or the fathomless naïveté of the doctors and the public who adopt them. Publicity has become such a powerful weapon that the worth of a treatment is now determined, not by its adoption after lengthy and serious clinical and laboratory experiments, but by the amount of advertising it is given.[19]

Frumusan would have witnessed the cynical advertising of drugs such as Antipon [7-5], which, it was claimed, offered weight loss 'without irksome dietary restrictions' or other forms of hard work: 'No distasteful dietary restrictions are enjoined…. Stout readers are earnestly entreated not to trifle farther with drugging, sweating and half-starving.' In 1903

7-5
Antipon.

the makers of Antipon, the 'King of Corpulence Cures', made the following claims for their product:

- 'within a day and a night of taking the first dose there will be a reduction of weight of up to 3 lb or even more'
- 'contains no injurious substances'
- 'permanent elegance and sounder health are the priceless gifts conferred by a short and economical and pleasant course of Antipon'
- 'without perfect health there is no physical beauty, and in giving back the one, Antipon assures the other'
- 'no irksome dietary restrictions to observe; the subject eats heartily'
- 'a permanent cure; it destroys the tendency to excessive fat development'.

Antipon was analysed in 1909 by the British Medical Association for the publication of *Secret Remedies*, an attempt to rationalise drug treatment and expose fraudulent claims for therapeutic substances. It was found to contain nothing more than citric acid diluted with alcohol, water and colouring. Although this analysis negates claims for the drug's efficacy, it nevertheless sold extremely well at 2s.6d (half-a-crown, now 25p or 50c) per bottle, more as a tribute to the power of advertising than the power of medical science. The claims made for Antipon, judged by today's standards, are not only outrageous lies, but also offensive and discriminatory against those who are obese, in their implication that corpulent individuals could possess neither elegance nor beauty. This attitude still existed in recent times; an advertisement from the *Journal of the American Medical Association* categorised patients with only two possible labels: 'Beauty and Obese'. However, a drug which bestows upon its user permanent beauty, grace, elegance and slimness without the need to diet or exercise is still what some patients expect to be prescribed when they appear at their doctor's surgery on a Monday morning. The makers of Antipon helped create the benchmark against which later remedies were compared, and the challenge facing modern drug companies is to manufacture a substance that lives up to the public's expectations.

The Association's *Secret Remedies* books were published in an effort to protect the gullible public and expose the fraudsters whom Frumusan had referred to as:

> Quacks and charlatans who made their fortunes by selling secret remedies to be used internally or externally, purgatives or iodized ointments, devoid of any therapeutic value whatsoever.... [They] must be put aside with a shrug of the shoulders, deploring, on the one hand, the facility with which this unfortunate country can be flooded with useless or dangerous secret remedies; and on the other, the naïve credulity of the public which is deceived by such claptrap.[20]

The British Medical Association analysed many 'cures' and found that the majority contained vegetable preparations, often *Fucus vesiculosus* (bladderwrack, a seaweed), which was not prepared to any official formula and which had dubious therapeutic merit. Its reputation for reducing corpulency seems to have been at variance with its use in Ireland, where it was widely used for fattening pigs. It contained large amounts of sodium salts and a small proportion of iodine. Iodine was discovered in 1811, and briefly prescribed for goitre in 1820. In 1859, an attempt was made to treat psoriasis with it, resulting in the observation of weight loss as a side-effect, leading to its widespread promotion in the medical and lay literature as a reducing agent.

Sucking lemons was another fashion that was said to reduce weight and citric acid was therefore an ingredient of some of the 'secret remedies' on offer. The purgative phenolphthalein was sometimes used under such names as Purgen, Laxoin, Laxatol or Laxen, and would lead to weight loss by virtue of its purging properties.

Quacks, charlatans and mountebanks have always preyed upon gullible people but the public is now fairly well protected against fraudulent claims, as advertising of drugs direct to the public is banned in many countries. Even where it is allowed, it is subject to tight legal restraints. But there are still individuals, methods and theories that slip through the net.

One of the most audacious advertising claims in history must surely be that of James A. Davis of Atlanta, Georgia, in 1916, with reference to his company's product Human Ease. So effective was Human Ease supposed to be, that it was backed by the statement:

WE GUARANTEE TO CURE ALL DISEASES BOTH IN AND ON MAN AND BEAST. TAKE HUMAN EASE THEN YOU CAN EAT WHAT YOU PLEASE.

Particular mention was given, in the accompanying leaflet, to obesity, diabetes, tuberculosis, paralysis, cancer, syphilis, mad dog bites and in-growing toenails. Human Ease contained no injurious substances 'Alkahols, Morphines, Opiates, Cocaine, Potash, or acids, or any sleepy or deadly poison that would do any harm to A BABY an HOUR OLD'. Dr W. S. Hubbard of the Bureau of Chemistry, Department of Agriculture, performed a chemical analysis of the substance, and announced that it was 95.5 per cent lard! The accompanying condemnation of the purveyor stated that the claims made for the product were astounding, as many of the diseases supposedly cured by it were in fact incurable.

Another quack, John Andreadis, was nothing if not persistent in attempting to conquer the market in obesity cures. Amongst his early products were the 'Glamour Mold Self-Massage reducing kit' and the 'Hollywood Two-Way diet plan'. Later in his career he founded the Wonder Drug Company, which manufactured 'propex' appetite suppressants. In 1959 he marketed 'Regimen' tablets, and sold millions of dollars worth of the tablets at $5 per pack, but his run of successful, if dishonest, business ventures ceased when he was eventually indicted for fraud by the US Food and Drug Administration.

Quackery and dishonest advertising went on in many forms. One hundred years ago an article from the *British Medical Journal* described how:

> an enterprising vendor of a specific for obesity had to stand, figuratively, in a white sheet for having, with more ingenuity than righteousness, used the portrait of a lady of a certain age to illustrate the condition of a patient before the use of his nostrums, and the portrait of the same lady when a young girl to show the effect of treatment.

Many quack obesity cures were 'puffed' or advertised in the early twentieth century, but exaggerated promises of rapid weight reduction were usually avoided for the nostrums or specifics in question because the recipients had to be encouraged to take the remedy for some considerable length of time – for the vendor's benefit. If a remedy claimed to cure obesity instantaneously, it would soon be revealed as a fraud. Prices were usually quoted for a small number of tablets or quantity of liquid medication to be supplied, but a discount was often available as an encouragement to purchase larger quantities – again, mainly to benefit the vendor. Testimonials from satisfied customers were important – and provided.

'Absorbit Reducing Paste and J. Z. Obesity Tablets' were advertised and sold by a 'Hygienic Skin Specialist' and were probably typical of the 'cures' on offer. The paste was a pink ointment consisting of purified ox bile, beeswax, lard, oil, carmine and a trace of perfume. The instructions for use were: 'Rub in a circular direction, at night, where needed, for five minutes or more; firm, even movements, and only use as much as the skin will absorb'. The price of the paste was 3s.6d for a jar containing just over 2 ounces. The estimated cost of the ingredients was 3d. J. Z. Obesity Tablets were flat, oval lozenges sold in boxes of 25 for 2s, and two were to be taken at night, dissolved in the mouth. The tablets were made up of sulphur, ginger, sugar and acacia gum, the main ingredient being sugar. The estimated cost of the ingredients for 25 lozenges was a half penny.

Russell's Anti-Corpulent Preparation vied with Hargreaves Reducing Wafers, Allan's Anti-Fat, Marmola and many other 'remedies' [7-6]. Different marketing strategies applied. Nelson Lloyd Safe Reducing Treatment offered a free trial for a fortnight. Only 6d for postage was required and a book entitled *The Scientific Treatment of Obesity* was to be sent, along with a promise 'that the treatment was not weakening, that it was permanent, and that it had no ill effects'. The tablets would 'at once put a stop to the fat-forming habit of the body'.

Cure-alls were popular, partly as a result of bold advertising and partly from the idea that if one elixir would treat many disorders, why not take that and deal with all one's discomforts at the same time and with less financial

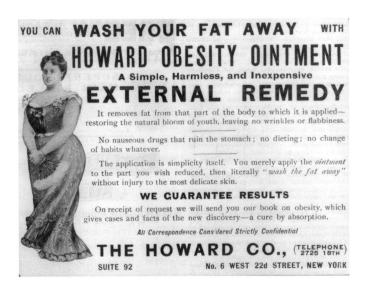

7-6
Howard's obesity ointment
promised that it 'removes fat
from that part of the body
to which it is applied…. No
dieting; no change of habits
whatsoever'.

outlay. For example, Dr Martin's Miracletts, supplied by a medicine company in London, were described as 'A real Elixir of Life in solid form. The world's greatest remedy.' A booklet supplied with the pills advised:

> Whatever you may be suffering from do not worry or fear, as Dr. Martin's Miracletts will be certain to cure you!
>
> Dr Martin's Miracletts make the weak and sickly become strong and healthy, and the aged become youthful and full of energy; the tired worn-out look being replaced by an appearance of cheerfulness and vivid health. The pale and wrinkled face with bad complexion gives way to rosy cheeks and a clear skin; the thin gain flesh, and the stout lose superfluous fat; indigestion quickly disappears, the appetite returns, and a *new life* is open to all.

Who could resist them! Furthermore, a guarantee was supplied which stated that any customer who had taken 18 tablets according to directions and was not satisfied with the results could have his money refunded. An additional note did comment that immediate results might not occur for long-standing ailments, but with patience and perseverance 'the result is SURE'. These miracle tablets consisted of quinine, zinc, iron oxide, menthol, kaolin and talc.

In 1911, the American Medical Association, following the example of the British Medical Association's *Secret Remedies*, published a volume called *Nostrums and Quackery*, in order to expose the 'Evil' fraudulent claims made for thousands of so-called remedies, often done in typically grandiose American style. The Foreword exudes common sense:

> Those who eat much and exercise little are likely to become obese, and no treatment that ignores the cause of the condition can or will

be effective…. Practically every 'fat cure', no matter to what type it belongs, is exploited under two specific claims: First that those who use it do not need to diet; second that they need not exercise. The most wildly extravagant representations are made by the dispensers of these worthless cures.

The American actress Texas Guinan was famed for being the first movie 'cowgirl', and became known as the Queen of the West. She amassed a fortune of around $700,000 in the 1920s, and during the Prohibition opened a speakeasy called the 300 Club, where 40 scantily clad dancers would mingle with the celebrity clients who somehow violated the ban on alcohol. It is said that the show *Chicago* is a homage to her. In 1913, she launched a new venture, Texas Guinan's World-Famed Treatment for Corpulency, price $20.00, after reducing her own weight from 204 to 134 pounds. Billed as a 'world-thrilling, perfect and positive fat-reducer', it induced 'a fresh new fairy slenderness of figure … lithe-limbed, small-waisted winsomeness from head to heel'. The liquid was designed to be applied and rubbed into the entire body or any of the fatty parts, leaving a dry powder residue. Laboratory analysis revealed it to contain 'thirty cents' worth of alcohol and alum'. In January 1914 Texas Guinan was declared guilty of conducting a fraudulent scheme. Judge Lamar summed up the case by saying:

> On the basis of an alleged reduction in weight by an actress by the use of the simple and well known drugs iodine, alum and alcohol, a wonderful and enticing story is built up, of a marvellous, new and positive cure for obesity … if Ms Guinan did in fact reduce her weight, it was due to hard work (the playing of ten shows a week), the abstinence from potatoes, and the massage given by her maid, rather than to the use of this mixture…. I therefore find that this is a scheme for obtaining money through the mails by means of false and fraudulent pretenses, representations and promises.

A fraud order was duly issued.[21]

Dangerous remedies in the early twentieth century

Whereas most quack remedies were fairly harmless – except to the wallet – but ineffective, many were highly effective in inducing weight loss but were also poisonous to varying degrees. In January 1914, *Good Housekeeping* published an article entitled 'Swindled Getting Slim':

> Overeating and under-exercising are the main causes of too much fat. Remove the causes and keep them removed. If you are not willing to do this, accept the fat and be jolly about it, and enjoy yourself; but don't spoil your digestion and general health, and waste your money, by patronizing advertised obesity cures. Better alive, fat and jolly, than svelte – and dead!

C-1
Daniel Lambert
pottery figure.

C-2
Daniel Lambert.

C-3
Lucky Strike advertisement
from the 1920s.

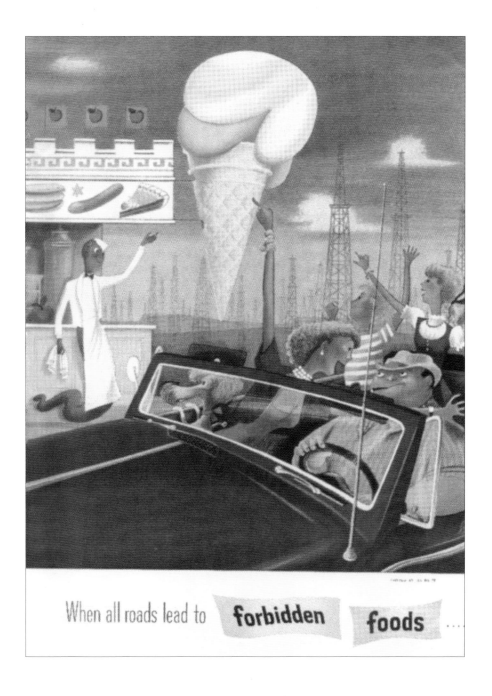

When all roads lead to **forbidden** **foods** ...

C-5
Adam and Eve, Cranach,
1526.

C-7
Central panel of *The Last
Judgement*, Bosch,
late fifteenth century.

C-8
The Last Judgement,
Fra Angelica.

C-9
The Fight Between Carnival and Lent, Breughel, 1559.

C-10
Resort, Gayle Chong Kwan, 2004 (c-type photograph, 31.5 inches × 40 inches).

C-11
Bacchus, Rubens.

C-12
Netherlandish Proverbs,
Breughel, 1559
oil on oak panel.

C-13
The Three Graces of the Primavera, Botticelli, 1482.

C-14
The Three Graces, Rubens, 1636–38.

X

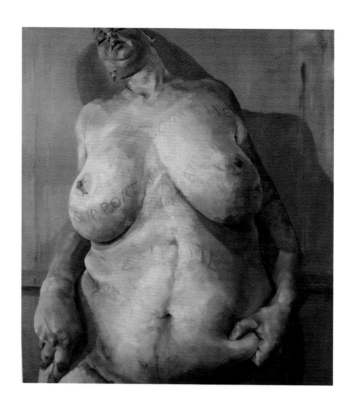

C-15
Branded, Jenny Saville, 1992
(213.4 cm × 182.9 cm).

C-16
I Am Too Political,
Martin Kippenberger., 1995.

C-17
Captain Obese.

C-18
Billy Bunter.

C-19
Exhibition 'Stare-Case',
Somerset House,
Rowlandson
(watercolour 15.7 in. ×
10.6 in., engraved c. 1800).

C-20
Strong Medicine, Kal, 1987.

C-21
Baron Grenville, Gillray,
1810. The print's full, proper
title is from Virgil: 'Tentanda
via est quame quoque
possium tollere humo…'
('some way must be tried by
which I too can raise myself
aloft and victoriously flit
through the mouths of men').

C-24
Lord Nozoo postcard.

C-25
Walt Munson,
'General Comics'.

C-26
Dance Macabre, Bernt Notke, in
St Nicholas' Church, Tallinn.

One such poison was pokeberry, used in various remedies for weight loss, including one called Phytoline. Its entry in a 1902 materia medica reads:

> *Phytolacca — Poke.*
> Source and Composition. The berry and root of *Phytolacca decandra*, (nat. ord. Phytolaccaceae), a N. American plant. It contains a neutral principle, *Phytolaccin*; also *Phytolaccic Acid*, tannin, starch, a fixed oil, etc.
> Preparations.
> > *Phytolaccae Fructus*, Poke Berry,—Dose, gr. x–xxx.
> > *Phytolaccae Radix*, Poke Root,—Dose, gr. j–v as alterative,—gr. x–xxx as emetic.
> > *Extractum Phytolaccae Radicis Fluidum*,—Dose, ᴹj–xxx.
>
> Physiological Action. Phytolacca depresses the heart-rate and the respiration, and is a paralyzer of motion by central action on the spinal cord. It is a slow and depressant emeto-cathartic, also somewhat narcotic and alterative. It irritates the throat and tonsils; produces tetanic convulsions in animals, and death by paralysis of respiration. Several cases of poisoning by this plant have occurred. Its action is antagonized by Alcohol, Ether, Opium, Digitalis. It promotes the absorption of adipose tissue.
>
> Therapeutics. Phytolacca is useful in—
> > *Mastitis*, to arrest the inflammation and prevent suppuration,—the extract may be applied locally and the fluid extract given internally.
> > *Varicose Ulcers*, and other ulcers of the leg,—it promotes healing.
> > *Eczema* of obstinate character,—has been cured by Phytolacca extract applied locally; also *Tinea Capitis*, and other skin affections.
> > *Chronic Rheumatism* of fibrous tissues,—used internally, it acts efficiently.
> > *Obesity*,—a resinoid preparation of the berries is sold as an 'anti-fat' remedy under the name *Phytoline*.
> > *Tonsillitis, Diphtheric Sore Throat* and *Chronic Follicular Pharyngitis*,—are affections in which Phytolacca has been much employed with good results, especially when high fever and pains in the head, back and limbs. In true adynamic Diphtheria it will do little good.[22]

King's American Dispensatory of 1898 warned:

> The berries, though poisonous, lose their toxic qualities somewhat when cooked, and some have gone so far as to make pies of the fruit – a practice which, however, should be condemned. Severe purging has followed the eating of the flesh of pigeons which had fed upon the berries.[23]

Pokeberry can still be found in some homeopathic remedies today.

Hundreds of different powders, pills, herbs, enemas and soaps were sold, some with the best of intentions, but others to defraud innocent customers. It was thought that using soap rectally, as an 'internal bath', would have the same effect as applying soapy detergent to a fat-covered dinner plate: emulsifying the fat and making it disappear. One can only guess at the extent of the deleterious effects of a soap enema, but weight loss would certainly not have been one of them!

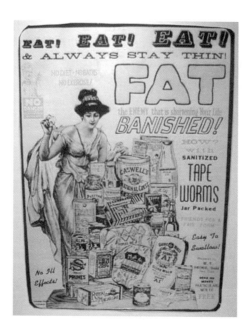

7-7
Tapeworm advertisement.

The use of tapeworms [7-7] at the start of the twentieth century to induce weight loss is legendary, although there is very little, if any, substantial evidence to suggest the practice ever occurred. Even Claudia Schiffer's name has been linked with the 'remedy'[24] and the opera singer Maria Callas was often said to have deliberately ingested the worm to shed pounds. By 1953, Callas was feeling humiliated by her excessive weight, and having experimented with crash diets and diuretics, all without prolonged success, she had even considered surgical remedies. But over the next two years she lost 66 pounds, reducing her weight from 210 to 144 pounds[25] without the help of any of these extreme measures, believing the cause was a tapeworm. However, this was unlikely to have been deliberately ingested and, given her propensity for eating rare and raw meat, it seems more likely that she consumed the tapeworm eggs inadvertently.

Reports that drug companies sold preserved tapeworm purporting to be diet pills have appeared from time to time. One claimed:

> A few years ago there was a company who put out sure fire diet pills, guaranteed to lose weight in no time. People began to take these pills, and in no time the people were losing weight. After a few weeks these people began to lose too much weight so the Government investigated. They opened the pills and found the head of a tapeworm.[26]

A search of the internet today will reveal tablets for sale purporting to contain tapeworm eggs. On close inspection, this has been found not to be true, and the advertisement is a hoax. Early advertisements exist openly claiming to contain the larvae of the worm, but whether they genuinely did so is uncertain.

Another successful but dangerous obesity cure was thyroid extract. George Bray, MD, described as the 'tireless world leader of obesity research and treatment', stated that:

> The beginning of 'modern' pharmacotherapy for obesity can be dated to 1893 when the use of *thyroid extract* was first reported. This crude preparation produced weight loss and its use has continued almost to the present time.[27]

An early, crude example was the Nelson Lloyd Safe Reducing Treatment,[28] mentioned above, from London, whose 'Special Tablets' contained bladderwrack, powdered liquorice, excipient (an inert substance added to the nostrum to make it suitable for administration) and moisture, but also 'proteid of thyroid gland'. The liquid version was predominantly extract of bladderwrack, glycerine and 'proteid of thyroid gland'.

The Mary Borden Company in New York concocted the aptly named Fatoff [7-8], the patent specifications for which included 'thyroid gland of sheep, tincture of iodine and extract of bladderwrack' to be used externally as a soap. But the actual patent application made no mention of obesity:

> The object of my invention is to provide or produce a new and useful composition, which when applied to the skin, will protect the covered part from the air, and at the same time operate as a cleanser or purifier for the removal of foreign matters or accumulations.

In contrast, the actual advertisement for the substance, aimed at highly gullible members of the public, stated:

> The discoverer of FATOFF considers herself one of Uncle Sam's 'assets' as a producer of something worth while. 'FATOFF', a product of Real commercial value at home and for export – and it's HONEST! YOU need it NOW if you're corpulent – take a FATOFF treatment to-night

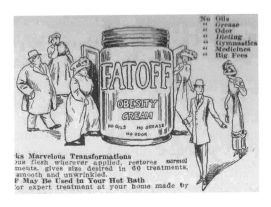

7-8
Fatoff advertisement.

and if you don't do enough extra business to-morrow to more than make up the cost you will be the first one.

However, when analysed, this so-called 'honest' treatment, far from representing the medical breakthrough it claimed, was found to contain nothing but soap and water, with not a trace of thyroid extract.

The volume *Nostrums and Quackery* carried the following warning:

> Thyroid extract was the basis of many of the 'fat reducers' first put on the market and this drug is still in use in some of them. The public however has been warned of the dangers of this powerful agent so it is becoming increasingly difficult for those who live on the fat of the land to sell remedies of this type.

Although sometimes clinically effective in inducing weight loss, the use of thyroid hormone is only appropriate in, and restricted to, cases of biochemically proven hypothyroidism, or underactive thyroid, where weight gain can be part of the presentation of myxoedema. Its use outside this condition can lead to overdose, and result in a severe, sometimes fatal, thyrotoxic crisis.

In 1894, before the nature of thyroid disease was fully understood, Professor Woods Hutchinson wrote that thyroid extracts 'cause, in some curious manner which we do not as yet understand, such an interference with the normal metabolism of the body as to cause the burning up and elimination of considerable amounts of body fat'. But he warned against losing more than 10 per cent of body weight – which he referred to as the 'movable' 10 per cent: the results of doing so, which we now understand to be thyrotoxicosis, would be injurious. 'The appetite becomes impaired, the sleep broken, and the heart's action irregular.' If treatment was prolonged, the drug would set up a 'serious and obstinate disturbance of the nervous system, and particularly of the nerves controlling the heart, accompanied by palpitation, sweating, weakness, and intense nervousness'.[29]

Charles Sajous of Philadelphia pointed out in 1916 that:

> thyroid preparations in sufficient doses promote the rapid combustion of fats.... We behold gradual emaciation beginning with the adipose tissues, which are the first to succumb. Hence the use of thyroid preparations in obesity.[30]

But the same author warned that such preparations should be used only for the treatment of obesity when that is linked with an underactive thyroid.

In August 1957 the *Journal of the American Medical Association*, the same body which had published the condemnatory volume *Nostrums and Quackery* nearly half a century earlier, demonstrated the ingenuity of the pharmaceutical industry of the era and its ability to think laterally to promote sales. The journal carried a full-page advertisement for Cytomel

"If a patient has signs and symptoms of hypometabolism, even if [she] has failed to respond to thyroid, a therapeutic trial with ['Cytomel'] should be carried out."[1]

Case History:[2] 32-year-old female. Presenting complaints—chronic fatigue, vague muscle pains, obesity. Her hair was thick and coarse. Laboratory findings showed a BMR of −21% and PBI in the normal range. Other laboratory and clinical findings were normal. The patient had been treated previously with three grains of desiccated thyroid daily for approximately six months. There was no change during this treatment.

Diagnosis: Metabolic Insufficiency—based on symptoms, signs and laboratory findings.

Treatment: Starting dosage: 5 mcg. of 'Cytomel' daily; increased to 10 mcg. daily in the second week; then gradually increased to 25 mcg. daily.

Results: After one week: there was marked improvement in her outlook and energy. After two weeks: the patient was "feeling fine" and "sleeping better." Her hair was silkier, and muscular aching had subsided. After six weeks: the patient reported "no complaints." She felt fine, had more energy, and no joint stiffness. At this time she had lost 9½ pounds, and her hair was soft and oily.

1. Helm, A.H.: Value of a Therapeutic Trial with Liothyronine, Internat. Rec. Med. & Gen. Pract. Clin. *170*:86 (Feb.) 1957.
2. Morton, J.H., and Callas, X.: Clinical Experience with L-triiodothyronine in Metabolic Disorders, Scientific Section of 105th Meeting of A.M.A., Chicago, Ill., June 11-15, 1956.

Smith, Kline & French Laboratories, Philadelphia

⭑T.M. Reg. U.S. Pat. Off. for liothyronine (L-triiodothyronine), S.K.F.

Cytomel⭑

a new hormone for treatment of hypometabolism

7-9
Cytomel advertisement.

[7-9], otherwise known as liothyronine – a synthetic version, triiodothyronine, of one of the hormones secreted by the thyroid gland, which is still in clinical use. However, Cytomel was being recommended outside the correct clinical guidelines drawn up by Sajous and others, for a 'convenient' condition the manufacturers called 'hypometabolism'. The advertisement cited a case of a 32-year-old woman 'Presenting complaints – chronic fatigue, vague muscle pains, obesity'. Her laboratory thyroid tests were normal, in particular her protein-bound iodine (PBI),[31] yet the modern equivalent of thyroid extract was nonetheless enthusiastically promoted. George Bray explained the anomaly, shedding light on the reasoning behind such a dangerous and inappropriate use of drugs:

> The use of thyroid extract could be justified because the 'metabolic rate' of many overweight people was said to be 'low'. It was widely believed that their low metabolism was the cause of obesity and that using a metabolic stimulant would 'correct' the problem.... It has [since] become clear that overweight people have higher metabolic rate.[32]

In the 1940s, the drug digitalis, manufactured from foxgloves to treat certain rhythm problems of the heart, was added to thyroid extract as a way to combat the racing pulse which hyperthyroidism induced. It also induced nausea and loss of appetite as a side-effect at very high doses, which added to its weight-loss effect. A drug similar to digitalis – strophanthin – was combined with thyroxine in a commercial product called Neo-Barine, advertised as 'a safe and dependable weight-reducing agent'. Despite its dangerous side-effects, Neo-Barine was used for weight loss until 1964, when it was revealed to be dangerous and removed from the market.

Pharmacology in the twentieth century

In the late 1920s, a new development in weight-loss drugs occurred with the evolution of the first ever synthetic anorectic agent. Its development was based on the observation during the First World War that workers in the chemical dye industry and in munitions factories who came into contact with dinitrophenol often lost weight. Dinitrophenol was used in the production of aniline dyes in clothes, especially pink and yellow hues, and was a major component in certain explosives. However, the compound is now known to be a metabolic poison and induces weight loss by increasing the body's metabolic rate. It was widely prescribed between 1933 and 1937, as Formula 37 and Corpu-lean, and heralded, as have many drugs before and since, as a wonder drug. After 1937 it was abandoned owing to side-effects, which included nerve damage and cataracts, as well as 'overheating' of the metabolism, which caused extreme increases in body temperature and ultimately death. Dinitrophenol is still used as an insecticide and wood preservative, and despite its poisonous nature is reportedly still used by some body-builders to improve their body morphology.

The next wonder drug was Benzedrine. Benzedrine was used as a decongestant and was studied as a cure for asthma, but was soon prescribed only to treat the sleeping disorder narcolepsy, and used by students to prolong their hours of studying. Patients receiving the drug were observed to lose their appetite and lose weight, leading to the drug being experimentally assessed and marketed for obesity treatment around 1938. The discovery of the effects of Benzedrine soon resulted in the introduction of a whole series of related compounds – amphetamines – which were marketed as 'anorectic agents', or appetite suppressants [7-10]. However, it soon became

7-10
Dexedrine: advertisement for
a weight-loss amphetamine.

clear that the amphetamines were beset by problems and side-effects: they worked only in the short term and their use was almost inevitably followed by rebound weight gain; they also caused the jitters, tremors, insomnia and restlessness. All of these drugs, including phenmetrazine, benzphetamine, phendimetrazine and many others, were classified as addictive, or potentially addictive, by the US Drug Enforcement Agency. One contributor to *Overeaters Anonymous* described the feeling induced by such agents:

> During a period when I was heavily addicted to diet pills I reached what I thought was the perfect weight for my five feet, seven inches: 95 pounds. My dream of being as scrawny as a Vogue model was finally realized. No more did I have to compare myself with other girls at parties and come out the one with the biggest hips. I felt gorgeous. Never mind such minor drawbacks as anaemia and malnutrition.

Another described the hyperactivity induced by the drugs:

> I found diet pills. They worked fine for two days. I came home on my lunch hour; cleaned the house, made the bed, did the dishes and ate lunch. The pills soon enabled me to eat faster – and more.

A third contributor, a professional dancer, described the rebound weight gain common on stopping therapy:

> I quit using amphetamines after my last show business job and gained 60 pounds. I tried every new diet I could find, went to hypnotists, psychiatrists and a fasting farm, but nothing could stop me. When I saw people I knew on the street, I hid in shame. I became almost violent if my parents or others who loved me tried to help. I hated myself and wished I would die.

7-11
Frances Farmer.

This third contributor also revealed the situation in which many show business celebrities found themselves, having to maintain a glamorous figure for the sake of the cameras and their careers. It has been alleged that film stars Judy Garland, Marilyn Monroe and Elizabeth Taylor were addicted to diet pills at some time during their careers. Gospel singer Dinah Washington died from an overdose of diet pills and Frances Farmer [7-11], a talented Hollywood and Broadway actress in the 1930s, was another person whose career was effectively ended by addiction to weight-loss drugs. She worried constantly about her weight and the roles she was playing, and started taking Benzedrine as an appetite suppressant. Her career declined, leading to increasingly antisocial behaviour. After several arrests, court cases and imprisonment, she was asked on one occasion if she had had anything to drink since her last court appearance. She replied 'Yes, I drank everything I could get, including Benzedrine'.

Another victim of the mania surrounding diet pills was circus fat lady Dolly Dimples (discussed in Chapter 3). Dolly was encouraged to try diet pills by her sister-in-law Alma, who, although not in Dolly's super-obese league, still had a major weight problem. In her autobiography, Dolly Dimples recalled the problems she and her sister-in-law experienced:

> I saw an advertisement in a magazine for pills that take off fat. I'm sure if we took them we could both lose weight and solve all our problems. I'd like to try them if you would. How about it?' The pills didn't work; 'I'm still as fat as a cow'; but after another sort of pill, and the use of a rolling pin, still without success, a third pill was successful. 'I think these pills are working' I told Alma, after we'd been on them for about ten days. 'That's what I think', she answered, 'my clothes seem loose to me.'
>
> In a couple of weeks Alma had lost a lot of weight, but she did not look well. Her face was drawn and yellowed. She confessed to me she had no appetite either.... Alma continued to lose weight. She looked haggard and I was worried.... When I got home that day I looked at my thighs and they were all puffed. I was scared.... It became so painful

to move around the apartment that I spent almost all my time in a chair or in bed. I heard that Alma was sick too, but I could not get any of the details. [My husband] Frank insisted that I call the doctor … I received the most awful shock of my life. 'There's something strange and similar about Alma's death and your illness' he said. 'What do you mean Alma's death' I shrieked.[33]

Thus Dolly describes both the side-effects and the fatal potential of amphetamines. Despite this they were used by millions of Americans for their energising effects, becoming widely known as 'hearts'. Users of these and related drugs included fighter pilots and long-distance drivers. They were even specifically advertised for use in pregnancy, a time during which weight loss is rarely, if ever, advised and the use of prescription drugs severely restricted.

The multimillion-pound pharmaceutical industry reached a low point in the field of anti-obesity medication in the 1950s with the drug Ambar, and other similar compounds. The 'Am' in the drug's name stood for amphetamine, still frequently used at the time, which had the anorectic effect of reducing appetite and increasing activity by its stimulant effect. The 'Bar' is an example of pharmaceutical company ingenuity, standing for barbiturate, which was added to calm the amphetamine-induced hyperactivity: 'weight loss without the jitters' was the proud claim, and consequently the cocktail of two of the most addictive, abusable and dangerous drugs was successfully marketed to an unsuspecting and vulnerable public. There were many such examples of similar agents, each one backed by massive advertising campaigns, often depicting healthy people engaging in healthy outdoor pursuits. Undoubtedly these drugs had the desired effect of weight loss, but at too high a cost: the side-effects were horrific, and the tendency to regain weight on stopping after the three-month licensed course, overwhelming. The drug Desoxyn, for example, was backed by a major high-profile and persistent advertising campaign, in which dozens of different glossy full-page advertisements [see C-4] appeared in high-profile journals such as the *Journal of the American Medical Association*. The advertisements featured an obese man or woman bravely resisting fattening food, but being presented with a tasty high-calorie treat by an evil-looking green character with a snake's tail, dressed as a waiter or other food provider: the Serpent of Temptation, who was either male or female, depending on the gender of its prey. Each advertisement has the Apple from the Tree of Knowledge hidden in it, and the implication is clear that the wonderful drug will conquer gluttony and temptation and be a saviour to hundreds of thousands of well meaning, but weak-willed victims. Drugs such as this were widely prescribed to millions of people worldwide.

The chemical profile of the anorectic agents did, however, improve; the addiction potential decreased and so the demand for them remained high.

The drugs were cheap to manufacture but were commonly to be found at vastly inflated prices in unscrupulous private slimming clinics, or even being sold from car boots in car parks. But it became clear that previously unidentified side-effects were linked with these agents, often fatal conditions such as heart valve defects and primary pulmonary hypertension. These led to the withdrawal of fenfluramine and dexfenfluramine from the market in 1997. Phentermine and ionamin, although not strictly amphetamine based, are throwbacks to that era of pharmacotherapy when the body of evidence required to launch such a product was much less challenging than today. The use of these drugs is highly restricted, especially in Britain, and they are licensed for three months only.

Today, modern, safe, effective, well tolerated drugs are under-used by doctors and patients alike, partly because there is a feeling of having been cheated by the marketeers in the past and encouraged to use drugs that turned out to be ineffective, or highly dangerous.

What now?

After a period during which no evidence-based drugs were available for the long-term management of obesity, modern therapies began to emerge in the late 1990s. Drugs called lipase inhibitors act on the bowel to prevent fat absorption; others act on the neurotransmitters in the brain to effect satiety, or moderate appetite, and also act peripherally on receptors which alter the body's metabolic processes. All appear to be effective and well tolerated, and are being increasingly widely prescribed. More and more pharmaceutical companies now have anti-obesity drugs in various stages of development, and their use as modifiers of cardiovascular and metabolic risk is increasingly widespread. Although the lessons of the past seem to have been heeded by the drugs industry, its products are unfairly tainted in the minds of healthcare professionals and patients, because of the harmful and destructive compounds of earlier eras and the cynical and dishonest advertising of previous generations of pharmaceutical entrepreneurs.

CHAPTER 8

Gluttony

The pleasure of the table belongs to all ages, to all conditions, to all countries and to all eras; it mingles with all other pleasures, and remains at last to console us for their departure. (Jean Anthelme Brillat-Savarin[1])

The words from Isaiah 22:13, 'Let us eat and drink, for tomorrow we shall die', may be apt for today's society of overindulgent eaters and drinkers. After the Second World War and the restrictions of rationing, and as different foods became more widely available, the 'pleasures of the table' increased. Fast-food franchises, thought by some observers to be the chief cause of the present obesity crisis, became part of the landscape of the developed world. The inevitable consequence of overindulgence for many is a degree of corpulence or obesity. As waistlines increase, so do the afflictions to which their owners are likely to succumb; gluttony reaps its own rewards.

William Combe wrote the following words to accompany Thomas Rowlandson's *Dance of Death* series of illustrations:

> There is no form which Vice puts on,
> None so distinguish'd – no, not one
> So nauseous none, in Reason's eye
> As the swoll'n shape of Gluttony.[2]

Change of bodily shape is just one of the perils of gluttony – a visible representation of conspicuous consumption. Chaucer made the following observation:

> O if men knew how many a malady
> Proceeds from gluttony and from excess,
> They'd be so much more moderate and frugal
> With what they eat when they sit down at table.[3]

The seven deadly sins

The ways in which gluttony has been viewed have changed over the centuries. The first or original sin committed by Adam and Eve [C-5], although essentially an act of disobedience, was regarded by some commentators as symbolically connected with eating. It was not concerned with the quantity of food consumed but the desire for what was offered, and so therefore still a form of gluttony. Graphic depictions of the biblical story from the Book of Genesis illustrate the Tree of Knowledge, from which Eve takes an apple and tempts Adam to eat. The long-term consequence of this act of gluttony was that suffering and death entered Paradise and all men and women were fated to carry the burden of suffering bequeathed to them by the sinful pair.

Gluttony or sloth (the subject of Chapter 9) – which one is the cause of the modern obesity epidemic? Both were regarded as deadly sins by early theologians and both contribute to obesity. Early theologians equated gluttony and sloth with immorality. Those who indulged themselves with an excess of food and drink were considered greedy and lazy; their gluttony was associated with overeating and with lust, and they ate whilst others went hungry. Their act was morally repugnant, not only because they ate in excess, but also because, by eating more than their fair portion, they deprived others. Worse still, as gluttons' thoughts were fixed upon their bellies, their minds were diverted from worshipping God. At the opposite extreme, those who practised self-starvation were regarded as holy, good and self-disciplined. Images of corpulence were signs or symbols of Christian immorality. A paunch was a symbol of carnality derived from an excess of sensual pleasure. By contrast, the gaunt features and almost cadaverous figures of the ascetics, who lived lives of austerity and aimed to achieve holiness through mortification of the flesh, were to be admired, although in the thirteenth century Thomas Aquinas [8-1] warned about the temptation to indulge in excessive fasting. The sin of pride might be invoked if those fasting sought to gain satisfaction from the suffering they endured. Excessive feasting and obsession with fasting, the latter usually associated with nuns, could both be associated with indulgence or temptation. Such nuns, who have been called 'holy anorexics', punished their bodies by starving themselves and indulging in all manner of inventive and frequently disgusting self-mortifications.[4]

In the fourth century, Evagrius of Pontus, who had protested against gluttony and had spent time fasting in the wilderness, described the sin as:

> the mother of lust, the nourishment of evil thoughts, laziness in fasting, obstacle to asceticism, terror to moral purpose, the imagining of food, sketcher of seasonings, unrestrained colt, unbridled frenzy, receptacle of disease, envy of health, obstruction of the passages, groaning of the bowels, the extreme of outrages, confederate of lust, pollution of the intellect, weakness of the body, difficult sleep, gloomy death.[5]

8-1
Thomas Aquinas.

In the sixth century, Pope Gregory the Great formulated the traditional seven deadly sins, which were ranked in a perceived order of severity: pride, avarice (greed/covetousness), envy, wrath (anger), lust, gluttony and sloth. Previously, in the early fifth century, eight sins had been described: vainglory had been considered as a sin along with pride; dejection was added to sloth or *accidia*, meaning spiritual gloom and heaviness, rendering the soul restless and unhappy; and envy was not considered at all. Seven was a convenient number of sins to name, however, as the number was supposed to be special and complete, and these were retained. The Roman Catholic Church in the West still commonly recognises these as the seven capital sins.

These were not necessarily the worst kind of sins in themselves. Their gravity was due to the power they had of generating other sins: covetousness, for example, might lead to theft and blackmail, anger to murder, and sloth to despair. Wrath, gluttony or lust could generate an intense level of heat in the body, upsetting bodily humours and leading to a frenzy or kind of madness. These sins warranted eternal damnation. According to popular medieval legend, the hermit John of Beverley was tested by God, who sent an angel to force John to choose one of three sins: drunkenness, rape or murder. John chose what seemed to be the lesser evil, drunkenness, but whilst in a drunken stupor raped and murdered his own sister.[6]

The word 'gluttony', derived from the Latin *gluttire* (to devour), applies to excessive eating and a glutton is one who eats excessively. Gregory the Great had described gluttony as applying to five different patterns of eating: eating too soon, too expensively, too much, too eagerly or too daintily – 'hastily, sumptuously, excessively, ravenously, fastidiously':

> Sometimes it forestalls the hour of need; sometimes it seeks costly means; sometimes it requires that food be daintily cooked; sometimes it exceeds the measure of refreshment by taking too much; sometimes we sin by the very heat of an immoderate appetite.[7]

Gluttony was not always bound up with fat, corpulence or obesity: a thin person might be a glutton. The act of overindulgence was the sin: being fat *per se* was not an issue.

Aquinas listed 'daughters' spawned by gluttony: excessive and unseemly joy, loutishness, uncleanness, talkativeness and uncomprehending dullness of mind. According to Thomas à Kempis, 'when the belly is full to bursting with food and drink, debauchery knocks on the door'.[8]

Gluttony had earned its place amongst the deadly sins and drinking excessively, or intemperance, would seem to be included in its remit, according to Aquinas:

> Drunkenness is the root of all kinds of sins…. Before all else, clerics should avoid drunkenness, which inflames and nourishes all kinds of sins. And drunkenness is a species of gluttony.[9]

The Christian Church constantly condemned intemperance, but many ecclesiastics set bad examples. In the eighth century, the Venerable Bede wrote to Egbert, Archbishop of York:

> It is commonly reported of certain bishops that the way they serve Christ is this. They have no one near them of any religious spirit or continence, but only such as are given to laughter, jokes, amusing stories, feasting, drunkenness and the other snares of a sensual life – men who feed their belly with meats, rather than their souls with the heavenly sacrifice.[10]

The practice apparently continued, as, about 50 years later, Boniface, Archbishop of the Germans, wrote to Cuthbert, Archbishop of York:

> It is reported that in your diocese the vice of drunkenness is too frequent; so that not only certain bishops do not hinder it, but they themselves indulge in excess of drink, and force others to drink till they are intoxicated.

Carvings in churches and places of worship were present as reminders of sinful behaviour. For example, images of grossly obese monks can be seen on a choir-stall seat in St George's Chapel in Windsor Castle defaecating demons as a symbol of their corruption. Lard-tub friars were lampooned; records of the rich and varied diets that monks consumed belied their frugal lifestyle.

In the Middle Ages some forms of music were associated by the clergy with lust and debauchery. Bagpipes especially were associated with lust – an association which also applied to pigs. Bagpipes were made from pigs' bladders and the two – pipes and pigs – can be seen in medieval carvings, for example in Beverley Minster.

At Westminster Abbey the monks were consuming in excess of the modern calorific recommended daily allowance even when they were supposed to be fasting. Studies of skeletons from monastic burials have found that monks were almost five times as likely to develop obesity-related joint disease as their secular counterparts.

Aquinas viewed gluttony less harshly as he grew older, possibly because he himself became obese, and known as the Dumb Ox of Sicily. The results of gluttony are not always easy to disguise, as it tends to enlarge the waistline. Aquinas was described at one time as 'a sort of walking wine barrel', and to him was ascribed the necessity of having a crescent cut out of a table to enable him to sit at it.[11] It was also necessary to cut a crescent out of the altar table from which he administered Holy Communion, to accommodate his increasing girth. Impressively, however, he continually overcame the handicap of his obesity and apparently still managed to levitate his gross bulk in his cell.

After Aquinas, gluttony came to be regarded in a more relaxed fashion. The sin was one of degree – with regard not to the actual consumption of food, which was, after all, necessary for maintaining life, but to the strength of appetite or desire for it and the pleasure derived from tasting it. Such desires and excessive preoccupations with all aspects of food and drink distracted from the more important, spiritual needs. St Francis of Assisi spread ashes on his food to destroy the pleasure to be obtained from eating it.

The Pardoner [8-2] in Chaucer's *Canterbury Tales* illustrates the kind of behaviour associated with or spawned by gluttony, to which Thomas à Kempis had alluded, when he describes how a company of youngsters from Flanders spent their time in dicing, dancing, eating and drinking to excess, laughing, swearing and blaspheming:

8-2
The Pardoner.

> And in there come the dainty dancing girls,
> Graceful and slim; harpers and procurers,
> The young fruit-sellers and confectioners,
> Who are in fact the Devil's officers,
> Who light and blow the fires of lechery,
> Which is so close conjoined with gluttony.
> I take Holy Writ to be my witness,
> Lechery springs from wine and drunkenness.[12]

Chaucer was born some time between 1340 and 1345. He began writing *The Canterbury Tales* about 1387 and continued to work on them until he died in 1400. He was a social commentator who held a mirror to contemporary society and reflected life in its variety, illuminating the humdrum and penetrating the motives and actions of men and women.[13] Chaucer wrote from a wide experience of life in different fields and through the medium of poetry described the pilgrims – ordinary men and women – who made their way from Suffolk to Thomas à Becket's shrine at Canterbury, amusing each other with stories on the way. Becket had been murdered in the Cathedral in 1170 and Canterbury became a place of pilgrimage. The characters of the pilgrims come alive in Chaucer's poetry and are similar to the characters of folk to be found anywhere in any age or place – 'everyman'. His poetry is full of humour, pathos and satire and through it can be seen contemporary views of the temptations to which man was liable. The seven deadly sins are represented through the stories told, gluttony and sloth amongst them. The Pardoner, in his tale, reiterates the teaching of the early Church and tells of the effects of the 'daughters of gluttony' as proclaimed by Aquinas. As part of the Pardoner's sermon, he engages with Adam and Eve, who were cast out of Paradise because of their gluttony, and reminds the pilgrims of this original sin. He refers to this episode of the Fall of Man using the story literally:

> O gluttony, full of all cursedness;
> O cause first of our confusion,
> O original of our damnation
> …
> Corrupt was all this world for gluttony.

He continues with his diatribe against overindulgence:

> Wine stirs up lechery and drunkenness,
> Is full of quarrelling and wickedness …
> … drink is the tomb
> Of a man's wit and judgement and discretion.
> For no one under the domination
> Of drink can keep a secret in his head.

In his sermon to the pilgrims about the seven deadly sins, Chaucer's Parson describes gluttony as an immeasurable appetite to eat or drink. William Langland, in *Piers the Ploughman*, written between 1360 and 1399, tells of the Confession of Glutton:

> And I have let myself go at supper, and sometimes dinner too, so badly that I have thrown it all up again before I have gone a mile, and wasted food that might have been saved for the hungry. On fast days I have eaten the tastiest foods I could get, and drunk the best wines, and sometimes sat so long at my meals that I've slept and eaten both at the same time. And to get more drink and hear some gossip, I've had my dinner at the pub on fast days too, and rushed off to a meal before midday.[14]

Thus, Glutton bewails his immorality and lack of moral fibre and seeks confession for the sin of gluttony.

Illustrations of gluttony

The earliest surviving British wall paintings of the seven deadly sins date from the first half of the fourteenth century, and can be seen at Cranborne in Dorset and Wootton Wawen in Warwickshire. An early sculptural series of the sins can also be seen on the Chapter House portal at Salisbury Cathedral, where a battle between Vices and Virtues is portrayed.

Many artists literally drew attention to the deadly sins, which were amongst the most popular themes of medieval art. At a time when few people could read, visual images provided basic teaching material. Initially only simple personifications of particular sins were produced, in church decorations and in the miniatures of manuscripts. An early representation in the form of a procession can be found carved in stone in the fifteenth-century medieval chapel at Rosslyn near Edinburgh in Scotland. This, it is thought, may have been the inspiration for the poem 'Dance of the Sevin Deidly Synnis' by the Scottish poet William Dunbar, written about 1496. The sins represented in the poem and those carved in procession at Rosslyn differ in their order from that set out by the Catholic Church. The standard order of the deadly sins was based on the extent to which they differ from love; pride is the furthest away from love and is therefore the most serious sin, whereas lust, a perverted kind of love, is closest and the least sinful. Part of Dunbar's poem reads:

> And first of all in dance was Pryd,
> With hair wyld bak and bonet on syd.
> Then Yre came in with sturt and stryfe,
> His hand was ay upoun his knyfe.
> Nixt in the dance followit Invy
> Next him in dans come Cuvatyce
> Syne sweirnes (Ydilness)
> Then Lichery
> Than the foull monstir Gluttony.

In the stone carvings, gluttony is shown with a large pitcher held up to his mouth; sloth is wearily dragging a bag along the ground.

Conventional representations of the seven deadly sins are in the form of a wheel or a tree, but Hieronymus Bosch's painting *The Seven Deadly Sins* (c. 1475–85) [C-6] is in the form of an eye, in the centre, or pupil, of which is an image of Christ – an all-seeing being – around whom scenes of the seven deadly sins are enacted. The words underneath the image of Christ ('Cave, cave, Dominus videt' – 'Beware, beware the Master sees') refer to God's omniscience: He sees and knows of all man's sinful actions. In the scene depicting 'Gula' or gluttony [8-3], everything in everyday life lies in disorder as the characters focus their attention on the only thing that

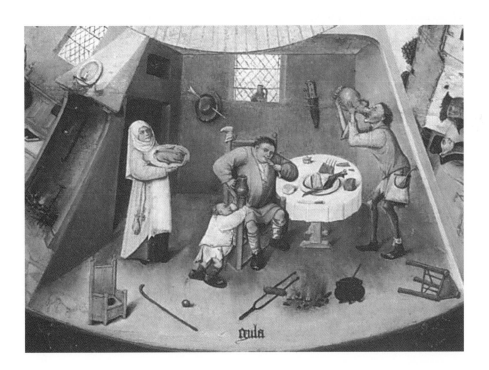

8-3
'Gula' (gluttony)
detail from Bosch's
The Seven Deadly Sins.

matters to them – food. Even the overweight child is sinfully reaching for food. The hat pierced by an arrow and hanging on the wall behind the gluttonous man is similar to that seen in some of Bosch's later pictures, though in those it is worn by torturers and tormentors. The nun bringing in more food seems to gaze at this symbol of the glutton's fate, the arrow pointing in his direction. This is a moralising representation of the sin, open to personal interpretation by the individual, and was intended to show the evil that men do in their daily lives in relation to the suffering of Christ. It is not an illustration of the punishments awaiting the sinner in the afterlife but, nevertheless, there is a medallion in each corner of the picture – a reminder or promise of things to come: death, judgement, hell or heaven.

Later images were more complicated, and attributes attached to a particular sin were added to images of animals. Contrasts were often made between sins and virtues, in a symbolic struggle between good and evil. Complicated and sophisticated allegories became part of the iconography of the seven deadly sins.

In his painting *The Last Judgement*, a triptych produced in the late fifteenth century, Bosch graphically presents the fate of the glutton. The artist produced a kind of work that was new to his followers and he populated his world with monstrous creatures and unconventional images. Although at this time knowledge of the earth's surface and about the human body and the animal and plant world was increasing, popular belief was still invested in devils and demons, who were held, along with their human accomplices, to be responsible for unexplained events, illnesses, deformities and epidemics. Those thought to be in league with evil forces would be tortured or burnt at the stake. Bosch's images were in line with popular imagination.

In the central panel of the triptych [C-7], character defects are acted out in dramatic fashion; certain sins are illustrated along with their predestined punishments. Sinners are delivered for their prescribed sentence to men depicted as monsters. For example, a gluttonous fat man is forced to drink from a barrel of freshly made latrine sewage [8-4]. The scene is one of hell on earth, with infernal torments delivered by strange beasts, insects, amphibious monsters, crawling beasts and other bizarre creatures or aspects of the Devil. Alternatively, those who were gluttons in life, according to Bosch, were cooked and eaten in death, in a variety of ways: roasted on a spit, sautéed in a frying pan, or simply boiled in a broth.

The fifteenth-century *Book of God's Providence*, a manual of virtues and vices, tells how, in the after-life, former gluttons sit round a burning-hot table, the hellish heat of which makes them thirst for urine to drink and hunger for straw and excrement to eat. They are then force-fed toads, lizards, vermin and other vile creatures. In late medieval morality plays, gluttony misled men to banquets in hell, where sauces were seasoned with sulphur and devils stuffed gluttons with toads from stinking rivers.

Warning to viewers against immoderation and overindulgence are implicit in the depictions of the last judgement by both Bosch and Fra Angelica [C-8, 8-5]. The images of those who were corpulent or had over-indulged during life are displayed for all to see; gluttons in the after-life were depicted as being presented with sumptuous feasts and banquets but were held back from eating them by the claws of demons and devils. In other interpretations of the punishments of gluttony, sinners were eaten whole by hellish monsters, only to be given birth, or defaecated, by them, to be consumed once more.

8-6
Gula, Breughel, 1558.

Pieter Breughel the Elder's series of engravings of 'The Seven Deadly Sins' was published in seven sheets by the famous Antwerp copperplate printing house of Hieronymus Cock in 1558. Breughel also produced disturbing landscapes inhabited by fantastic creatures developed partly from Bosch's images. Many thought that these were part of everyday reality. In Breughel's engraving of *Gula*, or Gluttony [8-6], the sin is personified by a woman in the dress of a Flemish burgher's wife. She is drinking from a jug. At her feet, her animal equivalent, a hog with the ears and hind legs of a dog, gorges itself on turnips and carrots. During the Middle Ages, each deadly sin was associated with a familiar barnyard animal, to help people to remember what the sins were. A pig or hog represented gluttony. 'Envy' sits at a table at which two naked humans are eating, one of whom is about to be carried off by demons. Behind the table is Envy's house – a dilapidated tent that partially covers a wine barrel, from which a monster wearing a monk's cowl is helping himself. Bagpipes, symbolising obesity, hang from the branches of a blasted tree nearby. In the right foreground is a bloated fish with its belly partially split open. The latter shows signs of having been repaired previously, but is bursting again as its owner consumes another fish. Another vignette is of a naked man trapped in a wine barrel with only his legs visible; he is being punished for his sin of drunkenness.

Meanwhile, by the side of a river, an obese man is destined to carry his distended abdomen in a cart as his punishment for overeating. Above him is a windmill made from a human face; sacks are being shovelled into the continually grinding mouth. 'Drunkenness and gluttony must be shunned', reads the Latin motto.

The French etcher, engraver and painter Jacques Callot produced his symbolic portraits of the seven deadly sins in 1619. Gula carried a flagon and a glass. A boar crouched behind her, with his snout protruding, the image of the pig or boar once again symbolising gluttony.

Feasting and fasting were an inevitable consequence of the way of life at this time. When harvests were good, or stores became available, or a court or monastery had a temporary surplus of food, overindulgence in both eating and drinking was the result. Times of hardship might follow, 'but let us eat and drink while we may'. The Church calendar acknowledged this pattern and to some extent regularised the situation by organising the liturgical year around a cycle of feasts and fasts. The year after producing his engraving *Gula*, Breughel painted an allegorical scene depicting this situation as a conflict between Protestants and Roman Catholics at a religious festival, *The Fight Between Carnival and Lent* [C-9, and details 8-7]. Fat versus thin is at issue. A gluttonous obese Carnival, representing Protestants in this *hors de combat*, rides astride a beer barrel, balancing a pie on his head and brandishing a stick on which a pig's head and other meats are impaled. The pig was again seen as a lustful and gluttonous animal and its presence – or that of its head – was an appropriate symbol. Carnival challenges a gaunt and haggard Lent, representing Roman Catholics, riding on a trolley with a

8-7
Details from *The Fight Between Carnival and Lent*, Breughel, 1559: Carnival (left) and Lent (right).

beehive on his head, bees being emblems of work and obedience to a royal master. The figure of Lent holds aloft a paddle, on which are two meagre fish. Feasting and frolicking take place on the left-hand side of the peasant scene, whilst piety and frugality are evident on the right. The flag is raised for battle to commence. Who will win – frugality or excess? In this scene, those who occupy the middle ground – the fish-sellers, bakers, shopkeepers and innkeepers – those not directly involved with the religious controversy – seem to be trading well. In the centre of the picture is a fool leading two people. He is bearing a lighted torch, although it is daytime. This is indicative of a world turned upside down, with people led astray by foolishness. Breughel caricatures both religious factions and offers moral lessons to each. Aristotle said that an excess of virtue is, in fact, a form of vice. What he championed was the golden mean: neither asceticism nor self-indulgence, but moderation.[15] Breughel also seems to advocate the middle way.

Depictions of the seven deadly sins continued to challenge artists. James Ensor, a Belgian, etched his version of the topic in an album that was published in 1904. Several of the etchings depict scenes in domestic environments as a reminder that depravity and corruption are part of the ordinary, everyday world, not just scenes that might occur in the afterlife. Some of his ideas hark back to the kind of images used by Bosch and Breughel and evoke revulsion and dismay. His etching *Gluttony*, for example, illustrates two men at a dinner table vomiting whilst waiting to be served with more food. A dish on which lies a severed head with a knife in its cheek sits on the table and is about to be served. A skeletal waiter stands by, holding a plate of scorpions to accompany this dish. A fat pig hovers above, in drooling imitation of the gluttons at the table, and a picture within the picture shows a sheep and a pig being eviscerated, their entrails lying on the ground with a dog feasting on the remains.

Graphic artists were not the only ones to paint pictures of hell and damnation. The poet Dante Alighieri painted his ideas through a different medium. Dante was born in Florence in 1265 but was exiled from the city in 1302. About this time he wrote his poetic work, the 'Inferno', part of the *Divina Commedia*. Dante's hell is divided into nine concentric circles, each smaller and lower than that preceding it, and each is devoted to the punishment of increasingly heinous offences or sins. Lust, gluttony, avarice and wrath were, according to Aristotle, 'sins of Incontinence' – sinful actions brought about by inadequate control of natural appetites and desires. Those guilty of such offences occupy circles 2 to 5 of Dante's hell.[16]

Dante is guided through this underworld by Virgil, and describes the conditions that he sees being suffered by the gluttons in circle 3:

> I am in the third round's den – deep there is the downpour,
> The timeless, cheerless rain, accurs'd and chillily falling,
> Which knows no change or renewal in nature or quality.

Heavy falling of hailstones, and foul water, and hell's sleet
Dank through the dark air continually drenching;
A filthy stench is from the ground and grievous,
That takes that falling.

Cerberus, the three-headed hound who is traditionally the watchdog of Hades, stands guard:

With his three gullets hideous, houndlike bays howling
Over the people submerged, immersed there in the mud.
Blood crimson his eyes are ablaze, black and greasy his muzzle
Both wide is his belly and big, and his hands with claws barbed.
He rends the spirits and wrenches them and rips them into quarters.[17]

'The lot of them lay there on the ground lubberly' – except one, who spoke to Dante. (A 'lubberly' man is an awkward, clumsy and lazy fellow, one who idles his life away.) His name had been Ciacco, meaning 'Porky-boy' – a well known Florentine glutton who had died when Dante was a young man.[18]

Gluttony was the fault, the foul sin I fell in,
Wherefore, as now you see, I am soaked in the rain's sluice;
And I, a soul here in sorrow, am not alone in this sadness;
Like pain and like penalty here is paid us who suffer
For sins of the same kind.

Dante wrote his *Divina Commedia* for an educated elite. His vision of the Inferno, Purgatory and Paradiso was full of symbolism and allusion based on his wide knowledge of philosophy, astronomy, natural science and history.

At this time, the emphasis was upon the act of gluttony and the punishment to be meted out in the after-life rather than upon its effects on the body during life itself. However, the physical effects of overindulgence can be clearly visualised through Edmund Spenser's *The Faerie Queen* (1596):

And by his side rode loathsome Gluttony,
Deformed creature, on a filthie swine;
His bellie was up-blowne with luxury,
And eke with fatnesse swollen were his eyne.
And like a Crane his necke was long and fine,
With which he swallowed up excessive feast.
… Full of diseases was his carcas blew,
And a dry dropsie through his flesh did flow:
Which by misdiet daily greater grew.[19]

Spenser thus associated gluttony with corpulence and morbidity. His writings were intended to illustrate the virtues necessary to fashion a gentleman, and his narrative style of poetry, looking back to Chaucer, covered important issues of the day, religious, ethical and moral. In a search for ideal virtues, the perils of a life of Christian immorality, including that of gluttony, were addressed.

The glutton's paradise

Pieter Breughel's scene *The Land of Cockaigne* (1567) [8-8] depicts the soporific effect of gluttony. Contemporary artists had usually depicted and mocked peasants as the gluttonous and drunken individuals in society, but in this scene Breughel indicates that anyone can be a glutton – and its concomitant – a sloth. He has portrayed a peasant, a knight and a scholar lying stupefied under a tree, around which a table has been fixed. A squire looks on from a shelter tiled with tarts. 'You must eat your way through a mountain of porridge to reach the land of Cockaigne, the proverbial "land of milk and honey". There, the fences are made of sausages, the geese lie ready-grilled on the plates, the pigs bring knives with them, and what one might take to be cacti are in fact oatcakes.'[20] This soporific trio have eaten their way through the porridge mountain and partaken of the foods provided in this mythical land. The proverbial land of Cockaigne features in many literary and graphic works. It is a fictional glutton's paradise.

A thirteenth-century French manuscript from the Bibliotheque Nationale in Paris is entitled 'Fabliau de Cocaigne', and describes a glutton's paradise which also encompasses a fountain of youth, as well as sexual gratification:

> The ladies there are forward belles,
> Both dowagers and demoiselles,
> Who with lubricious charms excite,
> The passion of each randy knight,
> And proudly yielding to his heat
> Pin a new ribbon to their sheet.

A poem entitled 'Land of Cokaygne' dates back to the early fourteenth century. The only copy is a manuscript in the British Library, thought to

8-8
The Land of Cockaigne,
Breughel, 1567 (wood,
52 cm × 78 cm, Alte
Pinakothek, Munich).

have been written in a friar's pocket book. The poem has been translated by different scholars, most notably Dunn and Byrnes.[21] It begins:

> Far in the sea to the west of Spain
> There is a land that we call Cokaygne;
> Under God's heaven no other land
> Such wealth and goodness has in hand
> Though paradise be merry and bright,
> Cokaygne is yet a fairer sight.

And later:

> The walls are all of pies,
> Of meat, of fish, and rich food,
> The most pleasing that a person can eat.
> All the shingles are cakes made of flour,
> On the church, the cloister, and the hall.
> The pegs are fat sausages,
> Rich food fit for princes and kings.
> One cannot eat enough of them,
> And can eat justifiably, without blame.

A Dutch poem from the fifteenth century is similar in vein, entitled 'Dit is van dat edele lant van Cockaengen' ('This is about that idyllic land of Cockaigne').

The concept of a 'gustatory heaven' has been commonplace throughout different cultures and races, the original forerunner being the Garden of Eden. Pherecrates and Telecleides, Greek poets of the Old Attic Comedy, described the Land of Bliss, where rivers flowed with wine, bread rolls grew on trees, fish flew in through the door and fried and served themselves, and roasted birds flew into open mouths. 'All men were fat and looked like Giants.'[22] Another Greek, Lucian, wrote of the similar 'Isle of the Blessed'. The Italians had the 'Paese di Chucagna', the 'Land of Cake', which boasted a lake of butter, ravioli trees, a cannon shooting nuts and a cloud of fried fowl. In 1530 Hans Sachs, the renowned Meistersinger of Wagner's opera, wrote of Schlaraffenland, the land of the lazy and idle, based on a tale by the brothers Grimm:

> In fabulous Schlaraffenland,
> The Sluggards sit in full command.
> It lies three leagues past Christmas day,
> And he who'd go must eat his way
> (Digging a tunnel like a mole)
> Through hills of porridge to his goal.
> But once he does, with breeches tight,
> He'll belch at all the wealth in sight.
>
> The Hogs you meet on every side
> Are sleek and fat and crisply fried:

> They carry knives – it's very nice–
> And stand by while you carve your slice!
> The very horses drop – poached eggs,
> And figs pile up by donkeys legs.[23]

Maps were even drawn of Schlaraffenland, resting between 'Bibonia', the Land of Booze, and 'Magni Stomachi Imperium'.

The idea of an ideal fictitious land for gluttons is not confined to Europe. In the folklore of the southern United States, the equivalent of these fabled countries is Diddy-Wah-Diddy,[24] the largest and best known of 'Negro' mythical places:

> [it is] way off somewhere and is reached by a road that curves so much that a mule pulling a wagon-load of fodder can eat off the back of the wagon as he goes. It is a place of no work and no worry for man and beast. A very restful place where even the curbstones are good sitting-chairs. The food is even already cooked. If a traveller is hungry all he needs do is to sit down on the curbstone and wait and soon he will hear something hollering 'Eat me! Eat me! Eat me!' and a big baked chicken will come along with a knife and a fork stuck in its sides. He can eat all he wants and let the chicken go on to the next one that needs something to eat. By that time a big deep sweet potato pie is pushing and shoving to get in front of the traveller with a knife all stuck up in the middle of it so he just cuts a piece off of that and so on until he finishes his snack.

Dreaming or imagining such a 'cloud, cuckoo land' was, perhaps, some compensation for the reality or harshness of life.

A twenty-first-century artist, Gayle Chong Kwan, explores rather different utopian ideas based upon the fourteenth-century myth of the glutton's paradise [C-10]. She presents photographic landscapes and images of historical monuments made out of foodstuffs which 'altogether combine to form a fantastical panorama', but, for example, the cheese and pasta and dried meat from which these images are made are beginning to sweat and rot, and the vegetables and salads are wilting. Her scenes undermine the desirability of food for its own sake; a glutton's paradise is a fleeting concept.

A brief history of gluttony and gluttons

As seen above, from the early Middle Ages until the early Renaissance, the danger of gluttony was seen to be in the effect it had of diverting attention from spiritual matters; the belly was worshipped as a god – an idol – to the detriment of the one and only true God. Punishment for committing this deadly sin came in the after-life, in the form of eternal damnation. Later, gluttony lost some of its stigma. The ability to dine extravagantly, to afford luxuries and to be able to display the signs and rewards of worldly success were important issues and no longer regarded as sinful.

Gluttony in the Roman world

In pre-Christian times, ancient Rome was an early setting for secular feasting and drinking; orgies and banquets were held to celebrate feast days and victories in battle and to honour visiting dignitaries, and for no reason whatsoever. The land, at least for the wealthy, seemed to be a veritable glutton's paradise. Overindulgence was encouraged. The extravagance of the food prepared was exceeded only by the exotic nature of some of the edible displays on offer: hummingbird tongues, dormice bathed in herbs and oils; quails, pigeons and peacocks vied with snails, truffles, artichokes, olives and oysters, followed by pastries and sweetmeats – all washed down with the best of wines – the nectar of the gods. Bacchus was the Roman god specifically connected with the fruit of the vine [C-11] and a bacchanal was an occasion on which to drink excessively – a drunken revelry to honour the god. Silenus, the foster-father of Bacchus, was pot bellied, bald and snub nosed. Rubens portrayed him as a sexual and sensual predator.

As the banquets went on for many hours, it was customary for guests to relieve their stomachs periodically in a special room – usually available in the houses of the wealthy – called a vomitorium. It is said that Nero had a personal physician who tickled his throat with a feather to induce vomiting. He was then able to return to the meal with appetite renewed. A chief cook in the days of Roman voluptuousness received the equivalent of £800 a year – a princely sum – and Antony rewarded the cook who pleased Cleopatra with his culinary delights with the gift of a city. Humans produce a litre of gas each day during the digestion of food, so a great deal of wind was generated at these feasts. In AD 41 the emperor Claudius planned to legitimise passing wind at banquets. Whether it had hitherto been banned is not known, but the offensiveness of such practice did not escape a later Italian courtesan, who would crush a vial of perfume when 'necessity' arose.

Three Romans particularly known for their gluttony and achievements in the gastronomical art were each named Apicius. The second and most famous of these lived under Augustus and Tiberius and was written about by such writers as Seneca, Pliny and Juvenal. He spent immense sums to satisfy his gluttony, invented several kinds of cakes which bear his name, and ran a school of cookery. However, in spite of having an annual income of the equivalent of about £80,000, he feared that he might have insufficient money to live on and so committed suicide.[25]

The Middle Ages, Renaissance and Enlightenment

Extravagant feasting was again prevalent in the late Middle Ages, when entertainment with eating and drinking was dispensed by the wealthy. Edward II failed to curb appetites with sumptuary laws that made it an offence to serve more than two or three courses at meals (depending upon the company kept). Overeating continued.

Henry VIII was noted for his size and his appetites. Size was considered to be important. As it was associated with heroic valour it impressed one's enemies and attracted the ladies. The monarch's suits were padded to add extra gravitas and superiority to his appearance. However, by the age of 56 his chest measured almost 60 inches. At this time, he was unable to walk unaided; his corpulence contributed to leg ulcers that would not heal, which meant that he had to be carried from room to room. His gluttony and debauchery left the wreckage of the man he had been.

Also in the sixteenth century, Catherine de Medici was known for her enormous appetite and frequent dyspepsia. In the seventeenth century, at Versailles, Louis XIV consumed prodigious amounts of food and became enormously fat. Whilst at his court the Princess Palatine died from overeating.[26]

Thomas Aquinas had derided overeating and also eating expensively. Henri IV of France fell into the latter category. He added gold and gems to his diet in the belief that gold led to immortality, rubies could prevent decay and sapphires could cure ulcers. As these substances were inert and would pass through the body unchanged, the main beneficiaries were probably the gentlemen of the bedchamber, who could recycle the gems for financial reward as they reappeared!

In 1630, the English Puritan Thomas Wright described gluttons as those who:

> think, talk, and earnestly procure to have great cheer [and] dainty dishes; they eat more than nature requires; at the table they will have the best; and in fine, the easy rule to perceive them, is to note their care and anxiety to fare daintily, to feast often, and therein delight much.[27]

Literary artists of the day still wrote about gluttony and its effects: Ben Jonson, for example, wrote a 'Hymn to the Belly', part of which praises the waistline:

> Hail, hail, plump paunch! O the founder of taste,
> For fresh meats or powdered, or pickle or paste!
> Devourer of broiled, baked, roasted or sod!
> And emptier of cups, be they even or odd!
> All which have now made thee so wide i' the waist,
> As scarce with no pudding thou art to be laced;
> But eating and drinking until thou dost nod,
> Thou break'st all thy girdles and break'st forth a god.[28]

Shakespeare wrote of the dire effects of overindulgence in *Henry IV, Part I*. Falstaff, a person of expanded paunch, has both endearing and reprehensible characteristics. Prince Hal sadly recognises this. Falstaff is a glutton and gluttony and sloth go hand in hand. Falstaff asks the Prince 'Now, Hal, what time of day is it, lad?' The Prince replies:

Thou art so fat-witted, with drinking of old sack and unbuttoning thee after supper and sleeping upon benches after noon, that thou hast forgotten to demand that truly which thou wouldst truly know. What a devil hast thou to do with the time of day? Unless hours were cups of sack and minutes capons and clocks the tongues of bawds and dials the signs of leaping-houses and the blessed sun himself a fair hot wench in flame-coloured taffeta, I see no reason why thou shouldst be so superfluous to demand the time of the day.[29]

Jonathan Swift alluded to a different aspect of gluttony in *Gulliver's Travels* (1726). Early theologians might condemn the meal prepared by the Laputians for Lemuel Gulliver as requiring excessive preoccupation with its preparation. Gulliver describes the dinner in question:

We had two courses, of three dishes each. In the first course, there was a shoulder of mutton, cut into an equilateral triangle, a piece of beef into a rhomboides, and a pudding into a cycloid. The second course was two ducks, trussed up into the form of fiddles; sausages and puddings resembling flutes and hautboys, and a breast of veal in the shape of a harp. The servants cut our bread into cones, cylinders, parallelograms, and several other mathematical figures.[30]

However, eating and drinking, even to excess, cannot always be said to be wrong or without benefit. Samuel Pepys commented that it was 'Strange to see how a good dinner and feasting reconciles everybody'. Many contracts, treatises, friendships and courtships have been conducted and negotiated during or at the conclusion of a good meal.

Some people said that the fire of London in 1666 was God's curse against gluttony. The fire had sparked and rolled across the city from Pudding Lane to Pie Corner. In Giltspur Street, West Smithfield, where the Fortune of War pub used to stand, the statue of the Fat Golden Boy perches above the pavement, hugging his round stomach, warning against greed.

The 'great eater of Kent' was Nicholas Wood, of Harrisom. In 1630, John Taylor wrote about him in *The Great Eater of Kent, or part of the admirable teeth and stomach exploits of Nicholas Wood, of Harrisom in the county of Kent, His excessive manner of Eating without manners in strange and true manner described*. Wood's gluttonous feats are recorded in great detail by the incredulous author. For example:

Once at Sir *Warham Saint Ledgers* house, and at Sir *William Sydleyes* he shewed himself so valiant of teeth and stomach, that he ate as much as would well have served and sufficed thirty men, so that his belly was like to turn bankrupt and break, but that the serving-men turned him to the fire, and anointed his paunch with grease and butter, to make it stretch and hold.

Taylor describes how Wood was known as a Tugmutton or Muttonmonger, for having eaten a whole sheep raw at a single meal except for the skin, wool, horns and bones. On another occasion he ate eight pounds of 'brawn', hot out of a new-killed boar's belly. He was apparently defeated on only one occasion, when a certain John Dale laid a wager that he would fill Wood's belly for two shillings. Dale dipped 12 penny white loaves in six pots of potent ale,

> the powerful fume whereof conquered the conqueror, robbed him of his reason, bereft him of his wit, violently took away his stomach, intoxicated his *Pia Mater*, and entered the sconce of his *Pericranium*, blind folded him with sleep; setting a *nap* of nine hours for manacles upon his *thread-bare eyelids,* to the unexpected winning of the wager.

Jack Biggers of Witney in England was also renowned for his ability to eat vast quantities. For a bet, he attempted to eat six pounds of bacon, a dish of greens, 12 suet dumplings, a loaf of bread and a gallon of beer in an hour. He almost won, but with only two ounces of bacon and half a dumpling left, he dropped dead.

The eighteenth and nineteenth centuries

In the *Spectator* of Saturday, 10 March 1711 [8-9], Joseph Addison writes of the existence of 'Nocturnal Assemblies' known as 'Clubs':

> When a sett of men find themselves agree on any particular, 'tho never so trivial, they establish themselves into a kind of Fraternity, and meet once or twice a Week, upon the Account of such a Fantastic Resemblance.

He goes on to describe a Club of Fat-Men that met not to entertain one another with sprightliness and wit but to keep one another 'in Countenance':

> The Room where the Club met, was something of the largest, and had two Entrances, the one by a Door of moderate Size, and the other by a Pair of Folding-Doors. If a Candidate for this Corpulent Club could make his Entrance through the first he was looked upon as unqualified; but if he stuck in the Passage, and could not force his Way through it, the Folding-Doors were immediately thrown open for his Reception, and he was saluted as a Brother.

It was said that although the Club had only 15 members, their combined weight was over three tons.

In opposition to the Club of Fat-Men, Addison describes one consisting of men of meagre dimensions. In his tale, the opposing parties eventually came to an 'accommodation': live and let live.

The *Spectator* purported to hold a mirror to society. Amongst other things, Addison declared that the human physique was glorious and that its Maker was to be venerated: 'How absurd, then, that through gluttony, drunkenness, luxury, ignorance, neglect and myriad other acts of commission and omission, God-given bodies were so abused'.

8-9
The *Spectator* on the Club of Fat-Men, 10 March 1711.

A wedding is always a good reason for eating and drinking and, as Pepys said, a feast was an occasion for courtship and friendship. Gustav Flaubert took five years to complete his masterpiece *Madame Bovary* (1857). He wrote slowly and savoured his words; this large man probably savoured every morsel of the wedding feast in his novel:

> The wedding-feast had been laid in the cart-shed. On the table were four sirloins, six dishes of hashed chicken, some stewed veal, three legs of mutton, and in the middle a nice roast sucking-pig flanked by four pork sausages with sorrel. Flasks of brandy stood at the corners. A rich foam had frothed out round the corks of the cider-bottles. Every glass had already been filled to the brim with wine. Yellow custard stood in big dishes, shaking at the slightest jog of the table, with the initials of the newly wedded couple traced on its smooth surface in arabesques of sugared almond. For the tarts and confectioneries they had hired a pastry-cook from Yvetot. He was new to the district, and so had taken great pains with his work. At dessert he brought in with his own hands a tiered cake that made them all cry out. It started off at the base with a square of blue cardboard representing a temple with porticoes and colonnades, with stucco statuettes all round it in recesses studded with gilt-paper stars; on the second layer was a castle-keep in Savoy cake, surrounded with tiny fortifications in angelica, almonds, raisins and quarters of orange; and finally, on the uppermost platform, which was a green meadow with rocks, pools of jam and boats of nutshell, stood a little Cupid, poised on a chocolate swing whose uprights had two real rose-buds for knobs at the top.[31]

The choice of wedding cake by a twenty-first-century bride and groom reported in *The Times* newspaper in October 2005 departed from the usual tradition and took the form of a three-tiered pork pie. Also on the menu at this wedding feast were fish and chips, sausage and mash and 'haggis, neeps and tatties' – a true cholesterol-laden meal with rather less poetic appeal than that enjoyed by Flaubert's fictional wedding couple.

On what is usually a more melancholy occasion, Tobias Smollett describes a funeral party in the Highlands of Scotland in his novel *The Expedition of Humphry Clinker* (1771) through the pen of Mr Bramble's nephew, Jery Melford. The latter writes to his friend in Oxford:

> Yesterday we were invited to the funeral of an old lady and found ourselves in the midst of fifty people who were regaled with a sumptuous feast, accompanied by the music of a dozen pipes. In short this meeting had all the air of a grand festival; and the guests did such honour to the entertainment, that many of them could not stand when we were reminded of the business on which we had met. The company forthwith taking horse, rode in a very irregular cavalcade to the place of interment, a church, at a distance of two long miles from the castle. On our arrival, however, we found we had committed a small oversight, in leaving the corpse behind....

> The ceremony was closed with the discharge of pistols; then we re-
> turned to the castle, resumed the bottle, and by midnight there was not
> a sober person in the family, the females excepted…. Afterwards, [our
> entertainer] seemed to think it a disparagement to his family, that not
> above a hundred gallons of whisky had been drank on such a solemn
> occasion.[32]

Dr Johnson declared: 'I mind my belly very well, for I look upon it that he who will not mind his belly will scarcely mind anything else.' However, on another occasion, he retorted 'whatever may be the quantity that a man eats, it is plain that if he is too fat, he has eaten more than he should have done'.[33]

It was often thought that obesity was essential to good health and strength and that plenty of food and drink enlarged the brain. George I liked his women to be well upholstered. Lord Chesterfield wrote 'No women came amiss to him if they were very willing and very fat…'.

It is said that Queen Anne became so fat through overeating that she hunted the stag in a special chaise strengthened to support her weight. A year before her death, she had put on so much weight that it was an ordeal for her to climb stairs, so she was lifted in her chair to the next floor by means of ropes and pulleys.[34] A similar means of transport was used in the nineteenth century to winch Parson Pike, a clergyman from Kirkby Mallory in Leicestershire, in and out of his pulpit.

In the late eighteenth century, the anatomist Dr George Fordyce main-tained that people were harming their health by overeating. Nonetheless, on 4 October 1791 he was reported to have been seen entering Dolly's Chop-house, where:

> As the clock strikes four, he seats himself at a table reserved for him,
> on which in readiness for his arrival are placed a bottle of port wine, a
> quarter of brandy, and a silver tankard of strong ale. The moment his
> loud step and loud voice are heard at the door, a solemn and orderly
> ritual is set in motion. As one drawer hastens to pull out his chair,
> the cook puts a pound and a half of rump steak on the gridiron and
> dishes up a trifle of broiled fowl or a dish of fish, which a second drawer
> lays before the doctor. Of this he disposes whilst the steak is grilling,
> and caps it with a drink of brandy. He then sets to work on the steak,
> washing it down with strong ale, and finally finishes off the brandy and
> drinks his bottle of port.

Dr Fordyce had been doing this for over 20 years. He had just one meal a day, spending one and a half hours over it, and then he returned to his house in Essex Street, calling at three hostelries on the way, at each of which he consumed a glass of brandy and water.[35]

Dolly's Chophouse was obviously a well known eating establishment; a reference to it also appears in Smollett's *The Expedition of Humphry Clinker*. Melford writes to Sir Watkin Phillips, Bart, at Oxford:

I take this opportunity to send you the history of this day, which has been remarkably full of adventures, and you will own I give you them like a beef-steak at Dolly's, *hot* and *hot*, without ceremony and parade.[36]

Roast beef and beer comprised the preferred diet of any patriotic Englishman, as Hogarth had illustrated in his print *The Roast Beef of Old England* (see page 249). This was what rendered the nation strong, with a healthy constitution and appetite. Henry Fielding wrote a song with that title, and the Sublime Society of Beefsteaks catered for those who appreciated this aspect of their diet. Parson Woodforde's last entry in his diary, that for 17 October 1802, recorded: 'Very weak this Morning, scarce able to put on my Cloaths and with great difficulty, get down Stairs with help.... Dinner to day, Roast Beef etc.'[37] The Parson died on New Year's Day, 1803.

Serious eating might prove to be a problem, but serious drinking could be even more so. This was no new phenomenon. William Vaughan had compared gluttony with excessive drinking of alcohol in his *Directions for Health* in 1607. On alcohol, he wrote:

> How shall toss-pots and swill-bowls be made to hate wine? Look on the countenance of a drunkard, and is it not disfigured? Does not his nose seem rotten, withered or worm eaten? Does not his breath stink, his tongue faulter? Is not his body crazy, and subject to gouts and dropsies?

And on food:

> for how is it possible, that the smoaky vapours which breathe from a fat and full paunch, should not interpose a thick mist of dullness between the body, and the body's light!

Many young Georgian men-about-town recorded their 'bottle days'. In his young days, the physician George Cheyne spent his time in coffee-houses, where young doctors built up their practices and hoped to become well known:

> nothing being necessary for that Purpose, but to be able to Eat lustily, and swallow down much Liquor; and being naturally of a large Size, a cheerful Temper, and Tolerable lively Imagination ... I soon became caressed by them, and grew daily in Bulk and in Friendship with these gay Gentlemen.[38]

Cheyne became 'excessively fat, short-breath'd, lethargick and listless'. He left London and went on a diet of greens, milk and seeds, as a consequence of which his excess flesh melted 'like a Snow-ball in Summer'. Cheyne had drawn attention to the evils of luxury and overindulgence in rich food, port, wine and brandy. His ideas ran counter to some contemporary practices. In the early eighteenth century, the idea was prevalent that dark melancholy was the result of self-denial and self-righteousness, a cold dry temperament

with too much thick, black and sour bile 'purged from the spleen' and too
little blood – in keeping with humoral theories – and it was thought that a
change to riotous living might provide a remedy. Cheyne opposed this idea
and claimed that, in his experience, the latter was the cause of the melancholy; decadence corrupted the passions.[39]

He himself had weighed 32 stone at one stage and needed a servant to
walk behind him carrying a stool on which to recover every few paces. Then
he saw the error of his self-indulgent ways and followed a milk and vegetable
diet. He felt that had he followed such rules himself during the previous 30
years he would have suffered less and had greater 'Freedom of Spirit' than
he had enjoyed. 'Certainly', he enjoined, ''tis easier to preserve Health than
to recover it, and to prevent Diseases than to cure them.' For preservation
of health and long life he made various observations and reflections on such
aspects as 'The Air we breathe in', 'Meat and Drink', 'Sleep and Watchful-
ness', 'Exercise and Rest', 'Evacuations and their Obstructions' and 'Passions
of the Mind'. Hippocrates had said much the same many years previously.

He issued a special word of warning to 'The Fat, unwieldy and over-
grown'. These individuals:

> should avoid all manner of Drink, strong and small, and even water
> itself, as much as possible. And if their Food be Vegetables and young
> Animals, they will have little Occasion for any Liquor.[40]

In spite of his 'rules', however, Cheyne's own weight went up and down
over the years. His book *The English Malady* (1733) was based on his own
experience and warned of the adverse effects of corpulence – both physical
and mental. His books were popular and his ideas of temperance became
widely accepted.

Ideas about health and longevity which were being promoted in the late
eighteenth century led to an increasing interest in diet and nutrition and
to the wisdom of eating and drinking in moderation. History, it seems, had
come full circle from Hippocrates' time. Benjamin Franklin, himself well
formed and strongly built, in his latter years inclining to corpulency, wrote:
'The Difficulty lies, in finding out an exact Measure; but eat for Necessity,
not Pleasure, for Lust knows not where Necessity ends'.[41] He also said 'I
don't so much mind being old, as I mind being fat and old'.

A nineteenth-century definition of a glutton seems to echo the words of
the early theologians:

> one who will eat as long as he can sit, and drinks longer than he can
> stand, nor leave his cup while he can lift it; or like the great eater of
> Kent who ... did eat with ease thirty dozen Pigeons at one meal, at
> another four score Rabbits, and eighteen Yards of Black Pudding,
> London Measure!!! – or a fastidious Appetite, only to be excited by
> fantastic Dainties, as the brains of Peacocks or Parrots, the tongues of
> Thrushes or Nightingales, or the teats of a lactiferous Sow.[42]

In the United States an entertainment specifically designed for the corpulent was the Fat Men's Clam Bake, held in Milford, Pennsylvania [8-10].

Another legendary eater, though in a different category, was the flamboyant Diamond Jim Brady (of the late nineteenth century), who has been described as the greatest glutton in American history. He consumed six meals a day, eating seven or eight steaks at one sitting. He acquired his name from his habit of giving out diamond jewellery on the slightest pretext. Originally a railway worker, then a runner for a finance company, Brady became a philanthropist and diamond collector in later life. He was said to sit down for his dinner with his belly six inches from the table, and to stop eating only when belly and table came into contact.

Depraved appetites

History is littered with examples of so-called depraved appetites. Depraved appetite might conceivably be considered as an aspect of gluttony, although it is not specifically mentioned by Aquinas. It could include, for instance, the drinking of human blood and cannibalism.

In 1771 a man named Goldschmidt of Weimar met a young traveller in the woods and accused him of cow frightening. Goldschmidt killed the young man with a stick, dragged the body to the bushes, cut it up, took it home in pieces and subsequently devoured it. He developed a taste for human flesh, and was eventually caught eating an abducted child. Another individual, from the Bicêtre hospital in Paris, had a penchant for eating decayed human flesh, and would haunt graveyards and eat the putrefying remains of the recently buried, preferring the intestines to any other part. Yet another deranged cannibal, Menesclou, was eventually caught with the forearm of a missing child in his pocket, and in his stove were discovered the child's head and half-burnt entrails. In his defence he claimed the situation was an accident.

The physician Bijoux describes a glutton at the Jardin des Plantes in Paris who ate a recently deceased lion from the menagerie, and later died of indigestion. The famous French glutton Tarrare once ate a dinner which had been prepared for 15 people, but this feat was nothing compared to his devouring of live cats (apart from the bones), serpents and dogs. On another occasion he ate a wooden box wrapped in plain white paper, which he defaecated the next day, the paper still intact. He took discarded meat from the butchers' shops away from the dogs, drank the bleedings from the hospital, and ate the dead from the dead-houses. Lastly, he was accused of eating a 14-month-old child. He, perhaps unsurprisingly, died of diarrhoea.

Gluttony today

The problem of those with uncontrolled appetites has not gone away and in this day and age gluttons remain. Some examples of grossly obese and gluttonous individuals have recently been televised. They have been described as 'temples to the god of fast foods and drink', admitting to a lifetime of overindulgence.

In the twenty-first century, gluttony is generally no longer regarded as a deadly sin. In some countries it has been transformed into a sport. The IFOCE, the International Federation of Competitive Eating, presides over speed-eating contests worldwide. This activity is, however, not entirely new. There are many instances of British gluttons from the seventeenth and eighteenth centuries, performers and others, who accepted wagers to consume food and drink – especially in the countryside. A good living and local fame was their fortune.

More recently, gluttony has been transformed from a sin that leads to other sins into an illness that leads to other illnesses. Illnesses such as diabetes, some forms of cancer and heart disease are just some of the fates that lie in store for the twenty-first-century glutton. Whereas the Romans had enjoyed their binge-eating, present-day binges can be associated with guilt and self-loathing. Punishment or retribution for overindulgence lies in the present life rather than in the hereafter. The increasing waistline, the induced slothfulness, the shortness of breath, the low self-esteem, the looks of pity or contempt from those who are slim and active are some of the other 'wages of sin'.

> Nowadays ... to what a stage have the evils of ill-health advanced! This is the interest which we pay on pleasures which we have coveted beyond what is reasonable and right. You need not wonder that diseases are beyond counting: count the cooks! All intellectual interests are in abeyance; those who follow culture lecture to empty rooms, in out-of-the-way places. The halls of the professor and the philosopher are deserted; but what a crowd there is in the cafes! How many young fellows besiege the kitchens of their gluttonous friends![43]

These words of Seneca still ring true in the twenty-first century, as does Pope Gregory's definition of a glutton: one who eats 'hastily, sumptuously, excessively, ravenously, fastidiously'. The present-day glutton may feel guilty for his overindulgence and may even do penance in the form of serial dieting or fasting, but in contrast to his predecessor he is unlikely to seek absolution for his sin.

CHAPTER 9

Sloth

He also that is slothful in his work is brother to him that is a great waster. (Proverbs 18:9)

Doe we not find by daily experience, that those which are more indulgent of their bellies and sleep than is meet, become so corpulent, grosse and ill-favoured, that their breast and chin even meet together? Wherefore it is no marvell that they become unhealthful and unlusty in their bodies, stupid and dull in their wits. (Tobias Venner, 1660[1])

The word 'sloth' means laziness and inactivity. To be slothful is easier today than it was for past generations – at least in Western society. Sedentariness or lack of physical activity is recognised as being a major factor in the rising level of obesity in the Western world. Many social changes in recent decades have contributed to slothfulness and to the development of the obesity epidemic. Transport by car, train and bus means that people, on the whole, walk less than previously; children are more likely to be driven to schools and clubs rather than to walk or cycle there. This may be done for a variety of reasons – for example, there is a perception that paedophiles and hit-and-run accidents are becoming more common – but the protection given by parents against such an eventuality reduces a child's opportunity for exercise. Many parents perceive danger in children playing outdoors; therefore more sedentary activities have largely replaced games in the streets, playgrounds or parks. Some children do not even have to rise from their chair or bed to switch on the television or to change programmes. In the 1970s, many school playing fields were sold, thereby reducing sports and games facilities, leading many young people to watch sports rather than to participate in them. A generation of 'couch potatoes' has been born.

Technological advances have made all our lives more effort free. After the drive to work, lifts make the transition from car park to office quicker and easier than climbing stairs, and the person in the next room can be e-mailed to save the time and inconvenience of walking. Shopping in malls is made less strenuous by the use of lifts and escalators; and most major supermarkets now deliver goods home following a telephone call or internet order; 'You shop, we drop', claims one store. Supermarket shopping has replaced visits to the local butcher, baker and greengrocer, when queuing and carrying goods home occupied a great deal of time and expended a large amount of energy. At home, housework has been made less labour intensive with the use of vacuum cleaners, washing machines, tumble driers, non-iron clothing and dishwashers. Smoke control regulations came into force in many areas in the 1970s with a consequent reduction in the use of open fires, which had to be cleaned out regularly. Central heating, once a luxury, is almost universal. Altogether, exercise and energy expenditure have been reduced. At the same time, convenience foods have become readily available, and high-energy snacks containing high levels of fat, sugar and salt are sold in vending machines in many locations. The search for food has never been easier and it is often to be found in larger portions. 'Two for the price of one' or 'Buy one, get one free' are present-day temptations to the glutton and the sloth.

The question has been asked whether it is sloth or gluttony that leads to obesity. The jury is, perhaps, still out on this, as the two are closely linked, 'but it seems reasonable to conclude that the low levels of physical activity now prevalent in Britain must play an important, perhaps dominant, role in the development of obesity by greatly reducing energy needs'.[2] It has also been said that: 'Fatness in the 21st century may not reflect the gluttony about which society has been so judgemental since Shakespeare's caricature of Falstaff, but rather a genotype for evolutionary survival wholly maladapted to its new environment.'[3] Animals spend more time asleep if they are overfed, confined in close quarters or otherwise bored, and the same can probably be said of man. Animals in the wild do not become obese; only when they are domesticated do they frequently become so.

Sloth as a deadly sin

Although sloth is still frowned upon today, it is not regarded in the same light as it was by some early theologians. Pope Gregory included sloth amongst his seven deadly sins. Thomas Aquinas thought otherwise. In his *Summa Theologica* from the late thirteenth century, he stated that sloth is not a capital vice, 'for a capital vice is one that moves a man to sinful acts'. He argued that sloth tends to discourage a man from taking any action – apathy – and is more likely to withdraw him from it, and therefore cannot be regarded as a deadly sin.

9-1
Accidia (sloth),
detail from Bosch's
The Seven Deadly Sins,
c. 1475–85.

Hieronymus Bosch illustrates human sins and vices – the evils that men do – actually taking place in *The Seven Deadly Sins*, and in this painting (a roundel – see C-6), he portrays these in relation to Christ's suffering. Sloth was a sin that was difficult to identify. The man sleeping in Bosch's scene might be meditating and studying, briefly resting or neglecting his duty, but the nun attending him is holding out a rosary and a book – standing for faith – and seems to berate him for his indolence, implying that he has other things to do than to sit by the fire sleeping, like the dog at his feet [9-1]. In the Middle Ages, sloth was a vice often attributed to monks – a vice which separated them from God. By neglecting his duty, the monk is turning away from the joy that comes from the love of God; he is denying the purpose of his existence. Another term for this kind of sloth is *accidia*. In addition to this is *pigritia*, meaning indolence, idleness, laziness or slackness. These might be termed sins of omission rather than commission and were considered to be moral issues.

9-2
'Desidia' (Indolence),
by Breughel. Detail from
drawing in the series
'Seven Deadly Sins'. Vienna
(Albertina), 1558.

Pieter Breughel the Elder produced two series of drawings, the 'Seven Deadly Sins' and the 'Seven Virtues', in 1558, not for wide circulation, but intended for a small circle of scholars who would understand the humour and satire portrayed and directed against the folly of the world. In the 'Desidia' (Indolence) scene [9-2], the sleeping woman reclining on the back of a recumbent donkey – the barnyard animal symbolising the sin of sloth – is a personalised Desidia. A number of symbols representing sloth surround her. For example, snails were believed to be born from mud and to feed on it. As they therefore made no effort to search for food they were perceived as being lazy, and the image of a snail came to represent such a sinner. An owl symbolises death, stillness and passivity, so the presence of the owl in this scene seems appropriate. The scorpion is a symbol of evil. Such a creature is carrying off two figures. Evil takes over when man slumbers.

The French artist Jacques Callot engraved personalised images of each of the deadly sins with their barnyard animal counterpart. For the depiction of sloth, Pigritia, Indolence, is shown sleeping by the side of her donkey [9-3]. The punishment of sloth was illustrated in 1496 in *Le grant kalendrier des Bergiers*, published by Nicolas le Rouge in Troyes, France: those indulging in it were thrown into a snake pit for eternity [9-4]. Although no one in

9-3
Jacques Callot's depiction of
sloth, Pigritia, Indolence.

9-4
The punishment of sloth as illustrated in *Le grant kalendrier des Bergiers*, published by Nicolas le Rouge, 1496.

the engraving appears to be obese, at least two appear to have tonsures, marking them out as monks, once again highlighting the prevailing view of their laziness.

Many carvings dating from the eleventh to the fifteenth century found in choirs and cathedrals in Europe depict both secular and religious scenes. Some of these can be found beneath the misericords (wooden rests) under the choir seats on which the elderly monks could perch or ease their *derrieres* during long services whilst still seeming to be standing.[4] There is a misericord carving in St Mary's, Fairford, Gloucester, of two men, one of whom seems to be dressed in a monk's habit, drinking from a cask of ale. They appear to be hiding and drinking in secret as they crouch beneath one of the monk's stalls.[5] Another carving is of a portly individual sleeping off the effects of a similar encounter with a cask of ale.[6] The cause of their slothfulness is there for all to see. Carvings and paintings in cathedrals and churches were intended to remind worshippers, whose thoughts might wander during services, of the reason for their presence there. At a time when few people could read, pictorial images were important. Although most of these were of religious significance, some, like the misericord carvings, drew attention to sinful practices. They also reflected a sense of humour held by some of the wood carvers and stone masons.

Amongst the stone carvings depicting deadly sins in Rosslyn Chapel, near Edinburgh, is one of Sloth dragging a bag along the ground [9-5]. His indolent expression and careless dragging of his bag (rather than hoisting it upon his shoulder and striding forth) illustrate a lack of effort or slothfulness.

There are frequent biblical exhortations regarding the sins of gluttony and sloth and such images were a constant reminder of the sin. About the middle of the eighth century BC the prophet Amos preached to the people of the northern kingdom of Israel, condemning them for their oppression of the poor and the injustices meted out on them. Religious observance was insincere and security was in name only. He admonished the people for their gluttony and sloth:

> Woe to you …
> You lie on beds inlaid with ivory
> And lounge on your couches.
> You dine on choice lambs
> And fattened calves
>
> You strum away on your harps like David
> And improvise on musical instruments.
>
> You drink wine by the bowlful
> And use the finest lotions,
> But you do not grieve over the ruin of Joseph.
>
> Therefore you will be among the first to go into exile;
> your feasting and lounging will end.[7]

9-5
Stone carving of 'sloth' in Rosslyn Chapel, Scotland. Copyright Antonia Reeve/RCT.

9-6
Slothful on terrace 4 in Purgatory.

According to Dante, the slothful end up on terrace 4 in Purgatory [9-6]. To absolve themselves of their slothful behaviour in life, the perpetrators, such as the 'abbot in St. Zeno', must now show great vigour in their degree of physical activity, and loudly proclaim examples of slothful behaviour and the opposing virtue of decisive zeal as they hurry around.[8]

> 'Henceforth it behoves thee thus to put off sloth,' said the Master, 'for, sitting upon down or under quilts, one comes not to fame, without which he who consumes his life leaves such vestige of himself on earth as smoke in air, or the foam on water: and therefore rise up, conquer thy panting with the soul that wins every battle, if it be not weighed down by its heavy body. A longer stairway needs must be ascended: it is not enough to have departed from these; if thou understandest me, now act so that it avail thee.'
>
> Then I rose up, showing myself better furnished with breath than I felt, and said:
> 'Go on, for I am strong and resolute.'[9]

Illustrations of sloth, from the Middle Ages to modernity

William Langland, a cleric in minor orders and a writer in the early medieval period, personifies sloth in his work *Piers the Ploughman*. In this, Langland portrays the ploughman as a dreamer who, whilst wandering in the Malvern Hills, has a vision of a high tower (Truth), a deep dungeon (Wrong) and a 'fair field full of folk' (the earth) between. These are the ordinary people of the time going about their daily tasks. The ploughman describes the people of the neighbourhood in terms of their personalities. Repentance moves the hearts of the people to seek confession for the seven deadly sins of which they are guilty and they set off on a pilgrimage to seek St Truth. The ploughman offers to guide them if they will help him to plough his half-acre. Sloth was one of the recognisable characters on his way to make his confession:

> Then came Sloth, all beslobbered, with his gummy eyes. 'I shall have to sit down,' he said, 'or I'll fall asleep. I cannot stand or prop myself up all the time, and you can't expect me to kneel without a hassock. If I had been put to bed now, you'd never get me up before dinner was ready, nor for all your bell-ringing – not unless nature called.
>
> Then, with a loud belch, he started his 'Bless me, father,' and beat his breast, but as he stopped to stretch, he yawned, grunted, and finally started to snore.[10]

Repentance and a change of ways are not easy.

Chaucer's approach to the topic of sin was also in the form of stories encompassing contemporary life, this time in poetic form. His writing has been described as the precursor of English literature. His style was satirical and earthy, and whereas Langland wrote about what everyman was like, Chaucer wrote of the particular man, such as the Franklin, the Pardoner and the Wife of Bath – each recognisable characters – but they still collectively embraced all humankind. In his *Canterbury Tales*, he holds the attention of his audience by relating stories associated with varying themes of morality. These were mostly in the form of poetry but the *Tales* end with a 'Prose sermon on the proper preparation for Confession and the true nature of the Seven Deadly Sins'. This, 'The Parson's Tale', was considered to be an appropriate ending to a pilgrimage from Southwark to Canterbury before the saint's shrine was reached. Accidie, the Parson preaches, does all tasks with vexation, slackly and without joy, and it is encumbered by doing good. It restrains one from prayer. It is the rotten-hearted sin of sloth. It leads to despair. The remedy is fortitude. In the Parson's words:

> Thanne is Accidie the anguish of a trouble herte; and Seint Augustin saith: 'it is anoy [does harm to, or troubles] of goodnesse and joys of harm.'
>
> Certes, this is a dampnable sinne; for it doth wrong to Jesu Crist, in-as-muche as it binimeth the service that men oghte doon to Crist with all diligence.
>
> Accidie is eek a ful greet enemy to lyflode [means of living] of the body; for it ne hath no perveaunce again temporal necessitee; for it forsleweth [wastes idly] and forsluggeth [spoils, allows to spoil], and destroyeth alle goodes temporeles by reacheleesnesse.
>
> Accidie maketh him hevy, thoughtful, and wrawe [peevish, fretful and angry].[11]

English society at the time, although deeply religious, distrusted the clergy and began to judge them by the standards they taught and sought to impose on others. The great monastic houses had become comfortable places for well born but landless men and women, indulgences could be granted and dispensations from the Pope allowed 'days off' from torment in Purgatory. Chaucer drew attention to rogues in clerical garb taking advantage of poor and ignorant people. Some carried phoney relics and promised blessings in return for money. However, not all clergy were corrupt and, altogether, this period was one of piety and religious belief.

The sloth, a mammal, lives up to its name [9-7]: it is a creature whose movements are sluggish and its habits nocturnal. It is inoffensive, silent and solitary. Its slothfulness, though, is its safeguard against predators – especially the eagle – its slow movements being difficult to detect from the air. Rather like the actions of the mammal, in the initial stages slothfulness may go undetected, but the effects of inertia, indolence and laziness can have wide-reaching significance. Neglect of duty, whether to God (as Bosch's picture [9-1] implies), to family, to the community or to self, can have dire consequences. 'Under the guise of deep study or meditation it [accidia or sloth] masks nothing less than a flight from the normal problems of life.'[12]

9-7
The sloth.

In some circumstances, slothfulness could become not only a way of life but also a means of making a living. A letter in the *Spectator*, dated Monday, 1 October 1711, tells of an advertisement seen in the *Daily Courant* concerning one Nicholas Hart, 'who slept last year in St. Bartholomew's Hospital, [and] intends to sleep this Year at the Cock and Bottle in Little Britain'. It seems that the gentleman concerned:

> is every year seized with a periodical Fit of Sleeping, which begins upon the Fifth of August, and ends on the Eleventh of the same Month; That
> On the First of the Month he grew dull;
> On the Second, appeared drowsy;
> On the Third, fell a yawning;
> On the Fourth, began to nod;
> On the Fifth, dropped asleep;
> On the Sixth, was heard to snore;
> On the Seventh, turned himself in his Bed;
> On the Eighth, recovered his former Posture;
> On the Ninth, fell a stretching;
> On the Tenth about Midnight, awaked;
> On the Eleventh in the Morning called for a little Small-Beer.

The letter goes on to say that this would seem to be the 'very natural Picture of the Life of many an honest English Gentleman, whose whole History very often consists of Yawning, Nodding, Stretching, Turning, Sleeping, Drinking, and the like extraordinary Particulars'. The writer recommends the practice to many other gentlemen who might rest their heads for even longer periods:

> Could one but lay asleep a few busy Heads which I could name, from the First of November next to the First of May ensuing, I question not but it would very much redound to the Quiet of particular Persons, as well as to the Benefit of the Publick.

Nicholas Hart, at this time aged 22 years, apparently 'gained his Livelihood by Sleeping and got last Year enough to support himself for a Twelvemonth'.[13]

Another way to escape from the normal problems of life was that described by Bernard de Mandeville in the eighteenth century. Gin, he claimed, was the 'grand preservator of sloth, Jeneva, that infallible antidote against care and frugal reflexion'.[14] Apathy, self-pity, despair and a sense of uselessness are all allied to sloth.

A popular pastime in the sixteenth century was collecting proverbs. Breughel's painting *Netherlandish Proverbs* [C-12] depicts more than 100 sayings or proverbs of the time. These include a woman who gazes through a window at a stork [9-8]. She may be hoping for a child, but the proverb describes her as wasting her time; she is idle. Breughel's 'earthy' scenes illustrate life as it was for the common people. There was no time for idle

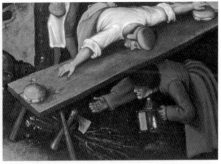

9-8
Two details from *Nether-landish Proverbs*, Breughel, 1559 (oil on oak panel).

day-dreaming. Another proverb tells of 'a lazy worker who always looks for his tools'. This one literally searches under the table for his hatchet [9-8].

A Spanish proverb is less condemnatory: 'How beautiful it is to do nothing, and then rest afterwards.'

'Never put off until tomorrow what you can do the day after tomorrow', said Mark Twain, alias Samuel Langhorne Clemens. This is not a proverb but could be the motto of the slothful. Mark Twain knew all about idleness and how attractive it is to small boys in particular. In *The Adventures of Tom Sawyer* (1876) he describes how Tom found ways to make his life easier [9-9]:

> Tom had been given the task of whitewashing the fence when he would rather have been spending the day idling in the sunshine and he did not want to be made fun of by the other boys who would see him working. He had an idea; by representing the whitewashing as an enviable task, boys who came along, paid for the privilege of doing the work for him....
>
> Tom gave up the brush with reluctance in his face, but alacrity in his heart. And while [his friend] worked and sweated in the sun, [he] sat on a barrel in the shade close by, dangling his legs, munched his apple, and planned the slaughter of more innocents. There was no lack of material; boys happened along every little while, they came to jeer but remained to whitewash. By the time Ben was fagged out, Tom had traded the next chance to Billy Fisher for a kite, in good repair; and when he played out, Johnny Miller bought in for a dead rat and a string to swing it with – and so on, and so on, hour after hour. And when the middle of the afternoon came, from being a poor poverty-stricken boy in the morning, Tom was literally rolling in wealth. He had besides the things before mentioned, twelve marbles, part of a jew's harp, a piece of blue bottle to look through, a spool cannon, a key that wouldn't unlock anything, a fragment of chalk, a glass stopper of a decanter, a tin soldier, a couple of tadpoles, six firecrackers, a kitten with only one eye, a brass doorknob, a dog collar – but no dog – the handle of a knife, four pieces of orange peel, and a dilapidated old window sash.
>
> He had had a nice, good, idle time all the while – plenty of company – and the fence had three coats of whitewash on it![15]

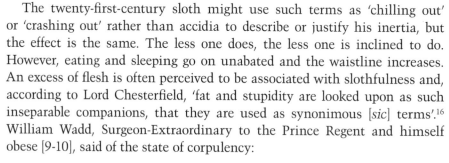
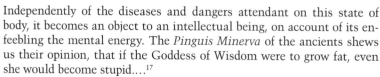

'AIN'T THAT WORK?'

9-9
Original illustration from
the first edition of *The
Adventures of Tom Sawyer*
(1876).

The twenty-first-century sloth might use such terms as 'chilling out'
or 'crashing out' rather than accidia to describe or justify his inertia, but
the effect is the same. The less one does, the less one is inclined to do.
However, eating and sleeping go on unabated and the waistline increases.
An excess of flesh is often perceived to be associated with slothfulness and,
according to Lord Chesterfield, 'fat and stupidity are looked upon as such
inseparable companions, that they are used as synonimous [*sic*] terms'.[16]
William Wadd, Surgeon-Extraordinary to the Prince Regent and himself
obese [9-10], said of the state of corpulency:

9-10
William Wadd.

> Independently of the diseases and dangers attendant on this state of
> body, it becomes an object to an intellectual being, on account of its en-
> feebling the mental energy. The *Pinguis Minerva* of the ancients shews
> us their opinion, that if the Goddess of Wisdom were to grow fat, even
> she would become stupid....[17]

According to Jean Anthelme Brillat-Savarin, the Duke de Luynes, whose
handsome countenance had become disfigured by fat, passed the last years

of his life in a nearly continual sleep.[18] Shakespeare spoke truly about sloth in *Cymbeline*:

> Weariness can snore upon the flint when resty Sloth
> Finds the down pillow hard.[19]

A biblical exhortation from Ecclesiastes (10:18) against laziness and sloth was part of a message or lesson on the virtue of good living: 'By much slothfulness the building decayeth; and through idleness of the hands the house droppest through.'

A series of books was published in the early twentieth century, called the 'Home Education' series, which set out to teach children the virtues of good living by self-management and self-perception. It describes the 'Riches of Mansoul' – a perfect kingdom of plenty – rich and beautiful. This kingdom seems based on that described by John Bunyan, a Nonconformist preacher, who wrote about a famous town in the country of Universe called Mansoul, in his book *The War for Mansoul* (1682). 'There is not an equal under the whole heaven', he wrote. This is an allegorical tale of a perfect and impregnable kingdom, 'Man's Soul', whose bountiful king cared for all the citizens. All was well until Diabolus, a mighty and ambitious giant, 'king of the blacks', who was initially as a servant to the king, wanted to be lord over all. He and his army of men were dismissed from the king's service for wrongdoing and, seeking revenge, set out to destroy Mansoul. Beelzebub recommended making the citizens' life easy: 'Let them grow rich and full.' 'When they grow full they ... may even fall asleep and neglect their watch tower and even their castle watch.' 'Cumber them with abundance.'

'Mansoul' is within everyone, the children are told. But there are perils in this kingdom, as the lesson from Ecclesiastes warns:

> Perhaps the most common evil is a sort of epidemic of sloth that spreads over the whole country. The scavengers sit with heavy eyes and folded arms, and let refuse and filth accumulate in the streets. The farmers and their labourers say 'What's the good?' and fail to go out with the plough or to sow the seed. Fruit drops from the trees and rots because no one cares to pick it up. The ships lie idle in the harbours because nobody wants anything from abroad. The librarians let their books be buried in dust and devoured by insects, and neglect their duty of gathering more. The pictures grow dim and tattered for want of care; and nobody in the whole country thinks it worth while to do anything at all.
>
> Sometimes the people still care to play; but play without work becomes dull after a time, and soon comes to a stop. And so the people, whatever be their business in Mansoul, sit or lounge about with dull eyes, folded arms, and hanging heads.[20]

If the children have not already fallen asleep by this stage, they are further warned of 'a sort of sloth or inertia which makes one unwilling to begin to think of anything but the small matters of everyday life'.

Sloth today

Attitudes towards sloth have changed to a certain extent. It is now scientifically recognised that adolescents who lie in bed until noon are not just lazy, but may have an excuse: their extra rest is said to be necessary for their growth and development. Nonetheless, exercise is also important for their growth and development, and an excess of sloth is still a contributory factor in the obesity epidemic. But, as Ogden Nash put it:

> How pleasant it is to sit on the beach,
> On the beach, on the sand, in the sun,
> With ocean galore within reach,
> And nothing at all to be done![21]

9-11
Postcard, Reg Carter.

THIS IS A FINE PLACE FOR SOLES

CHAPTER 10

Heavenly bodies

Perceptions of the ideal body shape have differed over time and place. This chapter looks at representations, largely of the female form, that have pointed to the desirability, or otherwise, of anything from a more rounded figure to an obese one.

Prehistoric figures

Prehistoric figures of naked women, in the form of bulging statuettes, have been found in Palaeolithic caves.

The Venus of Willendorf [10-1], a statuette discovered in Austria in 1908 during excavations in Willendorf on the River Danube, is said to be about 30,000 years old. She is made out of limestone, is 11.1 cm in height and was originally thickly coated with red ochre. She has enormous breasts, a huge abdomen, in the centre of which is a deep navel, and below that a fat vulva with enlarged labia. Large thighs taper to thin legs that are cut off at the ankles and thin arms terminate in tiny hands resting on the breasts. No face is shown and her head is bowed; she has an elaborate hairstyle. She is the most famous of a number of stone Venuses found across Europe which are characterised by the absence of feet and face, as well as by minutely represented arms.

Approximately 60 different images of 'Venus' have survived from the Palaeolithic era, named Venus as a sarcastic label by Austrian archaeologists because of their supposed ugliness. Contrasting statuettes show two different aspects of the naked female figure. The more famous Venus of Willendorf depicts an anatomically convincing 'apple', whereas the Venus of Lespugne demonstrates gluteal obesity of the thighs and legs, with a relatively modest abdomen. Much conjecture surrounds these figures; it has

10-1 (left)
The Venus of Willendorf.

10-2 (right)
The Venus of Laussel.
(Photograph of the original kept in Bordeaux museum, France. From Wikimedia Commons, http://commons.wikimedia.org)

been suggested that they were fertility symbols. An alternative theory is that they were the prehistoric equivalent of 'Playgirl of the month'! Some commentators have suggested that the Venus of Willendorf is pregnant, although the accuracy of the depiction of an abdominally obese woman actually offers no hint that she could actually be carrying a child.

On the other hand, the Venus of Laussel [10-2], a figurine from the Aurignacian or Gravettian period of the Palaeolithic era found in the Dordogne region, is relatively lean and slim and possibly pregnant – with a rounded belly and swollen breasts. She has maternal attributes but no facial features and she carries a bison's horn in her right hand – a fertility symbol. Other Venuses are slim, and not apparently pregnant. It may be that the obese representations were actually sex symbols – not pregnant and unlikely to become so, and therefore a safe proposition – and that the slim or gluteally obese versions were fertility symbols because of their greater likelihood of falling pregnant.

In the Later Neolithic period (8000 to 5500 BC), coinciding with the introduction of agriculture and the establishment of settlements, numerous 'mother goddesses' were made in many parts of Europe. They all have pendulous breasts and large abdomens and gluteal regions. These artefacts range in height from 2.5 to 24 cm, most between 5 and 12 cm.[1]

Some outstanding artefacts representing the human figure, which date back more than 5000 years, were discovered in the Maltese archipelago. One of the female figures found there, a statuette 10 cm tall, has been named the Maltese Venus and another the Sleeping Lady. These, too, are probably fertility symbols, although it has been said that such statuettes, like more recent Venuses, are merely representations of ideal beauty of the time.[2]

Classical, Renaissance and Enlightenment representations

Throughout history artists have felt that there must be some special formula by means of which a perfect human form could be depicted. According to Platonic ideas, a godlike man must conform to a mathematically perfect figure – the circle and the square – thereby having ideal human proportions, in keeping with the fundamental harmonies of nature. Strength, health and beauty were to be the accompanying attributes.

Proportion was the basis of classical sculpture. The Roman architectural theorist Vitruvius (first century BC) drew upon this idea with his 'Vitruvian man'. One of the most famous drawings that illustrate this perfectly circumscribed figure is that by Leonardo da Vinci, in which a naked man is depicted at the centre of the cosmos [10-3]. With his arms and legs extended he fits into the 'perfect' geometric forms, the circle and

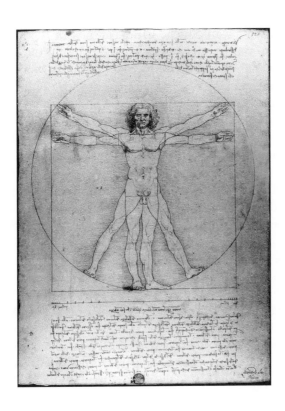

10-3
Vitruvian Man,
Leonardo da Vinci, c. 1487.

the square. Leonardo da Vinci said, 'the span of a man's outstretched arms is equal to his height. If a circle [with navel at the centre] be described of a man lying with his face upward and his hands and feet extended, it will touch his fingers and his toes.' Da Vinci makes his man 8 head-lengths tall with four concentric circles, each circle being one head apart. Whether artists make their figures 8, 9 or 12 head-lengths, the proportions remain constant. The symmetry of the human body shown in this drawing gives a sense of normal proportion, and for centuries Western culture considered that the secret of beauty was proportion.

In life, the human figure is usually 6½–7 head-lengths tall, but in art it may vary from 4 to 12 head-lengths, according to requirements. If an artist is primarily concerned with the muscles of the body, the head will not be considered important and will be small in proportion. If, however, the facial expression and features are important, the head will be larger.

The perfection of the human body with its ideal proportions was, according to the Greeks, in order that man might feel like a god. The athletes who performed at the Olympic Games were praised for their physical beauty as well as for their athletic skills; they were considered godlike and worthy inhabitants of the Olympian Heights. The perfect physique of a naked Apollo seen in ancient Greek sculptures was part of his divinity and the athletes, it was perceived, approached this state. Greek ideals dictated that physical fitness should be kept in peak condition, by such means as dancing, martial arts and exercising in the gymnasium with the help of trainers. It was thought that man should be neither too thin nor too fat. A vase in the British Museum has on it a scene in which an obese young man is facing a thin one. Two other men of rather more athletic build are shown, one throwing a discus and the other a javelin. The four men are naked, as was the custom in the gymnasium. Nakedness expressed their sense of wholeness; nothing which related to the whole man could be isolated or evaded.[3] Neither fatness nor thinness could be hidden or disguised.

Training in the gymnasium was for males only; women were excluded from public life. The fit, lithe, attractive warrior was admired and was often employed as an artistic model. Accompanying beauty and physical perfection were an 'ideal' moral attribute; the beautiful were good and, by extension, the ugly or unseemly were bad.

At the time of the Renaissance, in the sixteenth century, when artists looked back to classical Greek sculptures, Michelangelo's statue of David with his sling [10-4] personified the ideal physical beauty of youth at the time, supposedly embodying the perfection accorded to Apollo. Standing at a height of 15 feet 10½ inches, it is one of the most important statues in the history of the Renaissance. It is now claimed, however, that David's body is out of proportion: the upper part of his torso is anatomically too large when compared with the lower part. In addition to this, an art critic

10-4
David, Michelangelo,
1501–4.

and an ophthalmologist has written that David has deviating eyes, with the left eye fixating on the viewer while the right eye seems to be looking into the far distance. 'David – "a sublime balance of power, intellect and neoclassical beauty" – would probably have had problems successfully disposing of Goliath with a sling.'[4] Whatever defects David may have, his was regarded as a godlike figure and, as the basis of the ideal male body shape, that of an Olympian god probably still holds true.

Slight variations in the proportions accorded to male beauty have occurred since antiquity due to the changing taste of the time and to the skill, ideas and preference of artists or their patrons. However, depictions of the female nude were taboo in ancient Greece before the fifth century BC and sculptures of the goddess Aphrodite, for example, had to be covered in draperies to preserve her modesty.

The Egyptians sculpted figures that were to be displayed in open-fronted shrines. These idealised portraits were supposed to 'see' the rituals performed in front of them. The figures 'stride' forward with the left foot in front. The body was highly conventionalised and governed by a set of systematic, standardised proportions that were uniquely Egyptian.[5] Sheer and tightly designed garments reveal slim and 'perfect' female forms beneath.

Only much later was the Greek female body with a shapely geometric figure given some celestial status as a Venus in her own right, rather than being so-named retrospectively, as with the previous figures. The Venus de Milo [10-5] dates from about 100 BC. Although her marble height is 6 feet 2 inches, the perfect proportions of her body prevent any impression of excessive size and, artistically, she still represents the ideal female figure.

Greek women reputedly envied Etruscan women for their slim waistlines, but it does not seem that the Etruscan men were to be envied: Etruscan tombs, known as Obesii, 'depict the deceased male lying on top of his sarcophagus, half draped, resting on one arm, with his great big gut hanging out'.[6] It may be that the prominent abdomen had some symbolic meaning, but could just be the realistic depiction of the natural feature of many middle-aged Etruscan men.[7]

Figures from antiquity continued to provide the classical basis of the ideal body form and certain pieces of Greek sculpture became 'standards' for artists.

In the second half of the fifteenth century, Botticelli painted *The Three Graces of the Primavera* [C-13], derived from Ovid, to represent pagan divinities, the swirl of their flimsy draperies hinting at curves and sensuous flesh beneath. Their thinly veiled physical perfection was a revival of the classical ideal of Greek antiquity. The same artist's *Venus Rising from the Sea* (c. 1485) represents harmony and beauty [10-6]. Botticelli was the favourite painter of the Medici family and he painted the *Birth of Venus* for young Prince Lorenzo. Anatomically, her figure is incorrect; her body is

10-5
Venus de Milo, c. 100 BC.

Detail from
Venus Rising from the Sea,
Botticelli, c. 1485.

elongated as if in the act of 'rising up' and appears weightless – this was the Gothic version of the nude. According to Sir Kenneth Clark, art historian and critic, there were two basic models of the body – classical and Gothic – on which the whole art of the nude has been based.[8]

With the triumph of Christianity over paganism, 'the body ceased to be a mirror of divine perfection and became an object of humiliation and shame'.[9] After the Fall, Adam and Eve perceived that they were naked. Thereafter, nakedness was not the divine nakedness of the Greek gods but a pious Christian representation. This was the Gothic model: 'the body was often angular, sharp, and mean. Its gauntness was evidence of the mortification of flesh, punished for its power to entice the soul towards pleasure and away from grace.'[10] Lust lurked in nudity; the image of bodily beauty with a curve of the hip and buttocks was connected with desire and was to be expelled; lust, one of the seven deadly sins, was evoked. Instead, early Christians should admire the skeletal bodies of the anchorites or hermits, who retreated from the material world with all its temptations.

The Gothic nude had an elongated body with tapering limbs, extended torso and small breasts. Van der Goes's Eve in *Adam and Eve* has an elongated torso, her pelvis is wide, chest narrow, waist high and stomach rounded. Mannerist artists – those who sought to paint in the manner, but not the essence, of the Old Masters – produced such figures. In sixteenth-century France, 'Cellini's *"Nymph of Fontainbleu"* is so far from the antique canon of proportion that her legs alone are six heads long'.[11] (The legs of the classical model are three heads long.) These figures with their 'somewhat ridiculous shape – feet and hands too fine for honest work, bodies too thin for child-bearing, and heads too small to contain a single thought', were described by Clark as 'chic'.[12] He compared them with twentieth-century fashion models with their thin bodies.

Michelangelo's heroic figures, the young, strong yet graceful and poised men, painted on the ceiling of the Sistine Chapel between 1508 and 1512, were intended as mediators between the physical and spiritual worlds. Their physical perfection allowed them to fulfil this role in the same way that the physical perfection of the Greek athletes had enabled them to approach the Olympian Heights.

There was no agreement as to the actual form of 'ideal beauty' but general lines or rules were set down to which it must conform. The Old Masters of the Renaissance such as Raphael, Michelangelo and Leonardo da Vinci generally portrayed their figures along the lines indicated by the 'Vitruvian man'.

Studies of the nude female body did not take over from the male as an appealing art form until the seventeenth century. Since then, she has perhaps become a more popular model than the male and portrayed more often. The Greek ideals of female beauty were not universally acceptable; after some mannerist representations of Gothic proportions, many welcomed the more generous portrayal of the female form offered by Rubens, with his plump models: voluptuous, sensuous, full-bodied, glowing individuals, promising endless delights [C-14 – a study of the *Three Graces* that contrasts with Botticelli's a century and a half earlier]. His nudes 'seem at first sight to have been tumbled out of a cornucopia of abundance'.[13] Cellulite on large thighs, wrinkles and puckers on pink skin were more in keeping with the inhabitants of northern regions, who tended to carry more weight than their sisters from the warm south. In the twenty-first century they might be regarded as overweight or even obese. Slenderness was not fashionable in Flanders in Rubens' day; plumpness was. In the sixteenth and seventeenth centuries, gluttony and a certain amount of rotundity were widespread.

In eighteenth-century England, young artists were encouraged to copy works of the Old Masters and to study classical statuary; it was hoped that by doing so they would acquire a taste and idea of beauty and proportion. Hogarth, though, did not approve of the amount of time spent on copying works of the Old Masters, preferring instead to study from life itself. His one treatise on art, the *Analysis of Beauty*, published in November 1753, was written 'with a view to fix the fluctuating Ideas of Taste'. He searched for the basic fact of beauty and found it 'not in an abstract quality such as Grace or the sublime, but in a geometrical formula, an S-shaped curve, and upon this spiral rested everything that was beautiful, in nature or in art'. He called this 'the serpentine line' or 'the line of grace'. His ideas

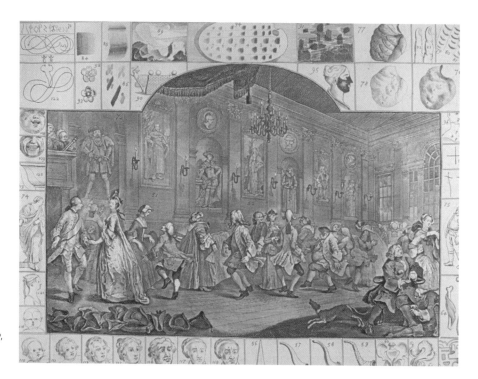

10-7
Plate 11, *The Country Dance*,
from *The Analysis of Beauty*,
Hogarth, 1753.

were based on the variety of forms seen in nature; he deplored regularity
and uniformity. He illustrated these ideas in *The Country Dance* [10-7],
in which he compared the elegance of couples dancing. In the margins of
the work he has drawn diagrams of the dancing couples reduced to their
linear equivalents, their relative elegance depending upon their reduction to
straight or curved lines. His 'heavenly bodies' were not so much dependent
upon proportions as on the elegance of their shape and line. This etching
and engraving of a ballroom scene shows how the elegant couple on the left,
with their regular 'serpentine' figures, compare with the sharp angularity
and ungainly lines of the couple on their right.

By the middle of the century, artists were encouraged to undertake 'life
drawings' as Hogarth had advocated, and in 1759 the Society of Arts offered
premiums 'for Drawings of Human figures from Living Models, at the
Academy of Artists in St. Martin's Lane, in chalks, by young men under 24
years'. At about the same time, the Duke of Richmond opened his sculpture
gallery to provide an opportunity for artists to study antique statuary.

The 'adaptation of classical statuary to the living model was … the only
viable means by which the human figure could transcend its inherently im-
perfect state', said Benjamin West, President of the Royal Academy, in 1796.
John Opie, artist and professor of painting at the Royal Academy in 1805,

10-8
La Baigneuse blonde,
Renoir, 1880.

told his students that such figures could be compared with 'the rank and vulgar redundance of a Flemish or Dutch female'.

Renoir's nude bathers, though not as robust as Rubens' models, were inclined to be 'deliciously plump'. His wife as portrayed in *La Baigneuse blonde* in 1880 was of this genre [10-8].

Cultural variation

The Venus de Milo might now be considered by Western standards to have hips too large to be of ideal dimensions, but tastes and fashions change and different cultures have different ideas of what makes an ideal figure. For example, India's sculptured goddesses have voluptuous curves and full breasts. Many modern Indian men still prefer their wives and daughters to be plump, as this reflects on the men's ability to provide for them.

A writer in the late nineteenth century describes one particular fattening process that was diligently pursued amongst many people who regarded an excessive accumulation of fat as an ornament of the female sex:

> Jewesses of Tunis, when scarcely ten years old are subjected to systematic treatment by confinement in narrow dark places, where they are fed

on farinaceous food and the flesh of puppies, until in a few months they expand to shapeless masses of fat.[14]

Moorish women were also said with equal rapidity to reach the desired roundedness on a diet of fresh dates and a kind of mead.

Utamaro's paintings of Japanese courtesans show them to be nicely rounded, and in some Polynesian cultures folds of fat are positively welcomed. The Pacific islanders of Tonga like their citizens to be weighty and once boasted the heaviest monarch, King Taufa'ahau Tupou IV, whose name appeared in the *Guinness Book of Records* in 1976 with a weight of 30 stone (420 pounds). Queen Salote Tupou III, who was on the throne from 1918 to 1965, was a large woman, at 6 feet 2½ inches tall and weighing more than 300 pounds. In a culture where feasting plays a major role and size is a status symbol, the royal family were esteemed for their size. Only recently have the perils of obesity been acknowledged there; according to the World Health Organization, Tonga – along with the South Pacific island of Nauru – has the largest obesity problem in the world (see Chapter 1).

Tonga was not the only nation that esteemed size; William Wadd tells of 'the Emperor of Mogul who is annually weighed upon his birthday; when, if it appears that since his former weighing, he has made any considerable acquisition of flesh, it is matter of public rejoicings throughout his whole dominion.'[15] Conversely, in ancient Egypt, princesses were valued as lithe and lean, as dancers.

In the 'Song of Solomon' in the Old Testament, King Solomon offers praise to the beauty of his bride:

> Thy neck is like the tower of David builded for an armoury, whereon there hangs a thousand bucklers, all shields of mighty men.
> Thy two breasts are like two young roes that are twins, which feed among the lilies.

And: 'This thy stature is like to a palm tree...'.

Fashion and fat

Fashion dictates body size to a great extent. For example, the ample figures – both male and female – of the early part of the eighteenth century in Europe gave way in female fashion to a 'new cult of the lithe, limber, slim body indicative of delicacy and fineness of sensibility'.[16] Thus, whereas seventeenth-century English portraits by the likes of Sir Peter Lely and Sir Godfrey Kneller had endowed their male sitters with large wigs and 'corporeal presence', a new, slimmer line came into being.[17] Breeches for men gave way to trousers, which became tighter and thigh-hugging, and for women layered petticoats with hoops and corsets gave way to light fabrics such as muslin, which, like the drapery of Botticelli's Graces, revealed and emphasised the body's contours.[18] Even under loose-fitting gowns, women wore laced stays, which were boned down the centre and side fronts to straighten the spine and push up the bosom.[19] This was deemed to help with deportment. Even very small girls were put into training stays to keep their backs stiff and straight. Comfort and health had to be sacrificed for the sake of fashion, but fashion was a hard taskmaster and shifted frequently.

Christopher Anstey wrote scathingly about this topic in *An Election Ball* in 1775 through the pen of his character Mr Inkle, writing to his wife from Bath:

> Lack a day! How her throat doth our MARGERY raise
> How shove up her bosom, and shove down her stays?
> For to make a young lady a true polite figure
> You must cramp up her sides that her breast may look bigger;
> And her's tho' a chicken as yet, my dear Dinah,
> Stand forth full as plump, and as jolly as thine are.[20]

Fat at this time was linked to successful motherhood, a state presumably attained by Mrs Inkle. An increase in weight was seen as natural after frequent pregnancies. It was also welcomed on stage, where it was regarded as voluptuous. If corsets were used, it was to accentuate roundness.

In contrast, by the middle of the twentieth century, playwrights eschewed fat stars. Noel Coward, for example, beseeched 'Mrs Worthington' not to put her daughter on the stage:

> She's a big girl, though her teeth are fairly good
> She's not the type I ever would be eager to engage,
> I repeat, Mrs Worthington, sweet Mrs Worthington
> Don't put your daughter on the stage.

Between 1860 and 1880, rotundity gained ground with both males and females. 'Actresses promoted fashionable plumpness, adding bustles to a corseting designed to stress ample bosoms and derriers.'[21]

A decade later, middle-class America began its ongoing battle against body fat, when 'willowy grace' was a sought-for ideal, but fashions changed frequently at this time. In the first decade of the twentieth century, a more natural body shape and waistline were the standard; brassieres were developed as an alternative and more comfortable garment to corsets. During the 1920s breasts 'disappeared' and a flat bosom was fashionable, a state often achieved with the aid of the new 'binding brassiere'. This slim, straight look was that of the 'flapper'.

Another decade later, a fuller bosom and slender waist returned. The breast line was enhanced with push-up brassieres, sometimes with foam-filled 'falsies' for extra effect. Later still, actresses like Marilyn Monroe were regarded as ideal role models [10-9].

10-9
Marilyn Monroe and
Jane Russell in *Gentlemen
Prefer Blondes*, 1953.

More recently, bottoms and thighs have drawn attention. Cellulite is now an accessory to be eschewed and a more athletic body is desired, with a slender but more muscular build. By the 1980s, however, fashion models had become waifs who sometimes appeared almost anorexic. The British Medical Association reported that models and actresses in the 1990s commonly had body fat levels as low as 10 per cent, when the average for a healthy woman is 22–26 per cent.[22] In 2007, the Model Health Inquiry was set up by the British Fashion Council to monitor the health and weight of young models. However, a slim, youthful and well dressed woman is still fashion's favourite even though reality indicates that there are an increasing number of people at odds with the fashion industry.

A long-term survey, using high-tech three-dimensional scanners which mapped the body shapes of more than 11,000 Britons, revealed that the average woman is now about two inches taller than in 1951, with slightly larger hip and bust measurements, but a waist size increased by almost seven inches.[23] The survey went on to report that, in the UK, a woman's average weight is 10 stone 3½ pounds (65 kg); in the United States, an average woman weighs 11 stone 1½ pound (71 kg). In 1951, the average weight of a woman was 9 stone 10 pounds (62 kg).

Fashions in dress, though, frequently have their origin in the wish to hide some disfigurement. The introduction of the crinoline has often been attributed to the Empress Eugenie, wife of Napoleon III, before the birth of the Prince Imperial, although ladies had worn a similar apparatus (a farthingale) in the sixteenth and seventeenth centuries. The daughters of Louis XI felt the need to hide their large feet; hence a fashion for trailing gowns evolved amongst society ladies. The wife of Philip III disguised her abnormally long neck with a high wimple, which soon became fashionable. At the beginning of the seventeenth century, James I started a fashion for wearing voluminous trunk hose as a means of concealing an unsightly malformation. English gallants followed suit. Breeches could be padded to help the wearer to conform to size. Carlyle told a story of an unlucky courtier who sat down on a nail. On rising to receive His Majesty, several pecks of bran leaked from his breeches, leaving the unfortunate gentleman in a shrunken state, with his breeches hanging in folds about him. The ruff became fashionable when the Prince Regent wished to hide the swollen tubercular glands in his neck, known at the time as scrofula or the king's evil.

Exquisite Dandies [10-10], a hand-coloured etching by Isaac Cruikshank, published in 1818, satirically illustrates the absurd lengths to which the Regency dandies might go to be considered as followers of fashion. What nature did not endow, art or artifice supplied. The Macaronis of the 1770s provided caricaturists with plenty of model appearances.

If beauty and perfection were to be perceived as moral attributes, the opposite also had to hold true: beauty equalled good; ugly was bad. Hence,

10-10
Exquisite Dandies,
Cruikshank, 1818.

to provide narrative detail to their work, artists could use images of defects in bodily shape and of facial features. For example, Roualt's painting of a naked prostitute in 1903–04 illustrates how he felt that nature could be defiled by nurture, that is, by the wrongful and sinful use of the body. Roualt's message was both religious and moral. The result is an obese, sullen and repugnant figure.[24]

Modern representations

Artistic ideas of the body have changed during the past century and some larger-than-life figures have emerged. Obese figures are now more prevalent, especially in the towns and cities, and some artists have found a new interest in portraying the extremes of body size and of human flesh. Obesity is opening up new areas of artistic exploration and expression.

During the twentieth century, a Latin American painter and sculptor, Fernando Botero, who moved to live and work in Europe, became popular with his monumental bronze sculptures of large female figures. Many of these statuesque figures stand in the square of his native Colombia; others can be seen in Paris. Botero has also produced super-sized interpretations of stylised Old Master paintings, giving generous curves to otherwise well known works of art, such as the Mona Lisa. Botero's images are rotund and out of scale, some figures resembling the solid body forms found in boxes of children's building blocks.

In her work as a sculptress, one artist, Joanna Mallin-Davies, is reacting against much of the pressure on women today to conform to 'fashionable ideals'. She believes that some of the blame for our society becoming increasingly fat or overweight is the negative attitude that there is towards people who are big, and the effect that being made to feel 'wrong' in oneself has on the mind and thus on the body. She is concerned with making beautiful objects; and to this effect, makes positive images of big, even fat, women as sensual creatures – the essence of female form and presence – with an innate self-possession, an inner contentment.[25] In line with these beliefs, Mallin-Davies's sculpture *The Three Graces* (2005) portrays a modern version of Canova's classical model [10-11]. Here, three overweight females are gracefully and self-confidently posed in similar fashion to their original prototypes.

10-11
The Three Graces, Joanna Mallin-Davies, 2005.

Beryl Cook (1926–2008) was another artist who liked to produce images of large people. In 1995, a series of Royal Mail stamps featured examples of her work. She painted from life and frequented clubs and bars in search of her pneumatic and humorous models. Her rendering possibly owes something to seaside picture postcards (on which, see Chapter 12).

Obesity has been portrayed 'as it is' in Lucien Freud's work, for instance the etching *Big Sue* (1996), an image that might be regarded as unsightly or even repulsive by some people. Her obese nude figure seems to merge into her surroundings. Freud is not concerned with an ideal figure here but makes the obese body an abstract idea. There is no background or chair on which the figure reclines and its identity seems to have become submerged as fat 'rounds off' the features. Freud painted many versions of this particular grossly obese woman and seems to be exploring or demonstrating the extreme of human form. He is interested in the craters, creases and crevices produced by uninhibited fat.

Jenny Saville, too, paints unidealised naked bodies 'stripped bare' of personality and context. She is fascinated with fat. 'Flesh is all things', she states: 'Ugly, beautiful, repulsive, compelling, anxious, neurotic, dead, alive. And it is nothing.'[26] She seems to anthropomorphise fat, to blame it for either empowering women or creating a neurosis. Her foreshortened figure in *Branded* (1992), for example, seems to expose an element of loathing of the female form, by exaggerating and distorting the figure – in this case, her own [C-15].

Martin Kippenberger, a twentieth-century German artist, produced an image of a large recumbent female nude by joining six canvases together as one image in a billboard-like design [C-16]. This image is said to 'operate as an anti-advert for itself, poking fun at the tradition of painting and the way it's been historically and ideologically subverted'. Perhaps a modern-day Venus?

The golden figure and the development of the body mass index

Fashion models in the twenty-first century bear little resemblance to the ideal figure of Venus de Milo and other classical studies of the female form; neither do their hip/waist ratios seem to conform to the 'golden figure' of fitness. Although body sizes have increased and obesity is literally and metaphorically widespread, the fashion industry illustrates thinness. The young, active, 'with it' image is all pervasive. Open any contemporary social magazine and there you will see that those people who are considered to be successful are slender, 'in fashion' and in the 'right' dimensions. Looking back at illustrations in social magazines over the past century, it is possible to see how fashion has been able to dictate what is considered to be the

10-12
Eye of the Beholder, Emma
Donnelly, 2009.

ideal bodily shape at a particular time. Few women would pretend to be,
or even aspire to be, like the Venus de Milo, or men to be like Apollo, but
many would like to be able to wear the latest 'designer' outfit.

What, then, is the ideal body shape? It is said that beauty is in the eye of
the beholder [10-12], but nature seems to play a part in deciding what the
beholder admires. Recent tests in which people were shown different body
images to find their preferred body shape found that the ideal body had a
ratio of waist to hip of 0.7, representing the 'golden figure'. This figure is
that of the most fertile and healthy person and therefore a fitting mate and
parent for a future generation.

There is a line between what is acceptable aesthetically as an ideal body
shape and what is acceptable physiologically. The margins of this line are,
however, not static: they change with fashion. In clinical terms, the ideal
body has historically been judged by weight alone, considered to be the
overwhelmingly important biometric factor. Height was taken into account
only as a secondary concern. The Belgian sociologist Adolphe Quetelet
applied modern science to the problem in 1833,[27] when he published
tables of average, maximum and minimum heights and weights for males
and females on an annual basis from birth until age 20, at 25 and then

for each decade from 30 to 80 years of age, now regarded as the original height–weight tables. According to Quetelet, 'apparently but little interest is attached to the determination of the stature and weight of man or to his physical development at different ages'.[28] This led him to improve the scientific methodology, based on the observation that in adults of normal size, weight is proportional to height squared – a calculation which became regarded as Quetelet's Index (QI), and was widely used as a measure of adiposity until 1972, when Keys *et al.*[29] coined the expression 'body mass index' (BMI) (expressed in kg/m²). This measure is still in common use today as a standard by which to judge the degree of body fat in an individual. A BMI of between 18.5 and 24.9 kg/m² is regarded as normal. A BMI of 30 or above is obese; a figure approaching 40 is considered morbidly obese. Associated health charts indicate ideal and healthy body size.

An additional and more accurate predictor of clinical risk is the measurement of the waistline. A figure of more than 40 inches (102 cm) for a man and more than 35 inches (88 cm) for a woman is designated as high risk, although the figure is less for some ethnic minorities, such as South Asians, who are at a higher risk at lower thresholds of waist circumference and BMI. As long ago as 1670, Johann Friedrich Held, who presented a doctoral dissertation on the topic of obesity at Jena, defined obesity by belt size, insisting that a waistline over 36 inches with a full stomach is technically obese.[30]

It is not enough, however, to know what the ideal body shape is like. How is it to be attained and maintained? It has been said that: 'Failure to live up to the new, standardised body image entails at least an appalling ugliness, at most a fundamentally flawed character.' With that in mind, is it any wonder that, as Brillat-Savarin says: 'to be exactly stout enough, neither too much nor too little, is for women the study of their life'.[31]

CHAPTER 11

Obesity on the page

> And Eglon was a very fat man.... And Ehud put forth his left hand, and took the dagger from his right thigh, and thrust it into his belly: And the haft also went in after the blade; and the fat closed upon the blade, so that he could not draw the dagger out of his belly; and the dirt came out. (Judges 3:17–22)

In this way, the left-handed Ehud delivered the children of Israel from Eglon, the King of Moab, who had oppressed them for 18 years. A bloody battle ensued; Moab was subdued under the hand of Israel 'and the land had rest fourscore years'. The defeat of the Moabs did not necessarily depend upon the size of Eglon, but the Old Testament story emphasises the fact that Eglon was 'a very fat man'. His abdominal obesity or paunch was perhaps recorded as a sign of his loss of control, with regard both to himself and to Israel. Jewish attitudes towards obesity centred on a lack of self-control or self-discipline, which was punishable.[1] This early reference to obesity in the Bible gives some indication of how the subject was regarded at the time.

The man who is 'very fat' in the twenty-first century, with a surplus of abdominal fatty tissue, may not suffer the same fate as the King of Moab, but his future is by no means secure. Abdominal fat is a danger to health; waist circumference is a surrogate marker for visceral fat, and diabetes, heart disease and stroke are just some of the problems that may ensue. Being overweight has not always been perceived as a reprehensible attribute, however; its contribution to life-threatening events such as diabetes and some forms of cancer was not fully recognised until comparatively recently and as long as the condition did not become one of true grossness or corpulence, or cause overt symptoms of distress, there was no obvious need for concern.

Perceptions of obesity have varied and changed throughout history. This can be seen through the work of literary and graphic artists; their character studies reflect society and its attitudes at the time in which they were written or drawn. Social historian Roy Porter comments:

> The truly obese had always been objects of literary and artistic satire – for grossness bespoke greed, lack of self-control and the vulgarity of temper associated with low life. But in traditional national, social and occupational stereotyping a certain stoutness was a positive property, betokening not just healthiness but the rock-solid strength of the gentleman, yeoman farmer, magistrate or citizen.[2]

To a large extent this is true, but, as can be seen in many literary works, descriptions vary and stoutness has not been viewed universally as a positive property. The portrayal of different characteristics under the guise of obesity even flourishes in literature for children, from books for the youngest onwards.

Childhood obesity

The tendency to spoil children with rewards of sweet foods – one of the causes of their obesity – was recognised and deplored by philosophers in the past. For example, Pamela, in Samuel Richardson's 1740 epistolatory novel of that name, offers to her husband her opinion of the writings of the seventeenth-century philosopher John Locke on the upbringing of children:

> This excellent author … justly disallowed of slavish and corporal punishment in the education of those we would have to be wise, good and ingenous [sic] men…. On the other side, to flatter children by rewards of things that are pleasant to them, is as carefully to be avoided. He that will give his son apples, or sugar plums, or what else of this kind he is most delighted with, to make him learn his book, does not authorise his love of pleasure, and cockers up that dangerous propensity, which he ought, by all means, to subdue and stifle in him…. To make a good, a wise, and a virtuous man, 'tis fit he should learn to cross his appetite, and deny his inclination to riches, finery, or pleasing his palate, etc. It is undoubtedly right to check an unreasonable appetite, and that at its first appearance.

Pamela deplores the practice of rewarding children with sweetmeats, but her objections are more on moral grounds than the effect on weight. The association with weight gain becomes more apparent later.

Differing perceptions of weight and obesity in relation to children range from the acceptable plump and playful characters who appear in the nursery to the more objectionable characterisations of plump or overweight individuals in comic strips and stories for older children. The many examples of those who are overweight in children's literature illustrate some of the problems associated with obesity in childhood in real life.

The prevalence of overweight and obesity in children and adolescents has increased over recent years. Obesity now overshadows all other chronic illnesses in adolescents. The International Obesity Task Force suggested that, in Britain in 2002, some 22 per cent of boys and 27 per cent of girls aged 2–15 were overweight, and 5 per cent of boys and 7 per cent of girls were obese; furthermore, there had been a marked acceleration in the trend from the mid-1980s onwards.[3]

Obesity in children's literature

Children are subjected to portrayals of stereotypical obese figures from the nursery; nursery rhymes abound with them. Old King Cole was a merry old soul, usually portrayed as being fat and jolly – a fat figure of fun. Like Santa Claus, he is somewhat daunting but is accepted because of parental approval. The rotundity of such figures signifies their importance and grandeur, yet remoteness to childish vision.

St Nicholas, the original Santa Claus, was a saint from the fourth century, a thin figure in historical documentation [11-1]. He became fat sometime between the thirteenth century and 1823, when he was described in verse by Clement Clarke Moore in a poem entitled *A Visit from St Nicholas*:

11-1
The traditionally thin figure of St Nicholas.

11-2
Santa Claus, as drawn by Thomas Nast for *Harper's Weekly*, 1862.

He had a broad face and a little round Belly
That shook when he laughed like a bowlful of Jelly.
He was chubby and plump; a right jolly old elf,
And I laughed when I saw him in spite of myself.

Thomas Nast drew him for *Harper's Weekly* in 1862 [11-2]. His obesity was probably not helped by copious consumption of sherry and mince pies left by countless children on Christmas Eve. The image of a rotund Santa was later used in an advertisement for a well known carbonated drink [11-3].

11-3
Santa Claus advertising
Coca-Cola.

The plump, stout, roly-poly or podgy character is familiar to all small children, from their own experience, and from most children's and classic literature in which different obesity-related characteristics are displayed. Children grow up with the reassuring presence of a plump teddy bear. He is warm, cuddly, comforting, non-judgemental and never changes. A. A. Milne's Winnie the Pooh, the anthropomorphised bear, is cuddly, bumbling and eccentric, designed to be as lovable and unthreatening as possible in order to send little ones off to sleep with happy thoughts in their heads. Pooh's body mass index has been estimated at around 35 kg/m^2 – in the 'obese' range – enhanced mainly through over-consumption, particularly of honey – as he seems to have a fairly active lifestyle. His enlarged abdominal circumference leads him to become trapped in Rabbit's doorway, a variation on one of the traditional comical fat situations. The predicament necessitates a starvation diet, which prompts him to ask Rabbit: 'How long does getting thin take?', to which Rabbit replies, 'About a week I should think'.

Many children know:

Jack Sprat could eat no fat,
his wife could eat no lean.
And so between them both, you see,
they kept the platter clean.

Accompanying pictures usually portray Jack as slim and his wife as obese. Although between them they ate everything, Jack's slimness, attained through his fat-reduced meals, and his wife's roly-poly figure offer obvious dietary recommendations.

The messages behind the images of obesity, however, are not consistent. For example, in J. R. R. Tolkien's *The Hobbit*, Bilbo Baggins displays the hobbits' inclination to be 'fat in the stomach', representing reassurance, stability of character and wisdom, whereas Lewis Carroll's bizarre identical twins Tweedledee and Tweedledum, men dressed as schoolboys [11-4] – also inclined to be 'fat in the stomach' – seem to display exactly the opposite characteristics, being unstable, aggressive and belligerent but ultimately cowardly.

Another classic figure is Toad from Kenneth Grahame's *Wind in the Willows*, whose abdominal obesity reflects his pomposity and arrogance, the

11-4
Tweedledum and
Tweedledee, as drawn by
John Tenniel for the original
illustration in Lewis Carroll's
Through the Looking Glass
(1871).

self-publicising 'popular and handsome toad, the rich and hospitable Toad, the Toad so free and careless and debonair' – Toad with 'a very elegant figure – for what I am'.

Most modern Western children know about the 'Fat Director', who is generally nameless, known for most of his career by his shape alone, and who gets promoted to 'Fat Controller' in Reverend W. V. Awdry's 'Thomas the Tank Engine' series of books. He is in the position of ultimate authority over the engines and their drivers, and displays corpulence in both appearance and character, but is frequently portrayed as a bumptious overblown fool. Although his true name is eventually revealed as Sir Charles Topham Hatt, the title of Fat Controller is the one that has entered literary history. His inflated ego and arrogant management of the working people and engines, who *really* run the railway, also earned him political fame, his name being used in parliamentary debate, and recorded in *Hansard* as an insult to over-inflated politicians.[4]

Fat characters in books for young children include Mr Greedy in the 'Mister Men' series, PC Plod and the Wobbly Man in Enid Blyton's 'Noddy' series, Beatrix Potter's Mrs Tiggywinkle and so on. The entire crew of Captain Pugwash's ship the *Black Pig* seems to be morbidly obese. Often fat individuals are introduced simply to provide contrast, but at other times their physical appearance is intended to suggest certain character traits. Fatty, the leader of the 'Five Find-Outers' from Enid Blyton's 'Mystery' series (and based on a real person) earned his nickname from his initials: Frederick Algernon Trotteville. He was, however, distinctly stout, as well as being wealthy, generous, a master of disguises, a skilled leader, orator and poet. Often referred to by grown-ups as merely 'That fat boy!', Fatty was admired by the rest of the group. Despite his obvious talent, popularity and status, Fatty's weight was recognised as a problem, clearly caused by over-eating, as his activity level as solver of mysteries was exemplary.

> Soon they were all sitting down enjoying a truly marvellous tea. Fatty's mother had handed out ten shillings as a reward for all their hard work, and that bought a very fine tea indeed – but wasn't quite enough to pay for ice-creams each as well, so Fatty delved into his own pocket as usual. 'I vote for scones and honey to begin with, macaroons to follow, and either éclairs or meringues after that, with ice-creams to end with' suggested Fatty.

But on another occasion:

> 'I vote we all go out to tea at the best tea-shop in the village. We'll be hungry after our hard work' said Fatty.
> 'Well, I'll pay for a good tea,' said his mother, laughing. 'I see you've forgotten that you want to take off some of your fat, Frederick.'
> 'Don't remind me of that, Mother, just when I'm looking forward to meringues and chocolate éclairs,' groaned Fatty.[5]

Enid Blyton's treatment of Fatty is worth closer inspection. In some ways he is the typical hero, brave, witty, charming, intelligent and, most of all, popular and admired, even revered. Given that particular cluster of characteristics, it is almost shocking to discover that he is obese and, frankly, a glutton. The cause of Fatty's excess weight is obvious: he clearly lacks discipline when faced with the reward of energy-dense, high-calorie, sugary treats after his day's mystery-solving exploits. Another fat Blyton character, Connie in the 'Malory Towers' series, is also an efficient, reliable and popular figure.

Unfortunately, many children's authors choose rather different stereo-types for fat children, either as horrible bullies, or clumsy and inept fools. In Carl Hiaasen's *Hoot*, for example, the hero, Roy, is mercilessly bullied by the large, lumpy, bulky, piggish, fat boy Dana, who would 'clamp a moist, ham-sized hand over Roy's face'. In Tim Kennemore's *Circle of Doom*, Max is bullied and robbed by Nathan, a piggy boy with podgy hands.

Sometimes, the obesity of an individual character is part of the portrayal of a grotesque, hideous monster with no redeeming features, either physi-cally or otherwise. Mr Swelter, the chef in Mervyn Peake's Gormenghast series, 'the pendulous horror ... like a moon-bathed sea-cow', is an example:

Abiatha Swelter, who wades in a slug-like illness of fat through the humid ground mists of the Great Kitchen. From hazy progs and flesh-pots half afloat, from bowls as big as baths, there rises and drifts like a miasmic tide the all but palpable odour of the day's bellytimber.... The arrogance of this fat head exudes itself like an evil sweat.[6]

Later, the chef becomes a 'catalyptic mass of wine-drenched blubber' covering an area of seven flagstones.[7] Peake does not miss the opportunity to eke out some obesity-related comedy slapstick from his character: 'In the dimness he flung his arms apart so that the buttons of his tunic were torn away, one of them whizzing across the room and stunning a cockroach on the opposite wall'.[8] Actor Richard Griffiths, who played the part of Swelter in a BBC adaptation (2000) of the 'Gormenghast' trilogy, likened the chef to Idi Amin, the Ugandan dictator of the 1970s, a monstrous figure who might be perceived as laughably comic and worthy of any derisory comment imaginable, but anyone under his control could die at any minute.

Griffiths plays the part of another irredeemably repugnant obese character in a film adaptation of a series of novels, Uncle Vernon Dursley in J. K. Rowling's 'Harry Potter' series, 'a big beefy man with hardly any neck'. Vernon is another literary example of a bully and a tyrant, who spends most of his time banging the table with a huge purple fist, or 'yelling at Harry, his face like a giant beetroot with a moustache'.[9]

Vernon's beloved son Dudley, like Swelter, is totally obnoxious, and is created to be as unpleasant as possible, both physically and in the way he behaves. Gross obesity is once again part of this portrayal, though rather than discriminating against the fat boy because of his weight, Rowling rails against the lifestyle that created this revolting creature – the idolising of an only child, who is spoilt and indulged at the expense of poor Harry:

Dudley looked a lot like Uncle Vernon. He had a large, pink face, not much neck, small, watery blue eyes, and thick blond hair that lay smoothly on his thick fat head. Aunt Petunia often said that Dudley looked like a baby angel – Harry often said that Dudley looked like a pig in a wig.[10]

The cause of Dudley's obesity is clear – sedentary occupation and too much food:

They were watching a brand new television, a welcome-home-for-the-summer present for Dudley, who had been complaining loudly about the long walk between the fridge and the television in the living room. Dudley had spent most of the summer in the kitchen, his piggy little eyes fixed on the screen and his five chins wobbling as he ate continually.[11]

He hated exercise 'unless it involves punching someone'.

Dudley is, predictably, the subject of comic descriptions and situations. Once, 'Dudley came waddling down the hall, his blond hair plastered flat to his fat head, a bow-tie just visible under his many chins'.[12] On another occasion, a pig's tail is attached to him to teach him a lesson. (The 'Piggy' epithet is common in children's books as an emblem of greed and grossness, the association of this plump, greedy animal being obvious to even very young children.)

Dudley is also stereotypically dull and stupid: adding two presents to 27 already in his possession, 'Dudley thought for a moment. It looked like hard work. Finally he said slowly, "so I'll have thirty … thirty…".'[13]

However, it is a third overweight character in the 'Harry Potter' series, the 'round-faced' 'fat cry-baby' Neville Longbottom, who represents possibly the most sinister stereotype of a fat person, the obese character whose sole reason for being overweight is to show the hero in a better light. Neville frequently loses his toads, breaks his cauldron and falls off his broomstick, and performs spells so badly they end in disaster, such as an eruption of boils, whereas heroes Harry and Hermione fare far better. When Neville succeeds in something, there is a sense of the hopeless underdog somehow succeeding despite being inept and lacking in any talent whatsoever.

This characteristic is displayed more pointedly in some American children's series of books. For example, Bess Marvin is the 'plump jolly girl' in the 'Nancy Drew' series, which started in the 1930s under a collective pen-name of Carolyn Keene. Bess has an obsession with food and a tendency to stay inactive at home rather than using up energy in facing danger. Psychologist Mildred Klingman in her book *The Secret Lives of Fat People* suggests that 'when a thin and a fat person are good friends, the thin person is often using the fat person as a backdrop against which he or she can look better'.[14] Thus Nancy, who is popular, clever, athletic and pretty – the perfect child – appears even more phenomenal compared with Bess's cowardliness and timidity. Nancy also appears to look even better by looking after Bess.

In Alice Emerson's 'Betty Gordon' series, 'Short, plump Libbie Littell' in *Betty Gordon at Boarding School* (1921) is the fat girl, similarly downtrodden. Louise comes to the rescue:

> 'You've been reading too many silly books,' scolded Bobby. 'Anyway, Libbie, you're too fat to look nice in a veil. Better get thin before you're old enough to be married, or else you'll have to wear a traveling suit.'
>
> Libbie eyed her scornfully and continued to parade up and down in her draperies.
>
> 'Betty would look pretty in a veil,' said Louise suddenly. 'Come on, girls, let's stage a wedding. Libbie won't sleep all night if she doesn't have some romantic outlet. I'll be the father.'
>
> She seized a pillow and stuffed it in the front of her dressing gown so that it made a very respectable corpulency.

Other discriminations, such as racial stereotyping, were often aired in books of that era. These are now generally considered unacceptable and in many instances passages have been deleted or revised in subsequent editions. It is interesting to note, however, that these modern, 'politically correct' editions of such books still refer to the shortcomings of the obese person. An excerpt from *Betty Gordon in Washington* (1920) reads:

> 'I cain't get the doors open,' announced the darky, after tinkering vainly with them. 'I reckon the lock's done got jammed. If I could get 'em open the lil girl under the seat could shinny up the wall and that would be one out, 'tannyrate.'
>
> Attention thus focused upon her, Libbie crawled from under the seat where she had dived, following an ostrich-like impulse to hide her head from coming danger. Her confusion was increased by the tactless comment of the operator who, seeing her 'full view' for the first time, exclaimed: 'Lawsy, Missie, you couldn't shinny up no wall. You is too fat.'[15]

Use of the word 'darky' would be deemed unacceptable today, but a reference to someone as 'fat' would probably pass without comment.

Alice Emerson's other famous series, the 'Ruth Fielding' books, boasts a plump character, named 'Heavy', whose real name is Jennie Stone, who is obsessed with food. The sight of a 'Whangdoodle Pudding' reduces her to ecstasies of delight. 'It's just scrumptious', she declares, rolling her eyes, and 'They laughed at Heavy's ecstasies, yet all did full justice to the pudding'.[16]

Chet Morton is the fat boy in Franklin W. Dixon's 'Hardy Boys' series. He is active, playing football and going on adventures, but his downfall is his eating and love of food, especially cooked by the Hardy Boys' mum, Trudy. Chet is just a little less brave, and a little more likely to succumb to accidents, than the others. Whilst the boys succeed in solving a mystery, Chet is generally on hand to perform the cooking and nurturing role.

The contrast between the lean hero and the fat backdrop is never more greatly emphasised than in Roald Dahl's *Charlie and the Chocolate Factory* (1964). Charlie Bucket is poor; the family go around 'from morning till night with a horrible empty feeling in their tummies'. Charlie desperately wants something more filling than cabbage and cabbage soup. Augustus Gloop, on the other hand, is

> a nine year old boy who was so enormously fat he looked as though he had been blown up with a powerful pump. Great flabby folds of fat bulged out from every part of his body, and his face was like a monstrous ball of dough with two small greedy curranty eyes peering out upon the world.

His only joy in life is eating; his mother, who, sadly, seems to represent some twenty-first century ill-informed, unmotivated parents of obese children, says 'he wouldn't go on eating like he does unless he needed nourishment would he? It's all vitamins anyway.' However, fate has in store for Augustus Gloop a punishment which could have been dreamt up by

Hieronymus Bosch as a reward for gluttony in the after-life: whilst drinking molten chocolate from a river in the Chocolate Factory, he falls in and gets sucked up into a chocolate production pipe, 'shooting up head first like a torpedo' and getting stuck because of his girth.

> The watchers below could see the chocolate swishing round the boy in the pipe, and they could see it building up behind him in a solid mass, pushing against the blockage. The pressure was terrific. Something had to give. Something did give, and that something was Augustus. WHOOF! Up he shot again like a bullet in the barrel of a gun.

Augustus was transformed by the pressure of the tube to a thin shadow of his former self.

> Augustus Gloop! Augustus Gloop!
> The great big greedy nincompoop!
> How long could we allow this beast
> To gorge and guzzle, feed and feast
> On anything he wanted to?
> Great Scott! It simply wouldn't do!
> However long this pig might live
> We're positive he'd never give
> Even the smallest bit of fun
> Or happiness to anyone....

Roald Dahl often uses a grotesque obese form as the exaggerated incarnation of horrendous personality traits. Aunt Sponge and Aunt Spiker from *James and the Giant Peach* (1961), whose appropriate names add value to their personalities, are both described as really horrible people, selfish, lazy and cruel. Right from the beginning they started beating poor James for almost no reason.

> Aunt Sponge was enormously fat and very short. She had small piggy eyes, a sunken mouth, and one of those white flabby faces that looked exactly as though it had been boiled. She was like a great, white soggy overboiled cabbage. Aunt Spiker on the other hand was lean, tall and bony.

Comic books

Comic books have always featured obese characters [11-5]. Because of the nature of the medium – cheaply produced and bought, quickly read and discarded – there is no great depth of quality to the writing. Quick laughs and obvious jokes are required, and fat people provide easy targets for this sort of humour, whether by being portrayed as clumsy, ugly, lazy, gluttonous or low in intelligence. Spadger, of 'Spadger's Isle', the cover story of the early *Wizard* comics, who existed between 1925 and 1956, had an enormous apple-shaped belly. He was looked after by black labourers called the 'Nigs',

11-5
Calamity James and Minnie the Minx meet obese characters in their strips within the *Beano*.

who fed him constantly: 'De boys and gals am eagerly lookin' forward to a stoopendous feast ob scrambled egg'; 'De second course am scrambled egg, and so am de third *and* de dessert'.

Knuck(les), one of the 'Bad(d) Lads' from the *Beezer* comic (1956–93), is a gormless, obese criminal who, on having a policeman's torch shone in his ear, is revealed to have an almost empty skull, with just a lonely spider and a brain the size of a baked bean inside it. Another *Beezer* favourite was Beefy Dan, the Fast Food Man, a lazy, sweaty, foolish cook. Hungry Horace from the *Dandy* comic, which first appeared in December 1937, loved unsuitable food ('Mmm! I like cake I do!'). However, the ultimate weighty comic book character is from the Spiderman superhero mould rather than the butt of the joke like most obese characters. He is Captain Obese [C-17], created by Apple Comics in 1988, 'Great Protector' of the world of Awe-San-Tan, and Alter Ego of Milman Trite, a much ridiculed victim of anti-obesity discrimination on Earth. He is owner of the Ring of Rings which amplifies *all* the wearer's emotions 10-fold, making him appear when angered to be a ferocious fighter, but when frightened a pathetic coward. In his superhero role he is enemy of the Mirk-Mire Swamp-Nads and, having conquered them, he has the opportunity to return to Earth:

> I can stay here [on Earth] where I'm a joke, where I'm treated like something fat and ugly stuck to the bottom of society's shoe, or I can return to Awe-San-Tan where I'm revered and treated like a hero – where I'm loved by one and all.

(Awe-San-Tan is the opposite of another science fiction world, that inhabited by the characters in Peter Carey's *The Fat Man in History*, where obesity is utterly abhorred – see below, page 227.)

Billy Bunter

Of all obese literary characters, the most blatant stereotype of them all is surely the 'Fat Owl of the Remove', Billy Bunter (11-6). He is vividly portrayed as the incarnation of everything that society despises about fat people; there is no opportunity to like Bunter, and there is no effort made to apply any sympathetic characterisation. The writing is crammed with opportunities to loathe and detest him, to ridicule and poke fun at him and to marvel at his ineptitude. The reader is swept along on a tidal wave of anti-obesity discrimination yet in spite of, or perhaps because of, the opportunities that are given to make fun of Bunter, he has become a popular anti-hero of juvenile comic fiction.

Created by Frank Richards in 1908, he made his debut in the first issue of *Magnet* comic [C-18], as an inept, short-sighted, bumbling child, but initially only 'a somewhat stout junior with a broad pleasant face, and an enormous pair of spectacles'. In 1911 Charles Henry Chapman took over

11-6
Peter Bridgmont in *Billy Bunter Shipwrecked*, 1961.

the artwork for the character, and Bunter became morbidly obese, a glee-fully grinning schoolboy with a 'Fat Owl' appearance. He appeared in many comics, such as *Valient* and *Knockout*, in strip cartoons and stories, as well as in numerous novels, stage and radio plays, and a television series, in which he was played by Gerald Campion.

The stories in *Magnet* are based on life at 'Greyfriars', a fashionable, old foundation public school, such as Eton or Winchester, and the main characters are boys from the fourth form who, over a period of about 30 years, never aged or changed. The atmosphere remained constant and the world outside Greyfriars is non-existent. Good, clean fun was the essence of the stories, in which practical jokes, canings, football, cricket and food – especially food, as far as Bunter was concerned – played a large part; sex and religion played no part.[17]

Bunter was not the only one at Greyfriars to be portrayed as a hackneyed social stereotype; his entire class seemed to be made up of obvious 'humor-ous' clichéd characters, in contrast to whom Bunter stands out as even more of a grotesque misfit. There are titled boys, who lend an air of snobbishness to the surroundings, foreigners, who provide opportunities for racial stereo-typing, and a token mildly handicapped deaf boy, whose hearing disability is trivialised for the benefit of a few feeble word jokes, to be enjoyed by the target audience of young teenagers.

However stylised and objectionable the Bunter stories seem today, as far as the medical model of childhood obesity is concerned they contain grains of truth. As is usually the case in real life, there is no doubt what-soever about the cause of Bunter's weight problem – enormous quantities of energy-dense food and a sedentary lifestyle, including endless 'frowsting' in bed, or in front of a warm fire, and avoiding any kind of physical activity.

On one occasion, whilst the 'Famous Five' (a group of Bunter's class-mates in the Remove form at Greyfriars School) had spent a strenuous day swimming and playing cricket, Bunter, having taken part in neither of these activities, nonetheless felt a similar need to his classmates for rest following his consumption of as many 'sticky things as could be accommo-dated within his extensive circumference'.[18] Indeed, he liked nothing better than eating and resting. On another occasion:

> Billy Bunter was much more agreeably occupied than in handling an oar. He had had only one breakfast that morning, and that was more than an hour ago. So he had vacancies to fill. And his lunch basket was packed with innumerable juicy, jammy sticky things, in which his fat heart rejoiced. With nothing to do but to loll on cushions and consume one tasty sticky morsel after another, life seemed very good to Bunter.[19]

In another parallel to modern life, the comments of Bunter's classmates fairly accurately depict the discriminatory beliefs common amongst peer groups and even some teachers:

'Bunter,' said Mr Quelch, the schoolmaster, with slow, grim thought-fulness.

'I have come to the conclusion, Bunter, that you are wasting your time here – and my time. You are lazy, idle, greedy, undutiful, slack in class, and slack at games – in no respect whatsoever a credit to this school.'[20]

Other less than complimentary remarks made by his classmates include 'fat, lazy, slack little porker', 'podgy pirate', 'bloated brigand', 'fat, frabjous, footling, frumptious foozler!' and 'a lazy toad, and a slacking fat frog, and a prevaricating fat porker'.

Several co-morbidities of childhood obesity are fairly accurately depicted in the stories. Bunter frequently gets short of breath on minimal exertion:

The Famous Five trotted. A trot around the sunny quad was pleasant and exhilarating, after Latin and Quelch. But if the active and strenuous Co. found it so, Billy Bunter did not. Breath was always in short supply with Bunter: and trotting was not in his line at all. A dozen yards were enough for Bunter ... Bunter came to a gasping halt ... the Famous Five trotted on, leaving him pumping in breath.[21]

And Bunter is a snorer; his daytime fatigue and somnolence almost certainly diagnose him as suffering from sleep apnoea secondary to the mechanical bulk of fat around his neck pressing on his airways. This leads to disturbed sleep at night, with loud snoring, and daytime tiredness, which, in the long term, will lead to raised blood pressure and the risk of increased cardiovascular disease. Sufferers from this condition classically snore, then stop breathing for a number of seconds, grunt loudly and restart a regular breathing pattern (the Pickwickian syndrome – see page 25). Bob Cherry shakes the sleeping Bunter's shoulder on one occasion, causing Bunter's snore to 'modulate into a grunt'. Elsewhere his snore is described as gargantuan and Wagnerian and an unmelodious rumble. Evidence of his daytime somnolence is also widespread:

Bunter was not easy to wake. Having settled down to slumber again after the visit of the Famous Five, less than a minute had sufficed to plunge him once more into the embrace of Morpheus. There were few things that Bunter could do well: but sleeping was one of the few. In that line Bunter had hardly an equal. Rip Van Winkle had little or nothing on Bunter – even Epimenides of old could scarcely have beaten him.[22]

Another co-morbidity of childhood obesity is joint pain, from which Bunter frequently suffered, though often as a means to avoid games, and he is no stranger to accidental injury, the incidence of which is significantly increased in obesity; Bunter commonly falls out of trees and breaks branches, bridges and floors.

Bunter seems to have escaped any major degree of depression, which is also a common sequel to obesity. His occasional 'indignant and morose frames of mind' were usually to be blamed on inability to find food rather than on genuine mental health problems. His self-esteem is remarkably high, despite his ineptitude. At football, for instance:

> 'I'll play,' said Bunter magnanimously. 'You've got a rotten team old chap; but one really good man in the side may pull it together.... One jolly good man makes a lot of difference.'

And in life in general:

> 'Well, I think you fellows might be pally, when everybody else is letting me down all round!' said Bunter, pathetically. 'Anybody would think that I was some sort of a rotter, really, instead of the most decent chap in the Remove'.

Unfortunately, in clinical practice, long-term weight management in childhood obesity is notoriously difficult. The school doctor's attempts to get Bunter to lose weight, not surprisingly, are doomed to failure, possibly because of a total lack of motivation on Bunter's part. Food and avoiding exercise are the only interests he has, and without any social network, or family to guide him, he has little or no chance of success. So much does he dread the loss of what he regards as his 'fine' figure that he even takes Flummox's Fattening Fluid to nullify the effect of the school doctor's pre-scribed diet.

Although most social commentators would abhor the use of anti-obesity discrimination, or any other type of discrimination, as a basis for a humor-ous series of sketches, and would have pity for poor Billy's predicament, the Bunter series can, nevertheless, be judged in its historical context. Looking back from a modern perspective, most of what happens to Billy Bunter fits in well with social and clinical patterns still occurring today. What is perhaps most surprising, compared with modern schools, where the obesity epidemic is gaining momentum with frightening speed, is that, apart from his equally obese and gluttonous sister, Bessie, who figures in the *Schoolgirl* comic, and brother Bertie (reflecting a familial tendency to obesity), there are very few other obese or overweight individuals in these stories: the Bunters stand alone.

Piggy

However much one might deplore the use of obese children as the objects of ridicule in humorous sketches and comics, there are circumstances and events concerning obese children in literature that form a substantial and relevant part of the action. Here, obesity is real and its consequences are stark and uncomfortable.

As children grow older, fatness and to be fat can have an even more threatening prospect:

His voice came first. 'Hi!' it said, 'Wait a minute! I can't hardly move with all these creeper things.'

The owner of the voice came backing out of the undergrowth. The naked crooks of his knees were plump, caught and scratched with thorns. He was shorter than the fair boy and very fat.

The boy was Piggy from William Golding's novel *Lord of the Flies* (1954). Piggy was very fat, wore glasses and had asthma. 'I was the only boy in our school what had asthma', he proudly declares. In addition to his asthma, Piggy has a protective aunt: 'I used to live with my auntie. She kept a sweet-shop. I used to get ever so many sweets. As many as I liked.'[23] He was not allowed to swim.

Piggy had worn glasses since he was three; they connected him with a blurred and hazy world outside himself, with a society in which he found it difficult to integrate. He was different from the other children because he was fat – Piggy – and they were thin. The glasses, however, gave him some value on the island on which the children had become stranded, because they could be used to start a fire. Without them Piggy was vulnerable and unable to function. In the end, after his death, Ralph recognised that he had lost a true, wise friend. The other children, who had reverted to savagery, merely saw him as a bag of fat. When Piggy was felled by rocks, 'his arms and legs twitched a bit, like a pig's after it has been killed'.[24]

Piggy demonstrates some of the social ramifications of juvenile obesity, the isolation, the disability and the inability to take part in activities, the derision caused by being fat, and the ignominy of being called 'Piggy'. The cause of his obesity can be traced back to his protective auntie and her sweet shop and to his lack of exercise. To most of his peers, Piggy died in an appropriate fashion.

Obesity in adult literature

Depictions of obesity in adult literature, as might be expected, are more complicated than those found in books for children. To consider a person merely fat, corpulent or obese is to oversimplify the issue. Through literature, one may gain some insight into the causes of the obesity, be enabled to visualise the person beneath the enlarged exterior and come to understand the problems experienced by that individual, both in coping with life as a fat person and in trying to reduce weight. In his book *Never Satisfied* (1986), Hillel Schwartz wrote 'No diet comes without a larger social agenda'.

Being fat or stout can sometimes be regarded as appropriate for someone in a position of authority. Charles Dickens recognised this. Oliver Twist [11-7] from the eponymous 1838 novel had dared to ask for more gruel and was ordered into instant confinement:

'Please, sir, I want some more.'

The master was a fat, healthy man; but he turned very pale. He gazed in stupefied astonishment on the small rebel for some seconds, and then clung for support to the copper....

'Do I understand,' asked a gentleman of the Board, 'that he asked for more, after he had eaten the supper allotted by the dietary?'[25]

Now Mr Bumble [11-8], too, was a fat man and choleric. He perspired as he walked and had to mop his brow and recover with the help of some gin and water that Mrs Mann, the lady in charge of the baby-farm, happened to have to hand. He also had a great idea of his oratorical powers and his importance; he had, in other words, swollen into a public character. He was the beadle who was to take Oliver, who had just attained his ninth year, from the branch workhouse, where he had been farmed out as an infant, to the parish workhouse. There, Oliver had to appear before 'the board'.

Oliver was conducted into a large white-washed-room, where eight or ten fat gentlemen were sitting round a table. At the top of the table, seated in an arm-chair rather higher than the rest, was a particularly fat gentleman with a very round, red face.

The members of the board were very sage, deep, philosophical men; ... they contracted with the water-works to lay on an unlimited supply of water; and with the corn-factor to supply periodically small quantities of oatmeal; and issued three meals of thin gruel a day, with an onion twice a week, and half a roll on Sundays.

Mr Bumble degraded in the eyes of the Paupers

11-7
Oliver Twist asking for more.

11-8
Mr Bumble.

Initially, under this regimen, expenses at the workhouse increased as undertakers' bills soared and as the clothes of the paupers had to be taken in to prevent them from fluttering round their owners' wasted shrunken forms. 'Please, sir, I want some more', Oliver had said, his diminutive size and wants highlighting the distance between the orphans and their superiors.[26] Dickens made good use of stereotypical images to describe his characters, many of whom had names associated with their characteristics or their employment. Mr Bumble seemed aptly named.

Another description of obesity representing overblown corpulence and megalomania in officialdom comes from Robert Browning's poem 'The Pied Piper of Hamelin'. The council members stand by whilst the rats run riot. The town folk complain:

> 'Tis clear,' cried they, 'our Mayor's a noddy;
> 'To think we buy gowns lined with ermine
> 'For dolts that can't or won't determine
> 'What's best to rid us of our vermin!
> 'You hope, because you're old and obese,
> 'To find in the furry civic robe ease?
> 'Rouse up, sirs! Give your brains a racking
> 'To find the remedy we're lacking,
> 'Or, sure as fate, we'll send you packing!'

Joe was another of Dickens's larger characters. He is to be found in *The Pickwick Papers* (1836).

> Fastened up behind the barouche was a hamper of spacious dimensions – one of those hampers which always awakens in a contemplative mind associations connected with cold fowls, tongues, and bottles of wine – and on the box sat a fat and red-faced boy in a state of somnolency, whom no speculative observer could have regarded for an instant without setting down as the official dispenser of the contents of the before-mentioned hamper when the proper time for their consumption should arrive.
>
> 'Joe! – damn that boy, he's gone to sleep again – Joe, let down the steps.' The fat boy rolled slowly off the box, let down the steps, and held the carriage door invitingly open ... waddled to the same perch and fell fast asleep instantly.
>
> ... 'Very extraordinary boy, that,' said Mr. Pickwick. 'Does he always sleep in this way?'
>
> 'Sleep!' said the old gentleman. 'He's always asleep. Goes on errands fast asleep and snores as he waits at table.' ...
>
> The fat boy rose, opened his eyes, swallowed the huge piece of pie he had been in the act of masticating when he last fell asleep, and slowly obeyed his master's orders.[27]

Other descriptions of Joe variously tell of how 'a train of nods which the fat boy gave by way of assent communicated a blancmange-like motion to his fat cheek'; he is a 'bloated lad' and is noted for 'the utter vacancy

11-9
Mr Pickwick.

of his countenance'. By contrast, Mr Pickwick [11-9], who was also fat, was a cheery, plump man 'charged with energy.... He bursts, he beams, he bulges.'[28] Dickens may well have visited freak shows such as those described in Chapter 3 and seen characters like Joe. On one occasion he describes how 'The object that presented itself to the eyes of the astonished clerk was a boy – a wonderfully fat boy – habited as a serving lad, standing upright on the mat, with his eyes closed as if in sleep. He had never seen such a fat boy, in or out of a travelling caravan.' Dickens had allegedly modelled Joe on one James Budden, who had bullied Dickens in his childhood. In 1956 C. Sidney Burwell and colleagues coined the term 'Pickwickian syndrome' because a patient of theirs had similar breathing and sleep problems to Joe (see Chapter 2).

Obese characters inhabit many different kinds of literature and their presence is usually of some significance to the plot.

Falstaff in Shakespeare's *King Henry IV, Part 1* (c. 1597) and *Part 2* (c. 1599), as well as *The Merry Wives of Windsor* (1602), is presented as a buffoon – a character who led Henry astray as a youth – a gross, fat, fellow with more wit than grace, 'a boaster and a coward', a glutton and a thief, always ready to cheat the weak and prey upon the poor. Henry describes him as 'the tutor and feeder of my riots'. He had made himself indispensable to Prince Hal by his perpetual gaiety and unfailing power of exciting laughter – 'levity which makes sport but raises no envy'. But Falstaff is intended as a positive warning to Prince Henry. The Prince has a choice of role model between the chivalrous Hotspur and the decadent Falstaff. In act II, scene iv, the Prince sadly recognises Falstaff for what he is:

> there is a devil haunts thee in the likeness of a fat old man; a tun of man is thy companion. Why does thou converse with that trunk of humours, that bolting-hutch of beastliness, that swoln parcel of dropsies, that huge bombard of sack, that stuffed cloakbag of guts, that roasted Manningtree ox with the pudding in his belly, that reverend vice, that grey iniquity, that father ruffian, that vanity in years?[29]

When the Prince becomes King, he rejects Falstaff and, symbolically, his old lifestyle:

> I know thee not, old man. Fall to thy prayers:
> How ill white hairs become a fool and jester!
> I have long dreamed of such a kind of man,
> So surfeit-swelled, so old, and so profane:
> But being awake, I do despise my dream.
> Make less thy body hence, and more thy grace:
> Leave gourmandising: know the grave doth gape
> For thee thrice wider than for other men.[30]

From a bragging soldier in *Henry IV*, Falstaff had become an aged fat being – and possibly a sexually depleted male and a comic old man in *The Merry*

11-10
Falstaff.

Wives of Windsor [11-10]. The happy corpulence of his youth had become the melancholic obesity of old age.

Impotence, erectile dysfunction and infertility are all associated with obesity and – in spite of boasting of his sexual prowess and the presence of the stag's horns (as an indication of cuckolding) – these were likely to be Falstaff's lot, symbolically implicated in his ultimate lack of success with the ladies. Sexually transmitted disease, the pox or 'clap', was also the probable outcome of his lifestyle ('consorting with whores'). The 'pox' was likely to be syphilis. The name 'French gout' was often given to syphilis and 'gout' could be used as a symbol of lust, the two factors not being entirely dissociated. Falstaff reflects upon his state: 'A man can no more separate age and covetousness than he can part young limbs and lechery. But the gout galls the one and the pox pinches the other'.[31] Shakespeare likened Falstaff's own bodily corruption with the disruption he could cause to the body politic or state if he continued to influence the prince.

Falstaff encompasses all aspects of a corpulent male body throughout his life. He is the epitome of British obesity and as such sets a benchmark for literary portrayal of the obese male body.

In contrast to the wishes of Henry, Shakespeare's Julius Caesar desired a fat man's presence rather than that of the gaunt Cassius in Shakespeare's play of that name. He was wary of the lean man, whom he perceived as plotting against him. The soothsayer had warned him to 'Beware the Ides of March'. His fear led him to say:

Let me have men about me that are fat;
Sleek-headed men and such as sleep o' nights;
Yond' Cassius has a lean and hungry look;
He thinks too much: such men are dangerous.[32]

Stereotypical figures are also shorthand for character references. Lady Bracknell in Oscar Wilde's *The Importance of Being Earnest* (1895) needs only her embonpoint to signify her own importance and stature. Portly elderly widows, aunts and mothers inhabit many nineteenth-century novels. Their size denotes their significance in the unfolding drama. Their physical inactivity, compounded by motherhood, age, obesity and habit, is contrasted with their lively machinations on behalf of the young, active, slender female members of the families in their search for suitable (rich and well appointed) husbands.

A description of a particular character, Mrs Musgrove, in Jane Austen's *Persuasion* (published posthumously in 1818), offers a rather unkind vision of one such fat woman:

[Anne Elliot and Captain Wentworth] were actually on the same sofa, for Mrs. Musgrove had most readily made room for him; they were divided only by Mrs. Musgrove. It was no insignificant barrier, indeed. Mrs. Musgrove was of a comfortable substantial size, infinitely more fitted by nature to express good cheer and good humour, than tenderness and sentiment; and while the agitations of Anne's slender form, and pensive face, may be considered as very completely screened, Captain Wentworth should be allowed some credit for the self-command with which he attended to her large fat sighings over the destiny of a son, whom alive nobody had cared for.

Personal size and mental sorrow have certainly no necessary proportions. A large bulky figure has as good a right to be in deep affliction, as the most graceful set of limbs in the world. But, fair, or not fair, there are unbecoming conjunctions, which reason will patronize in vain, – which taste cannot tolerate, – which ridicule will seize.[33]

Such words as 'ample', 'comely' and 'stout' are often used to describe these women. George Eliot's chubby Mrs Tulliver in *The Mill on the Floss* (1860) had, for a woman of 50, 'a very comely face and figure'. On one occasion when she had been in the act of brushing Maggie's hair and the girl had escaped her reach, Mrs Tulliver had been left 'sitting stout and helpless with the brushes on her lap'.

In Victorian literature it seems to be accepted that women will become overweight with age – fair, fat and 50. Mrs Peckover in Wilkie Collins' *Hide and Seek* (1854) is one such figure on whom 'time had lavishly added to her size'. Flora Finching in Dickens' *Little Dorrit* (1855–57), 'always tall, had grown to be very broad too, and short of breath'. Indeed, Flora, who had been a 'lily', had turned into a 'peony'. Recent research bears this out to some extent; it has been shown that body fat in elderly women is about 5 per cent greater than in young women.[34]

The more 'earthy' Mrs Gamp in Dickens' *Martin Chuzzlewit* (1843–44) was 'a fat old woman'; her size was of a different type than that of the more 'polite' maternal variety. 'The face of Mrs. Gamp – the nose in particular – was somewhat red and swollen, and it was difficult to enjoy her society without becoming conscious of a smell of spirits.' She was definitely not a lady; she was a low comic character who provided some relief in a time of trouble; as a monthly nurse or 'midwife', 'she went to a lying-in or a laying-out with equal zest and relish'. She was not comely, ample, broad or stout: she was just fat.

Another famous fat caricature is featured in the famous Geordie love song 'Cushie Butterfield', by George Ridley (1834–64):

> You'll oft see her down at Sandgate when the fresh herring come
> She's like a bag full of sawdust tied round with a string
> She wears big galoshes too and her stockings once was white
> And her petticoat's lilac and her hat's never straight
> She's a big lass and a bonny lass and she likes her beer
> And they call her Cushie Butterfield and I wish she was here.

Such characters as Mrs Gamp and Cushie Butterfield had no pretensions.

Having no elderly relative – fat or otherwise – to work on her behalf, wily Becky Sharp was on the lookout for her own husband in William Makepeace Thackeray's *Vanity Fair* (1848); she must make her own way in the world. 'If Mr. Joseph Sedley is rich and unmarried, why should I not marry him?' she asked herself before even having met this character. Her first sight of him was of 'a very stout, puffy man, in buckskins and Hessian boots, with several immense neckcloths, that rose almost to his nose, with red-striped waistcoat and an apple-green coat with steel buttons almost as large as crown pieces'.[35] This was the morning costume of a dandy of the day, as worn by such men as Beau Brummel. Joseph obviously liked to think of himself as quite a fellow, but:

> His bulk caused Joseph much anxious thought and alarm; now and then he would make a desperate attempt to get rid of his superabundant fat; but his indolence and love of good living speedily got the better of these endeavours at reform and he found himself again at his three meals a day. He had tried, in order to give himself a waist, every girth, stay, and waistband then invented. Like most fat men, he *would* have his clothes too tight, and took care they should be of the most brilliant colours and youthful cut.[36]

As did Milligan, in Carey's *The Fat Man in History* (discussed below): '[he] wears his clothes like corsets, always too tight. He says it is good for his blood, the tightness. But his flesh erupts in strange bulges from his thighs and stomach and arms.'[37]

Joseph Sedley is the 'pathetic fat boy whose body mirrors his weak character'.[38] This literary fat boy symbolises loss of moral control and weakness of will. These are demonstrated on a visit to Vauxhall, where Becky is expecting him to make a proposal of marriage. He lacks courage and, in a vain attempt to rise to the occasion, consumes the contents of a bowl of rack punch. The then inebriated 'fat gourmand' receives applause from those who have gathered round to listen to his singing and jesting. 'Brayvo, Fat un!' said one; 'Angcore, Daniel Lambert!' said another.[39] Readers at that time would have been able to identify Sedley with this enormous and popular figure (on whom see Chapter 2).

Many modern readers will be able to identify with Joseph's desperate attempt to get rid of his super-abundant fat – the good intentions to lose weight, the initial success followed by the overwhelming desire for food and an uncontrollable urge to eat. This is inevitably followed by a gain in weight. A short story published in 2003 illustrates the problem:

> For a solid year [Father Murray] held himself to eleven hundred exacting calories a day, eating two bananas for breakfast and a salad with vinegar for lunch. His weight plummeted; his profile shrank from Friar Tuck to Duns Scotus, and the waist of his trousers bunched like a paper bag.

Father Thomas Murray was a philosophy lecturer in a seminary in Erin McGraw's short story 'Ax of the Apostles'.[40] Fourteen months previously he had been warned by his doctor about his blood sugar levels and glucose intolerance and reminded of his family history. He had a 45-inch waist, extra chins and podgy fingers. His downfall came without warning; glasses of water and other tricks by which he had tried to stave off hunger no longer worked. One night he awoke and let his hunger 'propel him to the kitchen'. He ate two and a half pieces of cheesecake, went back to bed and slept as if pole-axed.

> Since then Father Murray had hardly gone a night without stealing downstairs for some snack – cookies, cake, whatever the seminarians and other priests, those wolves, had left. He stored his cache in a plastic bag and kept the bag in his desk drawer, allowing himself to nibble between classes, in the long afternoon lull before dinner, whenever the hunger roared up in him.

His hunger was becoming a kind of insanity. Food never left his mind.

> Nightly he ate directly from the refrigerator, shovelling fingerfuls of leftover casserole into his mouth, wolfing slice after slice of white bread. He dunked cold potatoes through the gravy's mantle of congealed fat, scooped up leathery cheese sauce. During the daytime he carried on the pretence of eating frugally.... For a week now he hadn't been able to button his trousers.

Father Murray's plight is typical of those suffering from binge-eating disorder (see page 31).

Although corpulence is usually contemplated with dismay, one immensely fat figure in fiction was considered by one particular lady as intriguing. In Wilkie Collins' *The Woman in White* (1859), Count Fosco, one of the main characters in the book, is described in the Introduction to the Everyman edition as 'the most convincing master criminal in fiction'. He, too, is a huge figure, though surprisingly light on his feet. Marian Halcombe, a heroine in the book, offers her thoughts about him:

> he is immensely fat. Before this time I have always especially disliked corpulent humanity. I have always maintained that the popular notion of connecting excessive grossness of size and excessive good humour as inseparable allies was equivalent to declaring, either that no people but amiable people ever get fat, or that the accidental addition of so many pounds of flesh has a directly favourable influence over the disposition of the person on whose body they accumulate … nevertheless, is Count Fosco, as fat as Henry the Eighth himself, established in my favour, without let or hindrance from his own odious corpulence.[41]

The peculiarity of Fosco's face intrigues Marian: she likens his features, on a large scale, with those of the 'great Napoleon'. His fat dominates his face; it is his fat that makes his face interesting. Brillat-Savarin (1755–1826), an author and connoisseur of the art of gastronomy and cooking, comments on how 'obesity fills up those hollows which nature formed to add highlights and shadows'.[42] Fatness, he maintains, usually makes faces 'insignificant' but not, apparently, in the case of Fosco, whose closely shaven physiognomy is smoother and freer from all marks and wrinkles than that of the commentator, Marian, though 'he is close on sixty years of age'. His wrinkle-free face, although intriguing to Marian, would, however, seem to fulfil Brillat-Savarin's prophecy with regard to obesity.

A successful twenty-first-century individual who sets out to catch villains can boast similar weight. This is the African lady Mma Ramotswe, in Alexander McCall Smith's *The No. 1 Ladies' Detective Agency*.[43] In a culture that values size and gives weight its due recognition, this lady sleuth is both respected and admired: 'Mma Ramotswe was not tall – being blessed with generous girth, rather than height'[44] and 'Her weight was hardly a confidential matter, and anyway, she was proud of being a traditionally built African lady, unlike these terrible stick-like creatures one saw in advertisements'.[45]

Investigating the suspicious behaviour of a client's husband, thought by his wife to be 'carrying on with ladies', Mma Ramotswe sets a trap for the amorous man. She meets him in a bar, has a few drinks with him and invites him to her home.

Then he put his arm around her waist, and told her that he liked good, fat women. All this business about being thin was nonsense and was quite wrong for Africa.

'Fat women like you are what men really want,' he said.[46]

The outcome of this case, though, was not quite what the betrayed wife expected and when she was confronted with a contrived photograph of the detective in the arms of her husband, her reaction to the fat woman was 'You fat bitch! You husband-stealer! Thief!' Beauty is in the eye of the beholder.

It is not difficult to 'behold' the vision of Mrs Manson Mingott, the venerable ancestress of Edith Wharton's *Age of Innocence* (1920). She is the literary embodiment of woman made flesh:

The immense accretion of flesh which had descended on her in middle life like a flood of lava on a doomed city had changed her from a plump active little woman with a neatly-turned foot and ankle into something as vast and august as a natural phenomenon. She had accepted this submergence as philosophically as all her other trials, and now, in extreme old age, was rewarded by presenting to her mirror an almost unwrinkled expanse of firm pink and white flesh, in the centre of which the traces of a small face survived as if awaiting excavation. A flight of double chins led down to the dizzy depths of a still-snowy bosom veiled in snowy muslins that were held in place by a miniature portrait of the late Mr. Mingott, and around and below, wave after wave of black silk surged away over the edges of a capacious armchair, with two tiny white hands poised like gulls on the surface of the billows.

The burden of Mrs. Mingott's flesh had long since made it impossible for her to go up and down stairs, and with characteristic independence she had made her reception rooms upstairs and established herself (in flagrant violation of all the New York properties) on the ground floor of the house.[47]

Mrs Mingott was an intrepid woman with an active mind and dominating will. She 'throned' in her cream-coloured house and people talked about her age and her spirit. This spirit was in evidence when, in spite of her corpulence-induced infirmities and the consternation of her relations, it had been rumoured that she would attend her granddaughter's wedding:

bets ran high at the clubs as to her being able to walk up the nave and squeeze into a seat. It was known that she had insisted on sending her own carpenter to look into the possibility of taking down the end panel of the front pew, and to measure the space between the seat and the front; but the result had been discouraging and for one anxious day her family had watched her dallying with the plan of being wheeled up the nave in her enormous bath-chair and sitting enthroned in it at the foot of the chancel.[48]

Her relations were greatly relieved when it was discovered that the chair was too wide to pass between the iron uprights of the awning that extended from the church door to the curbstone. The very idea of the monstrous exposure of her person had caused them much pain.

But later, in spite of her will and determination, Mrs Mingott succumbed to one of the consequences of obesity:

> at three in the morning the bell rang again, and the two servants, hastening in at the unwonted summons (for old Catherine usually slept like a baby), had found their mistress sitting up against her pillows with a crooked smile on her face and one little hand hanging limp from its huge arm.[49]

A stroke, such as that suffered by Mrs Mingott, is one of the co-morbidities associated with obesity, particularly when combined with lack of mobility, as was the case with regard to this venerable lady. It has, in fact, been suggested and widely accepted that inactivity can be considered as the fourth primary risk factor for stroke and coronary heart disease.[50] Obesity compounds the problem. Mrs Mingott, this wonderfully described character – like many of those who in real life have suffered a stroke – was never quite the same again.

In Peter Carey's surrealistic story of a fat-man revolution, *The Fat Man in History* (1995), the obese are rejected, outlawed and cast out from society. In this revolutionary society 'the word "fat" entered slyly into the language as a new adjective, as a synonym for greedy, ugly, sleazy, lazy, obscene, evil, dirty, dishonest, untrustworthy'.[51] 'It was unfair. It was not a good time to be a fat man.' Six fat men live together in a ramshackle house in a run-down, but once respectable, district of an American town. Only one of them earns his living – as a taxi driver; the others exist on their pensions and on stolen goods. Fantoni is the leader and driving force of the 'Fat Men Against The Revolution'. Alexander Finch is the Secretary but cannot bring himself to hate the revolutionaries as the others do. He has sadly realised that the way in which he viewed himself had changed with that of the world. He had previously thought of himself as possessing a lovable face and figure, known by such names as 'Cuddles', 'Teddy' or 'Teddy Bear'. But fat is now no longer acceptable. Viewing himself in a mirror, he sees 'four large rolls of fat descending like a flesh curtain suspended from his navel. His spare tyres. He holds the fat in his hand, clenching it, wishing to tear it away.'[52]

A plan of action is conceived by Fantoni whereby the fat men actually consume a senior member of the revolution (the establishment), or a monument of the revolution. This could be seen as a noble act, consuming what was good and excreting the bad. Fantoni digs a trench. Finch helps. Coke and wood are brought in for the barbecue but in the end it is not for a member of the revolution but for Fantoni. The fat man is consumed and another 'Fantoni' takes the leader's place.

Gustav Doré's depiction of
Don Quixote with his servant,
Sancho Panza.

The pairing of fat and thin is a device used by artists and writers alike. The first book of Cervantes' *Don Quixote* (1605) provides one example of this [11-11]. Cervantes drew from life and incorporated in his book ideas of the romance of chivalry in his day. The business of the knight-errant was to right wrongs, to succour the needy and to redress injuries. Quixote is the intrepid, mad, thin knight whose madness is confined to delusions on the subject of chivalry, who seldom eats because, in books of knighthood, knights are seldom seen eating; he becomes 'so long and lank, so hollow and lean', whereas his servant, Sancho Panza ('Mr Gut'), lives to eat and drink and does so whenever and wherever the opportunity arises. In contrast to Quixote, he has 'a big belly, short body and long shanks'. 'There is one part of you that wishes to be a hero or a saint, but another part of you is a little fat man who sees very clearly the advantages of staying alive with a whole skin.'[53]

Gigantism

Treatment for obesity forms part of the action in the satirical writing of the sixteenth-century monk turned priest and doctor François Rabelais. His novels in the series 'Gargantua and Pantagruel' (describing an eponymous father and son pair of giants) are allegorical skits on the extravagances and excesses of princes. Gargantua's father, Grangousier or Great Gullet, drank more than any other man on earth and ate large amounts of salted meat, which made him drink even more. Before Gargantua was born, his mother ate – despite warnings – '16 quarters, 2 bushels, and 6 pecks of dubious tripe'. Her pregnancy lasted for 11 months, after which Gargantua was born via her left ear. He proceeded to cry 'Drink, drink, drink', and 17,913 cows were ordered for his daily supply of milk. When he was 22 months old, on the advice of physicians, he was taken out in a special ox-cart.

> He had a fine face and almost 18 chins; and he cried very seldom. For he was amazingly phlegmatic in his actions, partly from natural character and partly for accidental reasons connected with overindulgence in the new wines of September. But he never drank a drop without reason. For if by chance he was vexed, angry, displeased, or peeved, if he stamped, if he wept or if he screamed, they always brought him drink to restore his temper, and immediately he became quiet and happy.

He became a by-word for gluttony and lust. Later, a sober regimen was devised for Gargantua, after he had been drugged and purged of his corrupt and perverse habits:

> This is the proper regime prescribed by the art of good, sound medicine, although a rabble of foolish physicians, worn out by the wrangling of the sophists, advise the contrary.... Gargantua's dinner was sober and frugal, for he only ate enough to stay the gnawings of his stomach. But his supper was copious and large, for then he took all that he needed to stay and nourish himself.

On wet days, when Gargantua and his companions got home for supper:

> they ate more soberly than on other days, of more desiccative and extenuating dishes, as a method of correcting the humid inclemency of the air, communicated to the body by necessary proximity, and so they might receive no harm from not having taken their usual exercise.

Rabelais's Gargantua was no ordinary obese man; he was a giant of a man, gigantic in all his qualities and appetites [11-12]. 'During the Renaissance the notion of the fat man as the condemned body on his way to Hell (as in Giotto's paintings) merges with the huge male body of Rabelais's Gargantua.' He was to be compared with the ascetics with their thin, gaunt features, which were a sign of moral virtue. Giants were not necessarily obese:

> [they] are huge because they consume everything, and they consume everything because they are huge. Food, and therefore gluttony, is central to their representation, yet they are not obese in the pathological sense, they are related to the medieval giants, who are simply oversized exempla of human beings.[54]

In *The Fourth Book of Pantagruel*, Rabelais introduces 'two sorts of troublesome and too officious apparitors, whom he very much detested.

11-12
Gargantua.

The first were called Engastrimythes; the others, Gastrolaters.' The former were 'soothsayers, enchanters, cheats, who gulled the mob, and seemed not to speak and give answers from the mouth, but from the belly'. And the Gastrolaters were:

> merry, wanton, and soft as so many milk-sops; … louring, grim, dogged, demure, and crabbed; all idle, mortal foes to business, spending half their time in sleeping and the rest in doing nothing, a rent-charge and dead unnecessary weight on the earth, as Hesiod saith; afraid, as we judged, of offending or lessening their paunch.

Pantagruel compared them to the Cyclops Polyphemus, whom Euripides brings in speaking thus: 'I only sacrifice to myself – not to the gods – and to this belly of mine, the greatest of all the gods'.

The Gastrolaters make sacrifices to a statue called Manduce, and caricature those who worship food and can think of nothing else. Therapist Mildred Klingman describes the modern-day equivalent:

When a fat person seems to be only half listening, when her mind seems to be wandering, when she's bored she's thinking about food. As a fat person, you have food on your mind almost all of the time. As soon as breakfast is over you begin to think about what you're going to have for lunch. After lunch, its time to think about dinner, or stocking the refrigerator for tomorrow.[55]

The Gastrolaters 'were followed by a great number of fat waiters and tenders, laden with baskets, dossers, hampers, dishes, wallets, pots, and kettles' as they worshipped their god, and provided him with over 100 courses, including chitterlings garnished with mustard, neats' tongues, hogs' haslets, powdered venison with turnips, pheasant and pheasant poots, peacocks, storks, woodcocks, flamingoes, cygnets, soused hogs' feet and whores' farts!

Gargantua's name lives on to describe what is overwhelmingly gross.

Rabelais is not confined to conventional language in his description of these obese, gluttonous beings; he describes them as 'lounging gulligutted Gastrolaters', 'lusty, gorbellied fellows', 'idle lobcocks'.

Another author who described obesity using combinations of sounds and syllables onomatopoeically was James Joyce in *Ulysses* (1922). His descriptions of fat people was from the gut rather than the dictionary, and allowed him to reveal his feelings unhampered by standard rules of grammar, allowing full emotional rein:

> Dullthudding Guinness's barrels. It passed statelily up the staircase, steered by an umbrella, a solemn beardframed face. The broadcloth back ascended each step: back. All his brains are in the nape of his neck, Simon Dedalus says. Welts of flesh behind on him. Fat folds of neck, fat, neck, fat, neck.
> Ben Dollard bulkily cachuchad towards the bar, mightily praisefed and all big roseate, on heavyfooted feet, his gouty fingers nakkering castagnettes in the air.
> (BEN JUMBO DOLLARD, RUBICUND, MUSCLEBOUND, HAIRYNOSTRILLED, HUGEBEARDED, CABBAGEEARED, SHAG-GYCHESTED, SHOCKMANED, FAT-PAPPED, STANDS FORTH, HIS LOINS AND GENITALS TIGHTENED INTO A PAIR OF BLACK BATHING BAGSLOPS.)

Obesity and gender in literature

It would seem that, in many instances, in literary terms, for men to be 'big' is commendable, powerful, rich and influential, but to be grossly big, obese or corpulent is to be set apart from the normal, and such men's habits and other attributes are more gross. Fat men in literature are extremes, and if not jolly or villainous are extremely weak-willed or socially inept. Thus the villain Fosco is more villainous than most villains and the clown in Falstaff more jolly, but his downfall more sad. Obesity can also be associated with lack of self-control, as in the character of Joseph Sedley – a young man who cannot be seen as a 'big', commendable and influential man. His excess weight and behaviour are seen as risible and his frequent attempts at dieting were unsustained and unsuccessful. Obesity is less acceptable in young women, although after middle age and childbearing some increase in weight is acceptable, even normal; obese older women, such as Mrs Mingott and Mrs Musgrove, may then be treated with indulgence, humour and tolerance. Some women, such as the Wife of Bath and Mrs Gamp, are crude enough and sharp enough through life experience to be confident despite obesity; they are the low-class comic characters who are set up as a foil to their 'superiors'.

Psychological aspects of obesity

Some more recent works of fiction draw attention to the psychological aspects of obesity. The storyline may be based on the hidden reason for uncontrolled eating and weight gain. For example, the central character in Fay Weldon's *The Fat Woman's Joke* (1967) is a woman who has an unrequited need for love and fulfilment. She turns to food as a substitute – an emotional crutch.

Conversely, a woman wishing to escape from the trap of marriage and maternity might become anorexic. Margaret Atwood's *Edible Woman* (1969) represents one such instance. Marian, the main character in the book, becomes engaged to marry a respectable and handsome man who is training to be a lawyer. By all appearances it is a suitable match, but Marian suddenly finds certain food distasteful to her: it seems to come alive. A piece of sponge cake 'felt cellular against her tongue, like the bursting of thousands of tiny lungs. She shuddered and spat the cake into her napkin.' Rice pudding, which she resorted to as her staple diet, suddenly became 'a collection of small cocoons. Cocoons with miniature living creatures inside.' This mental anthropomorphisation of food was accompanied by feelings of being taken over and 'consumed' herself. She visualised her future as fitting into a pattern but not one of her own making. She dreaded 'waking up in the morning one day and finding she had already changed without being aware of it'. Only when she literally ran away from the proposed wedding and afterwards said accusingly to her fiancé, 'You've been trying to destroy me, haven't you? You've been trying to assimilate me', was she able to eat normally again.

Louise in Andre Dubus' *The Fat Girl* (1995) typifies an insatiable desire for food. From childhood, her mother had sought to keep her daughter slim on the pretext that boys would not want anything to do with her if she were fat and she would never make a good marriage. Consequently, Louise went through childhood 'hungry and angry and thinking of food'. She became a secret eater.

Food can be a strong weapon. Its refusal can be a form of emotional blackmail; its consumption can be a source of revenge or self-punishment or of consolation and comfort. Many obese people, especially women, have poor self-esteem and a poor self-image. They tend to withdraw from social contact in order to avoid unpleasant remarks. Being obese unfairly invites dislike, rejection, criticism, ridicule and disparagement. Withdrawal from social contact means loss of friends and subsequent loneliness. Eating then becomes a form of consolation and a vicious circle is set up. It may be that, in some circumstances, obesity is an excuse to avoid sexual relations or to find a suitable job.

True grossness or corpulence was evident and literally on show in freak shows and circuses in the nineteenth and twentieth centuries, especially in America. Canadian writer Robertson Davies describes the lifestyle, as well as some of the physical and psychological problems, of one particular obese individual, Happy Hannah, in his novel *World of Wonders* (1975), the third novel in his Deptford trilogy. He describes a carnival show from 1918:

> A Fat Lady or Fat Man is almost a necessity for a show. Just as the public is fascinated by automata, it is unappeasable in its demand for fat people. A Human Skeleton is hardly worth having if he can't do something else – grow hair to his feet, or eat glass, or otherwise distinguish himself. But a Fat Lady merely has to be fat. Happy Hannah weighed 487 lb; all she needed to do was show herself sitting in a large chair, and her living was assured.[56]

Davies' fat woman follows closely with tradition: the name Happy Hannah combines light-hearted alliteration with the implication of a cheerful disposition at all times. Her performance was a 'loud harangue', introduced by her talker as '487 pounds of good humour and chuckles'; she 'wore a wig, a very youthful chestnut affair, curly and flirtatious; a kiss curl coiled like a watchspring in front of each rosy ear'. She wore a pink cotton romper suit.

Davies explores Happy Hannah's psychological make-up in great detail. How much of this is from genuine knowledge of fat ladies, and how much is his assumption of the truth of the cliché of fat jolly people being sad beneath the veneer is unclear. Either way, Hannah is far from happy. Her physical burden took its toll by 'copious sweating, in a person whose bodily creases may be twelve inches deep':

> Three or four times a day, Hannah had to retire to the women's part of the dressing tent, and there Gus stripped her down and powdered her in those difficult areas with cornstarch.
>
> [She] looked fairly jolly sitting on her platform, in a suit of pink cotton rompers, [but] a sorry mass of blubber when she was bent forward, her hands on the back of a chair; her monstrous abdomen hung almost to her knees, and her breasts hung like half-filled wallets of suet far down on her belly.

> A weekly event of some significance was Hannah's Saturday night bath. First Gus would bustle down the aisle with a large tarpaulin and an armful of towels. Then Hannah, in an orange mobcap and a red dressing-gown, would lurch and stumble down the car.... Gus spread the tarpaulin, Hannah stood on it hanging on to the wash basin, and Gus swabbed her down with a large sponge. Drying Hannah took a long time, because there were large portions of her that she could not reach herself, and Gus used to towel her down.[57]

Psychologically Hannah gave merely 'an impression of sunny good nature'. Elements of clinical depression are only hinted at in her depiction as an unhappy, humourless unpopular Bible-basher:

> She forced her laughter.... She pushed laughter out of herself in wheezing whooping cries, and her face became unpleasantly marbled with dabs of a darker red under the rouge she wore. Her collops[58] wobbled uncontrollably, her vast belly heaved and trembled as she sucked breath, and sometimes she attempted to slap her thigh, producing a wet splat of sound. Fat Ladies ought not to tell jokes; their mirth is of the flesh, not of the mind; a chuckle is all they can manage without putting a dangerous strain on their breathing and circulatory system.[59]

While this seems a jaundiced and discriminatory view of the subject, nevertheless the description of the circumstances of a super-obese circus fat lady stands up to scrutiny. Robertson Davies' stereotypical fat lady appeared outwardly jolly, but was inwardly sad and angry.

Conclusion

The obese have often provoked mixed reactions. Some have been regarded as jolly, pleasure loving but weak willed; others are seen as lazy and self-indulgent, even repulsive. Obese characters in literature mirror those of obese people in society as a whole; their problems are those of real people. Studying them may lead to some insight into the treatment and management of the social and psychological problems of obesity. Some sufferers may even gain some insight into their condition by reading about such characters as Marian and Louise.[60]

The characteristics described in obese literary figures generally reflect the more widespread subjective perceptions of obesity at the time the book was written. Such characters add substance and realism to a story in addition to providing a foil or contrast to what was perceived as 'normality'. Fat can be bloated and 'slothful' like Dickens' Joe; jolly, like Mr Pickwick; pathetic and the object of bullies, like Golding's Piggy; or a warning to others, like Falstaff.

The presence of obesity has become more prevalent in Western society during the past three decades and is increasing. Its presence in literature has, though, remained fairly constant. This may be because the obese person is depicted for a specific purpose in the context of the story and thus necessitates the inclusion of only a few stereotypical characteristics of obesity. However, as the obesity epidemic takes hold, some modern writers are beginning to recognise the consequences of obesity. The poet Conrad Hilberry, for example, writes in 'Fat' about a little girl who imagines her fat as something forced upon her in a car. The thin person inside wishes to get out:

> Wait. What you see is another person
> hanging here. I am the girl who jumps
> the Hodgman's fence so quick they never see me.
> Skipping rope, I always do hot peppers.
> But once on the way home I got in a strange
> car. I screamed and beat on the windows,
> but they smiled and held me. They said I could go
> when I put on the costume, so I climbed
> into it, pulled up the huge legs,
> globby with veins, around my skinny shins,
> Pulled on this stomach that flops over itself,
> I pushed my arm past the hanging elbow fat
> Down into the hands and fingers, tight
> Like a doctor's glove stuffed with Vaseline.
> I hooked the top behind my neck, with these
> two bladders bulging over my flat chest.
> Then I pulled the rubber mask down over
> my head and tucked in the cheek and chin
> folds at the neck hiding the seam. I hate
> the smell. When they pushed me out of the car,
> I slipped and staggered as though the street
> Was wet with fish oil. You see what this costume is.
> If you will undo me, if you will loan me a knife,
> I will step out the way I got in.[61]

CHAPTER 12

Popular images of obesity

Historians of medicine have traditionally been wary of the use of pictures as evidence of different aspects of medical practice because of the degree of artistic licence and personality cults often involved. Nonetheless, it is becoming increasingly clear that imagery is culturally determined and that the subjective perceptions of art and literature can be seen as part of the story of medicine and social history. As such, a study of obesity in art can provide useful information regarding the presence of obesity and perceptions of how it has been viewed over the years. However, account must be taken of the nature and the function of the images produced and these should be read not as straightforward documents but within a framework of recognisable artistic practices. For example, artists use images as part of their vocabulary to express meaning in narrative but their views may be biased and their images do not necessarily reflect the true picture in society as a whole. They might have a hidden agenda within their pictures, perhaps depicting obesity allied with immorality, as in the images of Degas's prostitutes, or incorporating some political, sexist or racist message.

Portraits conformed to the artistic conventions of the time and are usually sober and traditional. When to be stout and to have good embonpoint was equivalent to being prosperous and successful, obese figures in art seemed unremarkable, such as Frans Hals' group portraits of Dutch burgers, painted in the seventeenth century. Those who were successful could afford to commission portraits of themselves and had no desire to hide one of the markers of their success. However, such images do not represent society as a whole.

Apparent size, though, was not necessarily a sign of obesity; rulers, for example, often had padded clothing to add size and gravitas to their image. Any disfigurements or unacceptable attributes of a sitter were often omitted from the canvas.

To obtain a true picture of obesity in society as a whole over a long period of time, a wide range of images by different artists is required. In a short survey, as in this book, some selection of images is necessary and this has its drawbacks. Bearing this caveat in mind, representations of obesity in art do offer an interesting survey of the subject and give some indication of how public perceptions have changed over time. The focus here is not on fine art as such, but on three arguably more commercially driven forms of visual art: satirical prints and cartoons primarily from the eighteenth and early nineteenth centuries; political prints and cartoons from the same period and up to the present; and seaside postcards from the twentieth century.

Figuratively speaking: Hogarth and Rowlandson

> prints represent a pictorial rendering of the flow of events, moods and fashions and reflect social attitudes of the day.[1]

Until the eighteenth century, artists were restricted in the freedom of their work by the bonds of patronage, and young artists were encouraged to emulate the works of the Old Masters such as Raphael, Michelangelo and Leonardo, at the expense of original expression. Traditionally, paintings had consisted of religious, mythological, epic and historical themes, subjects that were considered by the art critics to be spiritually uplifting and of moral value to the nation. One artist rebelled against these ideas in the eighteenth century. He thought that such paintings were irrelevant to contemporary life and he sought free expression in his work. This was William Hogarth.

Hogarth produced series of engravings from his paintings and sold prints from them by subscription. He said these were 'Modern Moral Subjects' and they were narrative paintings of contemporary themes: every picture tells a story, or more than one story. The eighteenth century was regarded as the golden age of literary satire, the era of Gay, Swift, Pope and Fielding. Hogarth matched contemporary writers with his graphic works. Because his works were based on contemporary life, they provide valuable information with regard to perceptions of the time on many topics, including body images.

Once an ideal figure was defined (see Chapter 10), satirical artists such as William Hogarth could illustrate figures outside this norm to make some narrative point. To satirise and ridicule a subject in a work of art does not necessarily invalidate the use of that work as resource material for historical study. Satire, to be effective, has to be based on the truth if its message is to be understood. 'Prints reflect social attitudes of the day';[2] thus, amongst other things, they reflect social attitudes towards body size. Hogarth's 'Modern Moral Subjects' have also been called 'novels in paint' and they epitomise a way of life and warn against the evils of sin. They satirise the lifestyle of certain character types of the eighteenth century and

12-1
Detail from 'Marriage
à-la-Mode', Part 1, Hogarth,
c. 1745.

are often inhabited by well known contemporary figures in thin disguise. Hogarth frequently made use of stereotypical features for his characters and employed visual puns where appropriate.

Images of obesity or corpulence and leanness have often been used in graphic art as social indicators, increasing size denoting increasing social status. Hogarth was a social commentator *par excellence* and uses this device, for example, in the first of his series of paintings of 'Marriage à-la-Mode' (c. 1745), in which he also indicates recognition of the co-morbidity of gout [12-1]. The portly but financially strapped Earl is seen arranging the marriage of his son to a rich merchant's daughter and in the first scene is seen posed amongst his possessions, many of which – including his crutch – are branded with the mark of his coronet to denote his importance; even one of the dogs bears this mark on its flank. The nobleman points to a chart recording his family tree rising from the loins of William the Conqueror; his other hand rests over his heart, denoting sincerity. His heavily bandaged left foot rests on a gout stool.

Gout, in the seventeenth and eighteenth centuries, was considered to be a nobleman's disease and, even then, was recognised to be associated with obesity. The physician Thomas Sydenham (1624–89) said: 'they who are

Subject to this Disease have large Skulls, and most commonly are of gross Habit of Body, moist and lax, and of a Strong and lusty Constitution, the best and richest Foundation for Life'.[3]

To be effective in a narrative way, images portrayed by the artist had to be understood by the viewer. The stereotypical images associated with the Earl and his gout would have been recognised. Physician William Cadogan advocated diet as a treatment for gout and was vilified for so doing. He was accused of wanting to take away an Englishman's heritage. Gout was what made the nation strong. It was also considered a kind of mascot or amulet, which, if owned, would protect the sufferer from other diseases. Its presence was reassuring and even welcome if properly managed.

The City merchant in Hogarth's painting is of different stature and bodily size to the Earl. Even his sitting posture at the opposite side of the table, with feet set firmly in parallel instead of being placed at 'ten-to-two' in a more elegant position, were not what was expected in polite society. His inelegant deportment and gestures distance him literally and metaphorically from the nobleman. He is a dealer in commerce – a socially inferior occupation. His concerns are based more on financial and commercial matters as he negotiates a deal with the Earl that entails the marriage of his daughter to the Earl's son in exchange for money to complete a partially constructed building project that can be seen through the window. The clerk in attendance handing over documents is shown to be of even lower social status, with gaunt features and thin body. His clothes, too, mark him out as inferior. Such social signifiers as indicated by Hogarth separate the Earl, the merchant and the clerk in this narrative series of paintings; size denotes social status.

In another series, 'Industry and Idleness', Hogarth portrays many individuals accompanying a mayor and corporation [12-2]. They are depicted as rotund, pompous and greedy, big with ideas of grandeur and self-importance.

12-2
Detail from Plate 8 of 'Industry and Idleness', Hogarth, 1747.

12-3
Detail from *An Election Entertainment*, 'Election' series, Hogarth, 1754.

One such gentleman attending a banquet at the old Fishmongers' Hall is so obese that his coat will not button up over his paunch. His mouth is full and he has a large portion of food on his plate, as has his neighbour. His 'corporation' or paunch is symbolic of his greed for the trappings of office.

The mayor in Hogarth's *An Election Entertainment*, in which feasting plays a major role, is also portrayed as a greedy and corpulent individual [12-3]. He has succumbed to a fit of apoplexy – a reward for his gluttony – after eating a surfeit of oysters and is being bled by the barber-surgeon. This was a recognised form of treatment at the time. Part of the 'Poetical Description' of Hogarth's scene, written under his 'sanction and inspection' and published in 1759, tells how:

> The Mayor with oysters dies away!
> – But softly, don't exult so fast,
> His spirit noble to the last;
> His mouth still waters at the dish;
> His hand still holds his favourite fish;
> Bleed him the Barber-surgeon wou'd;
> He breathes a vein, but where's the blood?
> No more it flows its wonted pace,
> And chilly dew spreads o'er his face.[4]

The 'Election' series of paintings by Hogarth depicts a rowdy campaign in the general election of 1754, based on the notorious Oxfordshire election at that time. Ambition amongst politicians and the ensuing competition for votes led to innumerable corrupt practices, which were satirised by the artist. In the final scene, *Chairing the Member* [12-4], the triumphant

12-4
Detail from *Chairing the Member*, 'Election' series, Hogarth, 1754.

member's chair is toppled by a herd of Gadarene swine and the corpulent incumbent faces his own mortality in the form of the skull and cross-bones on the gatepost in front of him. In the actual election, the member's triumph is overturned because of a dispute in counting the votes.

An overweight judge in another of Hogarth's engravings, *The Bench* [12-5], is stuffed into his robes, his large size here lending him an appearance of sagacity, experience and wisdom. The artist's aim had been 'to depict *character* and to find his models in the *outré* of Nature herself, exemplified by the comic but not exaggerated physiognomies of the Judges'.[5]

Hogarth did not lightly dismiss opportunities to ridicule authority and the pompous, overblown, overweening and overweight establishment figures – usually with well lined pockets – get their just deserts. In twenty-first-century terms, such figures might be regarded as 'fat cats'. The mayor and corporation in a comparatively recent postcard provide some up-to-date humour in connection with corpulent officials (see the section below on seaside postcards, starting page 261, and 12-34).

12-5
Detail from *The Bench*, Hogarth, 1758.

12-6
Detail from 'A Harlot's
Progress', Plate 5, Hogarth.

A 'larger than life' figure in another of Hogarth's 'Modern Moral Subjects' is Dr Rock, a well known quack doctor who can be seen in the final scene of 'A Harlot's Progress' [12-6]. Oliver Goldsmith wrote about this man in his *Letters from a Citizen of the World to his Friends in the East*:

> The first upon the list of glory is doctor Richard Rock, F.U.N. This great man is short of stature, is fat, and waddles as he walks. He always wears a white three-tailed wig nicely combed and frizzed upon each cheek; sometimes he carries a cane, but a hat never.... He is usually drawn at the top of his own bills, sitting in his arm-chair, holding a little bottle between his finger and thumb, and surrounded with rotten teeth, nippers, pills, packets and gallipots. No man can promise fairer nor better than he; for, as he observes, 'Be your disorder never so far gone be under no uneasiness, make yourself quite easy; I can cure you.'[6]

The lean figure on the right of Dr Rock is another notorious quack, Dr Misaubin, a Frenchman known as M. Pillule. In Hogarth's satire, the English quack is superior to the French, confirmed by his more robust appearance and size. The Englishman conforms to the Hippocratic dictum that the physician must have a worthy appearance; he should look healthy and be well nourished, appropriate for his physique. This aspect was to reassure patients that their well-being was in safe hands. In whatever sphere

12-7
A Good Meal, Rowlandson.

of life one was employed, the visual attributes of success were socially and financially important. Corpulency, or at least a good measure of stoutness, was obligatory.

Artists frequently portrayed scenes of over-indulgence in food and drink as a metaphor for human folly in all spheres of life, and stereotypical signs of gout – the heavily bandaged foot of the overweight, well-to-do, wheelchair-bound individual – represented a lifetime of folly or, at least, of intemperance. In *A Good Meal* [12-7], by Thomas Rowlandson, the laden table and copious amounts of alcohol, the lascivious expression on the diner's face, the phallic glass and the presence of the plump waitress graphically portray the lifestyle of many wealthy individuals during the eighteenth and early nineteenth century. To allay the effects of a decadent lifestyle, many valetudinarians retreated to Bath or some other spa, such as Malvern or Buxton, to 'take the waters'. Hogarth's Earl would have felt at home there.

In the eighteenth century, Bath was a fashionable health resort and retirement town, where the ownership of a 'certain stoutness' was rife. It might be described as a microcosm of the wealthy, under-employed and self-indulgent. In 1798 Thomas Rowlandson produced a series of hand-coloured aquatints, 'The Comforts of Bath', which were later used to illustrate the 1858 edition of Christopher Anstey's *New Bath Guide* – first published in 1766 – a publication which claimed to be a guide to warn the unwary traveller of the 'whirlpools and rocks' in the voyage of life. The series satirically depicts the activities that took place in the spa – both medical

12-8
The Comforts of Bath, IV: The Fish Market, Rowlandson.

and social. In the typical Rowlandson style of drawing, with its disordered and unruly lines overflowing the canvas, overweight, gouty individuals are shown being examined by physicians, bathing in the King's Bath, drinking the water in the Pump Room, being wheeled in their bath-chairs, and being tempted and seduced by unsuitable food and young ladies. Fish roes, whitebait, sprats, sardines, herrings, bloaters and mussels, foods rich in purines, which may have contributed to the gout initially, are amongst the foods tempting the wheelchair-borne individual in Rowlandson's scene at the fish market [12-8]. Gout was also seen as a symbol of lust – illustrated as such in this scene by the image of the buxom wench and the phallic fish. Rowlandson's scenes conjure up a general impression of disorder, with leaning buildings, false perspectives and untidy, overweight people.

The Pump Room in Bath served as a meeting room for all those who had come to Bath in search of health [12-9, 12-10], and was a place where the spa water was usually drunk in the prescribed quantity and frequency for the 'patient'. Usually this was half to three pints in 24 hours. The sparkling mineral water was said to be beneficial for most ailments. Bathing in the waters was also recommended.

12-9 (left)
The Comforts of Bath, The Pump Room, Rowlandson, 1798.

12-10 (right)
The Comforts of Bathing, or The King's Bath, Rowlandson, 1798.

The physician George Cheyne wrote:

> I have often observed, with Admiration, the Wisdom and Goodness of Providence, in furnishing so wonderful an Antidote to almost all the Chronical Distempers of an English Constitution and Climate, which are chiefly owing to Errors of Diet, or rather, to Idleness and Fulness of Bread. The Rankness of the Soil; the Richness of the Provisions; the living so much on Flesh Meats; the Inconstancy of the Weather, and the indulging in Sedentary Amusements, or speculative Studies, directly leading thereto. To Remedy all which, kind heaven has provided Bath Waters.[7]

Dr William Oliver, a local physician, devised a special dietary biscuit to be consumed by those who had previously over-indulged themselves – the 'Bath Oliver' – a biscuit available at the present time that still conforms to the original recipe.

In the early seventeenth century, Tobias Venner was one of the first physicians to claim that the obese would benefit from visiting Bath. After listing the benefits to be gained for such sicknesses as 'Rheumes, Palsies, Epilepsies, Lethargies, Apoplexies, Cramps, Deafnesse, Forgetfulness, Trembling, or Weaknesses of any Member, Aches, and Swelling of the joints, etc.', he adds that the waters are also

> very profitable … to make slender such bodies as are too grosse…. Wherefore let those that feare obesity, that is, would not wax grosse, be careful to come often to our Baths: for by the use of them, according as the learned Physician shall direct, they may not only preserve their health, but also keep their bodies from being unseemly corpulent.[8]

Venner chides many of the visitors to the spa who claimed to receive no benefit from their stay there, some even finding themselves worse, both financially and physically: 'That sickness is a Symptom of Sin: And therefore first *Penitentiam agendo*, before you depart from home, make peace betwixt God and your conscience, and thus repair to the Baths.'

Once the season at Bath was over, Tobias Smollett, who shared some of Rowlandson's satirical views of the spa, describes the scene left behind and offers graphic images of the clergymen who stayed there. He does this through the medium of a letter written by Jerry Melford to his friend Sir Watkin Phillips in *The Expedition of Humphry Clinker* (1771):

> The music and entertainments of Bath are over for this season; and all our gay birds of passage have taken their flight to Bristol Well, Tunbridge, Brighthelmstone, Scarborough, Harrowgate etc. Not a soul is seen in this place, but a few broken-winded parsons, waddling like so many crows along the North Parade. There is always a great shew of clergy at Bath; none of your thin, puny, yellow, hectic figures, exhausted with abstinence and hard study, but great overgrown dignitaries and rectors, with rubicund noses and gouty ankles, or broad bloated faces, dragging along great swag bellies; the emblems of sloth and indigestion.[9]

12-11
Dropsy Courting Consumption, Rowlandson, 1810.

Fat versus thin was one of the subjects of Rowlandson's etchings depicting life's contrasts. Rowlandson's works required less interpretation than did those of Hogarth: the topic was instantly recognisable. In *Dropsy Courting Consumption* [12-11], a coloured etching from 1810, a corpulent man on his knees woos a thin woman who smiles and offers her hand. In the background the reverse situation applies: a thin man accompanies a large woman. They are admiring a statue of a heavenly body – a Herculean or Apollonian figure. The scene is enacted in the grounds of a mausoleum. Rowlandson makes the point that marked deviation from the ideal body state, in either direction, takes one nearer to death.

In contrast to the portly or robust characters to be found in Bath, scholars and clerks in holy orders were often portrayed as thin and underfed. Their bookish habits led to a lack of concern for bodily substance; they were living on pure thought and aspiring to the purely intellectual or spiritual. Thomas Rowlandson drew attention to the latter observation in a series of prints entitled 'Dr. Syntax's Tour of the Lakes' (1814–16), depicting the travels of an eccentric parson and schoolmaster. His prints were accompanied by verses that were provided independently by William Combe, a hack writer who spent many years in prison. The publisher, Ackerman, was responsible for coordinating the work of Rowlandson and Combe: the two men never actually met each other.

Dr Syntax was lean and spare in habit and fortune. He was hen-pecked and brow-beaten by his rather over-powering spouse [12-12], a lady of robust dimensions and ideas as described by William Combe:

12-12
Dr Syntax with his spouse,
Rowlandson, 1814–16.

The Doctor, 'midst his rumination
Was waken'd by a visitation
Which troubles many a poor man's life –
The visitation of his wife.
Good Mrs. Syntax was a lady
Ten years or more beyond her hey-day;

…

Her face was red, her form was fat,
A round-about, and rather squat;
And, when in angry humour stalking,
Was like a dumpling set a-walking.

It seems that those who considered themselves superior to others in moral, social or financial matters had physical proportions in line with the magnitude of this superiority. Thus, the bookseller to whom Syntax had been given a letter of introduction on the completion of the book about his tours received the doctor with some hostility:

… The master, who had fill'd his crop
In a smart room behind the shop,
On hearing a loud angry voice,
Came forth to know what caus'd the noise;
And left his wife and bottle too,
To see about this strange to-do.
He was a man whose ample paunch
Was made of beef, and ham, and haunch;
And, when he saw the shrivel'd form
Of Syntax, he began to storm.

Size is again seen as a signifier of success and of social status, and merchants who made their wealth through trade developed their paunches in line with their pockets. Learning was, to them, insignificant and therefore Syntax's lean and hungry look was in keeping with his perceived inferiority.

When the doctor had first arrived in Liverpool, he thought he would carry out a bit of commerce on his own behalf. He eventually found:

> Some one in whose sleek smiling face
> He could the lines of kindness trace:
> When soon a person he address'd,
> Whose paunch projected from his breast,
> And, looking with good humour fraught,
> Appear'd the very man he sought.

Alas! The well fed merchants of Liverpool, had no dealing with learning. One such individual remarked, as he headed for his dinner:

> To learning we make no pretence;
> But, Doctor, we have common sense.

Dr Syntax was a clergyman as well as a schoolmaster, so his sparse physical dimensions were appropriate on two counts. The honest clergyman was expected to be fleshless because he was ascetically floating heavenwards.

The women portrayed by Rowlandson in many scenes were of the large variety: they were plump, voluptuous and alluring. His *Exhibition 'Stare-Case', Somerset House* (engraved 1800) illustrates the humour attached to many of his drawings [C-19]. The actual staircase at Somerset House had been described as dangerous; it was steep and hazardous. Rowlandson's imagination almost amounts to lewdness as he depicts a cornucopia of plump bodies tumbling down the stairs – *en deshabille.*

The cognoscenti who bought or viewed such paintings or prints would understand the significance of the satirical points made. Fatness and thinness, good food and drink, and the consequences of overindulging (such as the mayor suffering from an attack of apoplexy) were part of everyday life. In eighteenth-century prints, at least, the stout seem to have been regarded with some humour, but without repugnance or vilification. (To be thin might be construed as being in ill-health or diseased, which was far less desirable.) Such prints would have been displayed in print-shop windows or in portfolios that publishers lent to the owners of country houses for the entertainment of guests. They cost about 6*d* each for black and white prints and 2*s* for coloured ones, a relatively high sum at a time when newspapers cost about a third of that price.

> In the eighteenth century prints were the primary way of conveying information visually on a widespread basis. Events were depicted and 'commented upon', personalities and buildings portrayed and various kinds of knowledge disseminated. Prints decorated rooms, taught lessons, presented fashions, proffered political views, provided illustrations for books and periodicals and gave entertainment.[10]

Body size was important.

The body politic: satirical prints and cartoons

> Medical representations, such as obesity, serve as metaphors, symbols and icons to order experience and construct social and cultural boundaries both within and beyond the culture of medicine.[11]

A stout individual can provide the image of prosperity, or greed, or sagacity and importance; or stoutness can be used in a symbolic way. Size speaks volumes. Variation in size tells other stories. One particular individual whose bodily dimensions varied according to the political climate was John Bull. He became a popular figure in the eighteenth century. At this time, the English were widely seen by the French as undignified, unstylish, gluttonous and morose, while the French were thought by the English to have affected manners and under-nourished bodies. Hostility between the two nations was rife in an age when the two great countries were imperial rivals. No opportunity was missed to pour contempt upon these neighbours across the Channel. Such attitudes are reflected in William Hogarth's painting *The Gate of Calais, or O, the Roast Beef of Old England* (1748) [12-13]. The large, well fed friar in this scene is drooling in anticipation of a roast beef dinner as a scrawny French cook's boy staggers under the weight of a huge haunch of beef that he is delivering to an English eating-house in Calais

12-13
The Gate of Calais, Hogarth, 1748.

12-14
French Happiness/English Misery, Cruikshank, published by Fores, 1793.

to feed English visitors. This contrasts markedly with the under-nourished French servants nearby, who are carrying a cauldron of *soupe-maigre* in the opposite direction to feed the locals. The English are being well fed, but who lives off the fat of the land in France? The lard-tub friar, usually regarded as a figure of fun and contempt, is one example.

In *Beer Street* (1750–51) Hogarth again contrasts the well-being of the English brought up on roast beef and beer (such as those held aloft by the corpulent English butcher) with the emaciation of the French sign painter who has arrived in their midst (see 4-3, page 70).

Isaac Cruikshank graphically illustrates a similar theme in his etching *French Happiness/English Misery* [12-14], published by Fores in 1793. The 'happy' starving Frenchmen share a frog and have only water to drink, whilst the 'miserable' Englishmen gorge themselves on roast beef, plum pudding and foaming tankards of beer. The French Tree of Liberty wilts in the background; the English need no such libertarian symbols. Such polemic prints were popular expressions of anti-Republican sentiments using body size as an indicator of well-being.

A popular song written in May 1757, 'The Beer-Drinking Briton', echoes the animosity between the two nations. It was said that beer was the natural beverage of the Englishman, and that wine and spirituous liquors were mere French inventions, calculated to corrupt and destroy British bravery and patriotism:

> Ye true honest Britons, who love your own land,
> Whose sires were so brave, so victorious and free;

Who always beat France when they took her in hand –
Come join, honest Britons, in chorus with me.

Let us sing our own treasures, Old England's good cheer,
The profits and pleasures of stout British beer;
Your wine-tippling, dram-sipping fellows retreat,
But your beer-drinking Britons can never be beat!

The French with their vineyards are meagre and pale,
They drink of the squeezings of half-ripen'd fruit;
But we who have hop-grounds to mellow our ale,
Are rosy and plump, and have freedom to boot,

Let us sing our own treasures, etc.

Should the French dare invade us, thus arm'd with our poles,
We'll bang their bare ribs, make their lanthorn jaws ring.
For your beef-eating, beer-drinking Britons are souls
Who will shed their last blood for their country and king.

Let us sing our own treasures, etc.

Beer-drinking and beef-eating were patriotic activities, corpulence often the result, but stoutness at this time was usually associated with prosperity.

The image of Daniel Lambert (see Chapter 2) was invoked as a patriotic figure whose size overwhelmed the puny image of Napoleon Bonaparte, owing, we are led to believe, to the consumption of English beef and beer. Napoleon had no chance of defeating such true English trenchermen. In 12-15, by an unknown artist, the well known trencherman Lambert, representing a true-born Englishman, has lunch with the French enemy or opposition, Napoleon, on the opposite side of the table. Lambert tucks into his roast beef and beer, whilst an under-sized Napoleon partakes of

12-15
The English Lamb and the French Tiger, by an unknown artist, published by Fores. Newarke House Museum, Leicester.

his meagre lunch of soup. Lambert's meal occupies the whole table, whilst Napoleon balances his bowl of soup on his knee.

The first person to define the typical Englishman was a Scot, by the name of John Arbuthnot. John Bull – as he named his Englishman – was conceived in 1712 and sired by this Scottish physician, writer and mathematician. Arbuthnot was called to see Prince George of Denmark, who had become ill whilst on a visit to Epsom. Following this incident Arbuthnot continued as a physician to the Prince. In 1705, at the special request of Queen Anne, he was made her Physician Extraordinary, and four years later he became Royal Physician-in-Ordinary. In the same year, he was elected a Fellow of the Royal College of Physicians. Whilst in London, Arbuthnot had become a close friend of Jonathan Swift. With him, he helped to form the Scriblerus Club – a group of satirical writers whose aim was to puncture pomposity and put what they saw as a proper slant on life. He wrote five allegorical political pamphlets, published in 1712, designed to advocate the end of the current war with France. In these satires, which, for a long time, Swift was thought to have written, Arbuthnot ridiculed the Duke of Marlborough, who had commanded the armies with success, but who wanted the war to continue. John Bull, as a tradesman, represented the English and the war was allegorised as his lawsuit, along with his linen-draper friend, Nicholas Frog (representing the Dutch), against Lewis Baboon (representing the French in the name of Louis XIV), for interfering with trade. The origin of the dispute is based on their selfish and narrow views. The various events of the war with the accompanying political intrigues are symbolised by the stages of progress of the suit, the tricks of the lawyers and the devices of the Principal Attorney (Marlborough) to prolong the struggle.[12] The pamphlets were later made up into *The History of John Bull*. These present a lively picture of the politics of the period whilst portraying the perceived characteristics of those taking part.

The wide circulation of Arbuthnot's satire fixed John Bull as a popular personification in many eighteenth-century literary and graphic works. The author describes his creation as follows:

> A blunt true-born Englishman, stubbornly independent of his social superiors and scornful of fine manners associated with the continental countries, because, for him, they symbolized the sycophancy of the countries as well as the abject submission to tyrants.

Arbuthnot continues:

> Bull, in the main, was an honest plain-dealing Fellow, Cholerick, Bold and of very unconstant Temper … he might be very apt to quarrel with his best Friends, especially if they pretended to govern him; if you flattered him, you might lead him like a child.… John's Temper depended very much upon the Air; his Spirits rose and fell with the Weather-glass.[13]

12-16
John Bull Taking a Luncheon,
Gillray, 1797.

The true-born Englishman was proud of his freedom to eat his own 'Beef and pudding' and drink his own beer, as Hogarth portrayed graphically, and to 'partake in football, cricket, cudgel-playing and such-like recreational activities'.

Arbuthnot provided the original words that defined John Bull, but visual images of the character did not appear until later. In the middle of the eighteenth century, he appeared by courtesy of graphic artists such as Gillray as a stout, good-natured and big-hearted individual who became a familiar figure as the personification of Old England. On 24 October 1797, following news of successive naval victories against the French, including Nelson's Victory of the Nile, James Gillray produced a caricature of *John Bull Taking a Luncheon* [12-16]. John is almost overwhelmed by the attention of naval cooks offering him such delicacies as 'fricassee a la Nelson' – a large dish of battered French ships of the line. John's dimensions increase drastically on his new diet of ships washed down with true British stout; he becomes grossly overweight.

In the same year (1797), Richard Newton published a political satire attacking the government for allowing the Bank of England to buy Spanish-American silver dollars [12-17]. These were stamped with the head of George III and they were circulated to make up for a shortage of silver coins. John Bull is being stuffed with the currency, both to his dismay and to his discomfort.

12-17
A Paper Meal with Spanish Sauce, Newton,
14 March 1797.

12-18
John Bull à la Rowlandson.

Although adding some of their own individual style to his portraits, different artists, including Newton, still kept the general character bequeathed by Gillray. Rowlandson, for example, added some coarseness and vulgarity to his character in typical Rowlandson-esque style [12-18].

A slimmed down version of John Bull came later under the burden of the French Revolution and the Napoleonic wars. John became downtrodden, reduced to poverty and almost cadaverous proportions by a diet of debt, taxation and oppression. His health or constitution was a political analogy with the British constitution. 'Constitution' was important – the foundation of individual well-being and security against illness and hard times. The body politic – the government – was often seen to undermine John Bull's constitution, although supposedly for the good of the country. During the conflicts he was portrayed as a rather stupid individual – but a victim – being purged, vomited or almost bled to death in an attempt by politicians to extract every ounce of value out of him in the cause of war. But John Bull's constitution was weakened; his dimensions became markedly reduced; being thin was unhealthy [12-19].

In this caricature, Lord Hawkesbury is supporting a sick John Bull whilst Prime Minister Henry Addington bleeds him. The blood issuing from his arm is labelled Malta and other conquests that were to be restored. John Bull submits to continuous demands made upon him with consequent reduction in his size. Bleeding and purging were frequent remedies for

12-19
Doctor Sangrado curing John Bull of Repletion, Gillray, 1803.

sickness or were used as a prophylaxis to keep the body in good working order – both for the individual and, in political cartoons, for the 'body politic'. Contemporary viewers would understand the underlying message.

Woodward portrayed a thin and impoverished John Bull [12-20] in an etching that was published at the time of the Peninsular War. John Bull is suffering from the burden of taxation and its effects. Nevertheless, he still clings to his stick of 'Wellington oak' and smokes his clay pipe. A Frenchman approaches him with the words 'By gar, Monsieur Jean Bull, you var much alter, – should not know you var Jean; I vas as big as you now!' John replies indignantly, 'Why, look you, Monsieur Parleyvou, though I have got thinner myself, I have a little sprig of oak in my hand that's as strong as ever; and if you give me any of your palaver, I'll be d—d if you shan't feel the weight of it.'

John Bull's patriotism was exploited to the full. But patriotism was in vogue and Bull was a heroic figure, with whom all patriotic Englishmen could empathise. He became the mouthpiece of the nation, with the ability to voice the criticism that many people felt towards the government and the hardships imposed. Public opinion was on his side. His country's triumphs, trials and tribulations were graphically portrayed through his image, and the dimensions of his body varied accordingly. Corpulence was thus indicative of well-being in the country; thinness represented the country in decline. As the symbol of the trueborn Englishman, John Bull emerged from the wars as an emblem of bellicose jingoistic pride. In the early 1800s he acquired a Union Jack waistcoat, which has remained a part of his wardrobe ever since.

In spite of the fluctuation in his fortunes, John Bull lives on; his diet and his size still vary according to the political climate but his appearances have become more sporadic. The treatment that he is given by his political

12-20
John Bull Rather Thin, Woodward.

doctors has changed somewhat along with medical advances. For example, in 1987, Margaret Thatcher gave him a strong dose of medicine via a hypodermic syringe [C-20]. He had to be put on the rack and strapped down to force him to take this treatment, which entailed such poisonous ingredients as the introduction of a community charge, a comprehensive reform of education and a new housing policy. He is remarkably reduced in size under this regimen, but the diet does not seem to suit him and he is not happy. Soon after this, he decides to change his doctor – a new Prime Minister.

At the present time he is well fed and prosperous and is sometimes seen in the company of Britannia – another national emblem [12-21]. Whereas John Bull came to be the embodiment of national character, Britannia was, and still is, the embodiment of national aspirations and ideals. She is older than John Bull. The Romans gave the provinces that they held feminine names; hence Britain became Britannia. Although the land was known by Julius Caesar a century previously, the name Britannia was not used until the reign of Emperor Claudius, and her pictorial debut was on the reverse of a Roman coin under Hadrian. She holds a sceptre in her left hand and a large round shield at her left side. In the reign of Antonius Pius she appeared as a classically draped figure and wore a plumed helmet (see also 12-25 for a nineteenth-century depiction of Britannia).

Like John Bull, Britannia has suffered physically under different political regimes. In 1793, for example, Thomas Paine, the author of *The Rights of Man*, in which he promoted 'a general insurrection among all people against Kings' and promulgated principles which were subversive of government and society in Britain, was caricatured fitting Britannia with a new pair of stays. Paine was originally a stay-maker from Thetford in England. In 12-21

12-21
Britannia in French Stays, or re-Form at the expence of Constitution, Gillray, 1793.

BRITANNIA in FRENCH STAYS,
or _ re-Form, at the expence of Constitution.

the lady is clinging to a tree and is in some discomfort as Paine attempts to get her into shape and fit her into his new, fashionable way of life. Stays were fashionable attire for reshaping the figure.

Like John Bull, Uncle Sam, as the familiar symbol of America, has changed in appearance and size according to the political and social climate. He first appeared in 1832, when he started life as little better than a country bumpkin.[14] With a make-over and change of clothes (both of which may have been influenced by frequent portrayals of Abraham Lincoln during the American Civil War), he acquired a statuesque body in the image of Lincoln, with the familiar top-hat and striped pants, and whiskers. Later cartoonists usually depicted him as tall and thin but varied his muscularity according to the message they wished to convey. 'The traditional, thin Uncle Sam is seen as often nervous and frequently inept. The muscular Uncle Sam is stronger, self-reliant and often aggressive.'[15] The traditional image has frequently been replaced in more recent time with a smaller, fat version in which 'He appears as unsure, gullible, dependent, weak and sometimes lazy and conniving'. This may be due to a change of national self-image and a more self-deprecating society. The image through the national looking glass no longer reflects a tall, thin figure; the obese figure is, perhaps, more representative of twenty-first-century American society [12-22].

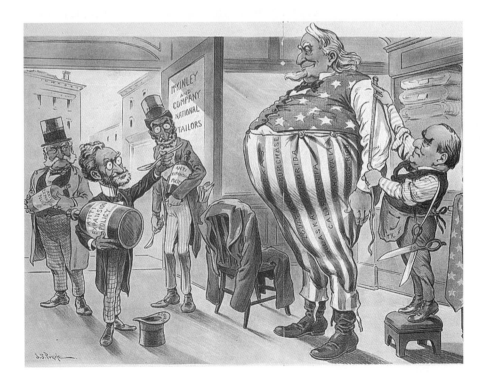

12-22
Uncle Sam.

12-23
A Voluptuary Under the Horrors of Digestion, Gillray, 1792 (British Museum).

Body size is a useful political indicator. The varying attributes of politicians lend themselves to cartoonists for satirical comment. Corpulence is a useful and easily recognisable attribute and can be used as a comment upon a ruler's character as well as upon the state of the nation. In contrast to the general treatment of John Bull, corpulence can be used to denote lack of control, weakness and ineffectiveness, as an emblem of dissolution and bad government.

James Gillray's print of the gross figure of the Prince of Wales depicts the heir to the throne in this light. *A Voluptuary Under the Horrors of Digestion* was published in July 1792 [12-23], at a time when the Prince was deep in debt in spite of having received grants from the civil list and from Parliament in 1787, and had promised to reform his ways. The obese Prince with bursting waistcoat is seen inelegantly sprawled in his chair, picking his teeth with a dinner fork in vulgar fashion; his paunch is a sign of incipient ills. The table is littered with the remains of a meal and dead wine bottles lie under the table. Underneath an overflowing chamber-pot on the close-stool behind him are numerous unpaid bills, the juxtaposition indicating the Prince's contempt both for those who send the bills and those who provide him with grants to pay them. Gambling dice lie on the floor alongside books of more unpaid debts. On the wall table behind the Prince, underneath a coat-of-arms displaying crossed knife and fork with phallic candles as supporters, is a display of nostrums for the treatment of venereal disease. The Prince was weak-willed and known for his voluptuousness; gluttony, lust and sloth were just three of the deadly sins to which he was prone.

Looking down upon this scene of extravagance and dissolution is a portrait of Luigi Cornaro, a noble Venetian, who, at the age of 40, gave up a life of indulgence and intemperance which threatened his life; 'by means of great sobriety, and a strict regimen in his diet, he recovered his health and vigour, which he preserved to an extreme old age'. Cornaro died in his hundredth year. He wrote four discourses on methods of attaining a long life, the first of which he wrote when he was 83 and which was published in Padua in 1558. English translations appeared about the time that Gillray's print was published. They proved popular and thus provided topical comment upon the Prince of Wales' condition and on how he should change his ways. Another print – the title of which, *Le cochon et ses deux petits or Rich Pickings for a Noble appetite*, appears underneath a scene in which the obese Prince is shown seated between two robust ladies – gives further indication of his lifestyle.

Gillray was famous for his etched political and social satires in which he ridiculed both Whig and Tory alike, and he took full advantage of the individual characteristics of the politicians involved. After the election in 1806, he satirised the new administration that had been formed on a 'broad bottom' and was to include 'all the talents' of the different parties. He addressed the political tensions which occurred following this and in 1807 portrayed members of this 'Ministry of all the Talents' (nicknamed the Broad-bottoms) in his etching *Political Mathematicians, Shaking the Broad bottom'd Hemispheres* [12-24]. Many of these literally broad-bottomed individuals can be seen dining lavishly on the largesse of office inside an inflated transparent pair of the late Charles James Fox's breeches. A tug of war between opposing parties threatens to topple the new ministry (represented by the breeches), and the latter are balanced upon the tri-feathered emblem of the Prince of Wales. The Ministry of all the Talents was mistakenly thought to be in league with the Prince of Wales and in Gillray's print rats gnawing at the base of this feathered edifice are undermining the foundations of the government. Napoleon watches from a distance, waiting for his opportunity to take advantage of the unrest, and the spectre of the late Charles James Fox, the previous owner of the breeches, peers out from his tomb in the foreground. Britannia watches the proceedings in despair.

12-24
Political Mathematicians, Shaking the Broad bottom'd Hemispheres, Gillray, 1807.

In his final etching of a political theme, in 1810, Gillray also makes use of the size of his political target by taking full advantage of the latter's physical dimensions. The politician in question is Baron Grenville, who was installed as Chancellor of Oxford on 3 July that year. He had been associated with Catholic emancipation, which was a topical issue but, in the print [C-21], the Baron, with a cross on his posterior, is ascending in a balloon, which fits snugly round his rotund form. He has thrown off a cardinal's hat, rosary and mitre and donned a tiara. He has conferred degrees on some of his past supporters and on his obese nephew, whose image just fits, full of hot air and farting 'Promisses', within the confines of the large balloon as they both rise upwards.

Recently, one of Lucian Freud's paintings of 'Big Sue' was put up for sale by auction, an occurrence reported in a number of newspapers. Identified in the painting's title as a civil servant – *Benefits Supervisor Sleeping* – she is portrayed reclining naked on an old settee. Her massive body fills the space available. Satirist Peter Brookes takes advantage of two coincidental news items and portrays Prime Minister Gordon Brown in an identical pose in his cartoon in *The Times* (12 April 2008) [C-22], also entitled 'Benefits Supervisor Sleeping'. In parenthesis beneath the caption are the words: 'while the economy goes down the pan'.

The line between stoutness and obesity was, and still is, a narrow one. It is bound up with character. The stoutness that is acceptable for an upright, philanthropic, good-natured and generous individual can become obese for the lazy, gluttonous, selfish and humourless one. Satirists made good use of these distinctions.

Seaside postcards

> in Vastness, *whatever be its nature*, there dwells sublimity. Why, therefore, may not the mountains of fat, the human Olympi and Caucasi, excite our attention? They *fill* a large space in society, are *great objects* of interest, and ought to afford us no *small matter* of amusement and instruction. (William Wadd, 1829[16])

William Hogarth wrote a section about 'quantity' in his one book on art, *The Analysis of Beauty* (1753). He notes that whereas a full wig gives dignity to the image of a person, if it is drawn twice as large again it immediately becomes 'a burlesque'; and if an 'improper person' wears it, it also looks ridiculous. In the margin of the first draft of his *Analysis*, Hogarth adds that when 'improper, or incompatible excesses meet, they always excite laughter'. This is the emotion elicited where saucy seaside postcards are concerned. Literally larger-than-life figures engage in ordinary but, as far as the individual is concerned, implausible holiday activities.

The seaside is a place of shifting identities, where the usual inhibitions that apply to everyday life may be lost or put into abeyance. 'Recreational activities' are pursued in a relaxed fashion, and sex, sea and sand are paramount.

Seawater bathing became popular in the late eighteenth century. 'Society', which had previously gathered in Bath, gradually transferred to Brighthelmstone (later to become 'Brighton'), largely because of the Prince of Wales, who first went there in 1782. Immersion in seawater became an acceptable alternative to immersion in the mineral waters of Bath. Smollett's fictional character Matthew Bramble went to Scarborough and extolled the virtues of the seawater there. His nephew, Jerry Melford, described the bathing scene in a letter to his friend:

> Betwixt the well and the harbour, the bathing machines are ranged along the beach, with all their proper utensils and attendants. Imagine to yourself a small, snug, wooden chamber, fixed upon a wheel-carriage, having a door at each end, and on each side a little window above, a bench below. The bather, ascending into this apartment by wooden steps, shuts himself in, and begins to undress, while the attendant yokes a horse to the end next the sea, and draws the carriage forwards, till the surface of the water is on a level with the floor of the dressing-room, then he moves and fixes the horse to the other end. The person within, being stripped, opens the door to the sea-ward, where he finds the guide ready, and plunges headlong into the water. After having

bathed, he reascends into the apartment, by the steps which had been shifted for that purpose, and puts on his clothes at his leisure, while his carriage is drawn back again upon the dry land; so that he has nothing further to do, but to open the door, and come down as he went up. Should he be so weak or ill as to require a servant to put off and on his clothes, there is room enough in the apartment for half a dozen people. The guides who attend the ladies in the water, are of their own sex, and they and the female bathers have a dress of flannel for the sea....[17]

An etching entitled *Venus's Bathing* in Margate in 1790, attributed to Thomas Rowlandson [C-23], sums up a less inhibited scene than that described by Smollett. This bather has no flannel dress but has other attributes to display, namely, her ample bosom, beefy thighs and her rather corpulent abdomen – all probably acquired from a wealthy lifestyle associated with 'taking the waters'.

Rowlandson's scene is more akin to some of the seaside postcards that were first produced in the early twentieth century and whose popularity continues today. For example, the 'Venus' at Morecambe portrayed by Donald McGill [12-25] possesses all the attributes of the eighteenth-century version, even though they are 'modestly' hidden in her bathing dress. A Peeping Tom keeps an eye on events in another version [12-26].

12-25 (left)
Donald McGill, 1914.

12-26 (right)
'Tron', published by
C. Richter Ltd, London.

12-27 (left)
Donald McGill.

12-28 (right)
'Comic' series, no. 494,
published by Bamforth & Co.,
Holmfirth, Yorkshire, details.

12-29

The images on seaside postcards are built upon stereotypes. They are usually based on sea, sand, sun and sex, although the last is often alluded to by means of *double entendre* [12-27]. The images themselves are often rather crudely drawn and brightly coloured – even garish – and the products are cheap to buy. A common stereotypical image is of the super-obese woman – often accompanied by a puny, rather downtrodden man [12-28].

The woman in question was often the object of worship by the puny fellow – an adoration perhaps suffused with an exciting and titillating element of fear. In 12-29 a small clerical gentleman with phallic hat leans towards his large *inamorata*, who eyes him with sidelong glance. The

12-30

women could be dominant, even ogres, frequently jolly and cheerful but never depressed or the subjects of discrimination.

Another recurring scenario is that of the lost child who can be seen in the shade or shelter of a fat woman [12-30]. Images such as this were repeated frequently but with slightly different captions. 'Have you seen my little Willy?' was one such *risqué* example. The woman with over-emphasised buttocks or enhanced belly or breasts whose dress clings tightly like a second skin was also a popular image [12-31].

'There can be no doubt that these pictures lift the lid off a very wide-spread repression, natural enough in a country whose women when young tend to be slim to the point of skimpiness'.[18] These words were written by George Orwell in the mid-1940s. He goes on to say that these figures are caricatures of the Englishman's secret ideal and that the brand of

12-31

"JIMMY, – WHICH PAIR OF BOOTS HAVE I GOT ON, THE BLACK OR THE BROWN?"

HIS COUNTRY SEAT.

12-32
12-33

humour exhibited only has meaning in relation to a fairly strict moral code. This may have been so at the time they first appeared, but cards featuring similar grotesque caricatures are still popular today, in a more liberal society.

Super-obese men are usually represented as foolish in some way; Lord Nozoo [C-24] has a ridiculous oversized bowtie and checked pantaloons as he swaggers along the promenade; skinny Jimmy has to tell his absurd corpulent companion which shoes he is wearing [12-32]; and the foolish yokel puffs on his clay pipe, leaning on a fence [12-33].

The mayor or other important figure might be portly, pompous and arrogant, as Hogarth had indicated (see pages 239–41), but his image could still be used for comic effect. A twentieth-century postcard [12-34] of the mayor with chain of office and large frontage pokes fun at the establishment and raises a few wry smiles with the visual pun '...And the whole of my corporation is behind me!'

Blank postcards pre-dated pictorial cards and were designed merely to accommodate a brief message to the recipient. An American, John P. Charlton, was the originator of these, which first appeared in America in 1861 and in Britain in 1870. The idea of decoration on the card came two years later, when Franz Rorich of Nuremberg printed his own engraved views of Zurich on the correspondence side of postcards. Even though this reduced the space for the message, the idea spread through Switzerland, Germany and Austria. In Britain, however, the Postmaster General forbade the transmission of any postcards other than those printed and sold by the Post Office and embossed with the requisite halfpenny stamp for postage. In 1894 regulations were relaxed and other cards were permitted, along with the use of adhesive stamps. Publishers responded by producing views of different parts of the country. The first picture postcards were not necessarily connected with the seaside, although a pictorial card from Scarborough dated 15 September 1894 is one example of an early seaside postcard.[19] It

" . . And the whole of my corporation is behind me ! "

12-34

The Sands, S. Shore, Blackpool

12-35
Blackpool postcard, 1914. Relatively early example of a photographic view on a picture postcard.

is of interest to see an early sepia-coloured card of the beach at Blackpool, dated 1914 [12-35]. All the holidaymakers on the crowded shore are fully clothed; just a few daring souls are paddling in the sea. On close inspection of this card, not one obese person can be seen. It would seem that the reality of Blackpool life before the First World War pre-dated the obesity epidemic.

Joke cards followed the earlier reality scenes; they originated in Paris and spread to other Continental cities. These 'French postcards', with their often erotic, or even soft-pornographic images, were frequently the objects of censorship or import difficulties, although, it was claimed, they were 'artistic' representations.[20]

The trade in joke cards evolved in Britain around 1900 and proved to be very popular. It was originally spawned from the pages of *Punch* and *Vanity Fair* and the earliest attempts at humour came from the pages of these magazines. Original drawings were then commissioned for the growing market, and up-to-date humour and topical subjects were covered.[21] From an initially sophisticated clientele, the market spread to all classes and the style of humour was adapted to a coarser and more popular type; the topical seaside postcard was born.

One particular comic artist, who died in 1962, Donald McGill, is believed to have created more than 3000 cards. He began designing postcards in 1904, to amuse a nephew of his who was in hospital, when he sketched humorous pictures on the back of plain postcards. The following year, he was introduced to the Pictorial Postcard Co. and his postcard career began. He later owned his own publishing company. His cards were immensely popular, with many bearing *double entendre* captions,

12-36
A 'Bamforth' comic,
no. 1403, Arnold Taylor.

although these were often considered to be in poor taste. Indeed, in 1954, McGill, then in his eightieth year, was charged with indecency under the 1857 Obscene Publications Act. A major trial was held in Lincoln, on 16 July of that year, at which some of his cards were described as disgusting, immoral and corrupting, and were, in fact, obscene. In his own defence, he argued that it was the public perception of the images and captions that was at fault, not his designs. He lost his case, however, and was found guilty to charges on four counts. He was banned from publishing the cards classed as obscene, but he continued to design and produce his well known cards for a number of years before his death.

Debate on the issue of vulgarity in seaside cards continues. Although the humour may be as crude as the artwork [C-25], it is hard to imagine anybody taking them seriously enough to arrest the artist as a criminal.

There were a number of publishers of cards, some of whom specialised in certain types or genres and artists did not necessarily design for only one publisher. Bamforth & Co. produced a line in comic relief cards that were quite distinctive in style [12-36]. Bamforth's heyday was in the 1960s.

Some cards in the seaside genre served an additional purpose. Advertising was a common theme and cards promoting an enjoyable – even an obese – lifestyle at a certain holiday resort were popular. Products also received some publicity, such as the plump child promoting toffees [12-37]. Some even acted as military propaganda. A postcard 'Made in U.S.A.' prescribes an 'Anti-Fat Remedy' [12-38].

12-37

12-38

12-39

The use of visual puns was another way of raising a smile; some were even quite witty [12-39]!

Making obesity a subject of humour in seaside postcards is not intended to discriminate against sufferers of the condition and ignores the medical and social consequences of being overweight, but many of the stereotypical images, perhaps inadvertently, draw attention to the different types of obesity in men and women. The 'apple' shape of an obese male, which is metabolically harmful and can lead to health problems, illustrates that excess fat is situated round the abdominal organs. The stereotypically obese female is 'pear' shaped. Her obesity resides in the bottom and hips, which is less dangerous and gives a metabolically protective element to her obesity. These types appear in many seaside postcards. The difference is recognised and hugely funny – at least whilst on holiday.

CHAPTER 13

Fat on film

> Our invention can be exploited for a certain time as a scientific curiosity, but apart from that, it has no commercial future whatsoever.
> (Auguste Lumière, pioneer of motion pictures, December 1895[1])

Unlike the portrayal of corpulency in literature or art, the advent of the cinema offered the unique opportunity to demonstrate the facets of obese characters in all their visual, moving, effectively three-dimensional glory, leaving nothing to the imagination. Obesity was a godsend to the producers of silent movies, who naturally relied on visual humour to ply their trade and who considered poking fun at the fat to be fair game.

Early films

One of the earliest examples in cinema of the mirth to be extracted from obese subjects is held in the archive of the British Film Institute, entitled *Fat Man on a Bicycle*, dating from around 1912. Fred Evans was well known as the amusing character Pimple, and in this early silent clip he teaches a fat friend to ride a bike, but, predictably, Pimple proves to be incompetent and crashes into a variety of innocent bystanders and trades people, who later exact their retribution.[2]

John Bunny was one of the earliest and most beloved of silent film stars. He was born in New York in 1863, weighed over 300 pounds at his peak, and possessed a distinctive bulbous nose. He starred in over 200 comedy shorts between 1910 and 1915, many with skinny actress Flora Finch to provide contrast; their collaborative works were known as 'Bunnyfinches'. His catalogue included *The Pickwick Papers* in 1913 and *Jack Fat and Joe Slim at Coney Island* in 1910. Unfortunately, few of his films survive.[3] During the first days of cinema, basic fat stereotypes were portrayed. Actors

13-1
Charlie Chaplin.

such as Frank Jaquet lurked in the background: short, extremely fat and jut-jawed, playing pompous windbags and slimy villains.[4] As the silent film genre developed, a broader spectrum of visual gags was utilised but, without the benefit of subtle wordplay, the humour remained fairly basic.

Charlie Chaplin [13-1] was born in London in 1889 and was admitted to the workhouse with his brother when only seven years old. His cinema career began in 1914 with the film *Making a Living* and in 1916 he signed a deal worth $10,000 a week with Mutual Film Corporation.[5] In the Chaplin film *The Idle Class* (1921), Charlie hits a golf ball into the mouth of a sleeping fat man. The ball appears and disappears as the man snores, necessitating Chaplin to stand on the man's belly and swipe the ball during pronounced expiration. In another film, Chaplin kicks a fat lady into a fountain. One critic explains Chaplin's appeal in such displays:

> He flirts with the pretty ladies in the park while simultaneously kicking the fat man up the arse.... In simple socio-political terms, he kicks the fat man up the arse because it's funny.[6]

In 1925 the Ton of Fun comedy team was created to perform silent two-reel slapstick comedies, starring three very fat comedians, Hilliard 'Fat' Karr (300 pounds), Frank 'Fatty' Alexander (350 pounds) and 'Kewpie' Ross (over 300 pounds). Apparently the sight of three very obese men walking abreast and engaging in slapstick hi-jinx was side-splitting hilarity for the early patrons of cinema.[7] The trio were said to have offered the most anarchic comedy per pound in films, including *The Heavy Parade* and *Heavy Infants*, in which they played incompetent and inept citizens, ending up in a mêlée of mirth and obesity-related destruction and chaos. The group continued filming until 1928, when Kewpie Ross retired.

The transition to the talkies

One character whose fame has been more enduring was Norvell Hardy, born in 1892, in Harlem, Georgia, USA. When Norvell was still a child, his father Oliver died and in his honour Norvell adopted his father's name, becoming known as Oliver Norvell Hardy. His on-screen partner, Arthur Stanley Jefferson, was born in 1890, in the town of Ulverston, in the English Lake District, later becoming famous by the name of Stan Laurel. Laurel made his stage debut at the age of 16 in Glasgow, as a 'golliwog', billed as 'Stan Jefferson – He of the Funny Ways'. He joined the legendary 'Fred Karno' and his troupe of comedians and toured America, alongside the young Charlie Chaplin.

As a duo, Laurel and Hardy [13-2] made films between 1921 and 1952. Oliver Hardy played the obese, arrogant and pompous, but oafish lead role,

13-2
Laurel and Hardy.

to Stan Laurel's small, submissive, gormless twit, ruffling his own hair and constantly on the verge of tears. They made the most of their starkly contrasting characters and physical appearances. Their career straddled the 'silents' and the 'talkies', and during both eras they managed to extract mirth and hilarity out of every possible fat-related scenario. Hardy would routinely fall through roofs, make cars tilt alarmingly to one side or collapse entirely on his mounting them, causing tyres to roll into view from off-screen. He would get stuck in a variety of embarrassing yet entertaining situations, usually remarking to Stan, 'Well, here's another nice mess you've gotten me into'.

The exploitation of the fat person for comic effect has been a recurring theme for as long as the performing arts have existed. Bucco was the traditional fat boy in the Atellan plays; Pulcinella and Il Dottore were traditional fat characters from the fifteenth-century Italian commedia dell'arte. Fat clowns have always been favourites in the circus ring, and in pantomime a cross-dressing pantomime dame is *de rigueur* at Christmas. As with Laurel and Hardy, a fat character is often teamed up with a thin partner or cast, such as Lou Costello in contrast to the lean Bud Abbott [13-3], or Curly Joe of the Three Stooges (although the Stooges *en masse* could be said to have had significant weight problems) [13-4]. Much more recently, show-business duos such as the Two Ronnies, Little and Large, Cannon and Ball, and French and Saunders have utilised the contrasting physique as a basis for their humour.

13-3
Abbott and Costello.

13-4
The Three Stooges.

13-5
Roscoe 'Fatty' Arbuckle

13-6
Buster Keaton.

The silent movie superstar Roscoe 'Fatty' Arbuckle [13-5] was born in Kansas in March 1887. His mother died when he was 12, and his father abandoned him soon after. He made ends meet by doing odd jobs at a hotel in San Jose, and was 'discovered' whilst singing in the hotel kitchen. His career began when he won an amateur talent contest in his local neighbourhood theatre, and he was soon in Vaudeville and destined to become one of the most popular and wealthy actors of the era. His first film was *Ben's Kid*, in 1909, and in 1913 he became a member of the slapstick Keystone Cops, and worked with Charlie Chaplin and other cinematic greats. (Buster Keaton [13-6], another silent movie star, learned his trade from Arbuckle, and the two remained lifelong friends.) Arbuckle attained a maximum weight of around 300 pounds, but still managed to be agile and nimble on his feet. He possessed a cherubic, versatile face, his expression ranging from broad happy smiles, to downright anger. His style was unashamedly slapstick, rowdy, gag-filled and raucous, with exaggerated physical humour which was immediately funny to children and adults alike, without too much critical thought being required.

In the film *A Noise From the Deep* he made slapstick history by being the first film comedian to be hit with a pie![8] In 1916 Arbuckle was earning $1000 a day plus 25 per cent of film profits, and in 1919 he signed a $1 million per year contract with Paramount; even his dog Luke was on $150 per week. His best work included films such as *Coney Island* and *Goodnight Nurse!*, but his workload was intensive – he sometimes worked on three films simultaneously. Arbuckle was an international sensation, but his career came to a shuddering halt at a Labor Day party he hosted in 1921. A young Hollywood starlet called Virginia Rappe gate-crashed the event, but died, ending the evening with acute peritonitis secondary to a ruptured bladder, later thought to be partly due to underlying syphilis.[9] However, a rumour spread through Hollywood that Fatty Arbuckle had raped the girl, and that his weight bearing down on her had caused the rupture of her bladder. Because of the value of a scandal to the media, the story was sensationalised. Arbuckle was indicted for first-degree murder but, three trials later, he was acquitted because of the complete lack of evidence against him. Nevertheless, his fans turned away, and the newly created Hays Code (a set of censorship guidelines for the industry) banned his films, removed them from circulation, and forbade him from ever acting again.

Broke, shunned and utterly demoralised, Arbuckle continued work surreptitiously under an assumed name, and friends such as Buster Keaton rallied round to provide employment of sorts. He directed several films using the name William Goodrich, his father's Christian names, but started drinking heavily and died aged only 46, in 1933. His reputation has still not recovered, despite the appalling miscarriage of justice he suffered, but his films are now belatedly and deservedly being recognised as amongst the very best of the silent era.

Large people in modern cinema

After the introduction of the talkies, the role of the fat person changed and expanded. The traditional silent-movie visual 'fat gag' was still alive and well, thanks to the Three Stooges and other groups, but the genre grew to include different aspects and characteristics associated with the corpulent persona. Some circus fat folk (see Chapter 3) appeared as cameos in some films. Todd Browning's 1932 classic *Freaks* [13-7] starred many genuine circus performers, including Half-Man and band-leader Johnny Eck, the limbless Prince Ranadian, pin-heads, midgets and an unnamed fat lady. In 1959 fat lady Marie King appeared briefly in *A Woman Obsessed*.[10] Howard Huge, also known as Fat Man Bruce Snowdon, appeared as himself in Tim Burton's film *Big Fish* (2003).

13-7
Freaks.

In a modern variation on the theme of movie fat ladies, Steven Spielberg and Robert Zemeckis' computer animated *Monster House* (2006) stars a house possessed by a circus fat lady, Constance the Giantess, who lies embedded in a shrine in the basement. Always an atypical fat lady, lacking the prefix 'Jolly' and being anxious and frankly paranoid, Constance was rescued from being goaded by children at the circus by the admiring Mr Nebbercracker, but died tragically when she fell into the foundations of the marital

13-8
Fats Domino.

home they were building, causing the house to become anthropomorphised by her spirit, eating humans, dogs, cars and toys in a gluttonous frenzy. The film also features a stereotypical foolish fat boy called Chowder.

In modern cinema, a famous or renowned fat actor will, by definition, always play a fat character and roles will generally be tailored for them. For instance, in 1957 Fats Domino [13-8] starred in one of the most famous rock'n'roll films ever, *The Girl Can't Help It*, as well as *Shake Rattle and Roll*, *The Big Beat* and *Jamboree*. An actor recognised as being obese will be selected for a role because of their build and reputation. Character actors such as Bill Maynard and Arthur Mullard had no option but to make their career exclusively playing corpulent individuals.

Other brilliant but obese actors were limited in the range of roles they could play by their build. In his prime Marlon Brando was described as

> amazingly beautiful – there is no other way of saying it…. He had huge eyes, a wide, deep brow, an angel's mouth, with the upper lip crested. And he could speak, softly, like breathing, so the mouth scarcely moved. But he was as male as a wild animal, hunky, husky, sensual, and incoherent or rhapsodic, depending on which style worked best with the young woman of the moment.[11]

Yet in his later years, despite his enormous talent, Brando had no choice but to play obese characters in films such as *Apocalypse Now* (1979) [13-9], *The Freshman* (1990) and *The Island of Dr Moreau* (1996). In his obituary in the *Guardian* following his death in 2004 at age 80, David Thomson

13-9
The younger and older
Marlon Brando.

commented sadly: 'he was a hulk, a wreck of obesity and self-indulgence, a hideously fat man – he who once had been so beautiful he altered our idea of maleness.'[12] Biographer Peter Manso agreed: 'The once-beautiful, most distinguished actor of our time has turned into a self-loathing slob, and left a lot of human wreckage in his wake'.[13]

Another such case was Orson Welles, who, by his own admission, 'started at the top and worked down'.[14] In his early masterpiece *Citizen Kane* (1941), Orson Welles, although not yet physically obese, plays an overbearing character who is corpulent in the sense of possessing great power and wealth. In later films, which were less critically acclaimed but still masterpieces in their own right, Welles was restricted by his build to playing physically corpulent – obese – individuals. By the time *Touch of Evil* was released in 1958, Welles was already developing an obesity problem [13-10], but required additional padding to play the grotesquely fat Quinlan. Critic Pauline Kael was appalled: 'By the 60s he was encased in make up, and his own fat, like a huge operatic version of W. C. Fields'.[15]

13-10
Orson Welles in *Touch of Evil* (1958).

Alternatively, an obese character from a novel or play will be transcribed and adapted for cinema, and the appropriate actor or actress selected accordingly. Obese actress Ayllene Gibbons was an example. Although a talented actress, she was far from being a star in her own right, but when the role of a fat lady was announced, she was high on the list of suitable candidates, playing Big Annie alongside Burt Reynolds in *Sam Whiskey* (1969) and the uncredited 'Fat Woman in Pub' in *My Fair Lady* (1964). Gibbons' moment of glory came in the film *The Loved One*, released in 1965, loosely based on the Evelyn Waugh novel. She played the bizarre and gluttonous Mrs Joyboy, pathologically obsessed by food and waited on by her son. She demolishes an entire suckling pig, tearing it apart limb from limb, and devours 'king chicken' and 'big boy crab' crudely and voraciously, even mouthing along to actors eating in television food advertisements.

Dom DeLuise made many appearances as the fat sidekick to someone else's starring role, such as in Mel Brooks' *Silent Movie* (1976) and *Blazing Saddles* (1974), but he starred only once, and was mauled by the critics, playing a food obsessive, in *Fatso* (1980).

The poet and critic Dana Gioia misses the good old days:

> In the Hollywood I love best, fat men filled the Silver Screen, innocent and unabashed.... Tinseltown was sweeter in those Great Depression days. The rich didn't grow hungry, and audience got more actor for their money. A roly-poly man wasn't clinically obese, but amiable.[16]

He lists some fat favourites: Edward Arnold, Monty Woolley, Charles Coburn, Sydney Greenstreet, Eugene Pallette, W. C. Fields, Charles Laughton, Wallace Beery, Robert Morley, Burl Ives and others [13-11, 13-12]. Gioia refers to Greenstreet and Pallette as pre-eminent. Greenstreet was born in

13-11
Clockwise from top left:
Edward Arnold, W. C. Fields,
Wallace Beery and
Charles Laughton.

Kent in 1879, and after careers planting tea and brewing beer, as well as many years of theatre acting, he turned to film acting at age 62, in 1941. His first film was his masterpiece, for which he is best remembered, playing the character of 'The Fat Man' Kasper Gutman in *The Maltese Falcon* (1941), alongside Peter Lorre; it was a pairing that would last for nine films, including *Casablanca* (1942), in which Greenstreet played the barman Signor Ferrari. Far from his obese slapstick predecessors, Greenstreet's characters were enigmatic and exuded evil; he also played the diabolical Count Fosco (see Chapter 11, page 225) in a film adaptation of Wilkie Collins' *The Woman in White* (1948).

Eugene Pallette was born in 1889. After a spell as a streetcar operator, he commenced his film career in the silent era as a slim, attractive lead man.

13-12
Greenstreet in *The Maltese
Falcon* (1941).

After a spell in the military during the First World War, Pallette returned to the cinema in more weighty roles [13-13], eventually expanding to at least 300 pounds. A prolific actor, he played Friar Tuck in *The Adventures of Robin Hood* (1938), co-starred with Shirley Temple in *Stowaway* (1936) and with Cary Grant in *Topper* (1937), amongst hundreds of other films in the 1930s and 1940s. He was also famed for his gravelly bullfrog voice. According to Gioia:

13-13
Eugene Pallette.

> Both Pallette and Greenstreet possessed a singular and striking personality. Pallette could anchor a scene just by walking downstairs.... One never loses Greenstreet or Pallette in a crowded scene. Their personalities radiate forth. (How dimly, by comparison, most current character actors glimmer.) … No actor ever carried his fat more magisterially than Greenstreet. Erect, urbane, and self-possessed, he presents corpulence not as a liability but an accomplishment. He is not obese but Olympian.... *Portly* seems insufficient and *tubby* too tame. Pallette came as close to globular as a human being can and still walk upright. Yet there was nothing flabby about his conspicuous girth. Round he may have been, but Pallette remained feisty and determined.[17]

One of the most famous fat people to appear in films was the obese director Alfred Hitchcock [13-14], who enjoyed playing cameo appearances in most of his own movies. He suffered from weight problems on and off throughout his life, but at his heaviest (in the late 1930s) he was around 300 pounds. He lost a considerable amount of weight in the early 1950s, for movies such as *To Catch a Thief*, in which he appeared remarkably thin. According to the Internet Movie Database:

> He had a hard time devising one of his signature walk-ons for *Lifeboat* (1944), a film about a small group of people trying to survive on a small boat. What he eventually came up with was to have his own picture in

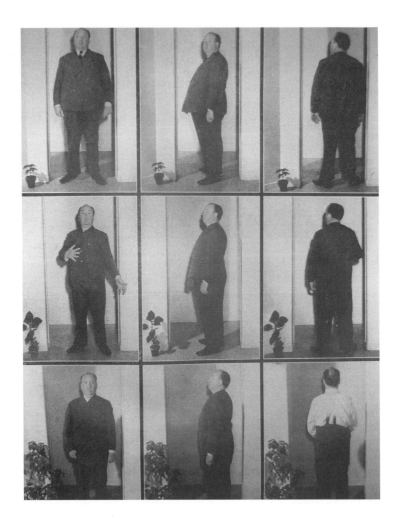

13-14
Alfred Hitchcock documented his weight loss for a magazine, in front, profile and rear views, together with time and weight: top row, 295 pounds at start; middle row, 273 pounds after three weeks; bottom row, 238 pounds after eight weeks.

a newspaper advertisement for weight loss floating amongst some debris around the boat. He had lost a considerable amount of weight from dieting around that time, so he was seen in both the 'Before' and the 'After' pictures.[18]

Born in 1908 in Wiltshire, Robert Morley was a quintessentially English gentleman, portly, double-chinned, usually pompous and jovial, who played quintessentially English characters. He would have fitted the role of a diplomat perfectly if he had pursued his original career choice, instead of ending up at the Royal Academy of Dramatic Art, studying acting. He made his London stage debut as Oscar Wilde in 1929, a role he would later portray on film. Two particularly memorable roles involved Robert Morley and food.

13-15
Robert Morley in
Theater of Blood (1973).

In the comedy horror classic *Theater of Blood* (1973), Vincent Price plays Shakespearian actor Edward Lionheart, who takes murderous revenge on his critics after failing to capture a coveted award, each murder representing a perverted re-enactment of a Shakespeare scene. Morley plays the effeminate critic Meredith Merridew, whose gory demise is based on the play *Titus Andronicus*, in which the character eats his own children baked in a pie. Since Morley has no offspring he is force fed to death on the next best thing – a pie made from his own two beloved toy poodles [13-15].

In *Who Is Killing the Great Chefs of Europe?* (1978) Morley plays Max, the rich, world-famous connoisseur of fine food, who cannot resist tucking in when top-quality food is served. However, he is under orders from his doctor to lose over 100 pounds in weight to avoid death from heart disease. Like most people, he finds the challenge difficult, especially in the presence of so many four-star European chefs. When the chefs in question start to be bumped off in unusual circumstances, each related to the chef's own speciality, Max is the prime suspect.

Morley had a fairly relaxed attitude to his health, commenting on physical activity:

> Exercise for the sake of exercise or in the hopeless quest of preservation is not to be countenanced in my book. Cats once they cease to be kittens never take an unnecessary step and live longer than dogs, who do. You too will be better advised to stretch out in front of the fire and turn the page.

And on nutrition:

> A diet is often brought on by wardrobe shrinkages. A dress or suit which fitted perfectly last summer is now unwearable, thanks to the extraordinary treatment it has received at the dry-cleaners.[19]

Caring for a morbidly obese mother and mentally handicapped brother is the lot of Gilbert Grape, the troubled teenager played by Johnny Depp in the 1993 film *What's Eating Gilbert Grape?* His mother was played by Darlene Cates on her debut, who weighed 500 pounds in real life. Her character has not left the house for seven years and spends most of her time on the couch watching television. She dies in her own bed, but the problem then arises of how to remove her body. The idea of having her body taken from the house by crane and risk becoming the laughing stock of the town is rejected by her family. Their solution is to empty the house of all their possessions and set it ablaze, thus cremating her body.

Obese, well loved British actor Richard Griffiths is the son of deaf mute parents.[20] He originally built a reputation as a Shakespearian clown, and played Henry VIII, Bottom and Falstaff during his extensive career. Although claiming to have 'always hated the way I look',[21] he has enjoyed critical acclaim, and an enormously high profile, most notably as the obnoxious uncle Vernon Dursley in the 'Harry Potter' series [13-16]. However, even Uncle Vernon was dwarfed by the massive figure of Robbie Coltrane, as the character Hagrid.

13-16
Richard Griffiths as Vernon Dursley in the 'Harry Potter' series of films.

One of the more outrageous manifestations of obesity in cinema was courtesy of the actor Harris Glen Milstead, who was born in 1945 in Maryland and became famous as shocking big-haired transvestite actress and recording artiste Divine. As a teenager, Divine idolised Elizabeth Taylor, but later said: 'All my life I wanted to look like Elizabeth Taylor. Now Elizabeth Taylor looks like me.'[22] He teamed up with film-maker John Waters in the 1960s and 1970s, in low-budget, sleazy films such as *Eat Your Makeup* and *Mondo Trasho*. Amongst their most famous and infamous work was *Pink Flamingos* (1972), in which Divine played Babs Johnson, the 'filthiest person alive', living in a pink trailer with her egg-eating grandmother, chicken-loving son and voyeuristic daughter. On the brink of superstardom after the hit musical *Hairspray* (1988), alongside Sonny Bono and Debbie Harry, Divine died at only 42, of respiratory failure, and possibly myocardial infarction, having suffered from obesity-related sleep apnoea for many years.[23]

Tragically, because of the health risks associated with obesity, an early death is far from uncommon amongst obese actors. As well as Divine, John Candy and John Belushi were two such cases. A Canadian actor, Candy died from a heart attack at age 44; his father Sidney suffered the same fate at age 35. Candy already had an impressive cinema portfolio and had an instantly recognisable face, but was destined for even greater things, until he died during the shooting of *Wagon's East* in 1994 in Mexico. John Belushi died even more prematurely, at age 33, but from a cause unrelated to overweight – cocaine and heroin overdose. Belushi [13-17], son of an Albanian immigrant to Chicago, was born in 1949, and achieved fame through the television series *Saturday Night Live* in 1975. He played the gluttonous

13-17
John Belushi.

beer-swilling slob Bluto in the hit film *Animal House* in 1978, and as Jake Blues in the 1980 smash hit *The Blues Brothers*, alongside Dan Ackroyd, as well as Ray Charles, James Brown and Aretha Franklin.

In a world where obese male actors are much more commonly seen than actresses, Hattie Jacques was a notable exception, but unfortunately she followed tradition by dying early of obesity-related illness. Born in 1922 in Kent, she was most famous playing Matron, opposite Kenneth Williams in the 'Carry On' films. She married and divorced *Dad's Army* star John Le Mesurier, and died at age 58 from a heart attack.

Putting on weight

Some actors have gained weight for the purpose of a film role, notably Renée Zellweger, who gained 25 pounds for the title role in the *Bridget Jones* films (2001 and 2004), and Robert de Niro in *Raging Bull* (1980), in order to resemble the boxer Jake La Motta in later life [13-18]. De Niro also put on weight deliberately for the role of Al Capone in *The Untouchables* (1987). George Clooney gained 38 pounds deliberately at age 44 for the film *Syriana* (2005), which led directly to bouts of depression.[24] Morgan Spurlock gained weight and caused his health to deteriorate by sticking to a fast-food diet in the documentary movie *Super Size Me* (2004).

Other roles have required actors and actresses to become obese through the skills of the make-up department. In *The Godfather* (1972), Marlon Brando puffed his cheeks out with cotton wool to produce the obligatory jowls for his character Vito Corleone. Later, the invention of the 'fat suit' allowed any naturally slim actor or actress to become obese for a role, or part of a role. The suit allowed fit young actors to experience the obese state for a day or two, and indulge in obesity-related slapstick and hi-jinx, and also encouraged the audience to belly-laugh at the fat fool, without any guilty feelings, knowing that a perfectly healthy person had climbed out of the suit at the end of the day's filming with nothing worse than a glow of perspiration and a profound thirst.

In *Shallow Hal* (2001) Jack Black plays the title role, and professes to want to judge women for their inner beauty, but his appreciation of physical beauty gets in the way. He visits a famous life-coach who hypnotises him into seeing people's inner beauty, not their external appearance. He then meets a woman who appears to him as slim and beautiful because she is kind and tender-hearted, but she is, in fact, very obese [13-19]. Eventually, after being released from his hypnotic state and experiencing some emotional turmoil, he realises that he does not need hypnosis to see people's true inner beauty. Gwyneth Paltrow plays Rosemary, the girl in question, in both states, slim and obese, with the help of a fat suit. Paltrow is the only actress in the film

13-18
Renée Zellweger, in the *Bridget Jones* films (2001 and 2004), and Robert de Niro in *Raging Bull* (1980), both of whom put on substantial weight to play their roles.

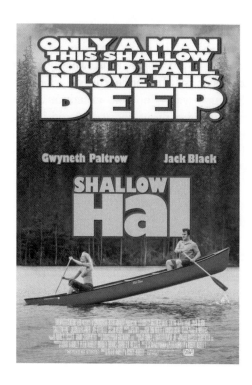

13-19
Shallow Hal (2001). The film poster showing Rosemary (Paltrow) seen as thin by Hal, but in reality obese and weighing down the boat.

to don a fat suit; others who are alternately observed as thin or fat are played by two different people. According to critic Karl Heitmueller:

> By burying Paltrow under latex and makeup, the film not only gives us an unconvincing obese girl, it lets the audience off the hook. We're not forced to truly deal with our attitudes toward obesity because we know Gwyneth the *actress* isn't fat.[25]

Other fat-suited actors include Eddie Murphy in *The Nutty Professor*, a Universal Studios production in 1996 in which Murphy plays the part of an obese genetics professor working on DNA experiments to make obese mice thin. The ultimate aim is to use his product on humans. However, when the professor falls in love, he cannot conceive that his love can be reciprocated whilst he retains his 400-pound frame. He drinks some of his experimental potion and turns into the slim, agile, handsome Eddie Murphy his fans know and love, but his condition is unstable and he may revert to his own fat self at any moment, in a Jekyll and Hyde manner. The animations in the film as his fat state re-emerges induce a sense of revulsion, horror and fascination with the fattening process. The girl in question has the choice of an unpredictable slim character, or a kind, thoughtful but obese one. She meets the professor's family – seven in total, all played by Eddie Murphy, all obese and all portrayed as generous, kind-hearted and good-humoured as well as vulgar, greedy and uncouth. How does a girl choose? In the end, she sees and chooses the one man who is kind, warm-hearted and thoughtful – the obese professor; his obesity has endearing qualities.

Julia Roberts donned a fat suit in *America's Sweethearts* (2001), as did Martin Lawrence in *Big Momma's House* (2000) and Kenan Thompson in *Fat Albert* (2004). In Karl Heitmueller's assessment:

> to the overweight person sitting in the audience, the experience must be similar to a black person watching an old blackface minstrel show. When the character is presented as mean-spiritedly as Mike Myers 'Fat Bastard' character from the 'Austin Powers' movies or scary thin Courteney Cox-Arquette's Fat Monica from flashback episodes of 'Friends' it becomes downright torture.[26]

The ultimate fat suit was worn by Terry Jones, playing the character of Mr Creosote in Monty Python's *The Meaning of Life* (1983). The outrageously obese character is first encountered entering a French restaurant, with the exchange:

> Maître D: Ah, good afternoon, sir, and how are we today?
> Mr. Creosote: Better.
> Maître D: Better?
> Mr. Creosote: Better get a bucket. I'm going to throw up.

He works his way through a meal of jugged hare ('Ze hare is very high, and ze sauce is very rich with truffles, anchovies, Grand Marnier, bacon, and cream'), moules marinières, pâté de foie gras, beluga caviar, eggs Benedictine, tart de poireaux, frogs' legs amandine, oeufs de caille Richard Shepherd ('mixed up togezer in a bucket with the eggs on top'), six bottles of Château Latour '45, a double jeroboam of champagne and the usual brown ales. However, the final tempting wafer-thin mint proves too much for Mr Creosote, who explodes cataclysmically, leaving his food and entrails all over the restaurant and diners, and his heart, still beating, dangling inside the remains of his ribcage. 'Terry Jones as Mr Creosote forces regurgitation to new highs (or lows) in a gross-out scene so expertly staged and performed that it becomes a triumph of excess'.[27] According to co-writer Michael Palin: 'Creosote, I think, was one of the best things that Python has ever done in terms of elevating some tiny idea to a sort of great Gothic extravaganza'.[28]

Animation

Another way of displaying obesity on film without worrying about stigmatising overweight actors or adverse audience reaction is by animation. Almost without exception, feature-length cartoons, stop-frame animations and computer-animated movies have used weight as a vehicle for inducing laughter from fat characters, often anthropomorphised animals. Their exact personality and role changes from film to film, but they are rarely, if ever, the leading role or love interest. Some are buffoons, like Baloo the bear in the *Jungle Book* or Mr Smee in *Peter Pan*, some evil, such as Ursula from *The Little Mermaid*, and Victor Quartermaine, the evil buffoon in Wallace and Gromit *The Curse of the Were-Rabbit*. Some are not very bright, including Winnie the Pooh, and the majority of the seven dwarfs. Disney villains tended to be fat, such as Ratcliffe from *Pocohontas*, and Edgar, the scheming butler from the *Aristocats*, has a prodigious pot belly. The longest-running Disney character of all was Pete, also known as Peg Leg Pete and Black Pete; his career spanned from the *Alice Comedies* in 1925 to *A Goofy Movie* in 1995. *Time* magazine referred to him as 'a monstrous mingling of common house cat and Long John Silver', and he was nemesis to Donald Duck and Mickey Mouse.[29] Stromboli is the evil and greedy and alarmingly obese showman in *Pinocchio*, who burns his puppets for firewood. According to the Disney archive, 'Walt Disney's Stromboli is a much more sinister Hollywood villain than the original character written by Italian author Carlo Collodi'. In the book, 'the Showman', as he is called, kindly sets Pinocchio free and even gives him five gold pieces to bring home for Geppetto. Bill Tytla's forceful animation of Stromboli is widely regarded as one of the pinnacles of animation acting, although the famed comedian W. C. Fields was reported to have criticised Stromboli's performance, saying 'He moves too much'.[30]

Homer Simpson has been an all-time television (and more recently movie) favourite for 20 years, and is a classical slob, combining overeating and inactivity with profound lack of insight. In one episode he turned into a doughnut and ate himself. Eric Cartman from the television series and movie *South Park* is another popular cartoon creation but, unlike Homer Simpson, is disgustingly obnoxious, except for an episode in which he is sent to a fat camp to lose weight and returns not only thinner but also much more mature and good-natured. However, he soon returns to his previous 'normal' self.

At least Mr Incredible from the Disney/Pixar film of the same name proves that even someone who has trouble doing up their belt can still be a useful member of society, if not always a superhero!

The dance of death

Fast and fear not, you'll need no drop or pill;
Hunger *may* starve – excess is *sure* to kill.[1]

William Wadd, who wrote this couplet, had pointed out in his book *Cursory Remarks on Corpulence* (first published in 1810) that sudden death is not uncommon in corpulent individuals. Hippocrates had noted this previously. The *Encyclopaedia Britannica*, in its ninth edition (published in 1880), had offered its view of death caused from over-indulgence: 'Hence it may be justly doubted, whether gluttony and intemperance have not depopulated the world more, than even the sword, pestilence, and famine'. Also in the nineteenth century, a physician named William Harvey also had warned of the dangers of obesity, but he offered a reprieve: 'it is important to remember that obesity may be either the cause of an early death, or merely a warning that a tendency to premature decay exists; in which case the time given for treatment may allow of the happiest results being produced'.[2]

'Death' itself offered no reprieve. Death was in the midst of life. 'Dance of death' and 'danse macabre' are terms which have been used since the Middle Ages to describe many different kinds of literary or artistic representations of a procession or dance in which the living and the dead take part – in which Death ushers mortals to the tomb. Man's mortality was and still is a common theme in literature and art.

In the dance of death, the dead might be portrayed by a number of figures or by a single individual personifying Death. Early artistic representations typically portray a procession of the living members of society in some order of precedence, such as a pope, cardinal, archbishop, or emperor, king, duke, sometimes with alternating religious and secular figures [C-26]. These range from the most important persons to the ordinary man in the street. The dance usually expresses some allegorical, moral or satirical point, drawing attention to the fact that all must die; death is no respecter of persons and the physical body and all earthly things are transient. Macabre figures or skeletons representing Death often retained their living expressions and conducted activities indicating the close link between life and death. The procession filed past Death, who summoned each mortal in turn to join in a dance to the grave.

An early representation of the dance of death can be found carved in stone in Rosslyn Chapel [14-1] (the chapel which featured in Dan Brown's 2003 book and the 2006 film *The Da Vinci Code*). These figures were probably carved in the mid-fifteenth century, and 16 figures with Death leading them in their 'dance' can be seen carved on ribbed arches inside the chapel. Such images in churches were a reminder that death was in the midst of life. *Memento mori* – Remember thou shalt die.

Hans Holbein completed his famous series of 41 wood engravings, 'The Dance of Death', in 1526, by which time Death had lost any remnants of skin and mummified flesh, which, until then, he had generally retained in various depictions. As a skeleton, he taunted his victims, leapt and danced, took perverse and sometimes erotic pleasure where he liked, and led his victims on a 'merry dance'. The engravings were produced in book form in Lyons in 1538 and by the time of Holbein's death in 1543 they were famous throughout Europe.

14-1
An arch in the Rosslyn Chapel, with a detail inset of the top couple from this dance of death, mid-fifteenth century. Copyright Antonia Reeve/RCT.

14-2
Rowlandson's print (March 1816) showing the banqueting hall, accompanied by Combe's couplet here 'This fine, hot, feast's a preparation / To some, for Death's last, cold Collation.'

In more recent times, Thomas Rowlandson produced a series of paintings entitled 'The English Dance of Death', published in 1816. William Combe, who had collaborated with Rowlandson in the series of paintings of 'Doctor Syntax', provided metrical text to accompany the series. These drew attention to the dangers that lay in store for those who led a less than blameless life, for example the glutton [14-2]. Combe gave warning that Death lurked in the banqueting hall, in a verse entitled 'The Dainty Dish':

> … in the proud, illumin'd hall,
> Where the Feast ushers in the Ball:
> Where the rich Banquet gives delight,
> And Beauty crowns the splendid night,
> DEATH sometimes will his step advance,
> Proclaim the Toast, and join the Dance.

Combe describes the gluttons who feast at these banquets:

> But these same cramming mortals meet
> With gloating eyes the various treat;
> In silence at their tables sit,
> Till they can't eat another bit;
> And when their well-crammed crops are full,
> They grow immeasurably dull.

And the narrator goes on to question the use of the glutton, whose sole enjoyment is to eat, to enjoy one meal, only to anticipate the next:

What is the good he e'ere bestows
From Morning's dawn to Evening's close,
Who boasts it as his sole delight,
To gorge his rav'nous appetite,
And joys, when he at noon can say,
'How lordly I shall dine today:'
Then fills his gullet, o'er and o'er
And sighs that he can eat no more.
…

These Corm'rants, when the stomach's still,
Weep for another paunch to fill.

The saga continues relating the plight of one such individual, who

At length his limbs, with hobbling gait,
Could scarce support the body's weight.
…

Then, calling for one slice more of his favourite dinner,

DEATH heard his call and soon obey'd,
And by his side the dish display'd;
When he exclaim'd, 'As I'm a sinner,
'One slice — and I have clos'd my dinner.'
The slice his eager knife supplies —
It will not pass — He choaks, — and dies.

Another of Rowlandson's 'Dance of Death' collaborative series is called 'The Kitchen'. Here, Combe informs us:

14-3
The Kitchen, from the 'Dance of Death' series, Rowlandson, 1816.

One day, DEATH, tempted by the scent,
Into Lord Ort'lans kitchen went,
Well-pleas'd he views the various show
Of *Fricasee* and *Fricandeau*,
Of ev'ry Flesh, and Fowl and Fish
Prepar'd to grace each silver dish,
Of roast and boil'd, of Grill and Stew,
Turtle and Ven'son and Ragout.

The sad end to this tale is the death of the cook, who tries to fend off Death with a roasting spit and ends up on the spit with a turkey. Rowlandson illustrates the scene [14-3], to which Death provides the caption:

Thou Slave to ev'ry gorging Glutton,
I'll spit thee like a Leg of Mutton.

Rowlandson's contemporary and collaborator George Woodward also produced 'Dance of Death' scenes, etched by Isaac Cruikshank in 1808 [14-4]. His scenes are drawn as a procession of contemporary figures dancing with death. Included amongst the victims are the Glutton, who does not want to be kept from his dinner, and the overweight bishop, who has his nose disrespectfully tweaked. None of them is ready to accompany Death.

14-4
George Woodward's 'Dance of Death', etched by Isaac Cruikshank in 1808, with detail ('If you detain me in this way my venison will be quite cold').

James Ensor continued the theme of death in association with the seven deadly sins in the engravings that he produced in 1904. The frontispiece of his work depicts a winged skull hovering over the images of seven people representing the sins, the separate portrayals of which are not overtly connected with the after-life but are contemporary scenes that show them enacted in everyday environments (see Chapter 8).

In another scene devised by Rowlandson and Combe, the spectre of alcohol looms in the 'Dram Shop':

> Indulge not in the liquid ill
> That flows from the empoison'd Still,
> Thither the Fiend loves to repair,
> And Death, too oft, attends him there.

This sentiment applies equally well to George Cruikshank's *The Gin Shop* [14-5], a print from 1829, which is full of allusions to drinking and its association with death. A skeleton holds up an hourglass in one hand and states 'I shall have them all dead drunk presently! They have nearly had their last glass.' He is referring to the drinkers who are standing inside a mantrap; one is a mother feeding gin to her baby, whilst a child drinks a similar potion by her side. A barmaid with a skeletal head upon her

14-5
The Gin Shop, Cruikshank, 1829.

shoulder and a skeletal foot protruding from her skirt is serving 'death' to her customers. All around are emblems of death by alcohol in the shape of coffins and posters. An open door behind the shop leading to the 'SPIRIT VAULTS' reveals a cauldron holding a death-head and around which are dancing 'spirits'. A book on the counter stating 'Open a Gin Shop' offers a prosperous way of life to such an owner, but to the consumer the ways out of the shop lead to the gibbet, the workhouse, the mad-house and the gaol. The effects of the consumption of alcohol in the twenty-first century might not be as desperate as they were in some areas in the eighteenth and nineteenth centuries, but there is no room for complacency.

Death has been reproduced in many forms but his presence in prints has probably attracted more attention to undesirable lifestyles than have many wordy treatises. Until the middle of the nineteenth century, the doctor was pictured in many death scenes – satirically acting as an accomplice to Death – but as medical education improved a new respect for doctors became apparent. Many death scenes then took on a more sentimental and realistic theme; Death could be welcomed as a friend bringing release to the sick and weary. He was not necessarily a ruthless destroyer of life.

For those who regard satirical images with a degree of scepticism, inscriptions on some tombstones might give food for more serious thought, or thought more seriously about food. A word of warning is recorded on the tombstone of one James Parsons, who was buried at Teddington on 7 March 1743. It was noted that he had often eaten a whole shoulder of mutton and a peck (two gallons) of 'hasty pudding' (a porridge made of flour and milk, or oatmeal and water). His weight, though, is not mentioned. Other church-yards contain details of the sudden death of fat people. Thomas Dollman is lamented in this way:

> Here lies the body of Thomas Dollman,
> A *vastly fat*, though not a very tall man;
> Full twenty stone he weighed, yet I am told,
> His captain thought him worth his *weight* in gold;
> Grim Death *who ne'er to nobody* shews favor,
> Hurried him off, for all his good behaviour;
> Regardless of his weight, he bundled him away,
> 'Fore any one 'Jack Robinson' could say.

The moral of the tale is told with regard to the late lamented John Holder:

> But why he grew so fat i'th' waist,
> Now mark ye, the true reason;
> When other people used to *fast*,
> He *feasted* in that season.
>
> So now alas! Hath cruel Death,
> Laid him in his Sepulchre.

> Therefore good people, here 'tis seen,
> You plainly may see here,
> That fat men sooner die than lean,
> Witness fat Johnny Holder.

The provision of extra-large coffins, such as were needed for some of the super-obese individuals described in Chapters 2 and 3, would be no problem today. A company in the United States is making mass-produced 'Goliath' coffins for bodies weighing up to 64 stone. Other Western countries will probably do likewise.

The corpulent were not immune to ridicule even in death. According to Wadd,[3] the fat physician Dr Stafford was not allowed to rest in his grave without a witticism:

> Take heed, O good trav'ller, and do not tread hard,
> For here lies Dr. Stafford, *in all this church-yard.*

It is well established that obesity, and not just super-obesity, leads to premature death; obese individuals will lose, on average, nine years of life. Some 30,000 deaths are estimated to occur in the UK each year as a direct consequence of obesity, and in the US this figure is increased 10-fold. In the UK, 18 million working days per year are lost to obesity-related illnesses, at an estimated cost to the economy of £2.6 billion.

It is perhaps time, in the twenty-first century, for a new set of *memento mori* images. The Fat, Gluttonous and Slothful are still dancing, or dicing, with Death.

Notes

Chapter 1. Introduction

1 William Combe, 'The Kitchen', from William Combe (text) and Thomas Rowlandson (illustrations), *English Dance of Death* (London: Ackermann, 1816). 'Corm'rant' (cormorant) in the last line means glutton.

2 Chi-Liang Eric Yen, *et al.*, 'Deficiency of the Intestinal Enzyme Acyl CoA:monoacylglycerol Acyltransferase-2 Protects Mice From Metabolic Disorders Induced by High-Fat Feeding', *Nature Medicine*, advance online publication 15 March 2009.

3 Foresight. *Trends and Drivers of Obesity: A Literature Review for the Foresight Project on Obesity*, p. 16. Available at www.foresight.gov.uk/Obesity/Literature_Review.pdf. The Foresight Programme is run by the UK government's Office of Science and Technology.

4 Thomas Short, quoted by Roy Porter, *Flesh in the Age of Reason* (London: Allen Lane, 2003), p. 233.

5 Traditionally, obesity has been measured using body mass index (BMI). The measurement was developed in Europe in the 1800s and was first used to monitor trends in overweight populations. It is calculated by taking an individual's weight in kilograms and dividing it by the square of his or her height in metres.

6 William Wadd, *Cursory Remarks on Corpulence; or Obesity considered as a Disease: with a Critical Examination of Ancient and Modern Opinions, Relative to Its Causes and Cure*, 3rd edition (London, 1816), p. 17.

7 A. Herbert, N. P. Gerry, M. B. McQueen, *et al.*, 'A Common Genetic Variant Is Associated with Adult and Childhood Obesity', *Science*, vol. 312 (2006), pp. 279–83.

8 Quoted in 'Paediatric Consultant: Body and Soul', *The Times*, 11 March 2006, p. 10.

9 *British Medical Journal*, 20–27 August 2005, p. 464.

10 *British Medical Journal*, 1 April 2006, p. 795.

11 Porter, *Flesh in the Age of Reason*, p. 234.

12 Principles of the School of Salerno, quoted by Magueloune Toussaint-Samat, *History of Food*, trans. Anthea Bell (Oxford: Blackwell, 1994), p. 755.

13 Hillel Schwartz, *Never Satisfied. A Cultural History of Diets, Fantasies and Fat* (London: Anchor Books, 1986), p. 8.

14 A. Prentice and S. Jebb, 'Gluttony or Sloth?', *British Medical Journal*, 12 August 1995, pp. 437–39.

15 Brett Silverstein, *et al.* 'The Role of Mass Media in Promoting a Thin Standard of Attractiveness for Women', *Sex Roles*, vol. 14 (1986), p. 519.

Chapter 2. The obese and the nature of obesity

1 *The Life of That Wonderful and Extraordinary Human Mammoth Daniel Lambert*, anonymous pamphlet (Stamford, 1883).

2 *The Life of That Wonderful and Extraordinary Human Mammoth Daniel Lambert*.

3 *Dimensions* magazine, '900 Club' (see www.dimensionsmagazine.com).

4 Anonymous, *Lives of Great and Celebrated Characters of All Ages and Countries* (Philadelphia, PA: Leary and Getz, 1854), p. 37.

5 *Lives of Great and Celebrated Characters*, p. 38.

6 Alison Barnes, *Essex Eccentrics* (Ipswich: Boydell, 1975).

7 Jon Bondeson, *Freaks* (Ithaca, NY: Cornell University Press, 2006), p. 131.

8 G. M. Gould and W. L. Pyle, *Anomalies and Curiosities of Medicine* (New York: Bell, 1896), p. 358.

9 Gould and Pyle, *Anomalies and Curiosities of Medicine*, p. 359.

10 See www.showhistory.com/FatPages/fat2.html.

11 James Mackenzie, *The History of Health and the Art of Preserving It* (Edinburgh: William Gordon, 1758), p. 32.

12 Mackenzie, *The History of Health*, p. 32.

13 Mackenzie, *The History of Health*, p. 33.

14 Obesity is commonly taken to be a body mass index (BMI) of over 30 kg/m². Morbidly obese denotes a BMI of 45–50 kg/m² and super-obese a BMI of over 50–60 kg/m².

15 Celeste 'Dolly Dimples' Geyer and Samuel Roen, *Diet or Die: The 'Dolly Dimples Weight Reducing Plan* (New York: F. Fell, 1968), pp. 184–85.

16 Joannes Baptista Morgagni, *Epistola anatoma clinica XXI: De Sedibuset Causis Morborum per Anatomen indagata* (1765).

17 William Wadd, *Lineaments on Leannes* (London: Ebers, 1829), p. 65.

18 Jean Vague, 'Sexual Differentiation, a Factor Affecting the Forms of Obesity', *Presse Medicale* (1947), pp. 339–40.

19 Contrasting statuettes, estimated to be 30,000 years old, show two different aspects of the naked female figure. The more famous Venus of Willendorf depicts an anatomically convincing 'apple', with expansive waistline, hands resting on large breasts, and relatively thin legs (see Chapter 10, page 186), whereas the Venus of Lespugne demonstrates gluteal obesity of the thighs and legs, with a relatively modest abdomen.

20 Mackenzie, *The History of Health*.

21 Sander L. Gilman, *Fat Boys: A Slim Book* (Lincoln, NE: Univeristy of Nebraska Press, 2004), p. 38, quoting from Herophilus, *The Art of Medicine in Early Alexandria*, ed. and trans. Henrich von Staden (Cambridge: Cambridge University Press, 1989), p. 298.

22 Jean Anthelme Brillat-Savarin, *Physiology of Taste, or, Meditations on Transcendental Gastronomy* (New York: Boni & Liveright, 1926; first published 1825), pp. 189–90.

23 G. Reaven, 'Role of Insulin Resistance in Human Disease', *Diabetes* (1988), vol. 37, pp. 1595–607.

24 Shadrach Ricketson, *Means of Preserving Health and Preventing Disease* (New York: Collins Perkins, 1806), p. 64.

25 Ricketson, *Means of Preserving Health*.

26 Diabetes simply denotes an excessive production of urine. Diabetes mellitus is a metabolic disorder relating to the hormone insulin. Type 1 develops in childhood and requires insulin injections. Type 2 typically develops in middle age and is associated with obesity; it involves decreased cellular sensitivity to insulin and is managed by diet and drugs. Diabetes mellitus can lead to kidney and nerve damage, as well as blindness.

27 Christos S. Mantzoros (ed.), *Obesity and Diabetes* (Toronto: Humana Press, 2006), pp. 3–13.

28 Mantzoros, *Obesity and Diabetes*.

29 Mantzoros, *Obesity and Diabetes*.

30 Robert Thomas, *The Modern Practice of Physic, Exhibiting the Characters, Causes, Symptoms, Prognostic, Morbid Appearances, and Improved Methods of Treating the Diseases of All Climates* (New York: Collins, 1811).

31 David Adler, *Life and Cuisine of Elvis Presley* (New York: Three Rivers Press, 1993).

32 See www.medphys.ucl.ac.uk/teaching/undergrad/projects/2003/group_03/history.html.

33 Geyer and Roen, *Diet or Die*, p. 194.

34 Mackenzie, *The History of Health*.

35 Thomas, *The Modern Practice of Physic*, p. 298.

36 Thomas, *The Modern Practice of Physic*, p. 301.

37 Thomas, *The Modern Practice of Physic*, p. 255.

38 William Buchan, *Domestic Medicine* (Philadelphia, PA, 1795).

39 Thomas, *The Modern Practice of Physic*, p. 527.

40 Mackenzie, *The History of Health*, p. 121.

41 Gilman, *Fat Boys*, p. 41.

42 Thomas, *The Modern Practice of Physic*, p. 392.

43 C. S. Burwell, *et al.*, 'Extreme Obesity Associated with Alveolar Hypoventilation – a Pick-wickian Syndrome', *American Journal of Medicine* (1956), vol. 21, pp. 811–18. Quoted in Neil J. Douglas, *Clinician's Guide to Sleep Medicine* (London: Arnold, 2002), p. 25.

44 Gilman, *Fat Boys*, p. 142.

45 William Shakespeare, *Henry IV, Part 1*, act II, scene iv, 25–26.

46 Wadd, *Cursory Remarks on Corpulence*.

47 W. Smith, ed., *A Dictionary of Greek and Roman Biography and Mythology* (London: John Murray, 1880). Quoted in Meir H. Kryger, 'Sleep Apnoea. From the Needles of Dionysius to Continuous Positive Airway Pressure', *Archives of Internal Medicine* (1983), vol. 143, pp. 2301–3.

48 I. Campbell and D. Haslam, *Your Questions Answered: Obesity* (London: Churchill Livingstone, 2005), p. 59.

49 Buchan, *Domestic Medicine*, p. 49.

50 Buchan, *Domestic Medicine*, p. 57.

51 Leslie Fiedler, *Freaks: Myths and Images of the Secret Self* (New York: Anchor, 1978), p. 126.

52 Mildred Klingman, *The Secret Lives of Fat People* (Boston, MA: Houghton Mifflin, 1981).

53 *Annals of Behavioral Medicine*, August 2002.

54 Fiedler, *Freaks*, p. 127.

55 Jean Frumusan, *The Cure of Obesity* (London: John Bale, 1924), p. 27 (first published in 1922 as *La cure de l'obésité*).

56 George Dupain, *Baffling Obesity: Outlining a Natural Form of Treatment for Extreme Corpulence* (Sydney: Briton, 1935).

57 Dupain, *Baffling Obesity*.

58 *Journal of the American Medical Association*, vol. 110, no. 16 (16 April 1938), p. 1261.

59 Gould and Pyle, *Anomalies and Curiosities of Medicine*, p. 361.

60 Gould and Pyle, *Anomalies and Curiosities of Medicine*, p. 362.

61 F. X. Dercum, 'Three Cases of Hitherto Unclassified Affection Resembling in Its Grosser Aspects Obesity, but Associated with Special Nervous Symptoms, Adiposis Dolorosa', *American Journal of the Medical Sciences*, vol. 104 (1892), pp. 521–35.

62 British Nutrition Foundation, *Obesity*, Task Force Report (London: Blackwell, 1999), p. 12.

63 A. K. Lindroos, *et al.*, 'Weight Change in Relation to Intake of Sugar and Sweet Foods Before and After Weight Reducing Gastric Surgery', *International Journal of Obesity*, vol. 20 (1996), pp. 634–43.

64 M. Sullivan, *et al.*, 'Swedish Obese Subjects (SOS). An Intervention Study of Obesity. I. Baseline Evaluation', *International Journal of Obesity*, vol. 17 (1993), pp. 503–12.

65 K. M. Carpenter, D. S. Hasin, D. B. Allison and M. S. Faith, 'The Relationships Between Obesity and DSM-IV Major Depressive Disorder, Suicide Ideation, and Suicide Attempts: Results from a General Population Study', *American Journal of Public Health*, vol. 90 (February 2000), pp. 251–71.

66 Anita Guerrini, *Obesity and Depression in the Enlightenment: The Life and Times of George Cheyne* (Norman, OK: University of Oklahoma Press, 2000).

67 Fiedler, *Freaks*, p. 131.

68 Daniel Mannix, *Freaks: We Who Are Not As Others* (New York: Powerhouse Books, 1976), p. 72.

69 British Nutrition Foundation, *Obesity*, p. 87.

70 S. Kenchaiah, J. M. Gaziano and R. S. Vasan, 'Impact of Obesity on the Risk of Heart Failure and Survival After the Onset of Heart Failure', *Medical Clinics of North America*, vol. 88 (2004), pp. 1273–94.

71 See the website of the US National Institute of Mental Health, www.nimh.nih.gov/health/publications/eating-disorders/binge-eating-disorder.shtml.

72 R. L. Spitzer, S. Yanovski, T. Wadden, *et al.*, 'Binge Eating Disorder: Its Further Validation in a Multisite Study', *International Journal of Eating Disorders*, vol. 13, no. 2 (1993), pp. 137–53.

73 Albert J. Stunkard, *The Pain of Obesity* (Palo Alto, CA: Bull Publishing, 1976).

74 Lord Byron, *The Works of Lord Byron, Letters and Journals*, vol. 1

75 Byron, *The Works*, vol. 1.

76 Jane Wilson, at http://secretstorm.blogspot.com/2004/04/great-big-man.html (posted April 2004).

77 See http://en.wikipedia.org/wiki/Carol_Yager.

78 See http://en.wikipedia.org/wiki/Patrick_Deuel and www.journalstar.com/articles/2004/08/12/nebraska/10053576.txt.

79 See http://dimensionsmagazine.com/dimtext/kjn/circus/baby_ruth.html.

80 Karl Niedershuh, 'The life and death of a big man', www.dimensionsmagazine.com/dimtext/hudson.html.

81 See http//insider.tv.yahoo.com/celeb/4136.

82 See www.rosaliebradford.com.

83 *The Life of That Wonderful and Extraordinary Human Mammoth Daniel Lambert*, pamphlet.

84 *The Life of That Wonderful and Extraordinary Human Mammoth Daniel Lambert*, pamphlet.

85 *National Register*, 25 June 1809, p. 415, col. 2.

86 *Dictionary of National Biography* (Oxford: Oxford University Press), vol. XI, p. 448.

Chapter 3. Fat folk on show

1 Rosemarie Garland Thomson (ed.), *Freakery: Cultural Spectacles of the Extraordinary Body* (New York: New York University Press, 1996), p. 130.

2 James Taylor, *Shocked and Amazed* (Guildford, CT: Lyons Press, 2002), pp. 82–88.

3 Geyer and Roen, *Diet or Die*.

4 Thomson, *Freakery*, pp. 127–30.

5 Robert Bogdan, *Freak Show: Presenting Human Oddities for Amusement and Profit* (Chicago, IL: University of Chicago Press, 1988), p. 55.

6 A. W. Stencil, *Seeing is Believing: American Sideshows* (Toronto: ECW Press, 2002), p. 3.

7 C. J. S. Thompson, *The History and Lore of Freaks* (London: Senate, 1996), p. 151.

8 Thompson, *The History and Lore of Freaks*.

9 Bogdan, *Freak Show*, p. 8.

10 Fiedler, *Freaks*, p. 125.

11 Bogdan, *Freak Show*, p. 12.

12 'An American Institution – The Circus'. Editorial in the *Plattsburgh Daily Press*, 9 July 1927. Reprinted in *Circus Scrap Book*, vol. 1, no. 2 (April 1929), pp. 3–5.

13 Alfred Trumble, *A Spangled World; or, Life with the Circus* (New York: Richard K. Fox, 1883).

14 Stencil, *Seeing is Believing*, p. 18.

15 Thomson, *Freakery*, p. 317.

16 Stencil, *Seeing is Believing*.

17 Bogdan, *Freak Show*, p. 205.

18 Stunkard, *The Pain of Obesity*, p. 75.

19 Fiedler, *Freaks*, p. 129.
20 Quotes from Geyer and Roen, *Diet or Die*, pp. 33, 46, 31, 1.
21 Frederick Drimmer, *Very Special People: The Struggles, Loves and Triumphs of Human Oddities* (New York: Bantam, 1973), p. 269.
22 Fiedler, *Freaks*.
23 Klingman, *The Secret Lives of Fat People*, p. 108.
24 Jana Evans Braziel and Kathleen LeBesco, eds, *Bodies Out of Bounds: Fatness and Transgression* (Berkeley, CA: University of California Press, 2001).
25 Thomson, *Freakery*, p. 323.
26 Braziel and LeBesco, *Bodies Out of Bounds*, p. 262.
27 Francis T. Buckland, *Curiosities of Natural History* (New York: Macmillan, 2005), p. 88.
28 Gould and Pyle, *Anomalies and Curiosities of Medicine*, p. 352.
29 Gould and Pyle, *Anomalies and Curiosities of Medicine*, p. 353.
30 *Medical Times and Gazette*, vol. 1 (1862), p. 363.

Chapter 4. A brief history of food and drink

1 Mark Twain, *Roughing It* (1872).
2 Reay Tannahil, *The Fine Art of Food* (London: Folio Society, 1968), preface.
3 Brillat-Savarin, *The Physiology of Taste*, p. ix.
4 Tannahil, *The Fine Art of Food*, p. 13.
5 Tannahil, *The Fine Art of Food*, p. 12.
6 Leviticus 11.
7 Hippocrates, 400 BC, *De Priscina Medicina*.
8 Charles Cooper, *The English Table in History and Literature* (London: Sampson Low, Marston & Co., 1929), p. 3.
9 Cooper, *The English Table*, p. 5.
10 Cooper, *The English Table*, p. 6.
11 Ann Hughes was a farmer's wife in Hertfordshire who wrote an account of her daily life from the beginning of 1796 to 1797. See S. Beedell (ed.), *The Diary of a Farmer's Wife, 1796–97* (London: Countrywise Books, 1964). Opponents of women's education were fearful of the effects this might have, but Ann was thankful that her mother had taught her 'how toe rite and figger'.
12 Derek Jarrett, *England in the Age of Hogarth* (London: Granada Publishing, 1976), p. 144.
13 James Woodforde, *The Diary of a Country Parson 1758–1802* (Oxford: Oxford University Press, 1935), p. 14.
14 Pliny the Elder, *Natural History*, Book XXII, Chapter 82.
15 *British Encyclopaedia*, 9th edition (1880), vol. V, 'Brewing'.
16 Fiona Haslam, 'Hogarth and the Art of Alcohol Abuse', *Proceedings of the Royal College of Physicians, Edinburgh*, vol. 22 (1992), pp. 74–80.
17 1 Timothy 5:23.
18 Proverbs 20:1.
19 Proverbs 23:29–35.
20 Luke 1:15.
21 *British Encyclopaedia*, 9th edition, vol. V, 'Brewing'
22 Quoted in Roy Porter, *English Society in the Eighteenth Century* (London: Penguin, 1990), p. 20.
23 Quoted in Porter, *Flesh in the Age of Reason*, p. 400.
24 Quoted in Porter, *Flesh in the Age of Reason*, p. 400.
25 *An Act for laying a duty upon the Retailers of Spirituous Liquors, and for licensing the Retailers thereof* to be enacted after 29 September 1736.
26 Marguerite Patten, *Victory Cookbook: Nostalgic Food and Facts from 1940–1954* (London: Chancellor Press, 2003): introduction.
27 Patten, *Victory Cookbook*.

28 Greg Critser, *Fat Land; How Americans Became the Fattest People in the World* (London: Allen Lane, 2003), pp. 9–11.

29 Critser, *Fat Land*, p. 14.

30 Critser, *Fat Land*, p. 22.

31 Critser, *Fat Land*, pp. 138–41.

Chapter 5. A brief history of physicians' views on obesity and diet

1 Hippocrates (c. 460–377 BC) is often called the Father of Medicine, but little is known of his life and there may have been several men with this name. Hippocrates may have been the author of only some, or none of the books that make up the Hippocratic collection (*Corpus Hippocraticum*). Douglas Guthrie, *A History of Medicine* (London: Thomas Nelson & Sons, 1945), p. 52.

2 Wilhelm Ebstein, *Corpulence and Its Treatment on Physiological Principles*, trans. A. H. Keane, from 6th German edition (London: University College Hospital, 1884), p. 72.

3 Mackenzie, *The History of Health*, pp. 67–68.

4 Mackenzie, *The History of Health*, p. 68.

5 Mackenzie, *The History of Health*, p. 72.

6 Mackenzie, *The History of Health*, p. 118.

7 Mackenzie, *The History of Health*, p. 125.

8 Mackenzie, *The History of Health*, p. 133.

9 Roy Porter, *Flesh in the Age of Reason*, p. 45.

10 Mark Grant, *Galen on Food and Diet* (London: Routledge, 2000).

11 Mackenzie, *The History of Health*, p. 176.

12 Mackenzie, *The History of Health*.

13 Carole Rawcliffe, *Medicine and Society in Later Medieval England* (London: Allan Sutton, 1995), p. 55, n23.

14 Quotes here and below taken from Geoffrey Chaucer, *The Canterbury Tales*, verse translation by David Wright (London: Folio Society, 1998).

15 Quoted in Rawcliffe, *Medicine and Society*, p. 41, n32.

16 Tobias Venner, *Via Recta ad Vitam Longam* (London, 1660), p. 231.

17 Venner, *Via Recta ad Vitam Longam*, p. 255.

18 Venner, *Via Recta ad Vitam Longam*, p. 285.

19 William Kitchiner, *Cook's Oracle* (London, 1817).

20 William Kitchiner, *The Art of Invigorating and Prolonging Life, by Food, Clothes, Air, Exercise, Wine, Sleep, etc...* (London, 1821).

21 Kitchiner, *The Art of Invigorating and Prolonging Life*, p. 188.

22 Wadd, *Cursory Remarks on Corpulence*, p. 122.

23 John Arbuthnot, *Essay Concerning the Nature of Aliments, and the choice of them, according to the different constitutions of human bodies. In which the different effects, advantages and disadvantages of animal and vegetable diet are explain'd* (Dublin: S. Powell, 1731).

24 Barnes, *Essex Eccentrics*, p. 62.

25 Barnes, *Essex Eccentrics*.

26 Ebstein, *Corpulence and Its Treatment on Physiological Principles*, preface.

27 Gilman, *Fat Boys*, p. 139.

28 *The Merry Wives of Windsor*, act III, scene v.

29 Thomas K. Chambers, *Lessons in Cookery. Hand-Book of the National Training School for Cookery. To Which Is Added the Principles of Diet in Health and Disease* (London: D. Appleton, 1878).

30 Horace Fletcher, *The New Glutton or Epicure* (New York: Frederick A. Stokes Co., 1909), preface, p. viii.

31 Quoted by David Lodge, *Author, Author* (London: Secker and Warburg, 2004).

Chapter 6. A brief history of physicians' views on obesity and physical activity

1 Dick Humelbergius Secundus, *Apician Morsels; or, Tales of the table, kitchen, and larder, containing a new and improved code of eatics; select epicurean precepts; nutritive maxims, reflections, anecdotes, &c.* (London: Whittaker, Treacher, & Co., 1829), p. 18.
2 Mackenzie, *The History of Health*, p. 248.
3 British Nutrition Foundation, *Obesity*.
4 Humelbergius, *Apician Morsels*, p. 42.
5 Humelbergius, *Apician Morsels*, p. 45.
6 Humelbergius, *Apician Morsels*, p. 45.
7 Humelbergius, *Apician Morsels*, p. 11.
8 Humelbergius, *Apician Morsels*, p. 73.
9 Humelbergius, *Apician Morsels*, p. 82.
10 Humelbergius, *Apician Morsels*, p. 108.
11 Humelbergius, *Apician Morsels*, p. 111.
12 Humelbergius, *Apician Morsels*, p. 115.
13 Humelbergius, *Apician Morsels*, p. 116.
14 Humelbergius, *Apician Morsels*, p. 141.
15 Humelbergius, *Apician Morsels*, p. 137.
16 Humelbergius, *Apician Morsels*, p. 155.
17 Gould and Pyle, *Anomalies and Curiosities of Medicine*, p. 357.
18 George Cheyne, *An Essay of Health and Long Life* (London, 1724), p. 98.
19 Mackenzie, *The History of Health*.
20 John Wesley, *Primitive Physic or An Easy and Natural Method of Curing Diseases*, (London, 1791), p. 31.
21 Humelbergius, *Apician Morsels*, p. 221.
22 Wadd, *Comments on Corpulency*, p. 29.
23 Kitchiner, *The Art of Invigorating and Prolonging Life*, p. 3.
24 Kitchiner, *The Art of Invigorating and Prolonging Life*, p. 7.
25 Ebstein, *Corpulence and Its Treatment*, p. 10.
26 Ebstein, *Corpulence and Its Treatment*, p. 28.
27 Ebstein, *Corpulence and Its Treatment*, p. 41.
28 Chambers, *Lessons in Cookery*, p. 136.
29 Chambers, *Lessons in Cookery*, p. 137.
30 Chambers, *Lessons in Cookery*, p. 155.
31 Chambers, *Lessons in Cookery*, p. 162.
32 F. A. Hornibrook, *The Culture of the Abdomen. The Cure of Constipation and Obesity* (London: Heinemann, 1933), p. 22.
33 Brian Mears and Ian Macleay, *Chelsea – Football Under the Blue Flag* (London: Mainstream, 2001).
34 http://www.golfing-scotland.com/history.asp#1
35 Hornibrook, *The Culture of the Abdomen*, p. 60.
36 See www.athleticscholarships.net/history-of-tennis.htm.
37 See http://uk.cricinfo.com/db/ABOUT_CRICKET/HISTORY/.
38 See http://content-www.cricinfo.com/ci/content/player/13424.html.
39 Michael Simkins, *Fatty Batter: How Cricket Saved My Life (Then Ruined It)* (London: Ebury, Press, 2008).
40 F. Cecil Russell, *Corpulency and the Cure* (London: Woburn House, 1896), p. 33.
41 Russell, *Corpulency and the Cure*, p. 34.
42 Edwin Checkley, *A Natural Method of Physical Training: Making Muscle and Reducing Flesh Without Dieting or Apparatus* (New York: W. C. Bryant & Co., 1892), p. 147.
43 Checkley, *A Natural Method of Physical Training*, p. 3.
44 Checkley, *A Natural Method of Physical Training*, p. 13.
45 Checkley, *A Natural Method of Physical Training*, p. 89.
46 Checkley, *A Natural Method of Physical Training*, p. 118.
47 Russell, *Corpulency and the Cure*, p. 12.

48 Chambers, *Lessons in Cookery*.
49 Peter N. Stearns, *Fat History: Bodies and Beauty in the Modern West* (New York: New York University Press, 1997), p. 20.
50 Charles Phelps Cushing, 'What Can a Fat Man Do?', *The World's Work*, vol. 32, no. 3 (July 1916).
51 See www.bernarrmacfadden.com.
52 Stearns, *Fat History*, p. 17.
53 *Physical Culture*, March 1932, p. 42.
54 *Physical Culture*, September 1937, p. 40.
55 *Physical Culture*, October 1932, p. 16.
56 *Physical Culture*, July 1936, p. 97.
57 *Physical Culture*, October 1932, p. 4.
58 *Physical Culture*, July 1936, p. 53.
59 Stearns, *Fat History*, p. 17.
60 Richard A. Friedman, attending psychiatrist and psychopharmacologist, Cornell-Weill Medical School, USA, quoted in *British Medical Journal*, 29 May 2004.

Chapter 7. A brief history of the use of drugs to treat obesity

1   Quoted in Wadd, *Comments on Corpulency*, p. 84.
2   Pierre Boaistuau, *Histoires prodigieuses* (1556). On the use of the medicinal leech (*Hirudo medicinalis*) to counter obesity, see P. C. A. Louis, 'Recherche sur les effets de la saignée dans plusieurs maladies inflammatoires', *Archives Générales de Médecine*, vol. 18 (1828), pp. 321–36.
3   Wadd, *Comments on Corpulency*.
4   Humelbergius, *Apician Morsels*, p. 11.
5   Gilman, *Fat Boys*, p. 12.
6   George Bray, *An Atlas of Obesity and Weight Management* (London: Parthenon, 2003).
7   Bray, *An Atlas of Obesity*, p. 21.
8   Wadd, *Comments on Corpulency*.
9   Russell, *Corpulency and the Cure*.
10 Russell, *Corpulency and the Cure*.
11 Schwartz, *Never Satisfied*, p. 97.
12 Klingman, *The Secret Lives of Fat People*, p. 78.
13 J. H. Baron, 'Illnesses and Creativity: Byron's Appetites, James Joyce's Gut, and Melba's Meals and Mésalliances', *British Medical Journal*, vol. 315 (20 December 1997), pp. 1697–703.
14 Schwartz, *Never Satisfied*, p. 109.
15 Schwartz, *Never Satisfied*, p. 181.
16 Chambers, *Lessons in Cookery*, p. 148.
17 Wadd, *Comments on Corpulency*, p. 80.
18 Wadd, *Comments on Corpulency*, p. 84.
19 Frumusan, *The Cure of Obesity*, p. 2.
20 Frumusan, *The Cure of Obesity*, p. 32.
21 American Medical Association, *Nostrums and Quackery* (1911), pp. 658–70.
22 Samuel Ottway Lewis Potter, *A Compend of Materia Medica, Therapeutics, and Prescription Writing* (1902), available online at www.henriettesherbal.com/eclectic/potter-comp/phytolacca.html.
23 Harvey Wickes Felter and John Uri Lloyd, *King's American Dispensatory* (1898), available online at www.henriettesherbal.com/eclectic/kings/index.html.
24 See www.snopes.com/horrors/vanities/tapeworm.htm.
25 Nadia Stancioff, *Maria Callas Remembered* (London: E. P. Dutton, 1987), p. 106.
26 R. Baker, *Hoosier Folk Legends* (Bloomington, IN: Indiana University Press, 1982).
27 Bray, *An Atlas of Obesity*, p. 21.

28 American Medical Association, *Nostrums and Quackery*, p. 687.

29 Laura Fraser, 'Ten Pounds in Ten Days: A Sampler of Diet Scams and Abuse', at www.ahealthyme.com/topic/dietscams.

30 C. E. de M. Sajous, *The Internal Secretion and the Principles of Medicine*, 7th edition (Philadelphia, PA: F. A. Davis Co., 1916), p. 724.

31 Testing for protein-bound iodine (PBI) in thyroid disease was developed in 1940. Thyroid replacement was not offered to patients unless the PBI level was abnormal.

32 Bray, *An Atlas of Obesity*.

33 Geyer and Roen, *Diet or Die*, p. 92.

Chapter 8. Gluttony

1 Brillat-Savarin, *The Physiology of Taste*, vol. VII, p. xxxiv.

2 Combe and Rowlandson, *English Dance of Death*.

3 Geoffrey Chaucer, 'The Pardoner's Tale'. Quotes from the *Canterbury Tales* here (p. 399) and below are taken from the Oxford World's Classics edition (Oxford: Oxford University Press, 2003).

4 Rudolph M. Bell, *Holy Anorexia* (Chicago, IL: University of Chicago Press, 1985), quoted by Francine Prose, *The Seven Deadly Sins: Gluttony* (Oxford: Oxford University Press, 2003), p.40

5 Prose, *The Seven Deadly Sins*, pp. 9–10.

6 Prose, *The Seven Deadly Sins*, p. 15.

7 Saint Thaumaturgus Gregory, *Fathers of the Church: Life and Works*, vol. 98, trans. Michael Slussor (Washington, DC: Catholic University of America Press, 1998), quoted in Prose, *The Seven Deadly Sins*, p. 7.

8 Herman Pleij, *Dreaming of Cockaigne*, trans. Diane Webb (New York: Columbia University Press, 2001), p. 377, quoted in Prose, *The Seven Deadly Sins*, p. 19.

9 Thomas Aquinas, *On Evil*, trans. Richard Regan, with introductory notes by Brian Davies (Oxford: Oxford University Press, 2003), p. 415.

10 Charles Nielson Gattey, *Excess in Food Drink and Sex* (London: Harrap, 1986), p. 33.

11 Prose, *The Seven Deadly Sins*, p. 39.

12 Chaucer, *Canterbury Tales*, 'The Pardoner's Tale', p. 398.

13 Chaucer, *Canterbury Tales*, Introduction, p. xviii.

14 William Langland, *Piers the Ploughman* (London: Penguin, 1959), p. 110.

15 Aristotle quoted in Robert J. Hutchinson, *The Book of Vices* (New York: Riverhead Books, 1995), p. 3.

16 *Dante's Inferno*, with translations, broadcast by the BBC Third Programme (London: BBC Publications, 1996), p. 303.

17 *Dante's Inferno*, p. 55.

18 *Dante's Inferno*, p. 304.

19 Edmund Spenser, *The Faerie Queen* (New York: E. P. Dutton, 1964), p. 58.

20 Rose-Marie Hagen and Rainer Hagen, *Pieter Breughel the Elder c. 1525–1569: Peasants, Fools and Demons* (London: Taschen, 2004), p. 74.

21 Charles W. Dunn and Edward T. Byrnes, eds, *Middle English Literature* (London: Routledge, 1990), pp. 188–92.

22 Hans Hinrichs, *The Glutton's Paradise* (New York: Peter Pauper Press, 1955), p. 14.

23 Hinrichs, *The Glutton's Paradise*, p. 6.

24 B. A. Botkin, *A Treasury of Southern Folklore* (New York: Crown Publishers, 1940).

25 Prosper Montagne, *Larousse Gastronomique: The Encyclopaedia of Food, Wine and Cooking*, eds Nina Ford and Charlotte Turgeon (London: Paul Hamlyn, 1968), p. 77.

26 Robert Klein, 'Fat Beauty', in *Bodies Out of Bounds*, eds Jana Evans and Kathleen LeBesco (Berkeley, CA: University of California Press, 2001), p. 33. Other leaders who famously suffered from obesity were: William the Conqueror; Charles le Gros; Louis le Gros; Henry I, King of Navarre; Henry III, Count of Champagne; Sancho I ('The Fat'); the King

of Leon; Alphonse II, King of Portugal; Frederick I, King of Würtemberg; Louis XVIII; Queen Victoria; and Winston Churchill.

27   Thomas Wright, *The Passions of the Mind* (1630), pp. 18–19, quoted in Stearns, *Fat History*, p. 6.

28   Ben Jonson, quoted in Hutchinson. *The Book of Vices*, p. 160.

29   William Shakespeare, *Henry IV, Part I*, act I, scene ii.

30   Jonathan Swift, *Gulliver's Travels* (London: Penguin, 1981), pp. 202–3.

31   Gustav Flaubert, *Madame Bovary* (London: Penguin, 1995), p. 41.

32   Tobias Smollett, *The Expedition of Humphry Clinker* (London: J. M. Dent, 1943), p. 305.

33   James Boswell, *The Life of Samuel Johnson* (London: Penguin, 1986), p. 300.

34   Charles Neilson Gattey, *Excess in Food, Drink and Sex* (London: Harrop, 1986), p. 72.

35   Gattey, *Excess in Food, Drink and Sex*, pp. 74–75.

36   Smollett, *The Expedition of Humphry Clinker*, p. 305.

37   Woodforde, *The Diary of a Country Parson*, p. 500.

38   George Cheyne, quoted in Porter, *Flesh in the Age of Reason*, p. 237.

39   George Cheyne, *Observations concerning the Nature and the due Method of Treating the Gout ... together with an Account of the Nature and Qualities of the Bath Waters* (London, 1720).

40   Cheyne, *Observations*, p. iii.

41   Benjamin Franklin, quoted in Schwartz, *Never Satisfied*, p. 14.

42   Kitchiner, *The Cook's Oracle*, p. 14.

43   Seneca, Epistles XCV, 23, quoted in *British Medical Journal*, 3 September 2005.

Chapter 9. Sloth

1   Tobias Venner, *Via Recta ad Vitam Longam, or, A treatise wherein the right way and best manner of living for attaining to a long and healthfull life, is clearly demonstrated and punctually applied to every age and constitution of body* (London, 1660), p. 306.

2   Andrew M. Prentice and Susan A. Jebb, 'Obesity in Britain: Gluttony or Sloth?', *British Medical Journal*, 12 August 1995, p. 439.

3   Terence J. Wilkin and Linda D. Voss, 'Metabolic Syndrome: Maladaptation to a Modern World', *Journal of the Royal Society of Medicine*, vol. 97 (2004), p. 511.

4   The word 'misericord' comes from the Latin for pity or mercy and heart.

5   Mike Harding, *A Little Book of Misericords* (London: Aurum Press, 1998), p. 36.

6   Harding, *A Little Book of Misericords*, p. 47.

7   New International Bible, Amos (6: 1–7).

8   See http://danteworlds.laits.utexas.edu/purgatory/06sloth.html.

9   Dante Alighieri, *The Divine Comedy*, p. 158.

10   William Langland, *Piers the Ploughman* (London: Penguin, 1959), p. 112.

11   Geoffrey Chaucer, 'The Pardoner's Tale', *Canterbury Tales*, Oxford World's Classics edition (Oxford: Oxford University Press, 2003), p. 512.

12   Carl Linfert, *Bosch* (New York: Harry N. Abrams, n.d.), p. 44.

13   Joseph Addison, *Spectator*, no. 184, 1 October 1711.

14   Bernard de Mandeville, *The Fable of the Bees* (1723).

15   Mark Twain, *The Adventures of Tom Sawyer* (London: Penguin, 1972), ch. 2, p. 19.

16   Wadd, *Cursory Remarks on Corpulence*, p. 55.

17   Wadd, *Cursory Remarks on Corpulence*, p. 53.

18   Brillat-Savarin, *The Physiology of Taste*, p. 198.

19   William Shakespeare, *Cymbeline*, act III, scene vi, line 33.

20   Charlotte Mason, '*Home Education*' Series (London: Kegan Paul, 1905), vol. IV, Introductory Chapter, p. 5.

21   Ogden Nash, 'Pretty Halcyon Days' (1945), lines 1–4.

Chapter 10. Heavenly bodies

1 H. W. Janson and Anthony F. Janson, *The Basic History of Western Art*, 7th edition (Oxford: :Pearson/Prentice Hall, 2006), p. 36.
2 Klein, 'Fat Beauty', p. 22.
3 Kenneth Clark, *The Nude: A Study of Ideal Art* (Harmondsworth: Pelican, 1960), pp. 19–21.
4 Saad Shaikh and James Leonard-Amodeo, 'The Deviating Eyes of Michelangelo's David', *Journal of the Royal Society of Medicine*, vol. 98 (2005), pp. 75–76.
5 Klein, 'Fat Beauty', p. 24.
6 Clark, *The Nude*, p. 362.
7 Klein, 'Fat Beauty', p. 24.
8 Clark, *The Nude*, p. 130.
9 Klein, 'Fat Beauty', p. 27.
10 Klein, 'Fat beauty', p. 28.
11 Clark, *The Nude*, p. 130.
12 Clark, *The Nude*, p. 130.
13 Clark, *The Nude*, p. 133.
14 Wadd, *Cursory Remarks on Corpulence*.
15 Wadd, *Cursory Remarks on Corpulence*.
16 Porter, *Flesh in the Age of Reason*, p. 243.
17 Sir Peter Lely (1618–80) was born in Germany of Dutch parents and arrived in England in the early 1640s and became the most influential of English seventeenth-century painters. Sir Godfrey Kneller (c. 1649–1723) came to England from Lubecke in Germany about 1676 and became a leading portrait painter.
18 Porter, *Flesh in the Age of Reason*, p. 241.
19 Jennifer Harris, 'Dress and Identity in Hogarth's London', essay in *William Hogarth (1697–1764): The Artist and the City* (Whitworth Art Gallery, University of Manchester, 1997), p. 55.
20 Christopher Anstey, *An Election Ball*, 2nd edition (1776), pp. 42–43.
21 Stearns, *Fat History*.
22 BBC News, 'Models Link to Teenage Anorexia', 14 November 2005. See http://news.bbc.co.uk/1/hi/health/769290.stm.
23 BBC News Magazine, 'Not-So-Little Britain', 14 November 2005. See http://news.bbc.co.uk/1/hi/magazine/3616904.stm.
24 Roualt's picture appears in Clark, *The Nude*, p. 130. Clark says that 'she belongs to a different world than the prostitutes depicted by Degas and Toulouse-Lautrec who convey the characters of an epoch and a society. Roualt's figure is a monstrous idol inspiring us with fear rather than pity.'
25 Personal correspondence with sculptress.
26 Suzie Mackenzie, 'Under the Skin', article on Jenny Saville's paintings in the *Guardian*, Weekend, 22 October 2005, p. 45.
27 Adolphe Quetelet, *Recherches sur le poids de l'homme aux differens ages* [*Researches on the Weights of Men at Different Ages*] (1833).
28 Emma Seifret Weigley, 'Adolphe Quetelet: Pioneer Anthropometrist – 1796–1874', *Nutrition Today*, April 1989.
29 A. Keys, F. Fidanza, M. J. Karvonen, N. Kimura and H. L. Taylor, 'Indices of Relative Weight and Obesity', *Journal of Chronic Disease*, vol. 25 (1972), pp. 329–43.
30 Johann Friedrich Held (1670), quoted in Ken Albala, 'Weight Loss in the Age of Reason', in Christopher E. Forth and Ana Carden-Coyne, eds, *Cultures of the Abdomen* (London: Palgrave Macmillan, 2005), p. 175.
31 Brillat-Savarin, *The Physiology of Taste*, p. 189.

Chapter 11. Obesity in literature

1 Gilman, *Fat Boys*, p. 46.
2 Porter, *Flesh in the Age of Reason*, p. 239.
3 See www.iotf.org/childhoodobesity.asp.
4 House of Commons, 10 May 2000, 9.19 p.m.
5 Enid Blyton, *Mystery of the Strange Messages* (1957).
6 Mervyn Peake, *Gormanghast* (1950), p. 9.
7 Mervyn Peake, *Titus Groan* (1946), p. 38.
8 Peake, *Titus Groan*, p. 34.
9 J. K. Rowling, *Harry Potter and the Philosopher's Stone* (London: Bloomsbury, 1997), p. 24.
10 Rowling, *Harry Potter and the Philosopher's Stone*, p. 9.
11 J. K. Rowling, *Harry Potter and the Prisoner of Azkaban* (London: Bloomsbury, 2000), p. 18.
12 Rowling, *Harry Potter and the Prisoner of Azkaban*, p. 22.
13 Rowling, *Harry Potter and the Philosopher's Stone*, p. 9.
14 Klingman, *The Secret Lives of Fat People*.
15 Alice B. Emerson, *Betty Gordon in Washington*.
16 Alice B. Emerson, *Ruth Fielding at Snow Camp* (New York: Cupples and Leon, 1913).
17 George Orwell, 'Boys' Weeklies', in *The Collected Essays. Journalism, Letters of George Orwell Vol. 1. An Age Like This. 1920–1940* (London: Secker & Warburg, 1968), p. 465.
18 Frank Richards, *Billy Bunter at Butlins* (1961), p. 146.
19 Richards, *Billy Bunter at Butlins*, p. 153.
20 *Greyfriars*, p. 52.
21 Richards, *Billy Bunter at Butlins*, p. 47.
22 Richards, *Billy Bunter at Butlins*, p. 108.
23 William Golding, *Lord of the Flies* (London: Faber & Faber, 1954), pp. 1, 8.
24 Golding, *Lord of the Flies*, p. 201.
25 Charles Dickens, *Oliver Twist*, autograph edition (London: Chapman & Hall, no date), p. 8.
26 Dickens, *Oliver Twist*, ch. 2, p. 6.
27 Dickens, *The Pickwick Papers*, Penguin Popular Classics (Harmondsworth: Penguin, 1994), pp. 75, 80, 81.
28 Dickens, *The Pickwick Papers*, pp. 126, 813.
29 *Henry IV, Part 1*, act II, scene iv, lines 498–507.
30 *Henry IV, Part 2*, act V, scene v, lines 51–59.
31 *Henry IV, Part 2*, act I, scene ii, lines 260–61.
32 *Julius Caesar*, act 1, scene ii, line 191.
33 Jane Austen, *Persuasion*, vol. 1, ch. viii.
34 See *Obesity Research*, vol. 9 (January 2001), pp. 17–20.
35 William Makepeace Thackeray, *Vanity Fair* (London: Penguin, 1985), p. 55.
36 Thackeray, *Vanity Fair*, p. 59.
37 Carey, 'Fat Man in History', p. 133.
38 Thackeray, *Vanity Fair*, p. 93.
39 Thackeray, *Vanity Fair*, p. 93.
40 Erin McGraw, 'Ax of the Apostles', in Donna Jarrell and Ira Sukrungruang, eds, *What Are You Looking At? The First Fat Fiction Anthology* (London: Harcourt, 2003), p. 102.
41 Wilkie Collins, *The Woman in White* (London: Dent, Everyman's Library, 1972), p. 193.
42 'Corpulence injures beauty by destroying the harmony of proportion established at first, because all the parts of the body do not enlarge equally. It also harms it by filling up cavities that Nature had destined to be in the shade; and so nothing is more common than to meet with faces formerly very interesting, and which fat has made almost insignificant.' Brillat-Savarin, *Physiology of Taste*, p. 197.
43 Alexander McCall Smith, *The No. 1 Ladies' Detective Agency* (London: Abacus, 2002), p. 141.

44 McCall Smith, *The No. 1 Ladies' Detective Agency*, p. 97.
45 McCall Smith, *The No. 1 Ladies' Detective Agency*, p. 193.
46 McCall Smith, *The No. 1 Ladies' Detective Agency*, p. 141.
47 Edith Wharton, *The Age of Innocence* (London: Chancellor Press, Great Classic Library, 1994), pp. 15–16.
48 Wharton, *The Age of Innocence*, p. 111.
49 Wharton, *The Age of Innocence*, p. 165.
50 Campbell and Haslam, *Your Questions Answered*, p. 112.
51 Peter Carey, 'Fat Man in History', in Jarrell and Sukrungruang, eds, *What Are You Looking At?*, p. 121.
52 Carey, 'Fat Man in History', p. 128.
53 Miguel de Cervantes Saavedra, *Don Quixote* (originally published in 1605) (London: Wordsworth Classics, 1993 edition). In Chapter 1, Don Quixote sets out on his travels; Sancho Panza joins him in Chapter 7 as his squire.
54 Gilman, *Fat Boys*, p. 53.
55 Klingman, *The Secret Lives of Fat People*.
56 Robertson Davies, *World of Wonders* (London: Macmillan, 1975), p. 576.
57 Davies, *World of Wonders*, pp. 584–85.
58 The wicked man in the book of Job (15:27) 'covered his face with his fatness, and maketh collops of fat on his flanks'.
59 Davies, *World of Wonders*, p. 592.
60 Sarah Shieff, 'Devouring Women: Corporeality and Autonomy in Fiction by Women Since the 1960s', in Jan Evans Braziel and Kathleen LeBesco, eds, *Bodies Out of Bounds* (Berkeley, CA: University of California Press, 2001), p. 214.
61 Conrad Hilberry, 'Fat', from *Shenandoah* (1976), reprinted from *The First Fat Fiction Anthology* (printed with permission of the author).

Chapter 12. Obesity in art prints and postcards

1 M. Dorothy George, *Hogarth to Cruikshank: Social Change in Graphic Satire* (London: Allen Lane, 1967), p. 13.
2 Ronald Paulson, *Hogarth's Graphic Works* (New Haven, CT: Yale University Press, 1965; revised edition 1989), p. 230.
3 Thomas Sydenham, *A Treatise of the Gout and Dropsie* from *The Whole Works of that Excellent Practical Physician Dr. Thomas Sydenham* (London, 1705), p. 340.
4 Paulson, *Hogarth's Graphic Works*, p. 230.
5 Joseph Burke and Colin Caldwell, *Hogarth: The Complete Engraving* (London: Alpine Fine Arts Collection, n.d.), no. 244.
6 Oliver Goldsmith, *Letters from a Citizen of the World to his Friends in the East*, Letter XXIV, c. 1761, from *The Works of Oliver Goldsmith* (Edinburgh, 1872), p. 202.
7 George Cheyne, *An Essay of the True Nature and Due Method of Treating the Gout ... together with an Account of the Nature and Qualities of Bath-Waters*, 6th edition (London, 1724), p. iii.
8 Venner, *Via Recta ad Vitam Longam*, p. 342.
9 Smollett, *The Expedition of Humphry Clinker*, p. 69.
10 Fiona Haslam, *From Hogarth to Rowlandson* (Liverpool: Liverpool University Press, 1996), p. 5.
11 Jean Comaroff, 'Medicine and Culture: Some Anthropological Perspectives', *Social Science and Medicine*, vol. 12 (1978), pp. 247–54.
12 John Arbuthnot, *The History of John Bull*, eds Alan W. Bower and Robert A. Erickson (Oxford: Clarendon Press, 1976).
13 Arbuthnot, *The History of John Bull*, p. lvii. 'Every facet of John Bull's character can be found established in traditional caricature and contemporary polemic' (p. lvii).
14 Thomas H. Bivins, 'The Body Politic: The Changing Shape of Uncle Sam', *Journalism Quarterly*, vol. 64, no. 1 (spring 1987), pp. 13–20, at p. 13.

15 Bivins, 'The Body Politic', p. 19.
16 Wadd, *Cursory Remarks on Corpulence*.
17 Smollett, *The Expedition of Humphry Clinker*, p. 170.
18 George Orwell, 'The Art of Donald McGill', in *The Collected Essays, Journalism and Letters of George Orwell, Vol. 2* (London: Secker & Warburg, 1968).
19 Alan Wykes, *Saucy Seaside Postcards* (London: Jupiter Books, 1977), p. 28.
20 Wykes, *Saucy Seaside Postcards*, p. 30.
21 Tonie Holt and Valmai Holt, *Picture Postcards of the Golden Age: A Collector's Guide* (London: MacGibbon & Kee, 1971), p. 91.

Chapter 13. Fat on film

1   www.csse.monash.edu.au/~pringle/silent.
2   www.screenonline.org.uk/film/id/730648/index.html
3   www.goldensilents.com/comedy/johnbunny.html
4   www.imdb.com/name/nm0418490/bio.
5   www.csse.monash.edu.au/~pringle/silent/chaplin/chaplin.html.
6   www.bfi.org.uk/sightandsound/feature/97.
7   www.imdb.com/name/nm0440070/bio.
8   www.silent-movies.com/Arbucklemania/KeyYears.html.
9   www.dvdjournal.com/reviews/b/bestarbucklekeaton.shtml.
10 www.circushistory.org/Query/Query06e.htm.
11 http://film.guardian.co.uk/news/story/0,12589,1252926,00.html.
12 http://film.guardian.co.uk/news/story/0,12589,1252926,00.html.
13 John Walker, ed., *Halliwell's Who's Who in the Movies* (London: HarperCollins, 2006), p. 65.
14 Walker, *Halliwell's Who's Who*, p. 490.
15 See www.imdb.com/name/nm0434461/bio.
16 Luc Sante and Melissa Holbrook Pierson, eds, *O.K. You Mugs: Writers on Movie Actors* (New York: Random House, 1999).
17 www.danagioia.net/essays/efatmen.htm.
18 http://imdb.com/name/nm0000033/bio.
19 Robert Morley, *Book of Worries* (London: Weidenfield and Nicholson, 1979).
20 www.imdb.com/name/nm0341743/bio.
21 www.imdb.com/name/nm0341743/bio.
22 www.imdb.com/name/nm0001145/bio.
23 www.imdb.com/name/nm0001145/bio.
24 www.exposay.com/george-clooney-depressed-while-filming-syriana/v/3227.
25 www.mtv.com/movies/news/articles/1514229/11212005/story.jhtml.
26 Karl Heitmueller, 'Rewind: Does the Fat Suit Really Fit Anyone in Hollywood?', at www.mtv.com/movies/news/articles/1514229/11212005/story.jhtml.
27 Kim 'Howard' Johnson, *The First 20 Years of Monty Python* (London: Plexus, 1989).
28 *The Pythons Autobiography* (London: Pythons Orion, 2003).
29 Disney Archive, http://disney.go.com/vault/archives/villains/pete/pete.html.
30 Disney Archive, http://disney.go.com/vault/archives/villains/stromboli/stromboli.html.

Epilogue. The dance of death

1   Wadd, *Cursory Remarks on Corpulence*, p. 115.
2   William Harvey, *On Corpulence in Relation to Disease: With Some Remarks on Diet* (London: Henry Henshaw, 1872), p. 102.
3   Wadd, *Cursory Remarks on Corpulence*.

Select bibliography

Albala, Kenneth, 'Weight Loss in the Age of Reason', in Christopher E. Forth and Ana Carden-Coyne, eds, *Cultures of the Abdomen: Diet, Digestion, and Fat in the Modern World* (London: Palgrave Macmillan, 2005).

Arbuthnot, John, *The History of John Bull*, eds Alan W. Bower and Robert A. Erickson (Oxford: Clarendon Press, 1976).

Arbuthnot, John, *Essay Concerning the Nature of Aliments, and the choice of them, according to the different constitutions of human bodies. In which the different effects, advantages and disadvantages of animal and vegetable diet are explain'd* (Dublin: S. Powell, 1731).

Baker, R., *Hoosier Folk Legends* (Bloomington, IN: Indiana University Press, 1982).

Banting, William, *Letter on Corpulence, Addressed to the Public*, 4th edition (Harrison, 1869).

Barnes, Alison, *Essex Eccentrics* (Ipswich: Boydell, 1975).

Baron, J. H., 'Illnesses and Creativity: Byron's Appetites, James Joyce's Gut, and Melba's Meals and Mésalliances', *British Medical Journal*, vol. 315 (20 December 1997), pp. 1697–703.

Bivins, Thomas H., 'The Body Politic: The Changing Shape of Uncle Sam', *Journalism Quarterly*, vol. 64, no. 1 (spring 1987), pp. 13–20.

Bogdan, Robert, *Freak Show: Presenting Human Oddities for Amusement and Profit* (Chicago, IL: University of Chicago Press, 1988).

Bondeson, Jon, *Freaks* (Ithaca, NY: Cornell University Press, 2006).

Botkin, B. A., *A Treasury of Southern Folklore* (New York: Crown Publishers, 1940).

Bray, George, *An Atlas of Obesity and Weight Management* (London: Parthenon, 2003).

Braziel, Jana Evans and Kathleen LeBesco, eds, *Bodies Out of Bounds: Fatness and Transgression* (Berkeley, CA: University of California Press, 2001).

Brillat-Savarin, Jean Anthelme, *The Physiology of Taste, or, Meditations on Transcendental Gastronomy* (New York: Boni & Liveright, 1926).

British Nutrition Foundation, *Obesity*, Task Force Report (London: Blackwell, 1999).

Burke, Joseph and Colin Caldwell, *Hogarth: The Complete Engraving* (London: Alpine Fine Arts Collection, n.d.), no. 244.

Burwell, C. S., *et al.*, 'Extreme Obesity Associated With Alveolar Hypoventilation – A Pickwickian Syndrome', *American Journal of Medicine* (1956), vol. 21, pp. 811–18.

Campbell, I. and D. Haslam, *Your Questions Answered: Obesity* (London: Churchill Livingstone, 2005).

Carey, Peter, 'Fat Man in History', in Donna Jarrell and Ira Sukrungruang, eds, *What Are You Looking At? The First Fat Fiction Anthology* (London: Harcourt, 2003).

Chambers, Thomas K., *Lessons in Cookery. Hand-Book of the National Training School for Cookery. To Which Is Added the Principles of Diet in Health and Disease* (London: D. Appleton, 1878).

Checkley, Edwin, *A Natural Method of Physical Training: Making Muscle and Reducing Flesh Without Dieting or Apparatus* (New York: W. C. Bryant & Co., 1892).

Cheyne, George, *An Essay of the True Nature and Due Method of Treating the Gout ... together with an Account of the Nature and Qualities of Bath-Waters*, 6th edition (London, 1724).

Cheyne, George, *An Essay of Health and Long Life* (London, 1724).

Clark, Kenneth, *The Nude: A Study of Ideal Art* (Harmondsworth: Pelican, 1960).

Comaroff, Jean, 'Medicine and Culture: Some Anthropological Perspectives', *Social Science and Medicine*, vol. 12 (1978), pp. 247–54.

Combe, William (text) and Thomas Rowlandson (illustrations), *English Dance of Death* (London: Ackermann, 1816).

Cooper, Charles, *The English Table in History and Literature* (London: Sampson Low, Marston & Co., 1929).

Critser, Greg, *Fat Land: How Americans Became the Fattest People in the World* (London: Allen Lane, 2003).

Davies, Robertson, *World of Wonders* (London: Macmillan, 1975).

Douglas, Neil J., *Clinician's Guide to Sleep Medicine* (London: Arnold, 2002).

Dunn, Charles W. and Edward T. Byrnes, eds, *Middle English Literature* (London: Routledge, 1990).

Dupain, George, *Baffling Obesity: Outlining a Natural Form of Treatment for Extreme Corpulence* (Sydney: Briton, 1935).

Ebstein, Wilhelm, *Corpulence and Its Treatment on Physiological Principles*, trans. A. H. Keane from the 6th German edition (London: University College Hospital, 1884).

Felter, Harvey Wickes and John Uri Lloyd, *King's American Dispensatory* (1898), available online at www.henriettesherbal.com/eclectic/kings/index.html.

Fiedler, Leslie, *Freaks: Myths and Images of the Secret Self* (New York: Anchor Books, 1978)

Fletcher, Horace, *The New Glutton or Epicure* (New York: Frederick A. Stokes Co., 1909).

Foresight. *Trends and Drivers of Obesity: A Literature Review for the Foresight Project on Obesity.* Available at www.foresight.gov.uk/Obesity/Literature_Review.pdf.

Frumusan, Jean, *The Cure of Obesity*, trans. Elaine A. Wood (London: John Bale, 1924) (first published in 1922 as *La cure de l'obésité*).

Gattey, Charles Nielson, *Excess in Food Drink and Sex* (London: Harrap, 1986).

George, M. Dorothy, *Hogarth to Cruikshank: Social Change in Graphic Satire* (London: Allen Lane, 1967).

Geyer, Celeste 'Dolly Dimples', and Samuel Roen, *Diet or Die: The 'Dolly Dimples' Weight Reducing Plan* (New York: F. Fell, 1968).

Gilman, Sander L., *Fat Boys: A Slim Book* (Lincoln, NE: Univeristy of Nebraska Press, 2004).

Gould, G. M. and W. L. Pyle, *Anomalies and Curiosities of Medicine* (New York: Bell, 1896).

Grant, Mark, *Galen on Food and Diet* (London: Routledge, 2000).

Guthrie, Douglas, *A History of Medicine* (London: Thomas Nelson & Sons, 1945).

Hagen, Rose-Marie and Rainer Hagen, *Pieter Breughel the Elder c. 1525–1569: Peasants, Fools and Demons* (London: Taschen, 2004).

Harding, Mike, *A Little Book of Misericords* (London: Aurum Press, 1998).

Harvey, William, *On Corpulence in Relation to Disease: With Some Remarks on Diet* (London: Henry Henshaw, 1872).

Haslam, Fiona, 'Hogarth and the Art of Alcohol Abuse', *Proceedings of the Royal College of Physicians, Edinburgh*, vol. 22 (1992), pp. 74–80.

Haslam, Fiona, *From Hogarth to Rowlandson* (Liverpool: Liverpool University Press, 1996).

Hilberry, Conrad, 'Fat', from *Shenandoah* (1976), , in Donna Jarrell and Ira Sukrungruang, eds, *What Are You Looking At? The First Fat Fiction Anthology* (London: Harcourt, 2003).

Hinrichs, Hans, *The Glutton's Paradise* (New York: Peter Pauper Press, 1955).

Holt, Tonie and Valmai Holt, *Picture Postcards of the Golden Age: A Collector's Guide* (London: MacGibbon & Kee, 1971).

Hornibrook, F. A., *The Culture of the Abdomen. The Cure of Constipation and Obesity* (London: Heinemann, 1933).

Humelbergius, Dick Secundus, *Apician Morsels; or, Tales of the table, kitchen, and larder, containing a new and improved code of eatics; select epicurean precepts; nutritive maxims, reflections, anecdotes, &c.* (London: Whittaker, Treacher, & Co., 1829).

Hutchinson, Robert J., *The Book of Vices* (New York: Riverhead Books, 1995).

Jarrell, Donna and Ira Sukrungruang, eds, *What Are You Looking At? The First Fat Fiction Anthology* (London: Harcourt, 2003).

Jarrett, Derek, *England in the Age of Hogarth* (London: Granada Publishing, 1976).

Kitchiner, William, *Cook's Oracle* (London, 1817).

Kitchiner, William, *The Art of Invigorating and Prolonging Life, by Food, Clothes, Air, Exercise, Wine, Sleep, etc...* (London, 1821).

Klein, Richard, 'Fat Beauty', in Jana Evans Braziel and Kathleen LeBresco, eds, *Bodies Out of Bounds* (Berkeley, CA: University of California Press, 2001).

Klingman, Mildred, *The Secret Lives of Fat People* (Boston, MA: Houghton Mifflin, 1981).

Mackenzie, J., *The History of Health and the Art of Preserving It* (Edinburgh: William Gordon, 1758).

Mantzoros, Christos S. (ed.), *Obesity and Diabetes* (Toronto: Humana Press, 2006).

Orwell, George, 'Boys' weeklies', in *The Collected Essays. Journalism, Letters of George Orwell Vol. 1. An Age Like This. 1920–1940* (London: Secker & Warburg, 1968).

Orwell, George, 'The Art of Donald McGill', in *The Collected Essays, Journalism and Letters of George Orwell, Vol. 2,* (London: Secker & Warburg, 1968).

Patten, Marguerite, *Victory Cookbook: Nostalgic Food and Facts from 1940–1954* (London: Chancellor Press, 2003).

Paulson, Ronald, *Hogarth's Graphic Works* (New Haven, CT: Yale University Press, 1965; revised edition 1989).

Porter, Roy, *English Society in the Eighteenth Century* (London: Penguin Books, 1990).

Porter, Roy, *The Greatest Benefit to Mankind* (London: Harper Collins, 1997).

Porter, Roy, *Flesh in the Age of Reason* (London: Allen Lane, 2003).

Potter, Samuel O. L., *A Compend of Materia Medica, Therapeutics, and Prescription Writing* (1902) available online at www.henriettesherbal.com/eclectic/potter-comp/phytolacca.html.

Prentice, A. and S. Jebb, 'Gluttony or Sloth?', *British Medical Journal*, 12 August 1995, pp. 437–39.

Prose, Francine, *The Seven Deadly Sins: Gluttony* (Oxford: Oxford University Press, 2003).

Rawcliffe, Carole, *Medicine and Society in Later Medieval England* (London: Alan Sutton, 1995).

Reaven, G., 'Role of Insulin Resistance in Human Disease', *Diabetes*, vol. 37 (1988), pp. 1595–607.

Ricketson, Shadrach, *Means of Preserving Health and Preventing Disease* (New York: Collins Perkins, 1806).

Russell, F. Cecil, *Corpulency and the Cure* (London: Woburn House, 1896).

Sajous, C. E. de M., *The Internal Secretion and the Principles of Medicine*, 7th edition (Philadelphia, PA: F. A. Davis Co., 1916).

Schwartz, Hillel, *Never Satisfied. A Cultural History of Diets, Fantasies and Fat* (London: Anchor Books, 1986).

Shieff, Sarah, 'Devouring Women: Corporeality and Autonomy in Fiction by Women Since the 1960s', in Jan Evans Braziel and Kathleen LeBesco, eds, *Bodies Out of Bounds* (Berkeley, CA: University of California Press, 2001).

Stearns, Peter N., *Fat History: Bodies and Beauty in the Modern World* (New York: New York University Press, 1997).

Stencil, A. W., *Seeing is Believing: American Sideshows* (Toronto: ECW Press, 2002)

Stunkard, Albert J., *The Pain of Obesity* (Palo Alto, CA: Bull Publishing, 1976).

Sydenham, Thomas, *A Treatise of the Gout and Dropsie* from *The Whole Works of that Excellent Practical Physician Dr. Thomas Sydenham* (London, 1705).

Tannahil, Reay, *The Fine Art of Food* (London: Folio Society, 1968).

Taylor, James, *Shocked and Amazed* (Guildford, CT: Lyons Press, 2002).

Thomas, Robert, *The Modern Practice of Physic, Exhibiting the Characters, Causes, Symptoms, Prognostic, Morbid Appearances, and Improved Methods of Treating the Diseases of All Climates* (New York: Collins, 1811).

Thompson, C. J. S., *The History and Lore of Freaks* (London: Senate, 1996).

Thomson, Rosemarie Garland (ed.), *Freakery: Cultural Spectacles of the Extraordinary Body* (New York: New York University Press, 1996).

Toussaint-Samat, Magueloune, *History of Food*, trans. Anthea Bell (Oxford: Blackwell, 1994).

Trumble, Alfred, *A Spangled World; or, Life with the circus* (New York: Richard K. Fox, 1883).

Venner, Tobias, *Via Recta ad Vitam Longam, or, A treatise wherein the right way and best manner of living for attaining to a long and healthfull life, is clearly demonstrated and punctually applied to every age and constitution of body* (London, 1660).

Wadd, William, *Cursory Remarks on Corpulence; or Obesity considered as a Disease: with a Critical Examination of Ancient and Modern Opinions, Relative to its Causes and Cure*, 3rd edition (London, 1816).

Wesley, John, *Primitive Physic or An Easy and Natural Method of Curing Diseases* (London, 1791).

Woodforde, James, *The Diary of a Country Parson 1758–1802* (Oxford: Oxford University Press, 1935).

Wykes, Alan, *Saucy Seaside Postcards* (London: Jupiter Books, 1977).

Index

Page numbers in italics refer to illustrations. Pages numbered in Roman capitals are in the colour section, which begins opposite page 134.